An American Crusade for Wildlife

A Boone and Crockett Club Book

Editorial and Historical Committee
James C. Rikhoff—Chairman   Ed Zern—Vice-chairman

An American Crusade for Wildlife

by James B. Trefethen
drawings by Peter Corbin

Published by
Winchester Press and the Boone and Crockett Club

I wish to express my gratitude to the many individuals who contributed to the completion of this book by offering suggestions, lending reference material, and providing illustrations.

Special thanks go to Dr. Durward L. Allen, Dr. Laurence R. Jahn, Dr. Daniel A. Poole, Kenneth J. Sabol, Dan Saults, Allan T. Studholme, and Lonnie L. Williamson for their review of the manuscript, in whole or in part, and for their contribution of facts and figures that might otherwise have eluded me.

Library of Congress Catalog Card Number: 75-9268
ISBN 0-87691-207-2

Library of Congress Cataloging in Publication Data

Trefethen, James B.
 An American crusade for wildlife.

 "A Boone and Crockett Club book."
 Bibliography: p. 383
 Includes index.
 1. Wildlife conservation—United States.
I. Corbin, Peter II. Title.
QL84.2.T73   333.9'5'0973   75-9268
ISBN 0-87691-207-2

Published by Winchester Press
205 East 42nd Street, New York 10017

Printed in the United States of America
Design by Karin Batten and Elliot Kreloff

To

C. R. "PINK" GUTERMUTH

Conservationist Extraordinary

Preface

Some fifteen years ago the Boone and Crockett Club commissioned James B. Trefethen to write a history of the club from its inception in 1887 under the tutelage of Theodore Roosevelt until the beginning of the sixth decade of this century. Mr. Trefethen, an associate member of the club and a professional wildlife specialist with the Wildlife Management Institute, immediately plunged into the research for his project and he soon realized that the task was larger and more complex than envisioned by the club's leadership.

The early history of the Boone and Crockett Club was in reality a chronicle of the first stirrings of the newly awakened conservation conscience in the United States. The club's activities in the latter part of the nineteenth century and the first decades of this one coincided with the launching of both government and private endeavors in the conservation and wildlife-management movement.

As his research reached forward into the 1930s, Jim Trefethen became increasingly aware of the magnitude and diversity of the record spreading out before him. What had started as a history of the Boone and Crockett Club soon assumed a much more significant position in the bibliography of conservation literature. In short, our story became a larger history—literally an epic of the crusade for wildlife in North America. The book became a standard reference in the field and one of the few chronological histories of the conservation movement available for research.

The United States—indeed, the world—has witnessed an almost unbelievable explosion in interest and concern about all things connected with nature since *Crusade for Wildlife* was published in 1961. "Ecology" has become a familiar word to millions. The old-line conservationist—often ignored or even ridiculed in the not-too-distant past—has found himself in the middle, often in the front, and sometimes left behind in a newly awakened body politic deeply committed to a better natural world about us.

It has become obvious to the Boone and Crockett Club that the world's awareness of today's conservation and wildlife problems is vastly stronger, more immediate, more urgent, and better-informed than it was in 1961. It has become equally apparent that it is time to restate and enlarge the history of the conservation movement in light of the rush of development and change in the last fifteen years. Fortunately, Jim Trefethen is still here to lend his wonderfully tuned hand and years of practical experience, tempered with deep philosophical insights and almost religious conviction, to the creation of a new book, appropriately entitled *An American Crusade for Wildlife*. This new book is no mere revision of the previous work but a completely new and, I believe, greater contribution from one of America's finest wildlife writers.

It is an honor and privilege for the Boone and Crockett Club and its Editorial and Historical Committee to have had a part in the compilation and publishing of this new book by James B. Trefethen.

James C. Rikhoff
Chairman, Editorial and Historical Committee
Boone and Crockett Club
August 1, 1975

Foreword

It is now fifteen years since the Boone and Crockett Club published its own history in a book entitled *Crusade for Wildlife*, authored with flair and diligence by James B. Trefethen. It quickly became evident that this was not just the story of a group of inspired sportsmen-conservationists founded in 1887 by Theodore Roosevelt. It was, indeed, one of the extremely few books that dealt systematically with the history of wildlife preservation and management in North America. As a reference work it literally dropped into an empty niche in student training programs, and it found ready acceptance among conservation scholars here and abroad.

Since 1961 the entire field of environmental science has blossomed, and great changes in government and society have affected wildlife and its place in our out-of-doors. It became evident to both the author and the club that the *Crusade* book must be expanded and updated, that it must become, across the board, a general history of wildlife in North America.

Jim Trefethen has steadily improved his impeccable credentials for this work. Conservation history has been his major interest, a field in which he made his first contribution while earning a master's degree at the University of Massachusetts. Since 1948, when he joined the Washington staff of the Wildlife Management Institute, he has been at the crossroads—one is tempted to say in the crossfire—of natural-resource activities on the national scene. He knew many of the actors in this drama personally, including, to a man, those revered and durable old-timers whose names were well known forty years ago and who remain active.

As a major annual responsibility beginning in 1953, Trefethen has edited the transactions of the North American Wildlife and Natural Resources Conference. No important problem in the field of renewable resources is neglected in these meetings, and the editor probably is the only person who ever read all the papers in this impressive shelf of books. It would be an incomparable education for anyone.

The facts in this new book attest that Trefethen has dug deeply into private sources to complete the record on many significant but superficially known events. In using his access to inner sanctums he brings out the unlooked-for elements of personality clash, group self-interest, wayward judgment, and chance occurrence that sometimes account for what did or did not happen. Often the course of destiny was guided by a thread of reason or unreason that had no reference to logic and public interest. Americans should understand better the narrow margin that sometimes separates great accomplishment from catastrophe. For many it may suggest a constructive role.

In this book there will be unexpected revelations for the outdoorsman, the environmentalist, the citizen conservationist. But its breadth and depth are such that it also has much to offer the most sophisticated professional. Its author knows well that in the '70s we left behind our long era of space and plenty. We encountered the verges of a new episode in the history of man on earth, a period dominated by abounding overpopulation. Great human needs and greater demands could override much of our progress toward rational resource husbandry. Wildlife of many kinds faces jeopardy in new and strange forms while we are bemused with overabundance in a few species.

Jim Trefethen's carefully researched accounts are a timely warning and good short-course preparation for the last and most critical quarter of the twentieth-century environmental crusade. All responsible Americans are involved. They would do well to review their record and ponder their future. These chapters convey a message that can help mightily in the tasks ahead.

Durward L. Allen
Purdue University
August 1, 1975

Contents

PART V: The Environmental Age

Part 1

Exploration
and
Exploitation

Chapter 1

Blood on the Prairies

The five riders reined in their mustangs on the crest of a grassy ridge. Ahead, the prairie rose and fell like a golden sea that rolled unbroken to the distant mountains. A variable wind riffled the manes of the horses and sent swirls and eddies scudding through the tall, dry grasses that clothed the landscape.

Without dismounting, the men conferred briefly and then fanned out to occupy widely separated posts. The bearded, buckskin-jacketed leader of the group kicked the flanks of his chestnut mare and cantered along the crest of the ridge for a quarter of a mile. Then, dropping down on the leeward side, he dismounted and ground-tethered the horse, pulled a heavy-barreled Sharps rifle from its boot, and hauled off the saddlebags. Leaving the mare, he climbed back to the crest, dropped the bags, and trampled the grass before them flat in a fan-shaped pattern. From one bag he took a stout fork of peeled alder and thrust its longer, sharpened end deep into the rich earth. From the other, he removed a buckskin pouch of cartridges and emptied it on the ground behind the fork. Then, placing the rifle on its improvised rest, he lay down behind it, fished a piece of antelope jerky from his pocket, put it between his teeth, and waited.

He did not wait long. From the west, a mile away, came the sound of the first shot, sounding in the prairie air, like an axe striking a hollow log. Then two, four, eight irregularly timed shots. At least two of his companions were in action before him. The man fitted the crescent buttplate to his shoulder, adjusted his hat brim to shade his eyes, and scanned the nearby pass between the hills.

He heard the buffalo before he saw them—the strident bawling of the calves, the deep-throated answers of the cows, the hoglike grunting of the bulls, and a muffled rumbling like far-distant thunder. The leaders of the herd, a massive bull and two cows, trotted through the pass. Pausing momentarily, they lifted shaggy heads to test the wind. Then they ran through the little valley that the rifleman was covering.

One of the cows passed within fifty yards. Without cocking, the man followed her with his rifle, holding the ivory bead of the front sight six inches below the ebony horn. When he swung the rifle back toward the pass, it was filled with brown, shaggy-maned bodies.

Again, he held his fire, although thirty or forty passed within easy range. He had hunted buffalo for three years now and knew from experience that if he let the leaders pass, those behind would follow.

Another band, larger than the second, poured through the saddle between the hills. This time the man hooked his thumb over the hammer and drew it back, pressing his cheek to the polished walnut. At the click of the rifle's action, a fat cow stopped and stared in his direction. He held behind her shoulder and squeezed off the shot. The recoil and the smoke of the discharge obscured his view, but the roar of the shot was echoed immediately by the thud of a solid hit. When the smoke cleared, the cow was on her side.

The hunter had already ejected the spent casing and jammed a fresh cartridge into the chamber. He aligned the sights with a bull's forehead, fired, and loaded again.

Two hours later he was out of ammunition. Scattered shots still came from his companions' rifles, and the prairies to the west were now speckled and blotched with bands of bison. But the bottom and sides of the little valley before him were studded with still, brown hulks. The hunter counted forty-eight. The skinners, waiting a mile or two away with their wagons and teams, would earn their money that day.

The year was 1876. It could have been 1870 or 1879. The place was western Kansas. It might have been the Dakotas, Wyoming, Texas, or Nebraska. All over the Great Plains, between 1865 and 1882, hundreds of other men played out variations of the same drama each year from early spring until winter blizzards temporarily ended the carnage.

Ever since the retreat of the great glaciers, the bison had been the dominant form of life on the western plains. Originally, there may have been sixty or even a hundred million occupying all of the natural grasslands between the Canadian subarctic and central Mexico almost from coast to coast. Fingers of their range extended deep into the great forests of the East along the Ohio River and its tributaries into Kentucky, Maryland, Pennsylvania, Virginia, and West Virginia. Sir Samuel Argall, later a deputy governor of Virginia, described "great stores of Cattle as big as Kine" in his exploration of the Potomac River in 1612.

But these scattered eastern bands were only offshoots of the great herds that occupied a vast ocean of grass that spread from the Mississippi Valley to the Rocky Mountains and from the taiga of western Canada through Texas to northern Mexico. In the Great Basin between the Rockies and the Cascades were similar extensive grasslands. Occupying these natural grazing lands and their adjacent parklands were a dozen or more loosely independent aggregations of plains bison, each herd numbering in the millions. Each herd migrated in a roughly circular route that covered a thousand or more miles. The pattern and timing of their movements assured the regeneration, before they returned, of the depleted grazing lands left in their wakes.

Flirting about the flanks of the moving herds and, at times, intermingling with them were bands of pronghorn antelope. The smaller ruminants may have been as abundant as their huge companions, although many early observers paid them scant attention because of the overwhelming conspicuousness of the buffalo.

Skulking around these masses of moving, milling flesh were the buffalo wolves, waiting their opportunity to pull down the straggler or the poorly guarded calf. As it does with all herbivores, predation helped mold the habits and behavior of the species. The wolf and the plains grizzly bear helped eliminate the less aggressive, the lone wanderer, the slow of foot, and the sick that could spread their infection throughout the herd.

The American plains Indian, even after he acquired the white man's horse, had little if any impact on the numbers and movements of the bison. If anything, the reverse was true. Zebulon Pike, one of the first Americans to see the Republican River and southern herds in their unspoiled glory in 1806 and 1807, reported that the buffalo along the Arkansas River could "feed all the savages in the United States for one century." At their peak, the combined population of the buffalo-hunting tribes numbered little more than 500,000 men, women, and children.

Before Cortes and his conquistadors involuntarily granted the Indian his greatest gift from the Old World, most of the natives of the plains—Arapaho, Blackfoot, Cheyenne, Cree, Kiowa, Mandan, Pawnee, and Shawnee—lived relatively sedentary existences as gatherers and tillers of the soil, in hogans of logs and sod. They hunted buffalo when buffalo appeared, but, limited to foot travel, were unable to follow them far. Apart from backpacks, their only means of overland transport was the travois, a framework lashed to a pair of trailing poles fastened to a harnessed dog. Even with this ingenious device, the largest dog could draw little more than his master could carry in a backpack. The weight of a bull buffalo on the hoof sometimes exceeds a ton.

Lack of mobility and an efficient transport system restricted the prehorse Indians in their use of the buffalo. Individual hunters, of course, killed individual buffalo by lying in wait in rock or brush blinds or by creeping within arrow range disguised in the hide of a wolf or antelope. But this was an uncertain and risky form of hunting even when a number of men teamed together to kill a selected animal. Unless the first arrow or arrows found heart, lungs, or spine, the intended victim would race off and become lost in the body of the herd to feed the wolves miles from its pursuers. Worse, the wounded animal could, and often did, turn on its tormentors to gore and trample them into lifeless pulp. For his main source of buffalo meat and hides, the unmounted Indian depended upon communal slaughter in which all members of the tribe played a part.

One common practice was for a group of hunters to segregate a band of buffalo from the body of the herd and drive it onto ice. On the slick surface, or if they broke through, the ponderous animals fell easy prey to lances and close-range arrows. Members of northern tribes, traveling on snowshoes, often killed large numbers of buffalo while they were floundering in deep snow. Those farther south drove groups of animals into marshes or quagmires.

Prairie Indian towns, by design, usually were situated near steep bluffs or precipices along traditional migration routes. At these strategic points, the Indians laid out two diverging lines of permanent rock blinds, each separated by a few yards, that extended from the edge of the precipice a mile or more out onto the open prairie. When a herd of buffalo approached, groups of men filed from the village, under cover of darkness, to man the blinds. Others infiltrated the buffalo herds outside the mouth of the great funnel formed by the lines of blinds. Still others, armed with bows and lances, with the women and older children, took up positions at the base of the cliff.

At daybreak, while the men in the blinds crouched silent and motionless, the crescent-shaped line of drivers began to move forward, slowly and quietly at first, to set in motion the animals they had cut off. As the buffalo approached the mouth of the funnel, the drivers began shouting and waving blankets and deer hides. When the buffalo entered the space between the lines of blinds, those manning the outer ends of the wings jumped into view, waving, whooping, and setting up a clatter with drums and rattles.

Now the buffalo were surrounded. Whether they turned right, left, or back, they were confronted by leaping, shouting men. Their only apparent route to safety was straight ahead. In full stampede, they raced forward in a compact mass, maddened by fear and blinded by dust and the bulk of those in the lead. The leaders may have tried to stop as they saw the abyss ahead, but within moments a cascade of flesh and bone flowed over the brink to break on the rocks below. If any survived, they were dispatched with arrows, lances, and axes while they lay stunned and helpless from their fall.

This was a highly efficient method of slaughter. It was also often wasteful. So many frequently were killed that the women, with their crude implements of obsidian and flint, could skin and butcher a relative few. They gave priority to the calves and cows, as these yielded the most pliable hides and the tenderest cuts of meat. The bulls often were divested only of their tongues and their carcasses left to the prairie scavengers. Successful drives were followed by days of gorging on fresh meat while the winter meat supply dried on racks over smoky fires.

The acquisition of the horse revolutionized the lifestyle of the buffalo-hunting Indians. By 1720, all of the prairie-dwelling Indians, through trade, theft, or conquest, had become hard-riding horsemen, each of whose individual wealth was counted in the number of ponies in his possession. The mounted hunter no longer had to await the coming of the buffalo; he could follow them at will. The dank, vermin-infested hovel of his father gave way to the airy tepee, the best designed and most comfortable of primitive living accommodations. It could accommodate a fire for cooking or heating without filling with choking smoke. In the warmer months, its skirts could be raised for full ventilation. Moreover, it could be struck within minutes and its poles used as the bases of a horse-drawn travois that could carry a whole family's possessions. On notice, an entire camp of a hundred or more tepees could be on the trail within an hour.

The horse also changed the hunting methods of the prairie Indian. Mounted, the Indian hunter could intercept the migrating buffalo herds again and again. He could race beside a running animal and drive arrow after arrow into its chest at close range until it dropped. Three or four horses with travois could drag its skinned and quartered carcass back to the village, even from miles away. It was a dangerous form of hunting in which carelessness, lack of judgment, or an unnoticed prairie dog burrow could mean death under the hooves of the stampeding herd or on the horns of a pain-maddened bull. But it was safer than stalking the bison on foot. For coursing buffalo with horses, the short-limbed Indian bow was superior to the firearms of the times. An accomplished archer could loose more than a dozen arrows in the time it took to reload a muzzleloading musket.

The settlement of the eastern portion of the North American continent by white men increased the number of Indians depending upon the buffalo for their survival. First to arrive, in the 1600s, were the Sioux, who had originated in the forests and parklands of Minnesota, where they had fished, raised corn, and hunted deer, moose, and caribou. Forced onto the prairies when their traditional enemies, the Chippewa, obtained firearms from the French, the Teton, Tetonais, and Yankton tribes of the Sioux Nation adapted quickly to the migratory life of the buffalo hunters. In time, they became the dominant people of the northern plains.

The population of the prairies was further swelled by forced arrivals of other eastern woodland people such as the Delawares, Cherokees, Chickasaws, and Seminoles. Many of these latecomers were assimilated into the ranks of the resident tribes. Others carved out hunting grounds of their own on the prairies of present-day Oklahoma and Nebraska.

To the newcomers, as with the resident tribes, the buffalo became the single staple resource. It was the beef, coal, iron, plastic, cotton, and wool of Indian economy, all in one. The woolly capes, tanned with a paste of buffalo liver, brains, and wood ashes, made warm robes and blankets. The hides of the cows were converted to durable garments, moccasins, and tepees. Stripped and braided, buffalo hides became whips, ropes, and cordage. Untreated hides dried hard as metal. Draped and fastened over a frame of saplings, one became a bull boat. When fresh or soaked, rawhide could be molded to form boxes, cases, quivers, shields, and saddles. Shrinking as they dried, strips of rawhide made strong, flexible fastenings for joining the parts of wooden structures and implements. The hollow horns were converted to cups, ladles, and ceremonial ornaments. Boiled with the hoofs, they formed a strong adhesive. The intestines became casings for pemmican and other food stuffs. The bladder and paunch could be used as water containers. The sinews were used as lashings, thread, and bowstrings. Bones, stripped first of their succulent marrow, could be fashioned into hundreds of implements, from needles and fishhooks to tent pegs and clubs. Attached to a wooden handle, the shoulder blade became a hoe, scoop, or shovel. Dried buffalo dung was the plains Indian's principal source of fuel.

All of these and many other uses of the buffalo were in addition to its primary importance as a source of food. It was this nearly total dependence on the bison by the prairie Indian that carried the seeds of destruction for both.

Exploitation of the buffalo by white men began early in American history. In 1540, García Lopez de Cárdenas explored northward, from a base established by Francisco Vásquez de Coronado in what is now New Mexico, to discover the Grand Canyon of the Colorado. From there he worked eastward across the Texas Panhandle to the plains of Kansas. There he found large herds of buffalo, and, presumably, he and his soldiers sampled the bison's meat. But Coronado's base camp had other significance in the history of the buffalo and its Indian hunters; it was the site of the first major livestock operation on the American prairies. The Spaniards brought with them 6,500 head of domesticated animals, of which five hundred were cattle. This was the beginning of an industry that would help crowd the buffalo from the American plains.

Before 1820, the pressure of the whites against the prairie buffalo had little more effect than that of the Indians. The bison outnumbered the hunters of both races by several thousand to one. Trappers and homesteaders along the frontier killed a buffalo or two when they needed meat. Army and trading posts usually were supplied with meat by civilian scouts or soldiers detailed to that work. Not infrequently, Army officers hunted the great wild oxen for sport, coursing them Indian-style and killing them at close range with pistols or carbines. The meat, consigned to the mess, was seldom wasted. The only significant effect of this subsistence hunting was the elimination, by 1800, of the comparatively few buffalo east of the Mississippi. These animals were especially vulnerable as they occupied the restricted acreages of natural grasslands in the predominantly forested East. These lands were coveted as pastures and homesites by the early settlers. Although white settlement had crossed the Mississippi into Iowa, Missouri, and Arkansas, the buffalo on the central prairies remained nearly as abundant as ever.

But things were already beginning to change. In April, 1833, Prince Maximilian of Wied-Neuwied began a prodigious fifteen-hundred-mile trek up the Missouri River from St. Louis to study the American aborigines in their native habitat. The German naturalist-prince was accompanied by a skillful young Swiss artist, Carl Bodmer, who left some of the most vivid pictorial records of early life on the American plains.

Bodmer recorded in his diary that, in the previous year, 43,000 buffalo hides had been shipped from Fort Union in Dakota Territory to St. Louis. Fort Union was only one of a string of trading posts that had been established by the American Fur Company deep in the heart of buffalo country. The majority of these hides had been taken by Indians and exchanged for cloth, firearms, hatchets, knives, and other necessities.

Ten years later, in the summer of 1843, John James Audubon retraced the route of Maximilian and Bodmer to Fort Union in a rickety steamer. Initiated into the sport of buffalo coursing by soldiers and traders at the fort, the aging artist participated in many exciting hunts. On one, he was charged by a bull that a companion dropped just before its horns made contact with Audubon's horse. His younger companion and associate, Lewis M. Squires, became so addicted to buffalo hunting that he pleaded with Audubon to let him remain at Fort Union throughout the winter. A fall from a horse ended Squires's brief and spectacular career as a buffalo hunter. But in his short stay on the prairies, the easterner killed so many buffalo that he later confessed he was "almost ashamed." From most of the kills, he had taken only the tongues.

Although the records left by Audubon and Squires indicate that bison were still abundant in 1843, even around trading posts where they were most susceptible to persecution, the artist-naturalist had noticed a "perceptible difference" in the size of the herds at the time of his visit and those reported by such earlier observers as Washington Irving, Meriwether Lewis, and Thomas Say. With insight remarkable for his time, Audubon foresaw the end of the great buffalo migrations. "Before many years," he wrote, "the Buffalo, like the Great Auk, will have disappeared; surely this should not be permitted."

Francis Parkman crossed the continent in 1846. His classic work, *The Oregon Trail*, contains some of the most accurate and eloquent records of life on the plains in the early 1800s. Parkman echoed Audubon's concern for the future of the buffalo and its effect on the buffalo-hunting Indians. "When the buffalo are extinct, they too must dwindle away."

To most of the trappers, prospectors, and settlers who crossed the prairies before 1850, however, the buffalo seemed an inexhaustible resource. But the beginning of the end already had come with the glint of gold in the millrace of an obscure California settlement. Within a year after James Marshall fished the first nugget from the tailwaters of Sutter's Mill on the American River in 1848, thousands of easterners abandoned families and jobs to seek their fortunes in the gold fields. Many traveled by sea. But just as many or more traveled overland on foot, on horseback, and in wagons across the plains and mountains.

As the wagon trains threaded their way westward in increasing numbers, obscure forts and trading posts along their routes blossomed into towns catering to the needs of the travelers. The sleepy mission towns of San Diego and San Francisco had become booming cities, and the population of California grew so rapidly in two years that it was incorporated into the Union in September, 1850. Hundreds of miles to the east, twelve thousand Mormons were clustered in and around a thriving community on the shores of the Great Salt Lake. Texas had achieved statehood five years earlier, and growing numbers of Texans were crowding the Comanches from their traditional hunting grounds, and replacing buffalo with cattle. Intensive settlement had flowed across the Mississippi deep into Illinois, Iowa, Missouri, and Arkansas.

With the population growth along the West Coast and in the patches of settlement in the western prairies and mountains came a natural desire to link the separated fragments of the nation with a transportation system more reliable than wagon roads and river barges.

There was also massive political pressure to open the western prairies to settlement. Many of the easterners who made the long trek westward to Oregon and California were farmers from worn-out hill farms in New England, and weevil-ruined cotton plantations in the South. These men recognized good soil and grass when they saw it. On the prairies the black loam sometimes lay to a depth of six feet or more under the sod. The grasses of the northern prairies often brushed the bellies of passing horses. When the dream of instant wealth faded, these men remembered the rich black earth and lush grasses of the central plains.

Even greater political pressure was building in the East. The flood-gates of immigration were wide open, and thousands of new Americans—from famine-ridden Ireland and strife-torn central Europe—English, Scots, Germans, Jews, Russians, Poles, and Scandinavians—were pouring through New York City to new lives in the New World. The population of the United States jumped from 17 million in 1840 to more than 23 million in 1850, and to 32 million in 1860. These people had to be fed and clothed. The eastern farmlands were all settled, and many had been drained of their fertility by overuse or ruined entirely by erosion. Horace Greeley's New York *Tribune* kept up a drumfire of editorials urging the opening of the western plains to settlement. They were echoed by powerful voices in the halls of Congress.

Two obstacles to these dreams gave a temporary respite to the buffalo and the Indian. One was the political maneuvering of northern and southern political factions. Government surveyors had already traced the routes of a number of feasible rail links between California and the East. Representatives of the slave-holding states wanted a southern route; the free states opted for a northern line. This political stalemate was broken only by five years of bloody war.

The second obstacle was the Indian himself. The nomadic hunters were resisting the invasion of their lands with growing intensity, raiding wagon trains, running off horses and cattle, and burning isolated camps and settlements. They were confined to the inadequate reservations to which the white man consigned them only by constant military vigilance.

The first obstacle to western settlement and a transcontinental railway was swept away with the conclusion of the Civil War. With the close of hostilities in 1865, the railroad construction crews started moving westward onto the prairies and eastward into the Sierras. With the slave-state/free-state controversy eliminated by the outbreak of the Civil War, the Congress established machinery through which the lands of the Indian and buffalo would be carved and divided by enacting the Homestead Laws of 1862. Most of these lands, legally, were in the public domain.

Congress had established the original public domain of the United States soon after the Revolutionary War by placing in federal ownership all territorial holdings outside the borders of the thirteen original states. To these first public lands were added the vast territories acquired through the Louisiana Purchase, the War with Mexico, the Oregon Compromise, the Gadsden Purchase, and the Purchase of Alaska, for a grand total of 1.8 billion acres. Approximately 120 million acres had been allocated to the individual states for sale as an aid to education. At a later date, 38 million additional acres were allocated to the states as an aid in the expansion of their railway systems, and 94 million granted to railway corporations as a direct stimulus to the transportation system. In 1850, the average price asked for these lands was fifty cents an acre. Many contained superb stands of virgin timber, priceless mineral rights, and some of the richest grazing and agricultural lands in the world.

With the exception of these lands and those set aside as Indian territory and Indian reservations, all of this vast acreage was thrown open to settlement by the Homestead Acts. Any American citizen who had not borne arms against the government could acquire title to 160 acres by living on it for five years and making minor improvements. Veterans of the Union Army and Navy were permitted to subtract their years of service from the residence requirements. A five-year veteran of the Union Army or Navy could acquire full ownership of a quarter square-mile of real estate simply by staking out the claim and filing with the nearest land office.

The one major obstacle to implementing the Homestead Acts on much of the central plains was the Indian. During the war, the prairie tribes were freed from intensive military control by the manpower demands of the eastern campaigns. Tribes that had been confined to reservations resumed their traditional nomadic lives. Attempts to move them back met forceful resistance. When the Civil War ended, the United States was confronted with another war—a war that had no fronts, no beginning, and, seemingly, no end.

Conditioned to hard riding and the use of weapons since early childhood, a tough veteran of intertribal warfare from the age of sixteen, the Indian was a durable and elusive enemy. He could strike at any show of weakness and disengage at the first show of superior strength. American cavalrymen, although they detested him as an enemy, admired his skill with horses. Some of the greatest called him the "best light cavalryman in the world."

The plains Indian warrior, however, had one major strategic weakness—his dependence on the buffalo. No one better understood this than Ulysses S. Grant, William Tecumseh Sherman, and Philip H. Sheridan, architects of the destruction of the Confederacy. They had cut the lifelines of the South, and they were to play prominent roles in cutting the lifelines of the Indian.

There is no evidence that these soldiers instigated the slaughter of the buffalo. The professional buffalo hunters who swarmed ahead of and around the growing rail lines needed no other incentive than the desire to make money while the opportunity still existed. But each of the military leaders had an opportunity to slow the killing and did nothing about it.

As late as 1871, when the slaughter was just beginning, buffalo were still spectacularly abundant in the areas that civilization had not touched. Colonel R. I. Dodge, leading a patrol along the Arkansas River in Colorado, encountered one herd that he estimated contained no fewer than four million head. It occupied a front of fifty miles and twenty miles or more in depth.

Second Lieutenant George S. Anderson, who later became one of the military superintendents of Yellowstone National Park, received his first command at Fort Hays, Kansas, in September, 1871. Within a few weeks after his arrival, the troop of the Sixth Cavalry to which he was assigned was transferred to Fort Lyons on the Arkansas River in Colorado. On October 12, their first day on the trail, the troopers passed scattered bands of buffalo. When they broke camp on the following morning, they could see "hundreds of thousands" of buffalo from the higher hills, black specks—singly, in pairs, and in dense clusters—mottling the golden brown of the autumn prairie.

On the 14th, an early blizzard roared down from the North and immobilized the soldiers in the mouth of a small ravine on the banks of the Smoky Hill River. As men and horses huddled together for shelter at the base of a low bluff, a living tide of buffalo piled up before the river barrier and surged about their camp. Throughout the night, the men, shivering in their bedrolls, were in constant danger of being trampled by the thousands of hooves that stamped and rumbled past them. Anderson later wrote:

> For six days we continued our way through this enormous herd, during the last three days of which it was in constant motion across our path. I am safe in calling this a single herd, and it is impossible to approximate the numbers tha: composed it. At times they pressed before us in such numbers as to delay the progress of our column, and often a belligerent bull would lower and shake his craggy head at us when we passed him a few feet distant.

But the rail lines were beginning to cut the range of these herds into fragments, and, for the first time, the railroads provided a reliable and relatively swift method for shipping buffalo products to the eastern markets. Before the rails penetrated the prairies, meat products usually spoiled by the time they reached the butcher shops by wagon or barge. The railroads themselves used prodigious amounts of fresh meat, at first to feed the construction crews and then as a staple fare in the dining cars. These needs were supplied by professional hunters.

Although a few professional buffalo hunters operated alone, most were members of teams with a larger complement of skinners who doubled as wagoneers. It was the task of the latter to strip off and process the hides, and butcher the carcasses after the hunters had made their kills. The most common method of procuring buffalo was to intercept an approaching herd from a strategic position and kill all animals that came within range of their powerful single-shot Sharps, Remington, or Springfield rifles. Although repeating rifles, notably the Spencer, had been developed before and during the Civil War, none could accommodate a cartridge of sufficient knockdown power to be reliable for killing a beast as large as the bison. But with the development of the self-contained metallic cartridge, a hunter could loose twenty shots a minute, even when armed with a single-shot rifle.

Other hunters preferred the more strenuous and exciting method of coursing, in which the animals were killed at close range with pistols or carbines. This was a favorite technique of the most famous of the buffalo killers, William F. "Buffalo Bill" Cody.

Cody obtained a contract in 1867 to supply the Kansas Pacific Railway with fresh meat. In the next eighteen months, by his own account, he killed 4,280 buffalo. Competing on a wager with another hunter, he slaughtered sixty-nine in a single day; his adversary managed a score of only forty-six.

Fresh meat, however, was a secondary product for most of the buffalo hunters. The hides and robes brought a price per pound as high as the better meat cuts, and they were much easier to preserve and transport. A wagon could carry only one or two butchered carcasses. It could carry a hundred or more robes and hides. At the height of the slaughter, huge mounds of baled hides waiting shipment to eastern tanneries were familiar sights at the rail depots of Denver, Hays, and Fort Kearney.

But many hunters bothered neither with hides nor meat. It took an hour or more for a pair of skilled skinners to remove, flesh, and stake out a hide. With two or three strokes of a knife, one man could remove a buffalo's tongue in seconds. Buffalo tongue was a prized delicacy that brought premium prices from restaurants, hotels, and railroad concessioners. The tongue was easily preserved in the field, even in hot weather, by salting or smoking, and a hundred or more could be packed in a barrel. Hundreds of thousands, if not millions, of buffalo were killed for their tongues alone—and half as many tons of good meat rotted in the prairie sun.

In 1867, the lines of the Union Pacific linked Council Bluffs, Iowa, and Cheyenne, Wyoming, splitting the range of the plains bison along the Platte River. Farther south, the Kansas Pacific was tracing the Smoky Hill River on its way to Denver, infiltrating and excising another huge segment of prime buffalo range. It was along and between these two routes that the slaughter of the buffalo first began in earnest.

In 1865, the estimated national buffalo kill had been a million head. With the arrival of the railroads on the prairies, the annual kill climbed steadily each year to a crest of nearly five million in 1871 and 1872. After 1873, only scattered bands remained south of the Platte, too few to support commercial hunting although cowboys, settlers, and prospectors shot the survivors whenever and wherever they encountered them. In less than eight years, nearly all of the millions of buffalo that had roamed the prairies of Arizona, Colorado, Kansas, Oklahoma, New Mexico, Texas, and Utah had been converted to meat, hides, and carrion.

North of the Platte, in Dakota Territory, Idaho, Montana, Wyoming, and the adjoining prairies of Canada, there were still a million and a half bison. They had been protected until then by a general lack of rail transportation, the bitter winter climate, and the fierce resistance of the Sioux and northern Cheyenne. With the destruction of the southern herds, the buffalo hunters turned their attention to those in the north.

One obstacle to the full exploitation of the northern herds fell soon after June 25, 1876, when George Armstrong Custer and his 267 troopers of the Seventh Cavalry died on the hill overlooking the Little

Bighorn River in Montana. The defeat of Custer was a great tactical victory for the united Indians of the northern tribes. But massive retaliation by the U. S. Army turned it into a strategic disaster. Now the full military might of the nation was brought to bear against the Indians, hounding some into Canada, fragmenting the tribes that remained, and herding the bits and pieces back into the reservations.

The second obstacle fell soon afterward when the Great Northern Railroad, pushing westward from Duluth to meet the Northern Pacific out of Seattle, penetrated the heart of the northern herd's migration routes in Dakota Territory.

Whatever public sentiment existed for saving sample segments of the great bison herds—and some such sentiment did exist—was overwhelmed after Custer's defeat by the resistance of military men who carried great political power. These men knew that if the buffalo were destroyed the Indians could never again leave their reservations and become a threat to the orderly development of the West. In 1874, President Grant, on the advice of General Sherman, pocket-vetoed a bill that had been passed by the Congress "to prevent the useless slaughter of the Buffaloes within the Territories of the United States."

When the Texas State Legislature considered a bill to impose a closed season on buffalo hunting, General Philip Sheridan, as commander of the Army in the Southwest, personally testified against it. Idaho's territorial legislature had enacted such a law in 1864, but since enforcement was vested largely in the military, its principal value was as a historical curiosity. Colorado and Kansas adopted closures in 1875—after the bison within their borders had been all but destroyed.

Even if there had been effective laws to prolong their existence, the migrating herds were doomed as soon as the railroads penetrated their range. Taking advantage of the generous homestead laws, settlers by the hundreds of thousands poured westward on the rails to stake out their claims on the prairies, tearing up the sod to make way for wheat and corn, and stocking the grasslands with their livestock. In an agricultural economy there was no place for an animal like the buffalo. To save one of the buffalo herds in something resembling its pristine glory would have involved setting aside a contiguous wilderness tract as large as Montana. After 1880, no such area remained in all of the United States.

By 1881 the buffalo hunters had killed themselves out of business. The northern herds had been reduced to a few scattered remnants. In the climate of the times, these had little hope for survival. In 1886, when a band of around forty was found in the Badlands along the Yellowstone River, the Smithsonian Institution sent an expedition to collect specimens for the National Museum of Natural History. The scientists collected twenty-eight.

In 1894, Dr. J. B. Taylor, a rancher, discovered a band of about forty head between the Rio Grande and Devil's River in Valverde County, Texas. Taylor immediately made plans to round up the animals and place them behind wire on his ranch in Tom Green County. He followed the band across the Mexican border into the Santa Rosa Mountains and found evidence that Mexicans had taken a heavy toll of the migrants. Whether these last survivors of the great southern herd ever emerged from Mexico is doubtful.

Three years later, in February, 1897, a pair of enterprising poachers discovered two bulls, a cow, and her bull calf in Colorado's Lost Park. Operating on snowshoes, they killed all four. The men were caught, heavily fined, and the hides were confiscated to become the principals in a habitat group in the Denver Museum of Natural History.

In August, 1889, William Allen, a cowboy, claimed to have encountered a band of four while hunting wild horses near the Mexican border in New Mexico. He shot one.

This left the small herd of mountain buffalo in Yellowstone National Park as the sole representatives of the millions of buffalo that had formerly roamed the grasslands of the United States.

Although it was inevitable, the destruction of the great migrating buffalo herds was the most brutal and wasteful chapter in the history of America's wildlife. One year the herds had blanketed the prairies like "a living robe." Somewhat more than a decade later, little remained except piles of bleached bones that the settlers were gathering to supplement their meager incomes through sales to the fertilizer makers.

If the buffalo, like a number of other American species before it, had simply withered away before the onslaught of civilization, its passing might have attracted little attention. As it was, its precipitous decline from abundance to near extinction shocked the sensibilities of men who had known it in its better days and who mourned its elimination from the American scene. One of these was Dr. George Bird Grinnell.

Grinnell was a New Yorker and, as editor and publisher of *Forest and Stream*, the nation's leading sportsman's magazine, a man with friends in high places. His interest in natural history had been stimulated early in life through an association with the widow of John James Audubon.

At the age of twenty-one, after receiving his bachelor's degree from Yale, Grinnell became a member of an expedition to the West, headed by Professor O. C. Marsh, to collect vertebrate fossils for the Peabody Museum. Because of the ever-present threat of Indian raids, an escort of Pawnee scouts, commanded by Major Frank North, accompanied the party. Throughout his first summer in the West, whenever he was unoccupied with his scientific duties, Grinnell spent his time conversing with the Pawnees, gaining a respect for and understanding of Indian culture that few others of his time shared. He found the experience so rewarding that he returned nearly every year. In 1875, he accompanied Custer's exploratory expedition as a naturalist to Yellowstone National Park and the Black Hills of Dakota Territory.

When Grinnell first traveled through the West, the buffalo slaughter was only beginning. On subsequent trips he witnessed the sordid final chapters in the history of the original herds and the people who depended upon them. As a result of his unique experience, Grinnell was able to view the tragedy, simultaneously, through the eyes of the naturalist, the sportsman, the plains Indian, and the soldier. His sentiments were expressed eloquently in a eulogy to the buffalo that was published in 1893:

> On the floor, on either side of my fireplace, lie two buffalo skulls. They are white and weathered, the horns cracked and bleached by the snows and frosts and the rains and heats of many winters and summers. Often, late in the night, when the house is quiet, I sit before the fire and muse and dream of the old days; and as I gaze at these relics of the past, they take life before my eyes. The matted brown hair again clothes the dry bone, and in the empty orbits the wild eyes gleam. Above me curves the blue arch; away on either hand stretches the yellow prairie, and scattered near and far are the dark forms of buffalo. They dot the rolling hills, quietly feeding like tame cattle, or lie at ease on the slopes, chewing the cud and half asleep. . . .
>
> Life, activity, excitement mark another memory as vivid as these. From behind a near hill, mounted men ride out and charge down toward the herd. For an instant the buffalo pause to stare, and then crowd together in a close throng, jostling and pushing one another, a confused mass of horns, hair, and hoofs. Heads down and tails in air, they rush away from their pursuers, and as they race along herd joins herd, till the black mass sweeping over the prairie numbers thousands. On its skirts hover the active, nimble horsemen, with twanging bowstrings and sharp arrows piercing many fat cows. . . . Returning on their tracks, they skin the dead, then load the meat and robes on their horses, and with laughter and jest ride away.
>
> After them on the deserted prairie, come the wolves to tear at the carcasses. The rain and the snow wash the blood from the bones, and fade and bleach the hair. . . . So this cow and this bull of mine may have left their bones on the prairie, where I found them and picked

them up to keep as mementos of the past, to dream over, and in such reverie to see again the swelling hosts which yesterday covered the plains, and today are but a dream.

So the buffalo passed into history.

To Grinnell and the few other people concerned about the future of wildlife in the United States in the 1800s, the bison became a symbol of a rallying point for action. In its destruction as a free-roaming animal, the buffalo carried the seeds of its own survival and that of a number of other species that otherwise might have passed from the American scene.

Chapter 2

The Original Heritage

The discoverers of America—and Columbus was only one of many —found a continent richer in plant and animal life than any of them had realized. Like the blind men feeling the elephant, each knew only a part of the whole.

Along the Atlantic Coast the bays were alive with oysters, lobsters, crabs, and fish, and the rivers in spring teemed with sturgeon, salmon, and shad. A man could slake his thirst in any stream or lake, and the air was clean and pure.

Westward across its midsection, the continent spread for more than three thousand miles. The eastern third was blanketed by a vast forest of huge trees, broken here and there by Indian clearings and lightning-set burns. From north to south this forest began with the sparse spruce-fir taiga in the Canadian subarctic and ended with the mangrove and palmetto thickets on Florida's subtropical tip and along the Mexican coast.

Below the boggy taiga lay a broad band of predominantly birch-maple-hemlock that covered what are now the Lake and Northeastern States. Two or three hundred miles south, this band merged with another made up primarily of beech, hickories, black cherry, and oaks of nearly two dozen species. In the South along the Atlantic and Gulf coasts and extending up along the larger rivers sprawled swamps filled with great bald cypresses, their gnarled limbs festooned with gray flags of Spanish moss. Along the drier areas of the Gulf, the forest was fringed on its southern side with massive live oak thickets.

On the sandier sites and those where windthrow or fires set by lightning or Indians had once opened the earth to the sun, great pines towered over the surrounding hardwoods—white and pitch pines in the North, shortleaf, longleaf, and loblolly in the South. Throughout the hardwood forest were huge specimens of American chestnut. On the river flood plains and on the well-watered lands near swamps and bogs, thick vines of poison ivy, bittersweet, and Virginia creeper climbed the trees like resting anacondas.

Beyond the green, tree-studded parklands at the western border of the forest were the prairies, treeless except along the streams and rivers where the earth received enough moisture for cottonwoods, alders, box elders, and aspens to set roots.

Past the prairies the Rocky Mountains rose tier on tier to craggy peaks perpetually cloaked in snow. Above the aspen parklands that covered their foothills, their slopes supported tall stands of ponderosa pine, fir, and larch. On the far side of the Rockies, the landscape dipped to the sumps and sagebrush flats of the Great Basin, robbed of most of its moisture by the peaks of the High Sierras to the west.

Along the Pacific was the most stately forest of all, the cathedral-like stands of redwoods of the California coast and the rain-drenched forests of the Pacific Northwest and coastal Canada where Douglas firs, sugar pines, and spruce towered two hundred feet in the sky from trunks ten to twelve feet thick at their bases.

Each of the different forest and grassland types supported a distinctive population of birds and mammals. Far above the northern fringe of the great forests, polar bears stalked seals and walruses on drifting ice floes, and bands of shaggy muskoxen roamed the icy shores. On the tundra, great herds of barren-ground caribou wandered in an endless search for lichens and sedges, trailed by Arctic wolves. The woodland caribou shared the taiga and northern coniferous forest with the moose, spruce grouse, ptarmigan, fisher, Canadian lynx, and Arctic hare.

The deciduous forests were home for the white-tailed deer, wild turkey, bobcat, black bear, ruffed grouse, cougar, and timber wolf. Here the passenger pigeon attained incredible numbers, migrating and searching for food in flocks that sometimes darkened the skies. Their nesting areas covered dozens of square miles with as many as fifty nests in a single tree.

The grasslands, with their enormous herds of bison, antelope, elk, and mule deer, supported one of the largest biomasses of any region in the world. The larger mammals shared the prairies with great flocks of prairie chickens, plovers, curlews, and blackbirds. Mice and prairie dogs, whose "towns" often covered many square miles, were hunted by foxes and coyotes, hawks, owls, eagles, and ferrets. Grizzly bears were common from the Mississippi Valley to the Pacific Coast.

The Rockies, Cascades, and coastal ranges held great flocks of bighorn sheep, and satellite populations occupied the Black Hills and the Badlands near the headwaters of the Missouri River. Ranging farthest north in the mountains of northern Canada and Alaska was the snow-white Dall sheep, whose range merged with that of the almost-black Stone sheep, the range of which abutted that of the Rocky Mountain bighorn. The deserts of California, New Mexico, Arizona, and Mexico were the domain of the desert bighorn sheep. The higher elevations of the northern mountains constituted range for the mountain goat. The wooded slopes also provided habitat for the spruce and blue grouse, the latter as large as a pullet. Bald and golden eagles, ravens, and peregrine falcons used the mountain ledges for nesting sites, and golden marmots, a favorite prey of the grizzly bear, abounded on the talus slopes.

The deserts of the Southwest had their own unique populations. The piglike collared peccary, or javelina, traveled in great herds through the thorny thickets. Chuckwallas, Gila monsters, rattlesnakes, and a host of lesser reptiles sought refuge from hunting roadrunners under the thorny paddles of *Opuntia* cacti. Great flocks of valley and scaled quail flushed at the approach of bobcat or coyote. Here jaguars competed with the cougar in hunting the desert mule deer. The deserts were the nesting grounds for the white-winged dove, but this species attained abundance rivaling that of the passenger pigeon in ebony and huisache thickets along the lower Rio Grande.

The spring and autumn migrations of the waterfowl were awe-inspiring sights to the first explorers who saw them. From the tundra and prairie sloughs and potholes still unseen by white men, swans, geese, and ducks of three dozen species streamed southward each fall to concentrate by the millions on the bays, marshes, and rivers of the South.

On this enormous wildlife resource, the American aborigine had little if any negative impact. The North American continent held only about a million Indians. While they used a wide variety of wildlife products as staples in their day-to-day economy, their needs were dwarfed by the magnitude of the supply.

The Indians of the plains had no effect one way or the other on the great buffalo herds. But those who inhabited the eastern forests practiced a primitive but effective form of wildlife management. Their principal tool was fire. Most of the woodland tribes were planters as well as hunters, living in semipermanent towns surrounded by communal or family fields in which the women cultivated corn, squash, and pumpkins with sharpened sticks and hoes fashioned from the shoulder blades of deer.

Lacking metals harder than copper, the Indian cleared his land with fire. He felled large trees by burning their lower trunks and chipping away the charcoal with flint axes until they fell. Except for an occasional dugout canoe—also shaped and hollowed by the burn-and-chip method—the eastern Indian had little or no use for big timber. He fashioned the frames of his bark huts and lodges from saplings and light poles. Many Indian towns were enclosed with palisades, but even these fortifications were of light timber. Bows, spear hafts, fish- and venison-drying racks, and handles of implements were more easily fashioned with stone tools from saplings. The straight, round sprouts of maple, birch, and red-osier dogwood were preformed arrow shafts. These types of wood were in short supply in the unbroken virgin forest. After dropping a large tree, the Indian burned it where it lay. If he salvaged anything, it was the slabs of bark from some species and firewood from the upper branches of others. But the ashes of the burned trunk became an excellent fertilizer for the corn and pumpkin patches that would occupy the site.

The Indians also cleared extensive areas around their communities that were not intended for immediate occupancy or cultivation. These broad, open beltlands provided protection from surprise attack by enemy warriors, for the Indian was perpetually involved in intertribal war.

The edges of the clearings produced wood of a size that could be readily converted to the products the Indian required. Fire stimulated the rapid growth of sprouts from stumps and roots, producing successively, withes for baskets, spear hafts, and lodge frames, often within a single season. In the North, the paper birch, which produced the tough, pliable bark used for building canoes and for fabricating drinking cups, boxes, and other containers, grew best on burned soils that had been opened to the sun. Blueberries, cranberries, grapes, and other fruits grew in profusion around the Indian clearings.

When the Indian set torch to the forest, he let the fire burn itself out in the standing timber, unless it threatened his crops at home. Dead, standing trees, girdled and killed by the flames, shed their limbs gradually, providing a reliable source of dry firewood.

Repeated burning by the Indians also created a diversity of food and cover close to their towns for a wide variety of game that otherwise could not have existed in the virgin forests. William Bradford, the second governor of Plymouth Plantation, mentioned the abundance of available grazing lands in the vicinity of the settlement. He and other early observers commented on the parklike nature of the neighboring forests, with stately, spreading trees scattered over grassy sod—an impression of the early American wilderness quite different from that usually imagined. Plymouth occupied the site of a town abandoned by the Wampanoags, who had been decimated by smallpox introduced by earlier European visitors to the New England coast.

These grasslands and parklike woodlands, which explorers found in many parts of the eastern forest, could only have resulted from repeated burning. Since elk and bison depend as heavily on grasses and forbs as on browse, this would account for their presence in forested areas of the East that could support neither species today. The grasslands of the Indian burns provided food and cover essential to many other species. Bobwhite quail, cottontail rabbits, plovers, and many species of waterfowl prefer to nest in grassy or herbaceous cover. Quail, wild turkeys, and ruffed grouse use such cover as a place to raise their young.

The sprout growth, shrubs, and brushy cover that developed on the less intensively burned lands provided food and cover for other species. Berry-burdened shrubs attracted bears and many species of birds, and the tender sprout growth was a nutritious and palatable browse for deer. The buds of aspen and birch are staples in the winter diet of ruffed grouse. Both trees are intolerant of shade and grow only where the forest canopy is broken by fire or logging.

The Indian's cornfields, of course, were attractive to many other species of wildlife. Raccoons, squirrels, deer, and bears must have been pests to the Indian farmer—and the swarming passenger pigeon a plague.

Thus the woodland Indian, through his manipulation of the forest habitat, contributed far more to the wildlife resource than the toll he exacted from it. It would take the whites four centuries of groping to rediscover the same principles.

Although it was certainly significant locally, there is no way to evaluate the overall extent of Indian influence on the forests and wildlife of America in precolonial times. Their beneficial impact, however, was compounded by the fact that the eastern tribes often shifted their village sites, abandoning the old ones to the elements. Lacking fertilizers, except wood ashes and decayed fish, the Indian farmer often wore out the soil. War and—with the coming of the whites—disease sometimes wiped out whole communities. The inhabitants of other towns were forced to move because of invasion of their lands by stronger hostile forces. The abandoned townsites and cropfields and the grassy clearings around them were soon invaded by shade-intolerant trees, such as white pines, birches, and aspen that could not have had much representation in the unbroken forest.

If the Indian population had been very large, most of the eastern forests would have been subjected to this treatment. As it was, many hundreds of thousands of square miles of forest remained untouched by the influence of man. Nature, of course, through the instruments of lightning, flood, insects, disease, and wind, frequently opened swaths through the forest canopy to permit the development of cover similar to that following land abandonment by the Indian.

Another important natural influence on the precolonial environment was the beaver, the only American mammal capable of modifying the habitat to meet its own needs. The beaver in early times was abundant over nearly all of North America between the Arctic Circle and the subtropics. It occupied the streams of the generally treeless prairies because their flood plains supported stands of aspen, cottonwoods, willows, and other hydrophytic plants, all of which are preferred beaver foods.

Through its dam-building activities, the beaver, like the woodland Indian, extended the ranges of many species of wild birds and mammals deep into the virgin forests. A beaver pond is more than a body of water supporting the needs of a group of beavers, but the epicenter of a whole dynamic ecosystem. With a surface area ranging from a fraction of an acre to several dozen acres, it is surrounded by a network of shallow canals through which the animals tow their winter food supplies and building materials for their lodges and dams. Felling trees for these purposes opens the forest canopy on lands surrounding the pond, permitting the development of shade-intolerant trees and shrubs, such as aspen, alder, elder, blueberries, and willows. Most of these are outstanding browse plants for moose, elk, and deer. Grouse of five species use aspen buds in winter and berries in summer.

Trees too large to be felled by the beavers' teeth frequently are killed by girdling or by flooding as the waters of the pond rise. As these large standing trees decay, their hollows and cavities become nesting sites for squirrels, raccoons, owls, wood ducks, or goldeneyes. Their insect-infested barks and trunks become feeding places for woodpeckers, brown creepers, and nuthatches. One of the larger trees may become the nesting platform for an eagle or osprey that finds fish easy to take from the still waters behind the dam.

The brush and sedge-covered margins of beaver ponds are favored nesting spots for black ducks, mallards, woodcock, snipe, and a wide variety of songbirds. The still shallows are hunting grounds for herons, egrets, and bitterns, and the muddy banks feeding places for spotted sandpipers, plovers, and other shorebirds. Each beaver pond supports a satellite population of muskrats, turtles, frogs, and salamanders.

This concentrated food supply invariably attracts predators—timber wolves, bobcats, lynx, foxes, hawks, owls, otters, and mink. When predators or Indians wiped out a colony of beavers, when a pond silted full, or when a freshet swept away a dam, the dewatered pondsite was quickly occupied by smartweeds, sedges, and grasses, berry-bearing shrubs, canes, and vines, and sprouts and shoots from the stumps of beaver-cut trees. Later, pines, maples, and other hard-woods occupied the site and began the long series of successional stages back to climax forest. Hundreds of thousands of these animal-created ecosystems, in various stages of succession, flanked the small-er streams of North America before the coming of the whites.

The early explorers of the Atlantic and Pacific coasts took note of this great and varied wildlife resource, and some were highly im-pressed. Jacques Cartier, on his exploration of the St. Lawrence River in 1545, noted:

> . . . a great store of Stags, Deere, Beares, and other like sorts of beasts as Connies [rabbits], Hares, Materns, Foxes, Otters, Bevers, Weasels, Badgers and Rats [muskrats] and exceedingly great and divers other sorts of wild Beasts.

This report, varying only in detail, was echoed by Captain John Smith and a dozen or more later explorers who reached America at other locations.

The early explorers of Spanish America, however, were preoccu-pied with an eternal search for gold, and their counterparts from England, Holland, Sweden, and France with a fruitless search for a passage to India and the Spice Islands. America's rich heritage of wildlife, as a result, remained almost untouched by the white man's exploitation for nearly a century after Columbus reached its shores.

Chapter 3

The Beginning of Exploitation

When John Cabot returned to England in 1497 with a report to Henry VII that he had found fish so abundant along the coast of Labrador that they "could be taken not only with the net, but in baskets let down with a stone," fishermen were quick to investigate his story. They found little, if any, exaggeration. They also found great pods of whales and herds of seals and walruses. Adapting and refining techniques long known to the Eskimos and coastal Indians, European whalers and fishermen were soon reaping rich harvests from the coastal waters of the New World.

"Trying out" the oil from whale blubber at sea was a hazardous process in the ships of the time because of the risk of fire. This had to be carried out on shore where firewood was readily available and where there was no danger to the ships. The Basque, French, and English fishermen also needed shore bases where their catches of cod, halibut, and haddock could be salted and air-dried on racks of willow saplings. The shore crews lived in dormitory-like huts constructed with lumber brought from Europe or with native logs and sod. These short-based communities were the first white settlements on the Atlantic Coast, although they were abandoned during the winter months. At a later date, these seasonal settlements dotted the coast as far south as Maine.

The European whalers and fishermen supplemented their spring and summer diets with the eggs and flesh of the seabirds that thronged the rocky shoreline. Gannets, auklets, puffins, and dovekies nested in such dense colonies that the gray granite usually resembled chalk.

One of these birds was the great auk, a goose-sized flightless bird, resembling a penguin and so trusting of man that it could be killed with a club. Hundreds of thousands were slaughtered and chopped up for cod bait. By 1840, the last known survivor of the species would die at the hands of a Danish skin collector on a rocky island off the coast of Iceland.

The fishermen and whalers supplemented their income by spearing polar bears for their hides and walruses for their tusks. Walrus blubber also produced a high-grade oil that was favored in Europe, and many tons of walrus fat also went into the trying pots. At later dates, ships and men specialized in gathering these commodities as they did in killing seals.

Far to the Southwest, the Spaniards were beginning to have their own peculiar impact on the wildlife resources of the continent. This came not so much from the conquistadors in their restless search for gold as from the padres who accompanied them in a quest for heathen souls. Part of their strategy in seeking to convert the Indians to Christianity involved changing them from hunters into shepherds. Sheep, goats, and European swine soon became important items in the economy of many of the southwestern tribes. All of these domesticated animals compete heavily with native wildlife for food, and are highly destructive of grassy and woody cover. The hog can be a serious predator on the young and eggs of ground-nesting birds. Domesticated goats and sheep carry diseases and parasites lethal to bighorn sheep, antelope, and deer.

Inevitably, in the course of Indian tribal wars or by accident, some of these animals escaped to form nuclei of feral breeding populations. Wild horses already had become well established in Mexico after abandonment or loss by Cortes and his men provided the initial breeding stock, multiplying in numbers and spreading their range northward to compete for grass with the elk and buffalo.

As soon as the Spaniards settled down and established settlements, cattle and sheep raising became the major industries, gradually spreading from Mexico into southern California and what now are New Mexico, Arizona, and Texas. The longhorned Spanish cattle were little more than wild animals. The common practice was to turn them loose to fare for themselves on the open range. Periodically, groups would be rounded up by the *vaqueros* for branding or slaughter.

Juan de Oñate's colonists in New Mexico made a short-lived and rather disastrous attempt at domesticating the American bison. On October 5, 1598, after locating a herd of 100,000 buffalo near their camp, they began erecting a corral of cottonwood logs large enough to accommodate ten thousand cattle. Weirlike wings extended from far out onto the prairie to an open gate in the side of the corral. Three days later, when all was ready, the riders confidently rode into the buffalo herd and began driving the band they had cut out toward the corral. Because of the "fact that when they run they look as if they were hobbled, taking small leaps, the men took their capture for granted." But as the buffalo approached the corral, they suddenly wheeled and "stampeded with great fury in the direction of the men and broke through them, even though they held close together; and they were unable to stop the cattle. . . . For a few days the men tried in a thousand ways to drive them inside the corral or round them up, but all methods proved equally fruitless. This is no wonder, because they are unusually fierce; in fact they killed three of our horses and wounded forty others badly. . . ."

In the Spanish colonies, bear-baiting and contests between various species of wild and domesticated animals—bulls against bears, wolves against dogs, and similar matches—became popular amusements. The wild contestants for these fights were acquired by cowboys, running down the animals on horseback, and roping them with lariats from either side. When dealing with grizzly bears, this must have been a hazardous form of predator control!

Wildlife played an important role in the establishment of the eastern seaboard colonies. Deer, turkeys, and other products of the chase provided a ready supply of fresh meat until the colonists could develop their own domesticated flocks and herds. The wild birds and mammals also became an important source of income. Furs, deer hides, and the down and plumes of birds brought high prices in European markets. All were readily available in the vicinity of the early French, English, and Dutch settlements along the Atlantic Coast.

Most of the first settlers were tradesmen, farmers, and professional men poorly equipped for wilderness hunting or for coping with the hazards of life in their new country. But they did know how to trade, and in the Indian they found an eager partner.

The English in Plymouth and Jamestown, the Dutch in Manhattan, and the Spanish in Florida possessed materials that to the native American's eyes must have seemed like gems from another planet. The glittering glass beads that the white man held in such low esteem were priceless jewels to a people who possessed nothing more brilliant than dyed porcupine quills and fragments of polished clamshell. To an Indian who had spent his life skinning deer with a sharpened stone chip, the cheapest of steel trade knives must have seemed like a gift from God. A battered trade matchlock gave him a sense of power that few Indians had known before. All of these priceless commodities and more—mirrors, metal pots, a scrap of bright calico—the white man was willing to relinquish for such mundane things as a few beaver pelts, a dozen deer skins, a haunch of venison, or land the Indian, by custom, did not individually own. While it lasted, this was probably the most rewarding trading relationship in history. Each side thought it was taking advantage of the other and obtaining priceless commodities in exchange for practically nothing.

Once he acquired the profit motive, the Indian no longer hunted for his own needs, but for those of the whites as well. The colonists had a prodigious need for fresh meat, and their demand for furs was insatiable. The European beaver, closely resembling the American species, had been nearly exterminated, and beaver pelts brought exceedingly high prices in London and Paris. The French in Canada and northern Maine were exploting this situation long before the first colonists set foot at Jamestown and Plymouth. John Smith wrote that, in one year, 1607, the French had shipped 25,000 furs, mostly beaver, to European markets.

Trade in fur between Plymouth and the mother country began with the return voyage of the *Mayflower*. Another ship, the *Fortune*, in 1621, "was speedily dispatcht away, being laden with good clapboard as full as she could stowe, and two hoggsheads of beaver and otter skins, which were got with a few trifling commodities brought with them at first, being altogether unprovided for trade; neither was there any amongst them that ever saw a beaver skin 'till they came here."

This deficiency in trade goods described by Bradford was soon remedied, for in 1634, "it pleased ye Lord to inable them to send home . . . in beaver 3366 waight . . . and of otter-skinnes, 346." Between 1631 and 1636, Plymouth settlers alone shipped more than ten thousand pounds of beaver skins to London. In these early years beaver pelts served as a medium of exchange between the colonists as they did among the Indians.

Bradford also intimated that there were some sharp practices in the fur trade. In 1622, he wrote, the master of a ship visiting the colony offered them two hogsheads of peas, which the settlers needed badly, for nine pounds sterling and "under 8 he would not take, and yet would have beaver at an under rate."

To exploit the fur trade with the Cape Cod Indians, the Pilgrims built a trading post called Patuxet, near the head of Buzzards Bay, soon after they established their permanent homes in Plymouth. In 1635, they erected another post at the present site of Hartford, Connecticut, moving its operations in 1638 up the Connecticut River to Windsor. After the beaver colonies along the coast began to decline,

William Pynchon, in 1636, built another post farther upriver at the present site of Springfield, Massachusetts, to trade with the Abenakis of the upper Connecticut River watershed. During the next six years, this post shipped to England 8,992 beaver pelts weighing 13,139 pounds.

Fur trading was a major occupation of the Dutch on Manhattan Island during their stay there between 1626 and 1664. Their little colony was strategically located to tap the rich fur fields of the Hudson Valley and Lakes Champlain and George to the north.

By 1650, most of the beaver between Maine and the Carolinas had been eliminated from all of the streams on the coastal plain and the lower St. Lawrence Valley. Without regulation of their take and the means of taking, beaver are easily overtrapped, and the Indian and white trappers of the 1600s operated under no restrictions. Because of its conspicuous influences on the local landscape, beaver was easily detected. By setting snares in the entrances to the lodges, trappers were almost assured of a quick catch. By making small breaks in the dams and setting traps or snares in the breeches, trappers made use of the beaver's instinct to repair his work. In this way, most of the streams east of the Appalachians were mined of their beaver before 1700.

Other species also suffered from overexploitation during the period of early settlement. Turkeys and deer, which had abounded around the Indian clearings, declined rapidly after whites occupied the same sites.

Most of the beaver and other furs were obtained through trade with the Indians. The colonists, however, took many of the turkeys they used themselves. As hunting arms for deer and other large game, their clumsy wheel locks and snaphaunce muskets were inferior to the bow. But for killing turkeys, waterfowl, and other flocking species of birds, they were meat getters, if the hunter could get within twenty-five yards of his quarry.

The whites adopted Indian hunting techniques as soon as reliable sources of powder and shot became available, and added refinements of their own. One method was to prebait an area until the birds became accustomed to feeding there. Then from the cover of a blind, the hunter lay in wait until a group of feeding birds was massed close at hand. A single charge of small shot, properly timed, might kill a half dozen at once. The shot-charged musket also was a handy instrument for knocking birds from their roosts at night. Most of the colonial farmers maintained log pen traps along the edges of their cornfields, which were highly attractive to wild turkeys. Through this method they might capture a whole flock in a single day.

As the white settler became more woods-wise under the tutelage of his red neighbors, he stalked wild turkeys by tracking them in the snow. "Some," wrote William Wood of Plymouth, "have killed ten or a dozen in halfe a day." If the white hunter, like the Indian, obtained more wild meat than he could use immediately, he could easily dispose of the surplus through sale. The prevailing price for large turkeys throughout the 1600s in most of the English colonies was four shillings.

Under this heavy hunting pressure, the turkey declined rapidly around all of the white settlements. In his *New England's Rarities Discovered* of 1672, John Josselyn wrote of the situation near Boston:

> I have also seen threescore of young Turkies on the side of a marsh, sunning of themselves in a morning beside, but this was thirty years since, the English and the Indians having now destroyed the breed, so that 'tis rare to meet with a wild Turkey in the Woods.

But the heaviest impact of white settlement in North America came not so much from the direct killing that attended it as from the wrenching changes in the prevailing habitat brought about by the intrusion of European farming into what had been unspoiled wilderness. The European colonist, poised on the shores of a wild continent, recognized no value in wilderness, which he faced with feelings of dread. He and his companions had left behind geometrically patterned landscapes of farms, pastures, woodlots, and villages, neatly compartmented by fences and hedgerows. His dream and, as he saw it, his God-given duty was to tame the wilderness and change the new land to conform to the old. He realized this dream sooner than anyone at the time could have thought possible.

Once the first few settlers at St. Augustine, Jamestown, and Plymouth, after tenuous and hazard-filled starts, proved that Europeans could live and prosper in America, others joined them. What began as a trickle of immigration soon became a flood. The first tiny bridgehead settlements grew rapidly in population as religious refugees, political dissidents, and people looking for a new way of life swelled the ranks of their inhabitants. The Spanish, of course, had been in America much longer than the English, and Spanish towns and missions were sprinkled along the Gulf Coast from Florida to Mexico and farther inland long before the settlement of Jamestown. Settlers sent out by Don Tristán de Luna in 1559 had established a town at Pensacola, Florida.

A settlement developed at Rye, New Hampshire, two years after the landing at Plymouth, and in 1623, Dutch settlers occupied New Netherlands at the mouth of the Hudson. By 1625, English settlers from Plymouth began carving homes from the wilderness at Pemaquid on the Maine coast. In 1630, Puritans joined the Pilgrims on

Massachusetts Bay at Boston. Two years after that, Catholic colonists sent over by Sir George Calvert, First Baron of Baltimore, landed on the shores of Chesapeake Bay to establish Maryland. In 1636, Roger Williams, banished from the Massachusetts Bay Colony, established a haven for religious dissenters in Rhode Island. Swedes, under Johan Pryng, were established in Delaware and Pennsylvania nearly a half century before the arrival of William Penn's Quaker colonists.

Each of these toehold settlements, as it grew in population, became the nucleus for a group of satellite towns. Salem, Lynn, Weymouth, Newton, and Concord, established soon after the landing of the Puritans, had their roots in Boston.

In their early years, these coastal communities had only three exportable commodities—fish, furs, and wood. Trade with the mother country in wood products, as the records left by Bradford show, began soon after settlement. Apart from agriculture-oriented enterprise, such as milling, the first commercial establishment in each settlement usually was a water-powered saw mill. The stately pines along the coast, some rising sixty feet to the first limb, made the best of masts and spars. The massive oaks with their sweeping, curved limbs provided the finest material for ships' knees, beams, keels, and planking. At an early date, agents of the Royal Navy were sent to America to seek out and mark with a broad-arrow blaze selected mast trees that were reserved for official naval use. This, perhaps, was the first faint glimmering of forest conservation in America. Clapboard and shingles, from the durable and easily split cedar and cypress, also commanded higher prices in Europe, and both species of trees were readily available in the coastal swamps near the settlements.

The early settlers made great demands upon the forests for domestic needs as well as for export trade. With the exception of stone and thatch for roofs, wood was the universal building material and the only source of fuel. Until the bog-iron deposits along the coast were discovered, all iron and metal products used in the colonies had to be imported from abroad. Nails were worth their weight in gold, and consequently wooden pegs were used for joining. Furniture, universally, was made of wood, and many of the colonists' eating utensils, bowls, and dishes were carved from maple or walnut.

As the colonists developed a system of roads between their communities, wooden bridges spanned the streams and rivers. Where the roads passed over boggy ground, they were paved with a corduroy of logs and limbs.

Shipbuilding blossomed into a major enterprise in all of the Atlantic coastal colonies soon after their establishment. This industry required prodigious amounts of timber.

In spite of their dependence upon the forests, the colonists wasted most of the timber resources near their settlements. One demand more immediate than commerce was the establishment of reliable domestic sources of food that could come only with the development of agriculture and animal husbandry. The forest was adapted to neither. Moreover, the European settler feared the wilderness. With the increased hostility of the Indian, the forests provided cover from which the red warriors could mount a surprise attack before the citizen soldiers could muster for defense. It was also a haven for the timber wolf, the scourge of the colonial livestock owner.

As a result of the demand for lumber and fuel and because of the need for expansion of grazing lands and cropfields, the early towns were soon surrounded by lands almost devoid of trees. Most were cleared by felling the trees, dragging them into windrows, and burning them. All that was salvaged was the heap of pearl ash that was used domestically in tanning processes or for fertilizer or shipped overseas for a small profit.

The white man adopted the Indian practice of burning the woods and letting the fires burn themselves out. The grasslands created by repeated burning and the opening of the forest canopy provided excellent forage for cattle and sheep. Livestock ran on the open range on common lands around each settlement under the care of a few herders whose principal function was to guard them from wolves and theft by Indians.

After the forests around each settlement fell, they rarely had an opportunity to replace themselves. Those cleared lands not usurped as homesites and cropfields by latecoming immigrants were incorporated into the common lands of the growing central town as grazing lands for the rapidly increasing numbers of cattle, horses, and sheep.

Colonial logging operations were normally separated from the settlement areas, and these cleared yet uninhabited areas undoubtedly favored an increase in deer, grouse, black bears, and moose. All of these species thrive best in young second-growth forests interspersed with openings where grasses, berry canes, and vines can develop.

Colonial agriculture favored another class of wildlife. The settlers brought with them seeds of many food plants that were foreign to America—wheat, oats, barley, and other grains, melons, certain clovers, and other legumes. Among them were the seeds of many other European plants generally regarded as weeds, but many of which are important foods for seed-eating birds. Waste grains left in the fields by the harvesters and threshers added to the imported wildlife food supply. The hayfields and brushy fencerows provided excellent nesting cover for bobwhite quail, cottontail rabbits, and many songbirds.

The colonial farmer fenced his fields, more to keep the livestock out of the cropfields than to confine them. The fences between fields were usually made of split rail in the zigzag snake design. Little attempt was made to check the growth of vegetation that developed naturally along these fencerows, and black cherries, American chestnuts, walnuts, hickories, and other fruit and nut trees soon thrust their heads above the mats of raspberries, blackberries, and grapevines that developed along the fences. These, with the woodlots that the farmer retained as a source of firewood and lumber, provided excellent habitat and food for squirrels. Farm wildlife must have attained high population levels soon after European agriculture reached America.

Few colonial settlers had much time for sport hunting. The myriad chores—all performed by hand—occupied their time from dawn to dusk, six days a week. And the strict religious code required everyone's presence in church on Sunday. But the colonial settler did take time to hunt wolves that killed his sheep and cattle, and to run down renegade bears that sometimes raided his hog sties.

The timber wolf was the bane of the colonial livestock owner. Wood called it "the greatest inconvenience in the country," and Bradford, fifteen years after the first landing of the Pilgrims in 1620, called it one of the most serious threats to colonization. He added a hopeful prediction ". . . that poyson, traps and other such means will help to destroy them." By all accounts, the wolf was abundant around all of the colonial settlements, and remained so long after its ancestral prey, the deer, had been eliminated from much of the same range. Conditioned by millions of years of evolution to prey on deer, the wolf found the fat, clumsy sheep and cattle of the colonists easy victims. The open-range grazing system favored in most of the colonies did not make its hunting difficult.

The settlers declared war on the wolf almost as soon as the first ships arrived from Europe. This war would last almost three centuries. Among the first acts passed by the General Court of the Massachusetts Bay Colony in 1630 was a law offering a reward to anyone who killed a wolf:

> . . . euy Englishe man that killeth a wolfe in any pte within the limmits of this pattent shall have allowed him ld [penny] for euy beast & horse & ob. for every weaned swyine & goate in euy plantacon, to be levied by the constables of sd plantacons.

A subsequent law, passed in 1635, replaced this with a flat bounty of one shilling. This was later raised to ten shillings and, in 1648, to twenty shillings.

In the meantime, Virginia had followed the lead set by Massachusetts by enacting its own wolf bounty in 1632. Instead of cash, the Virginia Grand Assembly at first favored incentives in the form of privileges and goods, although later payments were in cash. The first bounty law permitted anyone who killed a wolf "to kill also one wild hogg and take same for his owne use." The domesticated swine obviously had become established as a feral species in Virginia within twenty-five years after the settlement of Jamestown.

Like the bounty laws of Massachusetts, those in Virginia were amended, repealed, and reinstated frequently. By 1646, the reward for killing a wolf was one hundred pounds of tobacco, payable to Indians as well as whites.

These incentive laws were copied in various versions by every colony along the eastern seaboard, and by later units of government as settlement progressed inland. Many remained on the law books for three centuries or more, long after wolves were eliminated from most of the East.

To protect their livestock and to collect the rewards offered for wolf scalps, the settlers adopted a number of ingenious methods of control. Wolf pits—deep, steep-sided holes, often studded on the bottom with sharpened stakes and screened across the top with breakthrough lids of light poles and leaves—ringed all of the early settlements. These must have been hazards to the unwary traveler. In 1630, a woman from Lynn, Massachusetts, spent a restless night in one before she was rescued. Not long after she fell, a wolf dropped in beside her, and the mismatched pair passed the night cowering in opposite corners of the pit.

Equally dangerous to the unwary wanderer was the set gun, a pistol, musket, or fowling piece lashed to a tree or pair of stakes and activated by a trip cord or baited line leading to the trigger.

An especially inhumane method of wolf control was described by Josselyn: It consisted of binding four "machereal" hooks with thread, wrapping them in wool, and dipping the contrivance in melted fat to form a ball. The settlers scattered these about a recent kill of sheep or cow in the hope that the wolf, on returning, would gulp them down.

The cavalier settlers of Jamestown turned wolf hunting into a sport, coursing them on horseback, like the Spanish colonists, and catching them with ropes. Chroniclers tell of young Virginia bloods racing through village streets with live wolves tied to their horses' tails.

The more sedate settlers of New England usually hunted wolves on foot in drives involving most of the able-bodied men in several neighboring towns. With the clearing of the forests, the wolves usually found local strongholds in swamps or rocky country that civilization had bypassed. From these they ventured out at night to attack the livestock near the settlements.

On a designated morning, the men, armed with firearms, pitchforks, and pikes, surrounded the wolves' denning area and advanced into it from all sides. Sometimes wolves broke through the tightening ring, or escaped into rocky dens, but at other times the drives were highly effective.

Wolf driving apparently was used as a method of training colonial militiamen in forest warfare. *The Annals of Lynn* (Massachusetts) record that, in 1634: "On training day, Captain Turner, by the direction of Colonel Humfrey, went with his company to Nahant to hunt the wolves. This was a pleasant amusement for training day."

In spite of this relentless persecution, the wolf persisted along most of the Atlantic Coast for at least a century after the first settlements.

Other species, however, did not fare so well. The white-tailed deer, with its habitat usurped by growing numbers of cattle, sheep, and horses, and persecuted mercilessly for its flesh and hide, was soon eliminated from the vicinity of the coastal settlements. In contrast to the wolf, the deer was considered a major asset by the colonists. Its flesh was excellent fare, and its leather was ideal for many purposes. Buckskin made light, windproof mittens and gloves, and thornproof jackets and trousers for the soldier, surveyor, and woods cruiser who led the advance of civilization into America's interior. In the early days and later in the frontier, greased parchment made of deerskin substituted for glass in cottage and cabin windows. Deer antlers adapted themselves to many uses—knife and fork handles, chandeliers, clothing racks, and ornaments for personal wear. Colonists sometimes used deer hair for stuffing saddle pads and furniture.

Deer were snared as well as shot, and many must have fallen victims to the ubiquitous wolf pits and traps. The colonists in Massachusetts learned early the technique of deer snaring, even before they met the Indians who had devised it. After their first landing inside Provincetown's Race Point, the Pilgrims groped their way southward and westward along the northern shore of Cape Cod in search of Plymouth Harbor. On one of these extraordinary expeditions doughty William Bradford, soon to become governor of the colony, backed into a hidden noose and found himself dangling upside down from a tree limb. History and Edward Winslow, who witnessed and recorded the incident, tactfully neglected to record the Reverend Bradford's comments at the time, and the governor himself overlooked the embarrassing incident in his memoirs.

The destruction of deer and deer cover near the coast and in the river valleys, the improvement of cover through logging, and the exclusion of white settlement from the interior lands by hostile Indians led to a complete reshuffling of the deer range. Where, during the first years of settlement, deer had been common around every white village, they soon became scarce. In the interior, where they had been comparatively scarce, they became abundant.

This respite was only temporary, however, as the whites consolidated their bridgeheads along the coast and pushed their settlements deeper into the new continent, driving the Indians before them in a series of bloody wars. Except for the dates, the history of the forests and wildlife of the interior coastal plain and piedmont was the same as that which had occurred on the coast. The forests fell, villages and farms sprang up in the former wilderness, and livestock occupied the cleared lands not used for agriculture. Wild life was ruthlessly exploited.

Along the coasts, the former rich spawning runs of salmon, shad, sturgeon, and alewives were blocked from many streams by dams erected to power grist mills and sawmills or to ease the passage of logs and barges over rapids.

The segments of the passenger pigeon population east of the Appalachians suffered heavily during this white invasion. When the early settlements were being carved out of the forests of New England and the mid-Atlantic Coast, great nesting colonies of pigeons occupied the northern hardwood belt between the Great Lakes and southern New England. In autumn, as the acorns ripened, great flights poured down the Connecticut, Hudson, Delaware, and Potomac to wintering grounds farther south.

Both Josselyn and Wood used the term "millions of millions" to describe the flights they witnessed in Massachusetts in the 1600s. Josselyn wrote in 1673:

> I have seen a flight of Pidgeons in the spring, and at Michaelmas, when they return back to the Southward, for four or five miles that to my thinking had neither beginning nor ending, length or breadth, and so thick I could see no Sun.

During one of these flights, the members of a family in Lynn reportedly killed "a hundred dozens" by batting them from the air with poles. When another flight descended on Plymouth's cropfields in 1643, they destroyed so much of the ripening corn and grain that the colonists were threatened with famine. In 1648, however, the flights arrived after the harvest was in, and the birds themselves were heavily harvested by the settlers, ". . . it being incredible what multitudes of them were killed daily."

Most of the adult pigeons taken by the whites were caught in traps fashioned from fishnets and later from nets especially designed for their capture. These were erected on the edges of the cropfields or near their swarming nesting areas and roosts, one of which was situated within thirty-two miles of Boston.

The flightless squabs, almost as large as the adults at three weeks of age, made choice eating and commanded good prices in the markets of the colonies. Indians took great numbers by knocking them from their nests with poles and bringing them into the towns for barter. Those occupying nests too high to reach with poles often were suffocated with smudge fires placed beneath the nest trees.

This heavy attrition of young and breeding birds had its inevitable effect on the abundance of the pigeons. Josselyn reported that the New England flights were "much diminished" by 1672, although impressive numbers remained long after that time, especially in the Ohio Valley and in the Great Lakes region, which had been little affected by the march of civilization that was transforming the lands to the east.

To the credit of colonial legislators, some attempted to check the steady decline of the more valuable members of the wildlife communities. Most of the protective legislation was designed to save the deer, whose hide and flesh were important commodities in the colonial economy. On February 14, 1646, the town of Portsmouth, Rhode Island, ordered a closed season on deer hunting "from the first of May till the first of November; and if any shall shoot a deere within that time he shall forfeit five pounds. . . ." This ordinance established a pattern for laws that most of the colonies adopted before 1720.

The preamble of a law adopted by Connecticut reflected official concern over the future of the colony's deer herd:

> The killing of deer at unseasonable times of the year hath been found very much to the prediudice of the Colonie, great numbers of them having been hunted and destroyed in deep snowes when they are very poor and big with young, the flesh and skins of very little value, and the increase greatly hindered.

In 1705, the General Assembly at Newport, Rhode Island, noted that:

> . . . it hath been informed that great quantities of deer hath been destroyed in this Collony out of season . . . and may prove much to the damage of this Collony for the future, and . . . for the whole country, if not prevented.

There were scattered convictions of those who violated these early game laws, but these were exceptions rather than the rule. Enforcement, at first, was left to town-based county sheriffs or local constables. Most of the illegal deer killing was being done by independent settlers in the new frontier communities in whose environs the deer were still abundant.

Alarmed by the decrease in the numbers of deer, the General Court of Massachusetts acted in 1739 to put teeth in the poorly enforced deer-season law it had enacted in 1698. It instructed each town in the colony to appoint two "deer reeves" whose duty would be to enforce the closed season. Similar officers were authorized soon after that year by Rhode Island, Connecticut, New York, and North Carolina.

Penalties for violations of these colonial laws were heavy. In Massachusetts the fine was ten pounds, equivalent to several hundred dollars in modern currency. Half of the fine went to the deer reeve as his fee. This arrangement led to a greater number of convictions. In 1763, Azariah Seldon of Hadley, Massachusetts, was convicted in Northampton of having "willingly, with force of arms, killed one wild deer, and then and there had in his possession the raw flesh and skin of one wild deer killed since the 21st of December last, contrary to the laws of this province, the peace of said lord the King, his crown and dignity."

Azariah was assessed the full fine of ten pounds. But he was more fortunate than one Halbert who, unable to raise the fine, was put on the auction block and sold to the highest bidder for two months of forced labor. To the disappointment of the deer reeve who had apprehended Halbert, his services brought only thirty shillings.

Convictions such as these probably served as some deterrent to potential violators. But the continued destruction of deer habitat and the long open season without bag limit tended to nullify their benefits. Many towns in the colonies retained the office of deer reeve as a sinecure long after the deer had disappeared from their borders. By the time of the Revolution most jurisdictions had abolished the office because there were few or no deer left to protect.

The colonial deer laws were quite unsuccessful in achieving their objectives. But they did establish a mechanism that, in later times, would become a basic foundation for the protection and management of wildlife.

Chapter 4

The American Fur Trade

For more than a century, while the Atlantic coastal plain between Maine and the Carolinas was filling with farms and settlements, the Appalachians stood as a barrier to western expansion of English development. But farther north, the St. Lawrence River and the chain of Great Lakes from which it flowed provided for the French a direct water route to the center of the continent. While the English were grubbing their farms from the edge of the wilderness, the French were establishing forts, trading posts, and villages a thousand miles and more inland. Barges and cargo canoes ascended the St. Lawrence into the Great Lakes filled with trade muskets, knives, hatchets, and fishhooks. They returned laden with beaver, otter, and many other kinds of furs.

Even farther to the north, the English also were exploiting the fur resources of Canada through the "Governor and Company of Adventurers of England Trading into Hudson's Bay." This unwieldly name was shortened later to Hudson's Bay Company. Its charter required that the Company seek a northwest passage to the Pacific. But in exchange, the Crown granted it a full monopoly of the trade in all streams entering Hudson Bay and all traffic in any adjacent lands that the "adventurers" might enter. Additionally, the charter granted the Company full legislative, judicial, and executive authority in all of its trading lands. Within a few years after its establishment, it was doing a thriving business with the Indians and Eskimos of northern Canada. By the mid-1700s it had trading posts on James Bay and at the mouths of the Hayes and Churchill rivers. Its ships shuttled back and forth across the Atlantic to England, bringing trade goods in and loads of Arctic fox, beaver, and seal pelts out.

The French achieved a rapport with the American wilderness and the Indian that few of the more race-minded Englishmen ever attained. The exception was their relationship with the Iroquois, whose lasting hatred Samuel de Champlain had aroused by siding with the Hurons in a battle between the two tribes.

Unlike the English, the French found advantage in keeping much of their part of the new continent in an unspoiled state. They recognized immediately that their potential wealth lay in furs and fish rather than in gold, the search for which had preoccupied the Spaniards for nearly a century. The long Canadian winter limited the agricultural possibilities that the English were realizing in the South. The fortress town of Quebec was the only French post in Canada in 1627 when the Company of One Hundred Associates was established. Its principal interest was the exploitation of the fur trade. Montreal was established in 1642, and French traders were pushing deep into the interior to trade with the Chippewa and Illinois.

Under the Bourbon kings of France, Canada was sadly mismanaged. It was governed by autocratic royal agents who imposed heavy taxes and rigidly supervised the lives of the people. These agents also developed oppressive monopolies governing trade and commerce of goods needed by the citizens.

Although trade with the Indians and English was a prerogative reserved for the Crown, many of the more commercially minded French winked at the law. Some of the more ambitious deserted their lands and pushed into the wilderness to trade directly with the Indians. Many took Indian wives and adopted Indian ways. These *coureurs de bois*—tough, woodswise, and attuned to the wilderness—became the voyageurs, the backbone of the English fur trade after 1763 when the end of the Seven Years' War terminated French rule in Canada. They were the ideal ambassadors, negotiators, and mediators between the British and the Indians when the Hudson's Bay Company took over the trade relinquished by the French.

For a number of years, the British and their French-Canadian employees had the fur trade largely to themselves, the voyageurs penetrating the continent as far as the Rockies in their search for new beaver pelts. Their principal form of transportation was the *canot de maître*, a huge birch-bark canoe up to forty feet in length and seven feet across the beam, but weighing, unladen, only a few hundred pounds. The larger could accommodate a crew of twelve and five tons of cargo. Although it was fragile and required constant repair, it was swift and marvelously maneuverable. Its shallow draft permitted it to float over shoals and through rapids where heavier boats would ground. Its light weight made possible portages of miles where it was necessary to bypass dangerous rapids or to span land separating stream from stream or stream from lake.

On many of the lakes and larger rivers, the canoe often gave way to the flat-bottomed Mackinaw barge, which was propelled by six or eight oarsmen, sometimes assisted on open waters by a jury-rigged sail.

Home base for many of these craft was little Michilimackinac Island, lying in the narrow strait that separates Lakes Huron and Michigan. The fort and trading post commanded water routes leading west through the prairies, north to the Arctic Circle and south into Illinois and the Mississippi Valley. Spain claimed the lands south of Canada and west of the Mississippi when it acquired the Louisiana Territory from France at the end of the Seven Years' War in 1763. Except in the South along the Gulf Coast, it exerted little influence over these lands, and trappers from Canada regularly raided the fur resources of the northern portions of the region. In 1800, through a secret treaty, the region was again returned to France.

As soon as the Revolutionary War ended, American settlers began pouring through the gaps in the Appalachians to occupy Ohio, Kentucky, Tennessee, and other lands west of the mountains that hitherto had been virtually untouched. Foreign control of the Mississippi Valley, the most practical route for supplying the new settlements, was a matter of major concern to the American government. When Thomas Jefferson assumed office, he instructed his minister to France, Robert Livingston, to negotiate with Napoleon I's regime in an effort to open the Mississippi to American shipping. Livingston was authorized to purchase the town of New Orleans or to negotiate a treaty that would permit American craft to use the river. When Livingston made little progress, Jefferson dispatched James Monroe, then governor of Virginia, to Paris to assist him.

On April 30, 1803, after weeks of haggling, Charles Maurice de Talleyrand-Perigord, Napoleon's minister of foreign affairs, startled both Americans by offering abruptly to sell all French holdings in continental North America except Florida. Although they operated well beyond their authorized power, Livingston and Monroe seized the opportunity while it was in their grasp. For the sum of $15 million—about four cents an acre—they added 828,000 square miles to the area of the United States. This included all of the present-day states of Arkansas, Iowa, Kansas, Mississippi, Missouri, Nebraska, North and South Dakota, and Oklahoma; the lands west of the Mississippi in Minnesota and Louisiana, including New Orleans; and eastern Wyoming and Colorado.

The Louisiana Purchase extended the territory of the United States to the Pacific Ocean. The infant nation already claimed Oregon, which then included Idaho and Washington, through the explorations of Robert Gray, who, in 1792, had discovered the Columbia River. He had visited Oregon three years earlier on a round-the-world voyage. While there, he had found valuable and lustrous furs easy to acquire from the Indians and returned in 1792 for more. On Gray's first trip, British traders were in the area, also exploiting the sea otter trade. In 1789, Spanish warships commanded by Estevan José Martínez seized ships owned by a British trader, John Meares, in Nootka Sound on Vancouver Island. The incident went down in history as the "Nootka War." For reasons known only to themselves, the Spanish did not molest the American ships of Gray and John Kendrick, who were also trespassing in waters claimed by Spain and engaging in the fur trade, which precipitated the attack on the British.

The Russian-American Fur Company, based in Alaska, was also pursuing the marine fur trade with the coastal Eskimos and Indians at least as far south as Fort Ross, which they established just north of the present site of San Francisco. Sea otters and fur seals, providing some of the finest furs in the world, were abundant along most of the coast. They were especially valued by the Chinese, who prized the fur of the sea otter above all others in the world. Dozens of otters could be taken by drifting boats through the kelp beds and hauling them aboard with gaffs.

The Russian traders, by 1768, already had destroyed one of North America's unique species—the Steller's sea cow, a 24-foot-long relative of the manatee that occupied a few islands along the Alaskan coast. The sea cow had little if any commercial value, but its flesh was edible, and it was easily taken with harpoons. The species was discovered in 1741 when the German naturalist Georg Wilhelm Steller and Vitus J. Bering were shipwrecked on one of the Commander Islands named for Bering off the east coast of Kamchatka. The sea cow apparently was fairly common along the coasts of Kamchatka and Copper Islands. The discovery of the species and its extinction were separated by little more than a quarter of a century.

The sea cow's restricted distribution, large size, sluggishness, and lack of fear of man all contributed to its early demise as a species. The Russians harpooned sea cows from six- or eight-oared boats or from one-man boats drifted over the submerged feeding grounds of the animals. The sea cows were rarely killed outright, and many more were lost and wasted than were converted to food.

After the United States acquired Louisiana in 1803, the only northern settlement of any significance within the territory was St. Louis, strategically situated at the confluence of the Mississippi and the east-flowing Missouri. The first American agent for the Indians, Pierre Chouteau, Sr., a former *coureur de bois* and an accomplished trader in furs, made his headquarters in St. Louis. In one of his first reports to his superiors in Washington, Chouteau wrote uneasily of the large numbers of British fur traders moving up the Missouri into the lands of the Mandans and Sioux. He was particularly concerned about the large quantities of rotgut liquor the British intruders were carrying as a trade item to persuade the Indians to relinquish their furs.

This report, along with similar reports of British and Canadian trading operations in Oregon, were among many reasons that President Thomas Jefferson decided to confirm American sovereignty over the western territories by dispatching an exploratory expedition overland to the Pacific. Meriwether Lewis and William Clark spent two years in fulfilling the mission between 1804 and 1806.

Lewis's graphic reports of rich fur resources along the route stimulated interest by American speculators. One of those who listened most intently to these reports was John Jacob Astor of New York City. The explorers had suggested that beaver furs could be transported across the Rockies on pack horses to the Oregon coast and then transshipped to the lucrative markets of China. Astor's ships for a number of years had been carrying on a trade with the Orient by transporting silver, beaver pelts, and ginseng roots purchased in Montreal to Canton where these goods were exchanged for tea and silk. The route suggested by Lewis and Clark would remove thousands of miles from the voyage to China around Cape Horn. Additionally, his plan eliminated the need for negotiating with the sharp British traders in Canada. Astor also was aware of the opportunities for wealth that existed in exploiting the sea otter that swarmed in the kelp beds of the Pacific Northwest Coast.

Before Astor had an opportunity to formulate his plan of action, however, a group of independent traders operating in the Louisiana Territory and selling their furs to the Montreal-based North West Company, pooled their resources to form the Michilimackinac Company. In 1806, its officials dispatched David Thompson to the Pacific Coast to open trade with the otter-hunting Indians.

Astor, in 1808, received his charter for the American Fur Company. His first move was to try to buy the Michilimackinac Company and its trading rights on the Columbia. When the Canadians refused, Astor applied leverage by offering the use of his ships to the Russians to supply their trading posts in Alaska. Early in 1809, he asked Wilson Price Hunt to lead an overland expedition that would retrace the route of Lewis and Clark to the mouth of the Columbia to select the site of a trading post, while a seaborne expedition was being sent around Cape Horn.

Because of the Napoleonic Wars and the unsettled political climate in the British Empire, the United States Congress adopted embargos and anti-importation laws, which made it impossible for the British in Montreal to ship trade goods to their field base on Michilimackinac Island. This placed Astor in a favorable bargaining position for, if the British could form some sort of partnership with him, there was a possibility that the intent of the law might be circumvented.

Astor agreed to help them on the condition that the North West Fur Company purchase one-third of his Pacific Fur Company, which he was then organizing to exploit the riches of the Columbia River. The traders who were dealing directly with the Indians, however, cared little for the agreement reached by their city-based partners, for they wanted all of the upper Columbia River watershed as an exclusive field of operations. They dispatched a courier to intercept David Thompson, their advance agent, with instructions to proceed immediately to the Columbia and claim as much as possible of the Columbia for Great Britain and, of course, the North West Fur Company. The messenger intercepted Thompson near Fort William on Rainy Lake in present-day Ontario.

In the dead of winter, Thompson and a small band of followers headed for the Pacific, bypassing the hunting territories of warlike Indians, climbing the Rockies, and shooting the rapids of the treacherous Snake River canyons in hand-hewn canoes. On July 9, 1811, they reached the point where the Snake River meets the Columbia. Here they placed a stake, claiming the lands above for Great Britain and the "N. W. Company of Merchants from Canada."

In the meantime, the Congress of the United States had relaxed its restrictions on foreigners trading in the United States, and the North West Company had reneged on its agreement with Astor. By offering higher wages and greater benefits, the New York merchant retaliated by raiding the North West Company of many of its more experienced trappers, traders, and clerks. In September, the predominantly Canadian party sailed from New York Harbor aboard Astor's ship *Tonquin*. Seven months later it entered the mouth of the Columbia.

After unloading the men and their cargo at the site of a log fort named Astoria, the *Tonquin* sailed into Nootka Sound on Vancouver Island. Indians attacked it immediately, boarded it, and massacred the crew. The sole survivor, seriously wounded, managed to reach the powder magazine, set torch to it, and blow the ship, himself, and an unknown number of triumphant natives to pieces.

The loss of the *Tonquin* was a serious one to Astor and even more-so to the men at Astoria, as it cut off their principal contact with the East by sea. Then David Thompson arrived with documents showing that the North West Company owned one third of Astor's project. The Astorians, however, chose to ignore Thompson's staked claim to the upper Columbia and sent a party headed by Robert Stuart up the river to establish an inland post at the mouth of the Okanogan River.

While these developments were taking place, the voyageurs, headed by Wilson Price Hunt and Donald MacKenzie, were struggling over plains and mountains to the Columbia by the overland route. Scheduled to depart St. Louis well in advance of the sailing of the *Tonquin* and to reach the Pacific Coast ahead of her, Hunt had been delayed by recruiting problems and did not begin to move until the ship was ready to weigh anchor in New York.

Eleven hundred miles up the Missouri, the Hunt party's keelboats were overtaken by those sent out by the Missouri Fur Company, which had been organized in 1809 by Manuel Lisa, an American of Spanish blood. Among Lisa's partners were Pierre Chouteau; William Clark, the explorer; and Reuben Lewis, the son of Meriwether. For his services on the Lewis and Clark Expedition, Clark had been appointed a government agent for the Indians in the West. The Government also had awarded him a rank of brigadier general and placed him in command of the territorial militia, posts that gave him considerable personal influence in the affairs of Louisiana Territory. Lisa had acquired considerable experience in trading along the Missouri River, and Chouteau was an old hand at bartering with Indians.

When the rival parties met near the present border between North and South Dakota, the meeting was strained. It could have broken into open hostilities. But both were concerned about the reception they might receive from the Blackfeet, whose lands they were approaching. Of all the tribes on the northern plains, the Blackfeet had shown the most violent hostility toward white trespassers.

On his journey up the Missouri, Hunt had encountered and employed as a guide John Colter, a veteran of the Lewis and Clark Expedition and one of the most experienced frontiersmen in the West. Colter suggested that the Hunt party leave the Missouri, head overland to the Henry's Fork of the Snake River, and complete their trip to Astoria by boat. This would permit them to bypass the lands of the hostile Blackfeet. Lisa's primary interest at the time was trade with the Arikaras and other tribes of the east slopes of the Rockies with whom he had established good relationships.

Hunt's decision to leave the river broke the tension between the two groups. But the overland route selected by Colter required the use of horses. Lisa, eager to get potential rivals off the Missouri, of-

fered to sell him surplus mounts and pack animals from his herd at
Fort Mandan, his base of operations two hundred miles upriver.
While these were being brought back, Hunt purchased more, with
Lisa's help, from the friendly Arikaras. Hunt's party now consisted
of sixty-two men, the Indian wife of one of the trappers, and their
two children. In July, with eighty-two horses, they began the long
trek toward the Snake, crossing the Rockies at Union Pass to the
headwaters of the Green. On their march through the mountains they
found game scarce. But in the valley of the Green River, buffalo occurred in abundance. After taking and drying three tons of meat, they
proceeded northwestward through Teton Pass, reaching, in an October blizzard, the deserted cabin where Colter two years earlier had
wintered with Andrew Henry.

Here the voyageurs hewed dugout canoes from massive cottonwood logs. The relatively placid waters at Henry's Fork gave little or
no warning of the boiling rapids they would encounter as their frail
and tipsy craft reached the sheer-walled canyons of the Snake farther
downstream. Capsizings became almost daily occurrences, and a number of their brittle dugouts were shattered on the lava outcroppings.
One man drowned, and much of their cargo was lost. Faced with this
attrition on their supplies and a rapidly approaching winter, the
party split into smaller groups. Some stayed behind to trap beaver
and trade with the Indians. The others inched their way by various
routes to the coast. The first group, its numbers reduced by deaths
along the way, staggered into Fort Astoria in January, 1812. The
largest detachment under the command of Hunt arrived one month
later, and a third and final group straggled in in May.

Resupplied by another ship from New York, the Astorians who
had arrived earlier by sea were busily completing their trading post
and preparing to expand operations by building other forts farther up
the Columbia and along the coast. They had already opened negotiations with the Russians to purchase seal and sea otter pelts for ex-
portation to the Orient.

Along and east of the Rockies, Lisa's trappers were extending their
operations southward into New Mexico, which then included the area
of the states of Colorado, Utah, Nevada, Arizona, and New Mexico
and was claimed by Spain. Lisa's burning ambition was to open the
fur trade with Santa Fe. His efforts were plagued by disaster. Some
of his best trappers were killed by Indians. When rumors of a revolt
in New Mexico reached him, he dispatched a group to negotiate with
the new government—only to find that the Spanish were still in firm
control. His emissaries were imprisoned in Mexico for seven years.
Then the War of 1812 turned the Mississippi Valley into a battlefield.
Shock waves of the war swept through the Indian tribes of the West

and many tribes, formerly friendly to the Americans, aroused by British agents, turned against the American traders and trappers. Lisa was forced by the Minnetarees to evacuate Fort Mandan and other posts on the Missouri and withdraw his base of operations to Council Bluffs.

The war also affected the direction of John Jacob Astor's affairs. When hostilities broke out, the Congress passed the Non-Intercourse Act, which banned the activities of British traders in the American Northwest. This again brought the Montreal owners of the Michilimackinac Company to Astor with hats in hands. Again feeling that an American partner could use his influence to circumvent the law, they asked Astor to join forces with them. Astor accepted, but only on the condition that he receive half ownership of a new firm to be called the South West Company, which would trade west of Michilimackinac on both sides of the United States-Canadian border.

To the discomfiture of the Montrealers, however, the United States Government refused to allow any exceptions to the Non-Intercourse Act. But some trade goods did manage to filter past federal authorities to the Indians of the northern plains and mountains. In the opening years of the war, Robert Dickson, an English-Canadian, smuggled several loads across the border. This action convinced the Indians that the British were their friends, and they refused to deal with the legitimate American traders. Then word reached Astoria that a North West Company ship, the *Isaac Todd*, armed with cannon and letters of marque commissioning her as a privateer, had sailed from London to capture the post.

Duncan McDougall and Donald MacKenzie, who were the superior officers at Fort Astoria, decided to evacuate the post before the British arrived. The wooden stockade that surrounded it was proof against Indian arrows, but it could be battered to pieces by the smallest cannon. Moreover, the Indians, under the influence of Dickson's activities, were no longer bringing in furs. But their one ship, the *Beaver*, with Wilson Hunt aboard, was in Alaska. Hunt was purchasing fur seal pelts from Alexandr Baranov, manager of the Russian-American Company, for transshipment to Canton.

McDougall and MacKenzie did the only thing they could under the circumstances. They pulled their trappers from the upper Columbia and Snake and began gathering horses for the long trip east. Ships dispatched by Astor to strengthen the fort failed to arrive, and men of the North West Company were gathering across the river. When more Canadians joined the first, the uneasy McDougall decided that the time for negotiations had arrived, if the Pacific Fur Company was to salvage anything from its venture. He offered the Canadians the entire assets of his company at Astoria in return for safe passage across the Rockies. Under the agreement, the North West Company agreed to hire any Astorians who wished to stay and continue trapping.

Although Astor was furious at MacKenzie and McDougall when he received the news, he obtained at least some compensation. Soon after the Astorians began moving up the river, the British warship *Raccoon* crossed the bar at the mouth of the Columbia, ran up the Union Jack on Fort Astoria's flagstaff and renamed the post Fort George.

With the conclusion of the war by the Treaty of Ghent in December, 1814, war-weary Great Britain agreed to permit the boundaries between Canada and the United States to revert to their prewar positions. But the ownership of Oregon remained in doubt. Finally the two powers reached a compromise under which both British and American subjects could trade in the disputed territory for ten years, at which time negotiations would be reopened.

Two major territorial problems remained unresolved. One was Texas, where American freebooters had formed communities well inside the territorial lands of Spain. The second was East Florida, also held by Spain's moldering empire.

As soon as the war was over, the United States Government opened negotiations with Spain to purchase Florida. Andrew Jackson's imperious and impetuous raid into the peninsula—on which he insulted the Spanish governor and hanged a pair of British citizens—delayed negotiations. But in 1819 Spain and the United States signed the Adams-Onís Treaty that ceded Florida to the United States in exchange for a guarantee that the United States Government pay claims of the citizens of Florida against the Spanish Government up to a limit of five million dollars. This treaty was ratified in February, 1821. Texas, however, was a question that would be resolved a quarter of a century later only by the force of arms.

With the end of hostilities, settlers by the thousands poured across the Appalachians into the fertile lands beyond. The mountains, which had served as a dam to western expansion, were swamped under a flood of immigration. National borders, once a constant source of conflict on the frontier, had been stabilized. Indian opposition to the intrusion of white settlers had melted during the war, and what little of it remained was promptly squelched. The Iroquois had been driven into Canada. Tecumseh was dead, and his Shawnees and their Sauk and Fox allies were fragmented. Except for occasional violent outbreaks, such as the Black Hawk War in 1832, the eastern Indians were subjugated. In 1830, Congress passed the Indian Removal Act, which stripped the remaining tribes of their land and led to the genocidal Long March of the Creeks, Cherokees, Chickasaws, and those Seminoles who had not escaped to the swamps of Florida, to sterile reservations in Oklahoma.

The pattern of exploitation west of the Appalachians was much the same as that which had occurred in the East. Only the tempo changed. Between the censuses of 1810 and 1820, Ohio's population doubled. Indiana's rocketed from 24,500 to 147,178. The settlers came not only by alternately dusty and muddy roads that were beginning to link the West and the East, but by keelboat down the Ohio, and up the Mississippi by barge. The first steamboat on the Mississippi, the *New Orleans*, began traveling as early as 1812. Soon dozens of paddlewheelers, loaded with new settlers, farm equipment, and livestock were thrashing the waters of the Ohio, Mississippi, and Missouri.

Most of the hundreds of thousands of settlers fanned out over the lands between the Mississippi Valley and the crests of the eastern mountains to hew and burn farmsites, pastures, and cropfields from the forests. There was a prevalent belief that the only good agricultural lands supported hardwoods, and most of these new lands were filled with oaks, beech, and hickory. The forests fell swiftly before the advance of civilization.

In their first year or two, the frontiersmen lived largely off the land, eating venison and waterfowl, trapping beaver and other furs for sale or barter. The eastern elk and woodland bison of the eastern forests succumbed quickly to this human avalanche and its attendant flood of domesticated livestock. Those beaver that the Indian, French, and English trappers had overlooked lasted a little longer. Most disappeared by 1850.

In the West, along the Rockies and beyond, the fur trade had molded a new and unique breed of American—the mountain man— perhaps the most colorful to stride the stage of American history. Most were young men, in their twenties, and as lean and tough as Cheyenne quirts. They used American implements—traps, knives, and rifles—but most effected the practical fringed and beaded garb of the Indian, topped off with a felt hat or fur cap, often ornamented with a feather or two. Many married Indian wives or adopted Indian mistresses.

In the field, they led lives of almost total freedom, traveling alone or in small groups into every cranny of the West in an endless search for beaver. Each, unless he had an Indian squaw, was his own cook, food gatherer, tailor, and physician. When Thomas L. Smith, forever after known as "Pegleg," shattered his lower leg in a fall, he amputated the useless member with his skinning knife. Each was his own blacksmith, gunsmith, and mechanic. He lived a life of constant danger—from hostile Indians and Mexican patrols, from the elements, and from accident and illness. As simple an injury as a bad sprain or an infected scratch could mean death in the wilderness. Except for occasional contacts with others of his kind or military patrols, his links with civilization for months on end were almost nonexistent.

Many were "free trappers" who sold their catches directly to traders operating in or near their territories. The majority, however, were in the employ of the several major fur companies that operated in the West in the early 1800s. After the Adams-Onís Treaty relaxed tensions between the United States and Mexico, the American Fur Company realized Manuel Lisa's dream of opening the untapped trapping fields of New Mexico. On July 17, 1822, four American trappers arrived with wagonloads of New Mexican beaver pelts that Ramsey Crooks of the American Fur Company purchased for just under five thousand dollars.

This set off a rush of trappers to Mexican territory, a rush so great that in 1824 the Mexican Government decreed that only Mexican nationals would be licensed to trap beaver. The mountain men circumvented the law by accepting Mexican partners, applying for Mexican citizenship, or, more often, simply keeping out of sight of Mexican authority. Their base of operations was Taos, comparatively free from supervision from the territorial government in Santa Fe and close enough to the mountains to assure an abundant supply of beaver pelts. One of the trappers who started his career by working the New Mexican mountains and who left his mark on history was Kit Carson.

Three fur companies scoured the streams of the northern Rockies and plains in the 1820s. One was the Missouri Fur Company, whose trappers operated from Fort Benton at the meeting point of the Yellowstone and Bighorn rivers. The second was the French Fur Company, which traded with the Indians of the Great Plains from a base called Fort Lookout on the Missouri River in present-day South Dakota.

The third was organized in 1822 by two former mountain men, Andrew Henry and William H. Ashley. On February 13, they placed an advertisement in the St. Louis Missouri *Gazette*, addressed: "To Enterprising Young Men:"

> The subscriber wishes to engage ONE HUNDRED MEN to ascend the river Missouri to its source, there to be employed for one, two, or three years.—For particulars, enquire of Major Andrew Henry, near the Lead Mines in the County of Washington, (who will ascend with, and command the party). Or to the subscriber at St. Louis.
>
> Wm. H. Ashley

The terms offered by Ashley and Henry were generous at face value. Instead of offering wages, as many companies did, they offered the trappers the profits from fifty percent of their catch. This arrangement, however, was not disadvantageous to the partners. From his half, the trapper had to buy his traps, ammunition, clothing, liquor, tobacco, and other supplies—enough to last a year in the wilderness —from Ashley and Henry. The share system also spurred the trapper to take as many pelts as possible to increase his income. This worked more to the interest of the partners than it did to the trapper, as his desire for goods was proportional to his income. In the brawling binges at the rendezvous, where the trappers brought their bales of beaver pelts for sale to the traders, many blew their earnings for a year in a single week and returned to the traplines with little more to show for them than a few pounds of tobacco, a few gewgaws for the Indian women, and head-thumping hangovers.

Henry's trappers based their operations at Fort Henry on the Yellowstone River. His crew contained some of the most famous and skillful of the mountain men—Jim Bridger, William Sublette, and Jedediah Smith—who between 1822 and 1840 combed most of the mountains between Canada and the Rio Grande and from the Yellowstone to the Pacific, seeing lands that no other white man had ever seen.

In the meantime, in 1821 in Canada, the rival North West Company and Hudson's Bay Company had settled their differences by combining their companies under the standard of the Hudson's Bay Company. Under the firm leadership of John McLoughlin, who was placed in charge of operations along the Columbia, Fort George, formerly Astoria, was abandoned and a massive new base of operations, Fort Vancouver, constructed on the Willamette River, opposite the site of present-day Portland, Oregon.

Unlike the Americans, who were interested only in immediate profits, the Hudson's Bay Company for years had operated under a policy of conservative trapping to assure the perpetuation of a breeding stock of beavers. With the American trappers swarming over the Rockies, McLoughlin abandoned the conservation program and ordered his men to take every beaver they could from the Snake and upper Columbia watershed to discourage further penetration by the men of Ashley and Henry.

The Americans, advancing toward the coast, operated under no constraints, and were stripping the beaver from every stream they encountered. And with their wide-ranging operations, one or more of them encountered every stream in the West. No living resource could contend for long with the pressure exerted on the beaver in the United States. By 1830, trappers were culling the last surviving beavers from streams depleted by earlier trapping. The best streams had already been stripped. It was at this point that the bottom dropped out of the beaver market.

Before 1830, beaver fur was the only commodity prized by the hatters of London and Paris, and a fine prime pelt might bring as much as one hundred dollars in Europe. But they had discovered that the much cheaper nutria fur from South America was an acceptable substitute. But for hats, silk had become the ultimate material, and the floodgates to trade with the Orient were wide open. In 1831, beaver pelts brought six dollars a pound in St. Louis. Two years later they could be bought for half that price.

With the collapse of the beaver market, most of the mountain men turned to other pursuits. Many became guides for the military and for the increasing number of settlers and wagon trains that were crossing the Rockies to Oregon. Others became buffalo hunters, for the buffalo was beginning to gain the economic importance that the beaver had lost. The last rendezvous—a somber affair compared to the earlier gathering—was held in 1838 on Popo Agie Creek near the Wind River Mountains of Wyoming.

The collapse came just in time to save the beaver in the United States from extinction. Except for a few scattered colonies, the beaver had been eliminated from nearly all of the country east of the Rockies, and most of the western streams no longer held beaver.

Chapter 5

The Market Hunters

Wild meat quickly became an important part of the early American economy. It remained so for more than three centuries.

After the Indians became hostile to the white settlers because of their encroachment on the red man's traditional lands, white hunters assumed the task of supplying the settlements with meat. Bradford wrote that in Plymouth, in its early years, men were assigned to hunt deer, turkeys, and waterfowl to meet the protein needs of the colonists. Livestock did not reach Plymouth until 1623 when a bull and three heifers formed the nucleus of a dairy and beef herd. At a later date, men hunted for profit by choice, relishing the freedom from restrictions that wilderness living gave them. Many were social misfits or outcasts. Early ancestors of the mountain men, they learned their trade from the Indians and adopted Indian methods of hunting. Like the mountain men, they roamed ahead of the advancing waves of civilization, shooting, trapping, or netting whatever salable wildlife they could find.

Although others probably antedated him, Thomas Morton was the first member of the breed identifiable by name. Morton was probably the first European to appreciate fully the American wilderness in its unspoiled state. Where others found it depressing and frightening, Morton ecstasized over its beauty. Where contemporary settlers considered the American aborigines treacherous, dangerous, and dirty, Morton found them delightful and "more Christian" than his Puritan neighbors. In a New England society filled with religious intolerance and racial bigotry, he shines like a torch in a cave.

Morton was a lawyer by profession. He arrived on the southern shore of Boston Harbor in June, 1624, with a party of thirty men and their indentured servants under the command of Captain Wollaston, who established a settlement about thirty miles north of Plymouth on the present site of Quincy.

Intrigued by the wild country, Morton noted with enthusiasm the ". . . Millions of Turtle doves," the "sweet crystal fountains, and clear running streams," and the ". . . Fowles in abundance." The place was, he concluded, ". . . Nature's Master-peece. . . . If this land not be rich, then is the whole world poore." As articulate as he was enthusiastic, Morton, in his *New English Caanan*, left some of the most detailed and delightful descriptions of New England's wildlife resources.

Soon after he arrived at Mount Wollaston, Morton established friendly relations with the local Massachusetts and Wampanoag Indians, visiting their bark lodges, plying them with gifts, hunting with them, and trading with them for beaver pelts and deer hides.

Captain Wollaston soon found the settlement he had established less productive than he had hoped. In an effort to bolster his sagging financial status, he sailed for Virginia with some of his indentured servants, whose services he rented to the southern planters. This venture proved so profitable that he decided to devote full time to it. He abandoned Mount Wollaston, leaving a token force, including Morton, behind under command of a Mr. Fitcher.

Morton quickly assumed leadership of the settlers and servants left behind. Recognizing that Wollaston's abandonment of the settlement would lead to its dissolution, he promised those who would follow him freedom from all bondage and treatment as "equal partners and consciates." The rebels sent Fitcher packing on the trail to Plymouth and rechristened their settlement Ma-Re Mount, after its original Indian name. Almost immediately the name was corrupted to the delightfully appropriate Merry Mount.

On Philip and Jacob's Day, the rebels celebrated their new freedom ". . . with Revels and Merriment in the old English custom." They erected an enormous Maypole, topped by a pair of deer antlers and decorated with poems that Morton had composed to the goddess Maja. Around the ribbon-bedecked pole, they and their Indian friends —men and women—danced and frolicked, shouting, singing, banging on drums, and firing guns in the air. In the course of the day they consumed a barrel of beer and a case ". . . of bottles of other good cheer. . . ."

The "Visible Saincts," as the Plymouth Pilgrims called themselves, were shocked and horrified. Bradford wrote that ". . . Morton became a lord of misrule, and maintained, as it were, a school of Athisme."

Not only was he composing blasphemous poems to heathen gods but, worse, was following the *Book of Common Prayer of the High Church of England*, which the Pilgrims firmly rejected.

But the Pilgrims had more earthly grounds for opposing Morton. Through his friendship with the "Salvages," he was beginning to monopolize the fur trade. The mixture of Indian, gunpowder, and alcohol, also, was recognized early on the American frontier to be the substance of a high explosive. With justifiable anger, Bradford railed against Morton:

> And here I must bewail the mischief that this wicked man began in this district . . . notwithstanding the laws to the contrary. The result is that the Indians are stocked with all kinds of arms—fowling pieces, muskets, pistols, etc. They even have moulds to make shots of all sorts—musket balls, swan and geese shots and smaller sorts. It is well known that they often have powder and shot when the English lack it. . . . This goes on while their neighbors are being killed by the Indians every day . . . Oh the horror of this villainy!

Morton thoroughly enjoyed hunting and was an accomplished falconer. He turned these interests to neat profit each spring and autumn when the ducks, whistling swans, and Canada geese thronged the rivers and tidal estuaries near Merry Mount. He wrote that he often ". . . had one thousand Geese before the muzzle of my gun," and that frequently the profits from the sale of one week's take of feathers alone paid for all the shot and powder he used in a year. Wild goose and swan down was prized in Europe for stuffing feather beds and quilting.

When complaints against Morton to London elicited little more response than stifled yawns, the leaders of Plymouth decided to move against their sinful neighbors. In 1628, a force of militia under Captain Myles Standish (Morton called him "Captain Shrympe") raided the "den of iniquite" at Merry Mount, chopped down the blasphemous Maypole, and brought its leader to Plymouth for judgment. According to Morton they placed him on a barren island ". . . without gunne, powder, or shot, or dogge, or so much as a knife." But his Indian friends kept him supplied with food and water until he could hitch a ride to England on a passing fishing boat.

Authorities in London declined to bring charges against Morton and, to the dismay of the Visible Saints, he was soon back at his beloved Merry Mount, frolicking with the Indians, hunting for goose down, and resuming his generally profligate ways.

But during his absence, Morton's little settlement had been joined on Boston Harbor by another at Salem. Headed by dour John Endicott, this group of Puritans was even less tolerant of frivolity and sin than were the earlier arrivals in Plymouth. Endicott obtained a patent that gave his group control of all of the Massachusetts Bay Colony, which included Plymouth and Merry Mount. Almost as soon as he landed, he sent a force to suppress the revelry at Merry Mount, seize Morton's goods, and clap him in irons. Morton, however, fled to his Indian friends and sent word to Endicott that he was enjoying himself immensely and living well on venison and maize.

But the days of the Massachusetts wilderness were numbered. In July, 1630, a whole fleet filled with Puritan settlers arrived in Boston Harbor under the leadership of John Winthrop. Morton was captured, hauled before the General Court, sentenced to the stocks, and banished "with all speede" to England. The Puritans seized his goods and burned Merry Mount to the ground.

While in England, Morton wrote his *New English Canaan*, a caustic attack on the New England Puritans and a eulogy to the wilderness land he had learned to love.

In December, 1643, Morton, undaunted by his previous experience, arrived back in Boston; Winthrop had him jailed for a year. Financially ruined, the aging rogue fled to Maine, where he died in 1647.

Morton was one of the few early market hunters who emerge from history with names and personalities. The majority were anonymous, faceless men who prowled the wilderness and the outskirts of the towns and settlements with guns, traps, and dogs. As the deer and wild turkeys were driven from the environs of the villages by overhunting and competition with domestic livestock, the market gunners turned their attention to waterfowl and upland game. Ducks, geese, swans, and brant poured out of breeding grounds in the North in undiminished millions each autumn and returned in almost equal abundance each spring. Most of their northern breeding grounds were still unseen by white men's eyes. Apart from occasional mill ponds, which usually improved waterfowl habitat, alterations in the marshes, lakes, rivers, ponds, and sloughs on which the waterfowl wintered were beyond the engineering capabilities of the colonial settler. Colonial farming certainly improved the lot of rabbits, quail, and plovers.

Most of the game taken was trapped rather than shot as the early muzzleloading pieces and muskets were clumsy and awkward for wingshooting. Snares were used to take rabbits and grouse, and pound traps constructed from sticks and fishnets and baited with grain accounted for many of the waterfowl and quail. While waiting for the birds to enter his traps, the market gunner usually waited in a blind, covering a prebaited area until a flock was massed in front of the gun. Quick second shots were impossible with the firearms of the time, and the hunter made every shot count. But with patience and proper timing, he could kill a dozen or more at a single discharge. Quail were killed in much the same manner.

On occasion, when dense flocks of passenger pigeons and waterfowl passed close overhead, the hunter fired into their midst. The slow lock time of the flintlock, however, made precision shooting at individual birds in flight a near impossibility.

As the towns grew in number and population, there was a ready market for game, either through butcher shops or in direct sales to inns and housekeepers. Because of the general lack of refrigeration, the market hunters were forced to operate close to their point of sale, although they could venture farther afield in winter.

The market hunter operated under practically no restrictions. There were no closed seasons except those imposed by nature on migratory birds, most of which passed from the hunters' reach on their northern migrations. Bag limits were governed by the gunner's supply of ammunition and methods of taking only by the limits of his ingenuity.

In the nineteenth century new developments came rapidly. One was a great advance in the improvement of firearms. The flintlock, which was discharged by sparks from a flint striking a steel frizzen to ignite loose priming powder in a pan beside the breech, was highly susceptible to misfire. This was especially true in its use for wildfowling, as the hunter was constantly exposed to soaking by blown spray or by rain, and the best flights of waterfowl occur in foul weather. Even in dry weather, the hunter had to handle his firearm carefully lest the priming powder be lost. Loading was a tedious process. The hunter who could fire his second shot within two minutes of the first was agile indeed. But the flintlock system dominated the hunting and military scenes for two full centuries after 1620.

After 1820, the percussion system generally superceded the flintlocks. The percussion gun loaded through the muzzle, like the flintlock, but it was fired by a copper-encased cap of fulminate of mercury snapped over a nipple leading to the chamber. It was practically immune to wetness, and the primer stayed in place even under rough handling. With this development, many American gunsmiths were beginning to manufacture reasonably light double-barreled shotguns, which permitted the hunter to fire two shots in quick succession.

The principle of choked barrels—those with slight constrictions at the muzzle that control the spread of the shot charge—was not discovered until after the Civil War, and the open-bored shotguns were of limited range, although quite effective on quail, grouse, and shorebirds. To compensate for their deficiencies, most of the market gunners who hunted waterfowl favored single-barreled guns of large bore; 4- and 6-gauge shotguns were common, and a 10-gauge was considered a lightweight gun. Shooting from a boat or blind, the hunter was unaffected by the weight factor. By keeping two or three guns cocked and loaded at hand, the shooter could still get off multiple shots at a passing flock. Since his income depended entirely upon the number of birds he killed, the market hunter took every advantage of his game. The first shot usually was made at birds on the water after they had been baited or called into range, the second as they massed in flight.

The light sailboat was a favorite craft of the market gunners, especially for shooting the prized canvasback. Unlike the mallard and other so-called puddle ducks, diving ducks, like the canvasback, cannot spring directly from the water into the air. Before becoming airborne, they must race across the surface in a pattering takeoff into the wind. By running their swift cutters and sailing skiffs upwind of a feeding flock, the hunters could take the massed birds while they were skittering past the boats on the water.

The punt gun also made its first appearance early in the nineteenth century. This was essentially a light cannon with a bore of from 1¼ to 2 inches in diameter, and capable of throwing up to a pound of shot. In use, it was mounted on a low-sided, shallow-draft boat with ropes that held it in place and absorbed its enormous recoil. The gunner propelled the boat with short paddles while lying prone in the bottom beside the stock of the gun. These instruments of mass slaughter operated only at night. The gunner paddled silently to the edge of a feeding flock of birds, adjusted the position of the boat so the gun pointed at the thickest part, and pulled the lanyard as the birds began to take alarm. The resultant shot cut a swath of death up to eight feet wide and a hundred yards long. A hundred or more geese or ducks with a single shot was not unusual.

Another device, almost as deadly, was the sinkbox. This was essentially a coffin-shaped box supported by barndoor-sized wings that served as floats. In use, it was anchored over a bed of waterfowl food plants and sunk with weights placed on the wings until it would just support the hunter with only his eyes and forehead showing above the surface of the water while he lay on his back in the box. At a later date, the iron or lead weights were fashioned in the form of waterfowl, both as a lure to passing ducks and to further conceal the hunter. The sinkbox itself was painted to conform with the color of the water. When birds came in to the decoys, the hunter sat upright and fired as often as possible before the birds passed from range.

The first of these ingenious rigs, which was invented by an anonymous market hunter, made its appearance on Long Island Sound in the early 1820s. It proved so effective that it soon became used along most of the East Coast, in San Francisco Bay, and on the Great Lakes.

In spite of its effectiveness, sinkbox shooting was not the safest way to take waterfowl. Although the gunner always had an assistant waiting downwind in a skiff or sailboat to pick up his kill, a sudden squall could send the heavily weighted craft to the bottom in seconds. All sinkbox shooters favored long-barreled guns—for good reason. The hunter usually held one gun ready in his hands and leaned two or three others cocked and primed on the coaming at his feet. A short-barreled gun could easily slip, fall, and discharge within the box, sending the sinkbox and its occupant down into six to ten feet of icy water. Accidents of this kind were not uncommon and, in many, each accidental discharge also blew off the hunter's foot.

The use of live decoys also gained favor in the mid-1800s. The technique is said to have originated in 1840 with a group of shoemakers employed in North Bridgewater (now Brockton) in Massachusetts. Since they were paid by the piece, they conceived the idea of combining pleasure with industry by taking their lasts to the shore of a nearby pond where they built a shack to protect them from rain, snow, and cold behind a slabwood blind camouflaged with pine boughs. Here they worked until the geese came in. Then they dropped their hammers, needles, and awls and picked up guns. It was far more pleasant than working in the dingy factory and much more profitable. Geese were selling for between $1.50 and $2.50 each, a full day's wages for artisans of the time.

Whenever they downed a lightly wounded goose, instead of dispatching it for sale, they nursed it to health and tethered it before the blind to attract high-flying wild geese to the blind. Eventually, they developed a sizable flock. The experiment proved highly effective and was promptly adopted by other market hunters and sportsmen. Soon, live duck and goose decoys became standard equipment of the market hunters who plied the Atlantic Coast and the drainage of the Mississippi in the late 1800s and early 1900s.

A second major development that favored the prosperity of the market hunters was the development of the rail system, which began soon after the close of the War of 1812. The railroads permitted the market hunters to operate much farther afield and to ship game unspoiled to the city markets. The railroad and canal construction crews that were crisscrossing the eastern half of the country through most of the early 1800s provided immediate customers close to the point of supply. After the first primitive rail coaches blossomed into more commodious vehicles with dining cars and kitchens, game dishes became standard fare on their menus.

Venison, wild fowl, and other game were also staples in the cuisine of most American homes throughout the 1800s. Haunches of deer hung beside quarters of beef in the butcher shops, and the financial pages of the New York, Boston, and Chicago newspapers regularly quoted the current prices for braces of ducks, woodcock, snipe, and passenger pigeons.

Selling game to the railroads was so profitable that many boys and young men abandoned jobs and school to take up its pursuit. Henry William Herbert ("Frank Forester") wrote in 1848.

> All this is now changed—the railroads by which the country is everywhere intersected, enable the city pot-hunter to move about with his dogs, and to transmit the subject of his butchery to the market, easily, cheaply, speedily. Nor is this all—the country now bids fair to monopolize the trade of pot-hunting. The young men and boys, now-a-days, all shoot on the wing; many of them shoot exceedingly well; and knowing the country, and being at it all the time, the devastation they make is enormous.
>
> Their game is easily disposed of by the aid of the conductors, or other *employes* of the rail-roads, who share the spoils with the killers. The father, finding that the idle lad, who formerly did an hour or two of work, and bird-nested or played truant quite unprofitably all the rest of the day, now readily earns his three or four shillings by loafing about the woods with a gun in his hand and a cur at his heels, encourages him in the thoughtless course, and looks upon him as a source of both honor and profit to the family.

One major result of these activities was the extermination by 1848 on Long Island of the heath hen, the eastern race of the greater prairie chicken or pinnated grouse. Herbert wrote:

> The destruction of the Pinnated Grouse, which is total on Long Island, and all but total in New Jersey, and the Pennsylvania oak-barrens, is ascribable to the total and brutally wanton havoc committed among them by the charcoal-burners, who frequent those wooded districts; and who, not content with destroying the parent birds, at all seasons, even while hatching and hovering their broods; shooting the half-fledged *cheepers* in whole hatchings at a shot, and trapping them in deep snows—with a degree of wantoness equally barbarous, and unmeaning, steal or break all the eggs they can find.
>
> To this add the spring burnings of the forest land, and you have cause enough to account for the extermination of the Pinnated Grouse, or Heath-Hen; who is not now to be shot in such numbers as to render it worth the while to hunt for nearer than Michigan or Illinois.

By 1850, the heath hen was confined almost entirely to the island of Martha's Vineyard, off Cape Cod, where it would make its last stand as a distinct subspecies. The birds in Illinois and Michigan, of course, were greater prairie chickens of the western race, which in appearance were almost identical to the heath hen.

The concentrated flocks of the passenger pigeon made it an early and profitable target for the market hunter. In 1805, Audubon reported seeing schooners on the Hudson River loaded with pigeons on their way to markets in New York City.

The original abundance of the passenger pigeon would be unbelievable if it were not so well documented by so many competent observers scattered from Canada to the Gulf of Mexico. Alexander Wilson, the father of American ornithology, in 1806, saw one flight near the Green River in Kentucky that he estimated to be more than a mile wide, forty miles long, and to contain no fewer than 2,230,072,000 birds. On the assumption that each bird would eat a half pint of acorns a day, he calculated their daily food needs at 17,432,000 bushels.

Audubon, in the autumn of 1813, observed a flight on the Ohio River on a trip between Hardensburgh and Louisville that was so dense "the light of the noonday sun was obscured as by an eclipse." This flight passed over him in undiminished numbers throughout the 55-mile trip. He estimated that the number of birds he had seen that day was 1,115,136,000. The flight continued over Louisville for two more days.

Audubon also described a roost that he rode through for forty miles. He crossed it at intervals to determine its width, and estimated it to average three miles. The trees were so crowded with birds that the ground beneath them appeared to be covered with snow. Many trees up to two feet in diameter were broken off near their bases. The birds arrived at sundown, he wrote, "with a noise that sounded like a gale passing through the rigging of a close-reefed vessel," causing a great current of air as they passed. Throughout the forest as the birds poured in, he could hear trees and limbs crashing to earth under the weight of the swarming birds. The nesting colonies were even more impressive. One discovered in Wisconsin extended for more than a hundred miles with dozens of nests in every tree.

These dense concentrations in migration, feeding, nesting, and roosting, were tailor-made for exploitation by the market netters. The roosts, nesting places, and feeding grounds were easily located, and mass kills could be made with a minimum of effort. Although shooting into the concentrated flocks could bring down a dozen or more at each pull of the trigger, shooting was rarely used except by householders interested in meat for family use. The professional "pigeoners" used heavily baited drop or clap nets capable of taking hundreds at a time. These were erected around the edges of the roosts, nesting colonies, or feeding fields. As a further lure, they set out groups of live decoys, perched on T-shaped "stools," thus enriching the American vocabulary with the term "stool pigeon."

Although he gives no reason, Herbert was emphatic in stating that the passenger pigeon was not a game bird, and thus of little or no interest to the sport hunter. Possibly its sheer numbers and the ease with which it could be taken precluded its classification as game.

Even before the railroads began to crisscross the eastern United States, most of the nesting colonies near the larger towns and settlements had been eliminated by forest-clearing operations and overexploitation, although well after the Civil War flocks of enormous size streamed from nesting areas that civilization had bypassed. The last great nesting concentration in New York gathered in Allegany County in 1868, and a large roost was found in Steuben County in 1875.

Another roost whose birds had been traced to Missouri nesting grounds was destroyed by pigeoners near the upper Beaverkill River in New York in 1875. Tons of birds were shipped to New York markets from this roost and the netters used fifteen tons of ice to preserve the squabs.

The pigeoners were well organized, using the telegraph to keep one another informed of the location and movements of the birds. With the destruction of the eastern roosts and breeding colonies, all of those still in business concentrated their activities in the Lake States where the habitat of the birds could still be found in abundance. By 1878, the only productive roosts were in Michigan, and the pigeoners descended upon them *en masse*. Nets had increased steadily in size and efficiency, and some netters were using three or four in tandem. The record catch was 3,500 pigeons at a single spring of the net. The Mr. Osborn who reported it said that his own best catch was a little over three thousand.

One gang of netters, headed by a wealthy Ohio farmer who devoted half his time to pigeon netting, invaded a nesting colony in Newaygo County, Michigan, in 1875. Not only did they string their usual nets but they felled hundreds of trees, many containing up to fifty nests each, to obtain the squabs. The warehouse where the birds were stored for shipment was twenty by sixty feet, and most of this floor space was covered with squabs to a depth of three to four feet. The man estimated his total shipments during the nesting season at between forty and fifty tons of squabs. In the same year, netters in Oceana and Grand Traverse counties shipped two million pounds of squabs and 2,400,000 older birds to markets in American and European cities.

In 1878, the last great nesting colony was discovered near Petoskey, Michigan. Twenty-five hundred netters descended upon it. Within the space of a few weeks they marketed 1,107,800,066 pigeons. In 1881, Grand Traverse County yielded a million birds.

This was the end of the passenger pigeon as a viable species. A few scattered flocks persisted until after the turn of the century, but they dwindled in numbers each year. The last known survivor of the species died in the Cincinnati Zoological Garden on September 1, 1914.

Whether or not samples of the great flights of the passenger pigeon could have been preserved into the twentieth century is a moot question. Competent scientists have theorized that, without the dense colonies that it developed in earlier times, the species was psychologically incapable of breeding successfully. Certainly the market netters did not kill the last of the pigeons, as the hunters folded their nets after the destruction of the great concentrations made netting no longer profitable. In the absence of effective game laws, the surviving birds were harassed by gunners wherever they came within range of shotguns. But the determining factor was the destruction of the virgin forests that they required both for food and nesting sites. In the America of the 1900s there was no place that could support such seething masses of bird life without conflict with agriculture and other human interests.

But the passenger pigeon did not die entirely in vain. With its virtual extermination, coming as it did on the eve of the destruction of the bison herds, this loss became one more standard around which the pioneer conservationists of the time could rally.

Part 2

An Awakening Ecological Conscience

Chapter 6

The Emergence
of the American
Hunter/Conservationist

Until the middle of the nineteenth century, the line between the market hunter and the sportsman was hazy. Men who pursued game for pleasure often disposed of their surplus game through sale. Many of those who shot game primarily for profit enjoyed their work. Thomas Morton, for example, never did anything voluntarily that he didn't relish.

During the early years of settlement, the first men clearly identifiable as hunting purely for recreation were the planters of Maryland, Virginia, and the Carolinas. These men owned huge estates that were devoted to the culture of rice and tobacco and worked by crews of indentured servants and later by slaves. Obviously, such men did not have to hunt for their day-to-day needs for meat as did the hardscrabble settlers of the Northeast. They were the first Americans who could afford the luxury of leisure.

Many of these men were falconers, and others kept large packs of hounds and strings of hunting horses, which they used for coursing deer, foxes, and wolves in the forests around their estates. Some authorities argue that these men were responsible for introducing the red fox into America, as the European and American subspecies are almost identical. Records of the early explorers and fur traders dispute this contention, but the colonial hunters may have extended the range of the red fox southward by importation and release of European animals.

The colonial sportsman also owned fowling pieces made by the best English gunmakers. These were usually long-barreled guns with elaborately carved stocks and with locks and trigger guards orna- mented with gold and silver inlays or engraving.

There were neither bag limits nor closed seasons, and some of the early sportsmen made daily kills that today would seem astronomical. But on the colonial plantations of the South, the game was never wasted. The choicer pieces went to the kitchen of the manor house and the rest to feed the servants or slaves.

The distinction between the northern sportsman and the market and subsistence hunter remained fuzzy until well after the Revolu- tionary War. The booming period of prosperity and progress that followed the close of the War of 1812 gave rise to a new breed of Americans and a new kind of America. The impact of progress was most apparent in a great triangle running from Boston to Chicago in the north to Baltimore in the south. Within this triangle was centered most of the industrial might and financial wealth of the young nation. It contained nearly all of the country's resources of coal and iron, an abundance of water power, and, with unrestricted immigration, a seemingly inexhaustible supply of laborers, skilled and unskilled. Its bustling shipyards produced the largest and fastest ships—schooners, clippers, packets, and whalers—from timber cut in northern New England and the southern shores of the Great Lakes. Its rolling mills and smelters converted iron ore into rails and girders that eventually would span every river and weave a network of steel across the land. Its tanneries turned hides from the Pecos and Rio Grande into leather, and its shoe factories the leather into shoes. Back from the growing towns, the hills, largely denuded of timber, supported hundreds of thousands of sheep, whose fleece the woolen mills converted into blankets and yard cloth. Most of the cotton grown in the South emerged as cloth from the coastal factories of Massachusetts and Rhode Island.

This industrial revolution changed the face of the region, and from an esthetic point of view this change was not always for the better. Dams on the streams grew higher, blocking the annual spawning runs of salmon, shad, and sturgeon. The town or city, until that time, had been a quiet working place for the lawyers, physicians, trades- men, merchants, and artisans whose principal clients were the farm- ers who tilled the soil around them. Suddenly they became bustling cities. Each was now dominated by one or more factories whose chimneys belched black smoke into the once pristine air, and soiled the curtains of the workers' homes that crowded about them like chicks around a mother hen. Crowding brought sanitation problems. The factories spewed their wastes into the nearest river. In a time when the outdoor privy was the ultimate in waste disposal, the streets often ran with raw sewage that washed into the streams with every rain.

But industry, to many, also brought quick wealth. A few dollars invested in a new factory, steamship line, or railway could build into thousands in a matter of months. It was from the *nouveau riche* that the early-nineteenth-century sportsman emerged. The ordinary worker had little if any time to spend on outdoor recreation. The workman was expected to put in a ten- or twelve-hour day and the work week was six days long. Wages were low, and paid vacations were unheard of. Among the less affluent, only the farmer and farm hand had an opportunity to hunt, but the endless chores of nineteenth-century agriculture left them little time for sport.

The factory owner, the merchant, the financier, and the professional man were among the few in the early 1800s who could afford the time and money to hunt for sport. For those who could take advantage of it, the opportunities were excellent. Unspoiled marshes, teeming in autumn with ducks, geese, rails, and snipe, lay at the ends of the horsecar lines on the outskirts of New York City. Daniel Webster, an avid sportsman, frequently exchanged his frock coat for a hunting jacket in his congressional chambers after closing a debate, and finished the day hunting ducks and rails on the Anacostia Marshes, a short carriage ride from the Capitol. There were few if any suburbs, as such, and farms crowded close to the limits of the cities and towns. Their weedy fencerows and varied cropfields provided ideal habitat for quail, rabbits, and mourning doves.

If he wished, the wealthy sportsman could venture farther afield. The Adirondacks were the favorite vacation spot for hunters from New York City and Albany. Because their rough terrain made them unsuitable for agriculture, the Adirondacks had been largely untouched by the flood of progress that had flowed around their foothills and was then lapping at the edges of the Great Plains. Their forests harbored the only sizable deer herd remaining in the state. They also provided good black bear hunting, excellent grouse and woodcock shooting, and superb trout fishing. As the railroads extended their lines closer to the mountains, hotels and lodges were developed to cater to the sportsmen.

Bostonians favored Cape Cod or northern Maine, both of which had become readily accessible by rail. Cape Cod, with its sandy soils and sea-oriented population, contained extensive brushfields that supported several thousand deer, the only remaining deer in southern New England during most of the 1800s. Daniel Webster was a frequent visitor to Cape Cod, fishing for bluefish from catboats in late summer and hunting deer in autumn in the scrub oak barrens of the interior Cape.

Most of northern Maine was still an unspoiled wilderness. The loggers who were systematically stripping its timber were operating, for the most part, in the southern counties of the state. Moose, woodland caribou, white-tailed deer, and black bears were favorite quarries of the sportsmen, but, as in the Adirondacks, they combined big-game hunting with fishing and grouse shooting. The runs of Atlantic salmon were spectacular, and brook trout, lake trout, and landlocked salmon were found in all of the inland waters.

Hunters from Philadelphia, Baltimore, Washington, and Annapolis concentrated their attention on the rich hunting grounds of Chesapeake Bay. Throughout autumn and winter, its marshes and coves were blackened with ducks or so filled with whistling swans that they resembled snowfields.

Conflict between the sportsman and the market gunner first became apparent here. The market hunters, who operated by the hundreds on Chesapeake Bay, worked six days a week from dusk to dawn, and in the case of the punt gunner, much of the night. Their constant harassment made the birds skittish and decoy shy. To obtain quality hunting, the sportsmen, individually or in groups organized as clubs, began buying up choice shore areas covering the best passes along the waterfowl flight lanes, and posting them and their adjacent waters against trespass. The tough, independent market gunners, who operated on the outer fringes of the law anyway, ignored the signs.

To thwart the trespassers, the clubs and the wealthier individuals hired equally tough water men to guard their rights. These men were hard-fisted fishermen, oystermen, or former market hunters who thought little of blowing a hole through a trespasser's boat—or, on occasion, through the trespasser himself.

The first known sportsmen's club was the Carroll's Island Club, established in 1832 at the mouth of the Gunpowder River, fourteen miles north of Baltimore, by a Colonel William Slater. This club had a luxurious lodge and a staff of servants to cater to the whims of the members and their guests. Most of the shooting was at passing waterfowl from sunken blinds, each of which was equipped with a pump. A crew of guides with retrieving dogs brought in the birds as they fell to be plucked and iced by the servants. Clubs of this kind later monopolized most of the better shooting areas around much of Chesapeake Bay, Long Island Sound, and Cape Cod Bay.

Many of the market hunters found it more profitable and less laborious to serve as guides for sportsmen than to shoot for the market. Individual sport hunters, especially those in the cities, did not relish the work of maintaining an offshore brush blind or sinkbox, and few had the facilities for caring for a flock of live decoys. And both sinkboxes and live decoys were adopted and used by many sportsmen until the close of the first third of the twentieth century.

In 1844, a group of about eighty influential New York sportsmen banded together to form the New York Sportsmen's Club. This was no social group but an active band of militant conservationists. As its secretary, William S. Van Duser wrote to the editor of *Spirit of the Times* on June 1, 1848: "The objects and pursuits of the Club . . . are confined solely to the protection and preservation of game, and every dollar of its funds appropriated solely to those purposes. . . ."

The club had three major targets. One was the sale of game for the market, the second was the spring shooting of game birds, and the third the lax game laws. After the state legislature repealed the state game laws and turned responsibility for wildlife conservation over to the counties in 1846, the club drafted a model game law and had it introduced in the meeting of the Board of Supervisors of the County of New York. It provided a closure on woodcock hunting between January 1 and July 4, ruffed grouse between January 1 and September 1, quail between January 10 and October 25, and trout fishing between September 1 and March 1. The sale or possession of these birds and fish was prohibited in the closed season. Deer hunting was closed from January 1 through July 31 each year.

The law was adopted by the county that year and in 1848 by the boards of Orange and Rockland Counties. Its wording was based on a petition to the state legislature that had been drafted by Henry William Herbert, whose popular writings appeared regularly under the pen name of "Frank Forester" in *Spirit of the Times* and *Turf Register*, the leading sportsmen's journals of the day. Herbert was a young Englishman who had come to America in 1831, fallen in love with the country and its hunting and fishing, and decided to stay. He was a successful novelist, poet, and artist as well as the nation's first outdoor writer. His alarm over the rapid depletion of the wildlife resources in the Middle Atlantic States was reflected in his writings, which probably inspired the founding of the New York Sportsmen's Club and certainly motivated its members. His petition was presented to the state legislature through the club. It failed of enactment because of lack of interest among the legislators, an inadequate number of supporting signatures, and successful lobbying by the hotel owners, merchants, and railroad companies that were profiting from the traffic in game.

In a letter of apology to the club for failing to attend one of its meetings after a nasty spill from a horse in May, 1847, Herbert wrote: "I rejoice to hear of your success with the Game-killers; one or two more examples will work wonders."

This comment was based on the club's effective strategy of suing poachers, dealers, and hotel proprietors for the sale or possession of game killed out of season. The rights of citizens to sue violators of the game laws were an extension of colonial laws dating back to the time of the deer reeves in the early 1700s. Since there were no conservation officers and the sheriffs and constables paid little attention to their responsibilities in this field, the citizen suit was the only legal recourse for those interested in game-law enforcement.

A majority of the club members were attorneys, and they made effective cases. They located violators through personal detective work, scanning hotel menus, browsing in the markets, and following up tips from informers. Many of the latter were anonymous and signed "Anti-Poacher." Typical cases were listed in the secretary's report to the club on October 6, 1846:

> The Secretary would further report that judgment has been obtained in the Fifth Ward Court against E. W. Thompson for Ten Dollars and costs of court for a violation of the game laws for having in possession 2 Partridges on the 12th of October, and also in the same Court against Bardotte, the keeper of the Cafe Tortoni in Broadway for two penalties in two different suits for serving up 1 Partridge and 1 Quail on the 5th of October to the amount of $5. and costs in each suit. Also that there is now pending in the Court of Common Pleas, two suits against Amos Robbins of Fulton Market for a violation of the Game laws by having in possession on the 23rd of October Twenty Partridges and Five Quail. The evidence against him is complete and there can be no doubt as to the issue of the suit.

Although game, especially deer, had long disappeared from New York County and its environs, and the strengthened game laws applied only to three counties, New York City was the major outlet for game killed over a much larger area. By bringing suit against the owners of New York markets and restaurants, the club was able to strike at market hunters and poachers far removed from its own base of operations.

The New York Sportsmen's Club was so effective in its crusade against game-law violators that its approach was adopted before 1850 by newly formed groups of sportsmen in Boston, Massachusetts; Providence, Rhode Island; and Toronto, Ontario. Before the outbreak of the Civil War, similar sportsmen's groups, fighting for stronger game laws and bans on market hunting, came into being in most of the major cities of the East.

The critical situation that prompted the founding of these clubs was emphasized by Herbert. Spring shooting of upland game birds, prevalent in those times, was devastating to the breeding stock. Herbert was a dedicated woodcock hunter, and much of his concern was centered on that species. In 1848, he summarized the problem:

> . . . the ostentation, rather than the epicureanism of the rich New Yorker demands Woodcock; therefore, despite law, common sense, and common humanity, the bird is butchered at all times. . . . Within ten years to come, if some means widely different from any now adopted be not taken to save this bird, it will be extinct everywhere within a hundred miles of any city large enough to afford a market. Within fifty years from this day on which I write, I am satisfied that the Woodcock will be as rare in the eastern and midland states as the Wild Turkey and the Heath-Hen are at present.
> The Quail will last a little longer. . . .

Fortunately for the woodcock, quail, and other members of America's wildlife community, new means "widely different from any now adopted" were on the way. The nation, however, was on the verge of a period of divisive unrest, and the implementation of most of these new means would have to wait until the end of the War Between the States.

Chapter 7

Land for Wildlife

A new approach to wildlife conservation emerged soon after the guns at Appomatox had cooled and before the slaughter of the buffalo had reached its climax.

During the early 1800s, when the mountain men were trailing beaver across the unmarked tracks of Cabeza de Vaca, Coronado, and Meriwether Lewis, tales of a strange land deep in the Rocky Mountains filtered back to the East. Trappers told of an area between the Absaroka and Gallatin Ranges in the Northwest Territory where boiling water spurted from the shores of icy lakes, where the earth smoked and fumed in a ghostly landscape of yard-thick terraces of yellow glass, and where deep subterranean bellowings played bass to the bubbling of natural caldrons of multicolored mud. Men like Jim Bridger and John Meek were great spinners of yarns, and they told stories that intermingled fact with fiction so skillfully that few could tell where one began and the other ended. Everyone took their stories with handfuls of salt, although no one without suicidal tendencies called a mountain man a liar to his face. It was a good story well told, and after the tellers left, the townsfolk enjoyed a good laugh over the whole thing.

A few correspondents for eastern newspapers picked up these strange tales and sent them to their editors, only half believing what they themselves had written. The first written description of the thermal wonders of Yellowstone was contained in a letter by Daniel T. Potts, an employee of the Rocky Mountain Fur Company. It appeared in the Philadelphia *Gazette and Daily Advertiser* on September 27, 1827. This and later stories stirred little public interest.

It was with some surprise that the frontier skeptics learned that, for once at least, the mountain men had understated a case. In August, 1870, a formal exploration party of nineteen men ascended the Madison River. It was led by General Henry D. Washburn, surveyor-general of the Territory of Montana; Nathaniel P. Langford; and Lieutenant Gustavus C. Doane, the commanding officer of the cavalry detachment that provided protection for the group. The Washburn-Langford-Doane Expedition, as the party became known, spent nearly a month in the area, confirming the discoveries of the mountain men and making new ones of their own.

If the expedition had been headed by less public-spirited men, Yellowstone with all of its natural marvels would have been lost to the American public. On September 19, the explorers sat around their campfire at the junction of the Firehole and Gibbon Rivers debating what to do with their discoveries. There was talk of forming a corporation to exploit the area and of staking personal claims to the geysers and hot springs. All they needed to have done was to drive a few stakes and record their claims with the federal land office in Helena, and they would have been owners of the most valuable recreational land in the world. Among them, however, was a distinguished jurist from Helena who had a suggestion of his own. Judge Cornelius Hedges was both a far-sighted and eloquent man. The Yellowstone area, he argued, was too magnificent to be exploited for the profit of a few individuals. It should be held in trust for all of the people.

Judge Hedges's ideas were heartily endorsed by his companions and formalized in a report to the governor of Montana. Eventually they were incorporated in a bill that passed the Congress and was signed into law on March 1, 1872, by President Ulysses S. Grant.

The American people now owned 3,348 square miles of western real estate that had been set aside specifically for their personal enjoyment and use. But neither they nor the government had the remotest idea what to do with it. Just to reach the borders of the new park required a week or more of horse travel from existing rail lines through wild country inhabited only by outlaws and warlike Indians. After a party of federal geologists and surveyors had taken stock of the area, President Grant named Langford as superintendent of the park. With this, the Grant Administration dismissed the matter from its collective mind.

Langford, with practically no appropriations to support him, could do little actual work in the park. But he was a capable writer and lecturer, and was largely through his efforts in print and from the podium that the American people received some inkling of the value of the gift they had received.

Langford was succeeded as park superintendent on April 18, 1877, by Major P. W. Norris, who was provided with a minuscule appropriation to protect the park from fire and to make improvements in the road system. To round out his meager financial resources, he shipped huge quantities of geyser formations from the park for sale as curios. He fed his crews buffalo meat and venison, taken by professional hunters within the park. "He protected the wonders," according to Brigadier General George S. Anderson, a later superintendent, "by breaking them off with ax and crowbar and shipping them by the carload to Washington and elsewhere.

"The regulations permitted hunting for 'recreation' or 'for food,' which could always be made to cover the object of any captured poacher."

In spite of Anderson's caustic indictment, Norris's administration was not entirely bad. He did a reasonably good job of protecting the park from fire, and he built its first roads. At the close of his stay of office in 1883, the park became accessible for the first time when the Northern Pacific Railway ran a spur line south from Livingston to its northern entrance at Cinnebar, Montana.

The railroad brought the first wave of eastern tourists. It also brought vandals, exploiters, and market hunters who carried on their activities without fear of punishment. The Organic Act of March 1, 1872, which created Yellowstone National Park as a "pleasuring ground for the people," had serious inherent weaknesses. Although it authorized the Secretary of the Interior to make regulations for the protection of the park, it provided no authority for their enforcement. Poachers and market hunters roamed the plateaus and canyons, slaughtering the elk and buffalo, while vandals smashed and defaced the beautiful mineral deposits around the geysers and pools. The three civilian superintendents who succeeded Norris could do nothing except protest, wring their hands, and write reports to Washington, but Congress refused to provide funds for the park's protection. Yellowstone National Park, in short, was a park only in name, and it was in danger of destruction by the same public for whose benefit it had been set aside.

The impotent civilian supervision of Yellowstone National Park ended abruptly in 1886 when, as Anderson phrased it, David Wear was "legislated out of office." The civil appropriation bill for 1886–7 omitted the customary stipend for the protection of the park, and Wear, its fourth superintendent, submitted his resignation. Fortunately, however, an Act of March 3, 1883, authorized the Secretary of War, on request of the Secretary of the Interior, to dispatch troops to protect the park, with the commanding officer of the detachment serving as superintendent. Under this law, Interior Secretary L. Q. C. Lamar, of President Grover Cleveland's cabinet, appealed for help. A troop of the First Cavalry, commanded by Captain Moses Harris, arrived at park headquarters on August 1, 1886. From that point on, matters assumed a different aspect.

Harris found conditions in a deplorable state. For several months the park had been without even the nominal protection afforded it by the civilian superintendents. As Harris and his troopers trotted in, they passed wagonloads of logs being carted out. They found hunters camped by the springs and geysers and tourists gaily bearing off armloads of mineral specimens.

Harris, who had won the Medal of Honor in the Civil War, was a veteran of a dozen Indian campaigns. He was tough as only a frontier cavalryman knew how to be tough. Moreover, mixed with his strong sense of duty was a deep appreciation for the outdoors and for his new charge in particular. His orders were to protect the park, and to this task he applied all the skill and austere efficiency that he would have devoted to defending a position against an Indian raid.

Within hours after his arrival, he and his hard-faced troopers were roaming the back trails and canyons, flushing out hunters, woodcutters, and souvenir collectors. Guard details, under arms, were posted at each of the major points of tourist interest to halt the defacement of the geyser formations. Like his civilian predecessors, however, Harris labored under severe legal restrictions and impossibly vague orders. He could arrest a man for killing buffalo in the park, but there was no way to bring the poacher to trial. He could arrest a tourist for breaking or defacing geyser foundations but could not prefer charges against him. He could eject a timber thief from the park but could not prevent him from returning immediately. All he was empowered to do was confiscate government property that was being removed and, by a show of force, try to prevent attempts at further destruction of the resources of the area. This situation prevailed for nearly ten more years.

Upon his assignment to Washington and his replacement by Captain F. A. Boutelle in 1889, Harris became a member of the Boone and Crockett Club. This was a "club of American hunting riflemen" founded by Theodore Roosevelt in December, 1887. Roosevelt had traveled to North Dakota in the autumn of 1883 to hunt buffalo and antelope. At that time he was twenty-four, three years out of Harvard College and already a veteran member of the New York State Legislature. At a later date he wrote that if it had not been for his experiences in the Badlands of North Dakota he would never have become President. Whether or not that statement was true, it is indisputable that it was his life in North Dakota that whetted an already keen interest in problems involving soil, water, forestry, and wildlife. If his experiences in the West made Roosevelt the President, they also created Roosevelt, the conservationist. In the young man who went west to hunt buffalo, conservation was to find its most vocal, most colorful, and most influential leader, at a time when it needed leadership most.

Roosevelt, after much effort, finally took the buffalo head and robe that he sought; he and America gained much more. By the time he had completed his primary mission, he had fallen completely in love with the West and had begun negotiations that would lead to a more permanent link with that part of the country. Three weeks after his arrival in North Dakota, he and Sylvane Ferris, a resident Dakotan, formed a partnership and bought out the holdings of the Chimney Butte Ranch, with headquarters seven miles downstream from Medora, and purchased the Maltese Cross brand for their herds.

After his hunting trip in 1883, Roosevelt went back to New York City with the firm intention of returning to North Dakota at a later date, leaving the ranch in the care of Ferris and Arthur Merrifield, its original owner, whom the new owners had retained as foreman. His return was precipitated by tragic circumstances—the almost simultaneous deaths of his mother and his young wife in the winter of 1884. Reeling under this heavy double blow, he temporarily abandoned a promising political career at the close of the term of the state legislature the following June for the hard life of a frontier rancher. His original purchases in North Dakota had consisted of little more than a few head of cattle and a registered brand, but on his first hunting trip he had located an ideal spot for a ranch forty-two miles up the Little Missouri from his first holdings. There, in a grove of cottonwoods, he and his cowhands erected the cabins, stables, and bunkhouse that would be the headquarters of the Elkhorn Ranch.

During his two-year career as a rancher, Roosevelt had an excellent opportunity to observe the impact of civilization on a wild area, and the experience made a lasting impression on his character. The Northern Pacific had thrust its steel fingers through the Dakotas only three years before his arrival there. It brought with it market hunters who slaughtered all but scattered survivors of the once abundant buffalo, and reduced the antelope bands to remnants. The Audubon bighorn sheep, which inhabited the Badlands near Medora, had become so depleted that it ceased to exist by 1905.

The railroads also brought settlers who took up the carnage where the market hunter left off. The black bear, grizzly, and wolf were killed on sight as threats to livestock. Grazing animals were slaughtered for food and because they competed with sheep and cattle for forage.

The railroads also brought transient sportsmen who, in the absence of any legal checks, ran up large bags of trophies. To a sensitive naturalist like Roosevelt, this mindless butchery was repugnant. Although he relished the chase and took pride in a difficult shot, he rarely hunted during his stay in the West except when he needed meat or when he located an exceptional trophy.

While engaged in ranching, Roosevelt saw the ripening of the bitter fruits of unwise land use. He watched gullies grow where wild fire, excessive logging, and overgrazing had stripped the cover from the soil, and he saw the floods that these abuses caused. The knowledge and experience would have a profound influence on his thought and action at a later time when, in far different surroundings, he would make decisions affecting the entire nation.

In the winter of 1886, the school of hard knocks, in which Roosevelt had voluntarily enrolled, handed him his diploma in the form of a blizzard that roared down from Canada and left the grazing lands of the Dakotas littered with the frozen carcasses of cattle. Among the casualties were at least sixty percent of the animals with the Elkhorn brand. The previous year had been one of the best in the short history of the cattle industry on the northern plains and, like most of the ranchers, Roosevelt had overstocked his ranges. A few months before the tragedy, he had left the ranch in the care of a foreman and returned to New York to work on his writings and pick up the broken threads of his political career.

One of his first steps on returning east was to call a dinner meeting that was attended by some of the nation's leading explorers, writers, military leaders, scientists, and political leaders. These men had several things in common. Each was an enthusiastic big-game hunter, and each had traveled extensively in the West. They formed the nucleus of the Boone and Crockett Club, the principal function of which was to fight for the preservation of the big game of North America.

The deplorable conditions in Yellowstone National Park occupied much of the deliberations of the club in its early meetings. A number of the members had visited Yellowstone on one or more occasions. The acquisition of the outspoken Captain Harris as a member further strengthened the club's interest in the park and provided it with an authority who knew its problems more intimately than anyone else. Captain F. A. Boutelle, Harris's successor as superintendent of Yellowstone National Park, was succeeded in 1891 by Captain George S. Anderson. Both were elected to membership in the Boone and Crockett Club, bolstering the "Yellowstone bloc" at the club's meetings.

Although the club was a small group, limited to one hundred regular and around fifty associate members, it numbered in its ranks some of the most powerful men of their time—Senator Henry Cabot Lodge; Francis Parkman; Carl Schurz, former Secretary of the Interior and owner and publisher of a chain of leading newspapers; Owen Wister, the novelist; Albert Bierstadt, one of the nation's leading painters; and General William Tecumseh Sherman.

In Yellowstone National Park, Captain Anderson was having the same problems that had beset his predecessors, but his problems were aggravated by the growing number of visitors and the growth of towns on the edges of the park. He had asked repeatedly for more manpower to protect the forest and wildlife resources of the area. It is no coincidence that two months after the club passed a resolution endorsing this request a full troop of the Sixth Cavalry was assigned to Anderson's command.

Anderson's problems had been mounting for several years. The vandals, timber thieves, and poachers were still active and increasing in numbers as the towns around the park grew in population. Visitors were totaling nearly five thousand each season, and the construction of hotels and roads throughout the park spread people over a wider area, complicating the police problem.

In the absence of law, Anderson was forced to fall back on his own ingenuity in preventing the destruction of the park's resources. Vandalism had grown from a minor nuisance to a major problem. Much time and effort had to be spent curbing the propensity of the American male to carve or scrawl his name on any tree or rock, and that of the female to collect souvenirs. Under Anderson's orders, anyone caught breaking the geyser formations was brought before the superintendent, who administered a tongue-lashing of the sort usually reserved for laggard soldiers. The culprit was released with a warning that a second offense meant expulsion from the park.

Even rougher treatment was meted out to name carvers. When fresh names or initials were found on the geyser formations, troopers returned the offender to the scene of his violation. There he was handed a scrub brush and abrasives and, under the eyes of an armed guard, forced to polish away his mark. "One morning," Anderson reported with undisguised satisfaction, "a callow youth from the West was aroused at 6:30 a.m. at the Fountain Hotel and taken with brush and soap to the Fountain Geyser, there to obliterate the supposed imperishable monument to his folly." It was hard policy but effective. Open vandalism rapidly declined.

The fire problem also grew in magnitude with the increased popularity of the park, and fire patrol and suppression occupied much of the time of the soldiers assigned to park duty. One fire near Norris, apparently set by a careless smoker, required the efforts of every man in two calvary troops for twenty days and nights to bring under control. After that, Anderson ordered that anyone leaving a campfire unattended or carelessly disposing of smoking materials was to be summarily expelled from the park and forbidden to return. The troopers under Anderson's command carried out the orders with enthusiasm.

An even more difficult problem, however, centered about the protection of the park's wildlife. After 1885, the only wild bison herd of importance had found refuge there. Yellowstone held the largest elk herds in the country, and beaver were still fairly common on many of its streams. Outside its boundaries, these species had been nearly exterminated or greatly reduced in numbers. With the buffalo reduced to fewer than four hundred head, meat and hide hunting of the old mass-slaughter type was no longer possible. But anyone alert enough to avoid Anderson's troopers could still make a good living selling robes and heads to taxidermists in Billings, Helena, and Livingston. A bull buffalo head brought up to $500, and beaver pelts brought premium prices.

There was still no law through which poachers exploiting this illicit traffic could be jailed. The worst they risked was a little rough treatment from their captors, confiscation of their equipment, and expulsion from the park. Anticipating capture, many used scrub horses, ancient wagons, and cheap guns whose loss meant next to nothing. Anderson accumulated so much of this junk that he staged huge bonfires of the contraband near his headquarters.

Serious efforts to protect the wildlife, forests, and natural wonders of Yellowstone National Park had begun as early as 1883 when Senator George C. Vest of Missouri introduced legislation that would have made the park an inviolate wildlife refuge. Backed by Senator C. F. Manderson of Nebraska and Senator Joseph M. Carey of Wyoming, Vest, between 1883 and 1890, fought his bill through the Senate six times, twice by unanimous vote, only to have it buried and smothered in House committees. Opposition to the Vest Bills in the House stemmed from several sources, but it was led by a powerful lobby which, for years, had been fighting to force a railroad through the park. Leading this well-financed group were mining interests and real estate speculators in Cooke City and Livingston, Montana. Backing them were the market hunters and trappers, to whom crusty Captain Harris had referred in his reports as "our enemies to the north and east."

The chief argument of the lobbyists was that the regulation of the park should be left to state and local control, and they brought up the issue of states' rights whenever possible. They painted the park as a remote and inaccessible place that only millionaires could visit, a playground for the wealthy that was robbing poor but honest miners and hunters of their livelihoods. Every time one of the Vest Bills passed the Senate it emerged with a crippling rider that would have granted the controversial railroad right of way.

To the supporters of Yellowstone National Park, the idea of a railroad there was unthinkable. Apart from the destruction of natural features that construction would cause, there was real danger that the precedent established would make the exclusion of other lines impossible. Eventually, they felt, the park would be crisscrossed with steel.

The preservation of the park area during the railroad construction boom of the late 1800s was attributable largely to the foresight of Dr. F. V. Hayden of the U. S. Geological Survey, who had laid out the park boundaries through rugged mountain ranges. But when the Northern Pacific ran its spur line to Gardiner, Montana, in 1882, clamor for a hookup with that rail terminal originated in the mining town of Cooke City, just outside the northeast corner of the park.

Ten years later the scheme had grown to dangerous proportions, for the little mining town had acquired powerful allies in Livingston and Billings. Blocked in its efforts to force a right of way through the park, the railroad lobby, in 1892, obtained the introduction in Congress of a bill that would have restored the northern portion of the park to the public domain. Known as the "Segregation Bill," its passage would have excluded from the park borders the 622 square miles of land east of the Yellowstone River and north of the Lamar River and Soda Butte Creek, and removed the natural protection afforded by the barrier mountains to the north. This tract included some of the finest big-game range in the park.

The early interest of the Boone and Crockett Club in the park was as a refuge for big-game animals, and the club fought the Segregation Bill with vigor. Members testified at all of the hearings. One of the founding members, Dr. George Bird Grinnell, through his sportsmen's journal, *Forest and Stream*, published and sent to all of the major newspapers in the country a detailed brochure on the park and its problems. The pamphlet succeeded in raising support from all parts of the country. The Springfield (Mass.) *Republican* thundered editorially in a typical response to Grinnell's appeal:

> The town lot boomers and miners of both places [Cooke City and Livingston] are demanding the Park route, and they are aided by a floating crowd of hunters and trappers and prospectors, who want the rich northeastern corner of the Park thrown open to their depredations.

Club members elicited testimony from President T. F. Oakes of the Northern Pacific Railway, before congressional hearings, that ore deposits in the Cooke City area were not rich enough to justify rail access and that the route proposed by the lobbyists was impractical from an engineering standpoint. Captain Anderson predicted, in a published letter, that the construction of a railroad along the proposed route "would burn off the Park as black as your hat in six months." Anderson's concern over fire was justified. Indication of the bitterness that built up in this fight is given in the thinly veiled invitation to arson that appeared in an editorial of the Livingston (Mont.) *Post* on November 30, 1893:

> Everyone concedes that the destruction of the Park by fire would be a public, a national calamity, and the only way to avert such an impending danger would be for the Congress to grant the reasonable request of the people of the west and pass the segregation bill.

In spite of the efforts by its opponents, the Segregation Bill passed the Senate on February 23, 1893. There was a chance that it might have passed the House if P. J. Barr, the paid lobbyist for the Cooke City interests, had not made an error of judgment. He sent a wire to prominent Democrats in Montana asking them to bring full political pressure to bear on Speaker of the House Crisp in support of the bill. Grinnell obtained a copy of the telegram and reprinted it in full in a resounding editorial that put the Speaker in a difficult position. That ended the Segregation Bill for that session of Congress.

In spite of the setback, the hardy legislative perennial came up in each session of Congress until 1895, when it irrevocably died. The man largely responsible for killing it was an obscure market-hunting recluse named Edgar Howell.

The events that crystallized public opinion behind the defenders of the park were only remotely connected with the railroad issue. Cooke City was a snakepit of poachers who slipped into the park during the winter when patrol was most difficult. Three of these outlaws were regarded as especially dangerous, and Anderson assigned his single civilian scout to watch them closely.

Scout Ed Wilson, late in April, 1891, was patroling near Soda Butte when he found fresh signs of trapping activity along the Lamar River. Careful observation indicated that the poacher was tending his trapline at night and watching for pursuit through field glasses from the hills during the day. Under the cover of a wild blizzard, Wilson trekked forty miles in one night through deep snows on skis, coming upon his quarry at dawn just as the storm abated. He found the man, T. S. Van Dyck, asleep in his camp with traps, binoculars, firearms, and a camera arranged beside him. Wilson coolly photographed the sleeping poacher and his equipment with the man's own camera before awakening him and making his arrest. Taken to Fort Yellowstone, Van Dyck was thrown into the guardhouse and held while Anderson awaited instructions from Washington that never came. The poacher's property, valued at $350, was confiscated. After 34 days, Van Dyck was released with orders to keep out of the park, but without further punishment or formal arraignment. The scout who made this arrest disappeared one month after Van Dyck's release. His skeleton was found eleven months later.

The loss of Wilson was a blow to Anderson, who valued the scout over a full platoon of cavalrymen. He found a fortunate replacement, however, in Felix Burgess, another skilled and fearless woodsman who knew the park well.

One year after the Van Dyck incident Burgess reported to Anderson that a man named Pendleton had taken two new-born buffalo calves from the park in beer cases slung on the backs of pack animals. Both of the animals died before the poacher could get them to his home. When Pendleton returned for replacements he ran into the arms of a waiting patrol. Placed under arrest, he was held for a short time, and like Van Dyck, released for lack of a law under which he could be prosecuted.

Each of these cases gave the Boone and Crockett Club grist for its mill in its attempts to obtain legal protection for the big game in Yellowstone National Park. Grinnell kept up a drumfire of editorials relating to the cases in the pages of *Forest and Stream* and circulated reprints of them to all of the major newspapers. The cases were cited repeatedly at all of the hearings on the Vest Bills by members of the club, but they found their real *cause célèbre* in the activities of Edgar Howell, a sheep shearer turned poacher, who regarded the park as his private hunting preserve.

In October, 1893, Anderson, on an inspection tour of the eastern boundary of the park, found signs of a buffalo concentration near Pelican Creek, and knowing that this would serve as a natural magnet for any poachers in the area, assigned Burgess to keep an eye on that sector of the park. In March, 1894, Burgess, scouting Astringent Creek in Pelican Valley with a trooper named Troike, came upon a cache of six fresh buffalo scalps hanging in a tree. Both men were on skis, since the depth of the snow made any other form of travel impossible. A short distance downstream they found a tepee and, as they approached the camp, a string of six shots thudded in the distance. Climbing the slope into the cover of the timber, the men began stalking their quarry and, twenty minutes later, were looking down on the poacher from the cover of the lodgepole pines. The man was surrounded by five freshly killed buffalo. Burgess recognized the stocky figure of Ed Howell bending over the carcass of a fallen cow.

The poacher had every advantage except that of surprise. Burgess and Troike between them had only a single .38-caliber service pistol, while Howell was armed with a repeating rifle, which he had leaned against the carcass of a buffalo while he prepared to remove a cape from a second. He was also accompanied by a dog, although Troike and Burgess did not know that at the time. The only approach was down the open slope across the four hundred yards of open snowfield slashed by a ten-foot-wide gully. Burgess knew that Howell was a dangerous and desperate criminal who was possessed of tremendous physical strength, and Anderson had ordered his men to take no chances in dealing with him. Burgess, however, decided to try an approach.

Waiting until Howell was fully occupied with his butchering, Burgess, an expert skier, left Troike in the pines, and, pistol in hand, executed a swift, silent *schuss*, leaping the ditch on the way and cutting in between Howell and his rifle. The first inkling the poacher had that he was not alone in the wilderness was when he looked into the barrel of Burgess's revolver from a distance of eight feet.

Two things set this incident apart from the others. One was the utter flagrancy of Howell's actions. The second was the presence in the park of a team of reporters that had been sent by Grinnell, as editor of *Forest and Stream*, to spend a winter and to investigate the poaching problem. It was headed by Grinnell's ace reporter, Emerson Hough, who was accompanied by Billy Hofer, a guide, and F. Jay Haynes, the park's first photographic concessionaire and an official photographer of the Northern Pacific Railway. Between them, Hough and Haynes caught all of the drama of the case in words and on film. Hough interviewed all of the principals in the case from Howell to Captain Anderson. Haynes photographed the poacher's kills bloating in the snow and Howell himself, under guard, dragging in the evidence on his own toboggan. Hough's interview with Anderson caught perfectly the mingled elation, bitterness, and frustration that the superintendent felt when he learned of the capture:

> I have ordered [Burgess] to bring his prisoner on into the post as quickly as he can. Tomorrow I start out a party on snow-shoes to bring in the heads and hides of the buffalo killed. I have ordered Howell's tepee and supplies burned. His arms and outfit will be confiscated, and I will sock him just as far and as deep into the guardhouse as I know how, when I get him and he won't get fat there either. That is all I can do under the regulations. I shall report to the Secretary of the Interior and in due course the Secretary of the Interior will order me to set the prisoner free. There is no law governing

this park except the military regulations. There is no punishment that can be inflicted on this low-down fellow.

No one knew these facts better than Howell himself, and he talked freely to Hough when the reporter met him.

"I don't think I'll be there long," he bragged confidently on his way to headquarters over a phenomenal breakfast of twenty-four pancakes at the Canyon Hotel. "I haven't arranged my plans for the future. I may go back into the Park again later, or I may not. . . . I had been camped over on Pelican since September. It was pretty rough, of course. If you don't think it's a hard trail from Cooke City to Pelican Valley, you just try pulling a toboggan over Specimen Ridge. . . . If I'd seen Burgess first, he'd never have arrested me." He also told Hough that he "stood to make $2,000" and that the most he could lose was $26.50—the value of his equipment—and a little time in the guardhouse. He told Hough that he had killed eighty buffalo in the park, possibly one-fourth of all the wild buffalo left in the world.

Hough was a competent journalist, handling his story without sensationalism, and it was all the more effective as a result. As an added touch, he interviewed every taxidermist in the vicinity of the park. Each stated that he knew *other* taxidermists were buying heads from Howell, but that *he* would not think of such a thing.

Hough's story broke at a propitious time. The stumbling block of each of Senator Vest's repeated efforts to obtain a realistic law governing Yellowstone National Park had been the Public Lands Committee of the House of Representatives. All of the effort toward enacting legal protection had come from the Senate. But one week after the Howell case broke into print, Congressman John F. Lacey, a close friend of Grinnell and a member of the Boone and Crockett Club, introduced his version of the Vest Bills. It all but sailed through the House while a companion bill, introduced by Senator Joseph M. Carey of Wyoming, was romping through the Senate. Lacey was one of the few congressmen with a consistent record of supporting park protection, and he had a personal interest in the matter. He claimed that he had been a passenger on a stagecoach that was held up and robbed in 1882. Although the robber was apprehended, he was released because no one knew whether or not state law applied in the park.

Hough's coverage of the Howell case created a national sensation, and Grinnell accompanied the stories with dozens of editorials demanding action:

We suggest that every reader who is interested in the Park or in natural history, or in things pertaining to America, should write to his Senator and Representative, asking them to take a personal interest in the protection of the park.

The national press picked up the cry, and the response was overwhelming. Petitions and individual letters by the hundreds poured into Congress—from sportsmen and nature lovers, from people who had visited the park, and from people who hoped to visit it. The American people for the first time had begun to realize that they owned a national park, and they were determined to keep it. In a matter of weeks, the Cooke City-Livingston lobby found itself snowed in under a blizzard of public sentiment. Early in May, the Lacey Bill "for the protection of the Yellowstone Park" emerged from the Conference Committee, passed both Houses, and was signed into law by President Grover Cleveland on May 7, 1894.

The law was comprehensive, detailed, and explicit. It provided for the appointment of a resident commissioner of the United States circuit court and of Deputy U.S. Marshals assigned to park duty, spelled out offenses, and provided specific penalties. It made it a misdemeanor for any individual or stage or railroad company to transport birds, fish, or mammals taken from the park; provided jail sentences of up to two years and fines of up to $1,000 for killing wildlife, removing mineral deposits, or destroying timber; and made mandatory the confiscation of all equipment and vehicles used in such offenses. It even authorized funds for the erection of a jail at the park headquarters.

The enactment of the law changed completely the enforcement situation within the park, and there appears to be some poetic justice in the fact that the first man arrested after the law was passed was Edgar Howell. On July 28, the redoubtable poacher swaggered into a hotel in the park and was promptly arrested. Hauled before the newly appointed commissioner, J. R. Meldrum, Howell was given a month in jail and fined $50 for violating Anderson's order for him to stay out of the park. He appealed the case and subsequently went free, as his violation was clearly *ex post facto*. But the incident served notice on all poachers that a new day had dawned in Yellowstone National Park.

Under the Yellowstone Park Protection Act, the park became, in addition to the first national park, the first inviolate wildlife refuge in the nation—one of the few places where wildlife could roam freely without fear of or competition with human activity. The concept was a new one and it caught the imagination of the conservationists.

The creation of Yellowstone National Park had a precedent in Yosemite, which Congress had transferred to the State of California for safe-keeping as early as 1869. In comparison with Yellowstone, its wildlife potential was limited, but it contained some of the most spectacular scenery in the world. One of its first proponents was Horace Greeley, who after visiting the valley in 1859 called it the "greatest marvel of the continent." The original preserve consisted only of eight square miles which included the valley and the Mariposa Grove of redwoods. Settlers soon swarmed into the unreserved areas, stringing fences, building cabins, and grazing horses and cattle on the valley floor.

John Muir, a Scot geologist who had immigrated to America in 1849, visited Yosemite in 1868 on a walking tour of the Sierras. His constant barrage of articles was largely instrumental in the enactment by Congress of the Yosemite National Park Act of 1890. Kings Canyon and Sequoia National Parks, also in California, came into being in 1890. Two years later, Muir founded the Sierra Club, the original members predominantly Californians who wanted to save some of the state's spectacular scenery before it could be destroyed by the miners, loggers, and sheepmen who were grubbing, chopping, and chewing it to bits. Many square miles of California had been run through sluice boxes during the Gold Rush between 1848 and 1855.

The first objective of Muir and his Sierra Club was to obtain appropriations for Yosemite to protect its scenic values. During most of the 1890s, the valley was overrun with sheep and cattle, and most of its original elk and deer had been driven out by overgrazing, or killed for meat by the homesteaders. To provide grazing lands for their flocks and herds, the livestock owners burned over the valley each year. The latter practice, like the overgrazing, was deplored by Muir although more recent evidence suggests that the impacts of livestock were far more destructive. The scenic vistas, meadows, and park-like stands of trees that so impressed the white discoverers of Yosemite Valley were maintained largely by annual burning by the resident Indians for centuries before their arrival.

In 1898, Congress provided the first appropriations for administering Yosemite National Park. Cowboys hired with these funds drove thousands of sheep and cattle from the valley while cavalrymen cut the fences and herded out the squatting homesteaders.

Although it was not apparent at the time, the establishment of the Sierra Club represented a dichotomy in the philosophy of the infant conservation movement, with one side advocating full protection and nonuse, at least of selected areas, the other favoring regulated use or management. The rift between the two was rarely wide, and on many issues closed completely.

Chapter 8

Saving America's Forests

The success of Yellowstone National Park as a wildlife refuge, particularly for the American bison, whose existence it had saved, prompted Theodore Roosevelt and other early conservationists to try to extend the principle to other natural areas. Their attention focused on the 13-million-acre national forest reserves.

With the exception of the four national parks, these were the only lands in the United States that had been set aside in public ownership for future use.

During the latter half of the nineteenth century, nearly all of the larger forms of wildlife were confined to the undeveloped western lands of the growing nation. The white-tailed deer, now abundant nearly everywhere in the East and Middle West, reached its low point in numbers between 1870 and 1900, and east of the Mississippi during this period there were only scattered patches of occupied deer range in the Appalachians, the northern counties of the Lake States, and scattered swamps and mountains throughout the South. Black bears and wild turkeys had been reduced to even lower levels. There were remnant populations of moose and caribou in northern Maine and Minnesota, but all of the big-game animals maintained relative abundance only in the West. The majority roamed lands that were highly vulnerable to exploitation through entry under the Homestead Laws.

The objectives of the Homestead Laws, under which nearly all of the remaining strongholds of America's big game were thrown open to settlement, were commendable. But their administration and results were deplorable. The General Land Office in the Department of the Interior, which administered the public domain, was understaffed for its monumental task and, in the absence of a civil-service system, was filled with political appointees who often took advantage of their short stays in office to pad their purses through graft. Supervision from and communication with Washington were inefficient, and local field officers often interpreted the law as they saw fit.

Timber operators and livestock owners took advantage of this confused situation to build empires of their own. In many instances, huge tracts of the public domain were stripped of their timber or appropriated for grazing lands without payment of tribute or taxes to the federal government. Homesteaders who staked out legitimate claims on these lands often found themselves "trespassing" on the private domain of a latter-day baron. The standard answer to a complaint to the local official of the General Land Office usually was, at best, a shrug of the shoulders. At worst, it was a shot from ambush and a burned-out home.

Much of the problem was attributable to the wording in the Homestead Laws themselves. A hundred and sixty acres of land in much of the semi-arid West could never provide the necessities of life for a farmer and his family. That limitation had been written into the law by eastern legislators, who had applied standards of Illinois, Ohio, and Maryland to a region that ecologically was entirely different. Hundreds of thousands of disillusioned settlers who had gone west with visions of fortune sold out to the first land speculator who made them an offer. In an attempt to correct this deficiency in the basic law, Congress amended it to permit a homesteader to "preempt" a second 160 acres of land. This merely compounded the problem. Many homesteaders "proved" on two or more new claims and sold the extra land to the highest bidder. Unscrupulous landowners assigned their employees to file on lands containing valuable water rights and timber and appropriated the claim from the "dummy" as soon as he had received title. Others built shacks and fences in such a way that these required "improvements" could be shifted rapidly from one claim to another.

In 1873, the law was again amended to permit "tree claims" of up to 480 acres of forest land. Most of these claims were filed for the sole purpose of merging them at a profit into the holdings of the large timber operators. Some of the finest stands of virgin timber, among the best wildlife range in the West, and a number of potential national parks went into private ownership through this publicly sponsored grab bag. By 1891 the abuses of the tree-claim law had become so flagrant that it was repealed by an aroused Congress.

The first serious efforts to reform the General Land Office had come in 1877 with the appointment by President Rutherford B. Hayes of Carl Schurz as Secretary of the Interior. Schurz was an immigrant political refugee from Cologne, Germany, who, in conservation matters, was way ahead of his time. A capable journalist, he had thrown in his lot with the Republican Party, had been appointed minister to Spain by Abraham Lincoln, and then resigned his diplomatic post to raise a brigade of German-Americans which, under his leadership, served with distinction in Sigel's Corps at Second Manassas, Chancellorsville, and Gettysburg. He had served as a senator from Missouri from 1869 to 1875.

Schurz's interest in forestry dated from his youth in his native Germany, where the art was well advanced, and in his new post of responsibility he fought for reforms in the land laws. He was among the first public officials to recognize the interrelationships among land use, forests, and water supplies and the first to advocate a system of forest reserves and the establishment of a professional federal forestry agency. He selected his personal assistants on the basis of merit by competitive examination rather than for their political influence. Because of the nature of the times, most of his ideas reached fruition after he left public office. The Civil Service Commission was established in 1883, in the year that Theodore Roosevelt made his first trip to the West and two years after Schurz returned to private life. The first forest reserves were not set aside until 1891, and the U. S. Forest Service did not come into being until 1905, a year before Schurz died.

During his administration as Secretary of the Interior, Schurz struck hard at the abuses and mismanagement of the public lands that had been placed in his charge. When he took office, the western public lands were being systematically looted by timber thieves, ravaged by wild fire, and appropriated through fraud by lumber companies and livestock owners. His investigators turned up one company that had set up a complete mill town on the public domain, from which it was doing a thriving business by shipping overseas government-owned timber for which it had not paid a cent. Shocked by these abuses, Schurz, who, from his observations in Europe, knew the values of forests in checking soil erosion, maintaining water supplies, and stabilizing the economy of the nation, wrote in his first annual report as Secretary of the Interior:

> All timber lands still belonging to the United States should be withdrawn from the operation of the pre-emption and homestead laws, as well as the location of the various kinds of scrip. Timber lands suitable for agricultural purposes should be sold, if sold at all, for cash . . . value of the land.

Schurz also recommended the reseeding and reforestation of lands needed for watershed protection or as timber reserves. Later in a speech before the American Forestry Association on October 15,

1889, he called for a uniformed protective force, made up of soldiers mustered out of service in the Indian wars, to patrol the public lands to prevent timber theft, fire, and the slaughter of the wildlife. He called the destruction of the public forests "murder of our future prosperity" and decried "this wanton, barbarous, disgraceful vandalism" and a government "careless of the future and unmindful of a pressing duty." "But," he added in his memoirs, "I found myself standing almost solitary and alone. Deaf was Congress, and deaf the people seemed to be."

This farsighted German-American got almost nowhere in his attempts to reform the land laws or to initiate a system of forest conservation. The Americans of the time were more interested in extracting as much profit as possible from the forests rather than saving them for posterity. Before 1890, the timber crews that had stripped the virgin pines from the hills of New England had slashed huge swaths through the forests of the Lake States and were hacking their way through those of the Northwest from Montana to the Pacific Coast. In Washington, Oregon, and California, Douglas firs, ponderosa pines, and redwoods, some more than three hundred feet high and up to fifteen feet through the trunk, were thundering to earth. The hills of the West were echoing with the curse of the bullwhacker and the ring of the feller's axe.

Fire was an ever-present campfollower of the logger, sweeping through the mounds of dry tops and slash left by the cutting operations and often through the standing timber beyond, burning the fertility from the soil and leaving an aftermath of destruction and death —death to trees and grass, to big game and small, to trout, salmon, and grayling.

Fire had been present in North America's forests for hundreds of thousands of years, and it had been responsible for some of the most impressive stands of trees—the sequoias, the white and red pines of the North, the lodgepoles of the Rockies, and the long-leaf pines of the South. These fires had been set by lightning or by Indians, and they occurred with sufficient frequency to prevent the buildup of an inflammable understory. They burned gently through the forests until checked by rain or a river. Logging set the stage for forest fires of a magnitude the continent had never seen before.

At Peshtigo, Wisconsin, more than twelve hundred people died on October 8, 1871, but this blazing horror had little if any effect on the nation's apathy. The disaster went little noticed in the press, as it occurred on the same day Chicago burned, and Chicago had a "better press." In Wisconsin alone, during the 1880s, 2,500 separate fires burned an average of a half-million acres each year. There was no federal agency charged to manage the publicly owned forestlands or to educate the public on the losses that wild fire can cause. A few of the eastern states, under the urging of the recently formed American Forestry Association, organized poorly financed agencies to protect their woodland, but the nation at large regarded forest fires as mildly exciting spectacles, the inevitable aftermaths of logging.

As fire followed the logger, so flood and soil erosion followed the fire. Beautiful rivers that had flowed cool and pure since the Ice Age became clogged overnight with silt and logging debris, and flooded their banks after every shower. With the vegetation gone from the watersheds, many smaller streams disappeared completely. On the barren hills where lumberjacks and fire had done their worst, rills and gullies appeared as the soil flowed downhill to the streams. Millions of acres of mountainous country that, under modern forest management, might have produced periodical crops of timber forever were so badly damaged during this period that it would be nearly a century before they would support anything more noble than stunted brush.

There had been a few rays of light in the generally murky forest picture before 1890. Governor Sterling Morton of Nebraska, in 1872, had instituted Arbor Day to stimulate the development of woodlots and shelterbelts on the treeless prairies of his state. The idea spread rapidly across the nation. In the following year, Congress had passed the Timber Culture Act, granting 160 acres of prairie farmland to anyone who would devote one fourth of the claim to tree production. Congress, by creating Yellowstone National Park, had set a precedent for itself under which, whenever it desired, it could set aside other selected portions of the public domain for specified purposes. Also, in 1872, the New York State Forest Commission had been established to advise the state legislature on laws needed to protect the state's woodlands.

The American Association for the Advancement of Science had taken an early interest in the nation's natural resources. In 1873, under the leadership of Dr. Franklin B. Hough, it had petitioned President Grant to authorize the Secretary of Agriculture to employ an adviser on forest affairs. Hough himself was appointed to this post three years later and, by 1881, the tiny organization he had built around himself with an annual appropriation of $2,000 a year, evolved into the Forestry Division—"the germ," as Gifford Pinchot later called it, "of the present United States Forest Service."

On September 10, 1875, the American Forestry Association had come into being. Led by Dr. Bernard E. Fernow, its secretary, it had become the rallying point for those interested in the protection of the nation's forests. The combined influence of the AAAS and the AFA had been strong enough to obtain, as early as 1876, the introduction of bills in Congress that would have withdrawn forested lands to protect the upper watersheds of the nation's largest rivers but not potent enough to push the bills through Congress.

The first legislative breakthrough in the movement to create a system of federal forests, after repeated false starts and failures, came fully fifteen years later. The Sundry Civil Service Act of March 3, 1891, slipped through both houses of Congress with a rider that authorized the President of the United States to create forest reserves by executive order. The amendment was made at the request of Secretary of the Interior John W. Noble, acting upon a suggestion of Edward H. Bowers, special agent for the General Land Office, and Arnold Hague of the U. S. Geological Survey. The Boone and Crockett Club strongly supported this legislation as an extension of its campaign to obtain protection for Yellowstone National Park.

The first reserve established by President Benjamin Harrison under this Act was the Yellowstone National Park Timberland Reserve, embracing a million and a quarter acres, as suggested by Hague, who had defined the boundaries in his original suggestion to Noble. This vast reserve created defense in depth for the eastern and southern boundaries of the park and protection for the summer range of the herds of elk that wintered in the park. Before he left office Noble, through Harrison, was responsible for the withdrawal of more than thirteen million acres of forest reserves in the western states and territories.

On April 8, 1891, the Boone and Crockett Club gave a testimonial dinner for Noble and presented him with a resolution in which the members "most heartily thank the President of the United States and the Honorable John W. Noble" for setting aside the Yellowstone National Park Timberland Reserve and Sequoia National Park. Resolved:

> That this Society recognized in these actions the most important steps taken in recent years for the preservation of our forests and measures which confer the greatest benefits on the people of the adjacent states.

Unfortunately, the people of the adjacent states saw matters in a different light. Their screams could be heard all the way to the Potomac River. Western congressmen, taken by surprise by Harrison's bold action, rose almost as a man to launch an angry retaliatory counterattack against the President of the United States and his Secretary of the Interior.

There was perhaps as much justice in their stand as there was in that of the Administration. Harrison's withdrawals of the land made no provision for their use other than for watershed protection, which was then understood only vaguely, if at all, by the western frontier settler. All commercial use of the reserves was prohibited. It was illegal to cut the timber—even a cord of firewood for an adjacent treeless homestead; it was against the law to run livestock on the reserves, even though a rancher might have been using the lands for grazing for a generation or more. It was illegal to remove minerals, or to shoot game, or even to walk across the invisible fences that the law erected along their hastily defined borders.

Paradoxically, the one thing that saved these early reservations, the nucleus of the present national forest system, from the wrath of the West was that there was no enforcement of these unrealistic regulations. The frontier settlers did exactly what frontiersmen always have done when they disagreed with a law that was not backed by force—they simply ignored it. Timber thieves and market hunters continued their operations without even pausing to read the law, as though no forest reserves existed. The western congressmen, who *had* read the law, realized that without supplementary legislation, the government could do little to alter the *status quo*, and permitted their anger to simmer to apathy.

The Boone and Crockett Club, however, was far from apathetic. Following cold logic and the best scientific opinion of the day, it demanded full protection for the reservations whose establishment it had supported. As easterners, even easterners better informed than most about western attitudes, its members failed at first to realize the dangers inherent in trying to force acceptance of the reserves on the people of the West. The club's attitude at the time is best reflected in an article prepared jointly by Theodore Roosevelt and George Bird Grinnell in 1893:

> We now have these forest reservations, refuges where the timber and its wild denizens should be safe from destruction. What are we going to do with them? The mere formal declaration that they have been set aside will contribute little toward their safety. It will prevent the settlement of the regions, but will not of itself preserve neither the timber nor the game on them. The various national parks are watched and patrolled by Federal troops. . . . The forest reservations are absolutely unprotected . . . they are still without government and without guards.
>
> This should not be. If it is worth while to establish these reservations, it is worth while to protect them. A general law providing for the adequate guarding of all such national possessions should be enacted by Congress . . . supplemented by laws of the states in which the reservations lie. The timber and game ought to be made the absolute property of the government, and it should constitute a punishable offense to appropriate such property within the limits of the reservations.

Grinnell followed up with a strong editorial in *Forest and Stream* demanding that the reservations "be protected from the incursion of trespassers and from fire. . . . [The law] should authorize the Secretary of War to furnish to the Secretary of the Interior, on his request, such troops as may be necessary for the purpose of efficiently patrolling and permanently protecting each of the reservations."

The origin of these ideas is not difficult to trace. Military protection had worked well in Yellowstone and the other national parks, at least as a stop-gap, and the distinction between the parks and the newer forest reservations was not clearly defined. Hough, Fernow, Schurz, and the American Forestry Association all favored military or semi-military protection, and they were the leading authorities on forestry in the New World. Moreover, there appeared to be no middle ground between full protection by the military or abandonment of the reserves. Under nineteenth-century terminology, use of a forest meant its eventual destruction—first by logging, then by fire, and finally by sheep and cattle.

Gifford Pinchot was the Moses who led American forestry out of this wilderness of confusion. At Vanderbilt Forest in North Carolina, he had demonstrated clearly that the use of a forest did not necessarily mean its devastation and that, in fact, forest management could improve wildlife range, provide protection for watersheds, and produce sustained crops of commercial timber indefinitely. Like Fernow, whom he succeeded in 1898 as chief of the Forestry Division in the U.S. Department of Agriculture, Pinchot had received his training in Europe, as no courses in forestry were presented at American universities. But unlike his predecessor, Pinchot was an American who approached his formalized studies with American problems clearly in mind. The few other professional foresters in the United States were all Europeans, most of whom failed to realize that there was as much difference between the cultured forests of Germany and France and those of America as there was between a Grand Duke's thoroughbred and a prairie mustang. Fernow and his followers had the foresight to fight hard and effectively for the establishment of the forest reserves, but they had no recommendations for their management beyond saving them for the future by keeping the public from using them.

Pinchot came into government employment through a circuitous route. In February, 1896, Hoke Smith, Secretary of the Interior, wrote to Dr. Wolcott Gibbs, president of the National Academy of Sciences, requesting information on the forest situation in the United States. As a result of this letter, a committee of seven known as the Forest Commission of the National Academy of Sciences and later as the National Forestry Commission, was appointed by Gibbs. In addition to Gibbs, himself, the members were Dr. Charles L. Sargent, professor of arboriculture at Harvard University; General Henry L. Abbott of the Army Engineers; Dr. Alexander Agassiz, curator of the Harvard Museum of Comparative Zoology; Dr. William H. Brewster, professor of agriculture at Yale; Arnold Hague of the Geological Survey; and Pinchot. The composition of this committee is revealing. Although its members represented the best scientific minds concerned with forest conservation in the country, Pinchot was the only member with practical experience in forest management.

The circumstances that threw Hague and Pinchot together on this committee marked a beginning of a change in attitude of the Boone and Crockett Club, to which both belonged. Hague, though a geologist without training in forestry, was a man of perception. As he and Pinchot traveled together on Commission business, the things that Pinchot pointed out to him made sense. The two became close friends.

Sargent and Abbott were strong proponents of non-use backed by military force. Pinchot, however, recognized that public opposition to the forest reserves in the West had to be taken into consideration if the reservations were to be saved. The center of the political power in the nation was moving daily toward the Mississippi River. He argued for opening the forest reserves to regulated use under the supervision of trained foresters. This, he felt, would assure protection for the forests while deriving maximum benefits from them, and win friends for the principle of forest preservation. Lock up the reserves by force, he predicted, and western opposition would uproot the frail seedling of a forest program that had been planted by Harrison, Cleveland, Noble, and other pioneer conservationists.

Hague had spent much time in the West and recognized the validity of Pinchot's arguments. He knew that the western settler, only a few years removed from the law of the six-shooter, would never take lying down what he was certain to consider imposition by easterners. Pinchot, Hague, and Brewer formed themselves into a liberal wing of the Forest Commission that diametrically opposed the views of Sargent and Abbott.

Cleveland, in his request to the National Academy of Sciences, had left the door open to the establishment of a forest management program and had indicated that he personally favored the creation of a career service to manage the reserves. With this in mind, Pinchot, Hague, and Brewer drew up an elaborate plan recommending a study of the forests with a view toward these ends. Sargent and Abbott, however, were immovable. They had opposed, from the start, the liberal views of the President, and they rejected the proposals of the younger Commission members.

Meeting in Hague's home in Newport, Rhode Island, on October

24, 1896, the Commission drew up its report. The one point on which all members agreed was that more forest reservations should be established and that Mount Rainier and the Grand Canyon of the Colorado should be protected as national parks. Ten days before he left the White House, Grover Cleveland signed a proclamation based on these recommendations, adding 21,279,840 acres to the forest reserves.

Cleveland's action, more than doubling the area of the already unpopular forest reserves, came as a complete surprise to the members of Congress most intimately concerned, and to nearly everyone else. For some reason, Sargent and Abbott had insisted upon keeping the deliberations and even the existence of the Commission a secret. Western reaction to Cleveland's action, as it had been to that of Harrison, was all but explosive. As Pinchot wrote: "Under existing interpretation of the law . . . the only possible conclusion was that this vast area was to be locked up, settlers were to be kept out, and all development permanently prevented. No wonder the West rose up."

Six days after Cleveland's proclamation, Senator Clarence D. Clark of Wyoming angrily slammed into the hopper an amendment to the Sundry Civil Service Appropriations Bill that called for the nullification of the President's action and restoration of the forest reserves to the public domain. The bill passed the Senate the same day.

This reaction was exactly what Pinchot had predicted and feared. With everything they had been fighting for at stake, he and Hague rushed to Washington. In Congress, in John F. Lacey, who had done so much for Yellowstone National Park, they found the friend they needed. With the help of his callers, Lacey wrote his own amendment to the appropriations bill that would authorize the Secretary of the Interior "to make sales of timber on any forest reservation now or hereafter proclaimed, for mining or domestic purposes, under such regulations as he may prescribe, and to make all needful rules and regulations in furtherance of the purposes of such reserves, for the management and protection of same." Lacey's document, hastily written under pressure, nevertheless contained wording almost identical to that of the order that, eight years later, would establish the United States Forest Service in its present form.

In conference, the Congress rejected the Clark amendment and adopted a somewhat altered version of the Lacey rider. Then Cleveland, unexpectedly, let the whole bill die in a pocket veto; but the forest reserves, for the time at least, had been saved.

With the inauguration of President William McKinley, the westerners renewed their attack on the forest reservations with increased vigor. But, meanwhile, Pinchot and Hague had enlisted the support of Hague's superior, Dr. Charles D. Walcott, director of the Geological

Survey and an astute politician in his own right. Walcott, Pinchot later wrote, was "the man who actually saved our bacon." It was he who succeeded in convincing a number of western congressmen and senators that the forest reserves, properly managed, could be a tremendous asset to the West.

With Pinchot, Hague, and Walcott, and the American Forestry Association carrying on the fight on the Washington front, the Boone and Crockett Club pressed it into the home territories of the western congressmen by circulating petitions in support of the forest reserves. Addressed to the President of the United States, these petitions called the reserves:

> . . . necessary for the preservation of the timber and to secure the continuous and equitable flow of streams and the prevention of floods and water famine. Ranching and stock raising are both at stake when the water supply is threatened. We are informed that legislation will be proposed for the full development of all the resources of the reserves. This is the proper method of relief. We therefore sincerely hope that while enacting laws that will open them to the reasonable use of the people, you will maintain the reserves, which are essential to the prosperity of our state.

This document is not so remarkable for the results it achieved as it was a reflection of the change in attitude of the club leadership toward the reserves in the two years since the appearance of Grinnell's "troops for the forests" editorial. Obviously Pinchot had worked strong medicine in the short time that he had been a member.

In the vicinity of the forest reserves, however, the early hard-nosed approach that had been advocated by Sargent and Abbott had created so much bitterness that compromise was now difficult. A letter addressed to Archibald Rogers, a member of the club, by a rancher friend near Billings, Montana, reflected the attitude of the average well-informed westerner:

> I understand the necessity of preserving the timber, but it will be utterly useless for me to attempt to get signatures. The western settlers are peculiar people and insanely jealous of what they call interference with their rights by the East. A perfect storm of indignation swept over the West when Cleveland's proclamation of creating Forrestry Reserves were [sic] published.

The future of the forest reserves in 1897 depended almost entirely on the attitude of Cleveland's successor. By vetoing the Sundry Civil Service Appropriations Bill, Cleveland, in effect, had dropped a hot potato into the hand of William McKinley. The main bill was "must" legislation, and some version of the rider affecting the forest reserves was certain to be appended to it. McKinley had two choices—abandon the forest reservations and restore them to the public domain as the West was demanding, or fight for a realistic plan of management. In the red light of western anger, the former would have been the easier course; but the backfires set by Pinchot and his friends were taking effect. McKinley courageously decided to fight for the reserves.

The new Secretary of the Interior under McKinley was Cornelius N. Bliss, who was treasurer of the Republican National Committee, a coincidence that had a profound effect on the fate of the forest reserves. When lobbyists for the Homestake Mining Company, the largest gold-mining company in the nation and a major political force in the West, complained to Bliss that the enforcement of a rigid forest-reserves system would deprive the company of its source of supply of mine props and fuel, Bliss told them, in effect, "Just keep cutting timber as you have in the past. What difference does it make whether we call the lands forest reserves or public domain?" As a result, all of the steam disappeared from Homestake's attack on the reserves. It dropped back first to a position of neutrality, and then, under the persuasion of Charles Walcott, threw its considerable weight in favor of a program of sustained-yield management.

One of the leading opponents of the forest reserves had been Senator Richard F. Pettigrew of South Dakota, where Homestake's major holdings were headquartered. Taking a hurried glance at the new and unexpected tack that Homestake had taken, Pettigrew tore up a handful of speeches denouncing the forest reserves and introduced a surprisingly liberal amendment to the new Civil Service Appropriations Bill. The new rider called for regulation of the reserves by the Secretary of the Interior, who was "to regulate their occupancy and use and to preserve the forests therein from destruction."

On April 6, the Forest Commission was summoned to the White House, where McKinley laid matters on the line. Accept the Pettigrew Amendment, he told them, or risk losing all of the forest reserves. The Commission suggested a few changes in the amendment, and on the following day the revised bill was introduced. On June 4, 1897, it was signed into law. It authorized the Secretary of the Interior to sell "dead, matured, or large-growth trees from the forest reserves." It knocked the wind from the sails of the enemies of the reserves by permitting "bona fide settlers, miners, residents, and prospectors for minerals to remove needed fuel and timber for personal use."

This, in effect, was the basis of the program for which Pinchot had been fighting from the start. While he disagreed with some of the wording, he hailed the amendment as the first step toward a national forest policy.

In a report to the Boone and Crockett Club on January 8, 1898,

Pinchot opened a campaign to coordinate the existing forest programs of Agriculture and Interior under one cabinet head:

It will be little use to hold the reserves unless they can be properly administered. It is the quality of this administration which is now the main object of concern. We shall undoubtedly have some sort of forest service, but that is not enough. Very unfortunately, a disposition is manifest, on the part of the General Land Office, to assimilate the coming forest service, through the appointment of Special Agents, to the system of political appointment which obtains there. The result of such action would not only be to destroy the favorable opinion which is now forming in the West, but to retard the whole progress of forest preservation in the United States.

The Pettigrew Amendment opened the forest reserves outside California to entry under the Homestead Laws for one year, after which those not filed upon were to revert to their former status as national forest reservations. During this period of suspension, largely through the influence of Hague, Pinchot was appointed a "confidential forest Agent" by Secretary of the Interior Bliss, to investigate conditions in and the needs of the various reserves. He spent much of the following year touring the western forests, gaining first-hand knowledge of the great reservations and the problems involved in their protection. Upon his return to Washington on July 1, 1898, he was appointed chief of the feeble and politically harassed Forestry Division. His entire organization, including the Forester, consisted of ten men.

Secretary of Agriculture, James "Tama Jim" Wilson, however, was one official who recognized the importance of forests, and he gave Pinchot a free hand in building his little organization, while serving as a firm buffer between the Forester and the swarms of patronage-hungry politicians. Because of Wilson, Pinchot was able to recruit and hold nearly all of the newly trained foresters available in America. His Division of Forestry soon boasted the highest morale of any agency of government.

In 1900, Pinchot founded the Society of American Foresters, an organization designed largely to nourish the *esprit de corps* of the small but growing number of men engaged professionally in forest management, and to win standing for the profession in the eyes of the public. Theodore Roosevelt and Arnold Hague were charter associate members and attended many of the society's weekly meetings at Pinchot's home in Washington, D.C. Roosevelt regarded Pinchot so highly that, after he became President of the United States, he broke precedent for a Chief Executive by continuing his attendance at meetings of the Society in Pinchot's home.

When Pinchot was selected to head the Division of Forestry, the forest reserves were administered by the Department of the Interior, while the professional foresters—the "whole two of them," as Pinchot phrased it—were in the Department of Agriculture. Under earlier administrative procedure, this had made little difference, as Fernow had regarded his little agency as an educational group rather than a body of practicing professional technicians. Pinchot had other ideas, and the Pettigrew Amendment made mandatory the management of the public forests.

During the 1800s, the General Land Office of the Interior Department was almost traditionally a dumping ground for political misfits whom newly elected congressmen "had to make a place for," and the burial ground of incompetents from other agencies who, for one reason or another, could not be fired outright. It provided no environment for the growth of the strong public-spirited agency that Pinchot was trying to build. Obviously, the forests and the foresters had to be brought together under one cabinet head.

Pinchot, therefore, through the newly organized Society of American Foresters, the Boone and Crockett Club, and the American Forestry Association, opened an all-out campaign to place the Division of Forestry under the jurisdiction of the Department of Agriculture, where, at least as long as Tama Jim Wilson was around, he would receive protection for his staff from political raiders.

In 1900, against his own wishes, Colonel Theodore Roosevelt, governor of the State of New York, hero of the Spanish-American War, and a rising force in the Republican Party, was named as the running mate of William McKinley for the anonymity that the Vice-Presidency then imposed. He nevertheless campaigned vigorously, and the McKinley-Roosevelt slate swept the field. Less than a year later, fate, in the form of a crazed anarchist named Czolgosz, propelled Roosevelt overnight from his reluctant duties as President of the Senate to the highest office in the land. One of his callers at the White House was Gifford Pinchot, whom he summoned to help him with his first message to Congress. Delivered on December 2, 1901, it stated: "the fundamental idea of forestry is the perpetuation of the forests by use. . . . The various functions (pertaining to the management and protection of forests) should be united in the Bureau of Forestry in which they properly belong." On February 2, 1902, he appointed Pinchot a special agent and Forester in the Department of the Interior while retaining him as Forester in the Department of Agriculture.

The Boone and Crockett Club was in a highly favorable position. It was in the enviable position of having its founder and first president as Chief Executive of the United States and one of its prominent members in full charge of the forest affairs of the nation. Members of the club enjoyed easy access to the President's office and a sympathetic ear to their request that wildlife refuges be established on all of the forest reserves.

Soon after Roosevelt delivered his inaugural message, he summoned to the White House, Dr. C. Hart Merriam, chief of the Biological Survey and his assistant Dr. T. S. Palmer; Congressman John F. Lacey; and Pinchot. Lacey by that time had attained the chairmanship of the House Committee on Public Lands. Shortly after the meeting, he introduced a bill providing for the transfer of the forest reserves to the Department of Agriculture and "to authorize game and fish protection in forest reserves, and for other purposes." This bill, to which was added a crippling states'-rights amendment that would have given the governors of the various states veto powers over the establishment, enlargement of, and management plans for the forest reserves, failed of enactment after a bitter floor fight. Western opposition, led by powerful Joseph G. Cannon, chairman of the House Appropriations Committee, could not be overcome. What was needed by the friends of the forest reserves was something dramatic to mobilize public support behind the federal forest program.

The opportunity came in 1905, when, on January 2-6, the American Forestry Association staged the American Forest Conference. The AFA had developed into the most powerful popular conservation organization in the country. It commanded widespread respect, and its Forestry Conference was a great success. Presided over by the Secretary of Agriculture, it represented all of the many interests concerned with forest resources—railroads, mining companies, timber operators, livestock associations, irrigators, and recreational interests.

As a direct result of the Forestry Conference, the next bill calling for transfer of the forests to the Department of Agriculture slipped easily through the legislative mill. President Roosevelt met it on February 1, with poised pen. His signature marked the end of a major campaign in Pinchot's fight for multiple-use forest management. Enactment of the Transfer Act made possible the establishment of the United States Forest Service, and 86 million acres of forest reserves—now national forests—were for the first time placed under the control of men qualified to manage them.

Secretary of Agriculture Wilson, who had supported Pinchot staunchly under two presidents, spelled out in a detailed letter to the forester what he expected in the way of management of the new national forests:

. . . where conflicting interests must be reconciled, the question will always be decided from the standpoint of the greatest good for the greatest number in the long run.

Chapter 9

Building the Framework for Wildlife Conservation

During much of the nineteenth century, concerned citizens groped and fumbled toward a meaningful and effective system for protecting the nation's dwindling wildlife resources. Before 1870, their numbers were relatively few and their efforts, like those of the New York Sportsmen's Club, generally localized.

Before the Civil War, the efforts of the organized sportsmen, a few scientists, and an even smaller body of concerned nature enthusiasts, which then constituted the conservation activists of the nation, centered on obtaining closed seasons for the various game species. Most states and some of the territories adopted such laws during the early 1800s. As early as February, 1791, New York had enacted a law to protect the heath hen between April 1 and February 5 each year. Massachusetts passed a similar law in 1848. Nearly all of the states, especially those in the East, had laws protecting deer, with closed seasons that represented extensions of colonial legal codes or enactments made by state legislatures soon after the formation of the Union.

These laws were ineffective for a number of reasons. Most were based on the principle of town or county option and had been pushed through the legislatures by sportsmen's groups centered in the larger towns and metropolitan centers. The rural counties, in which the wildlife lived, usually considered game laws an infringement on personal liberty, and exempted themselves from the protective legislation. In 1837, when the Massachusetts State Legislature passed a law providing full protection for the heath hen for four years, the Town of Tisbury, where most of the remaining heath hens found refuge, voted in town meeting to exempt its citizens and permit the hunting and sale of heath hens during a ten-day open season. When, occasionally, a game law applied statewide, without exceptions, it was usually ignored by the market hunter and rural pothunter and observed only by the real sportsman.

There were no game wardens, and the constables and sheriffs rarely ventured into the hunting fields. Except when one of the growing numbers of game-protective associations, patterned after the New York Sportsmen's Club, brought suit against violators, there was no effective law enforcement.

Public interest in wildlife and in nature in general, however, broadened greatly throughout the nineteenth century. With improvements in printing techniques, books, magazines, and newspapers became common household items, while earlier, they had reached only the wealthy. Literacy rates climbed sharply throughout the century. As a result, the writings of men like Henry David Thoreau, Alexander Wilson, Thomas Nutall, Audubon, and others sparked an interest and appreciation for the natural world that no earlier generations of Americans had known. Americans, for the first time, were beginning to look upon wildlife as something other than things to eat. Evidence of this broadened public concern is found in the law of 1851 of the State of Vermont protecting songbirds. By 1864, similar laws were adopted by eleven other states.

The concept of a central authority for the conservation and management of fish and wildlife did not emerge until after the Civil War. In 1871, Congress set up the United States Fishery Commission and charged it with rehabilitating the nation's depleted fisheries. The agency was headed by Dr. Spencer Fullerton Baird, assistant secretary of the Smithsonian Institution and a former professor of natural history at Dickinson College in Pennsylvania. Under his enthusiastic guidance, the federal government and the states launched extensive propagation and transplanting campaigns that reshuffled completely the ranges of a number of native fishes and added some newcomers— not all of them entirely desirable.

One of the latter was the German carp. The carp had become well established in the Hudson River through introductions from England in the 1830s. It was a popular food and game fish in Europe and no less an authority than Izaak Walton had extolled its sporting qualities. It grew rapidly to enormous size in waters with much less oxygen content than those tolerated by native fishes, it was abundantly prolific, and its primary food was aquatic vegetation. All of these qualities seemed to make it the ideal fish to supplement America's native fauna.

The U. S. Fishery Commission pushed carp "farming" to the hilt, promoting its propagation through literature and through demonstration breeding pools installed on the grounds of the Smithsonian Institution in Washington, D.C. Between 1871 and 1880, nearly all states, emulating the federal government, created fishery commissions of their own. Each vied with the next in encouraging carp propagation. Farmers throughout the nation, assured of quick wealth by the well-intentioned fish commissioners, released carp in their stock ponds, tanks, irrigation ditches, and reservoirs. Within a few years all of these waters were teeming with fish ready for harvest.

Carp farming was an enormous success—except for two things. One was that few Americans ever developed a taste for the bony flesh of carp. And the American angler—with ready access to a large number of sporty native fishes—rarely regarded the newcomer as a game fish. The result was that the carp, within ten years after 1871, became established in nearly all streams in the country, crowding out the native species, roiling the waters, and consuming tons of food needed by waterfowl, muskrats, and other aquatic animals.

The federal and state fish commissions achieved more public approval for their efforts toward redistributing the native game fishes. In 1872, the U. S. Fish Commission established the first federal trout hatchery at Baird, California. In the same year, it released eastern brook trout from New Hampshire in Alameda Creek, a tributary of the American River in California. In 1873, rainbow trout eggs from California were shipped to the newly established Caledonia State Trout Hatchery in New York State. Brook trout flourished in the West and rainbow trout in the waters of the East.

Until the mid-1800s, the smallmouth black bass was confined largely in the drainages of the Ohio River and the Great Lakes. In 1850, through the efforts of an individual sportsman, it was successfully stocked in one small pond in Wareham, Massachusetts. In 1853, General W. W. Shriver brought smallmouth bass across the Appalachians from Wheeling Creek, West Virginia, in the tender of a Baltimore and Ohio Railroad locomotive and released them in the Potomac River. But, under the auspices of the state fishery commissions and with the full encouragement of the federal commission, black bass were introduced into nearly every pond, lake, and stream in the country.

The success of the fish commissions with artificial propagation and transplanting inspired others to try the same techniques with game birds. In 1877, California constructed a game farm where it tried unsuccessfully to propagate wild turkeys to extend the range of the species west of the Rocky Mountains, where the bird had not occurred in pre-settlement times.

In 1881, Judge O. N. Denny returned to his native Oregon from his consulate office in Shanghai. Accompanying him were twenty eight Chinese ring-necked pheasants that he had purchased from street vendors in the Chinese city. He released the birds near his home in the Willamette Valley. The success was phenomenal. By 1891, the pheasant occupied a bridgehead 40 miles wide and 180 miles long, and Oregon declared the first pheasant hunting season in North America. Hunters took thousands of birds.

The success in Oregon caught the interest of sportsmen's groups and official agencies across America. Farmers and market hunters in Oregon found that live-trapping and transshipping pheasants could return high profits from many willing buyers. By 1900, the newcomer was well established across the northern United States and southern Canada from coast to coast. Many of the birds used to start the nucleus flocks in the East originated from a game farm operated by Gene Simpson of Corvallis, Oregon, who was the first to demonstrate the feasibility of raising game birds in captivity.

Maine was the first state to employ salaried game wardens. In 1852, it appointed one man from each of seven counties to enforce the deer- and moose-hunting regulations. They were paid between $25 and $75 a year. In addition to its closed season on deer and moose, Maine was probably the first, in 1873, to impose a bag limit on deer. In that year, it enacted a law that limited each hunter to a maximum of three a year. Then in 1880, it placed its game-law enforcement officers under the jurisdiction of the existing fish commission, essentially establishing one of the first state game and fish commissions.

Some states, finding that protection of the game animals during the breeding seasons was not checking their decline, tried new approaches, the more promising being adopted by other states. In 1878, Iowa decreed that no man could kill more than twenty-five prairie chickens in a single day—the first upland-game bag-limit law in the United States. Other states applied the same principle to other game species, although the bag limit was not adopted universally for many years. As late as 1895, Michigan's five-deer season limit was considered revolutionary. Wisconsin had pioneered in prohibiting the use of dogs for hunting deer in 1876, and in 1881, Michigan outlawed the use of traps, snares, and pitfalls—favorite instruments of the market hunters hired by logging camps—for taking deer and banned shooting deer in water. In the same year, South Dakota passed a law prohibiting hunters from leaving the carcasses of big game in the field, action that may have been inspired more by reasons of public health than of conservation. Open seasons on big game gradually were pared from the six-months-long season that prevailed before 1865 to an average of two months in the 1890s.

During the late 1800s, the by-now numerous local game-protective associations banded together to form state associations that fought for game laws that would be less subject to county or local veto. In nearly every state, local or county governments could still exempt their citizens from the application of state game laws, and most of those with appreciable wildlife resources usually did so. County officials also often enacted ordinances that sometimes contradicted state laws, excluded hunters from other jurisdictions, and caused a welter of confusion. There were virtually no restrictions in the manner by which wildlife could be taken, and in their absence, hunters who called themselves sportsmen adopted methods that the real sportsman abhorred.

One of Winslow Homer's most famous paintings—*Hunter and Hound*—shows a youthful Adirondack deer hunter in a guide's boat, looping the antlers of a half-drowned and obviously wounded buck while shouting encouragement to the swimming hound that had driven the deer to water. The artist's skillful brush caught with photographic accuracy the drama, action, and excitement of a typical New York State deer hunt in the late 1800s—the buck driven to water by hounds, shot from a boat while swimming, and secured before the swirling water could claim the kill. Homer was not moralizing; he was merely reporting. This sort of hunting, and jacklighting as well, were accepted hunting practices throughout the range of the white-tailed deer.

W. W. Greener, the great British gunmaker, reported disapprovingly that: "The deer are often shot within ten feet of the boat, and it is said that in some instances, the boatman has had hold of the deer's tail before the hunter fired."

The New York Association for the Protection of Game, the statewide outgrowth of the old New York Sportsmen's Club, under the leadership of Robert B. Roosevelt, TR's uncle, fought hard for reform. In 1879, it succeeded in pushing through the Legislature an "Act for the Preservation of Moose and Wild Deer, Birds, Fish and Other Game." This law established a uniform state game code and removed the power to make game laws from the towns and counties. It made the possession of game in closed season an offense, although enforcement was left in local hands.

After this major legislative success, the New York Association for the Protection of Game went into a sharp decline. The trapshooting craze was sweeping the nation, and many of the old game-protective organizations that had fought long and hard for wildlife conservation became preoccupied with the new sport to the extent that it dominated their programs. By 1890, the annual business meeting of the New York Association for the Protection of Game was little more than a formal preliminary to the annual trapshooting matches.

The leadership of the Boone and Crockett Club, whose program, in part, had been patterned after the older state organization, sought to get the game-protective association back on its rails. It needed the support of a large membership organization to push through reforms of its own drafting. Grinnell ran a number of editorials criticizing the leadership of the association for its backsliding. But it was General D. H. Bruce of Syracuse who proposed the ultimate solution that satisfied both the trapshooters and the conservationists in the state association. He suggested that the association hold two separate annual meetings—one a trapshooting tournament and the other a business meeting at which the pressing problems of game and fish conservation would be tackled. This placed two strong citizens' groups in the field fighting for reform of the game laws.

Reform was badly needed. The New York deer-hunting season in 1895 ran from August 15 through November 1 without limit, and night hunting was legal throughout the season. The use of dogs was permitted between September 10 and October 10, and the only restriction on the means of taking deer was a loosely worded and even more loosely enforced prohibition against shooting deer at salt licks.

The same situation prevailed in nearly all states, although Michigan and Wisconsin already had taken the lead in outlawing some of these unsportsmanlike methods.

On January 13, 1894, Civil Service Commissioner Theodore Roosevelt wrote to Grinnell from Washington, and in one of his personal postscripts, which frequently are more revealing than the bodies of his dictated letters, wrote:

> Don't you think the executive committee plus Madison Grant, might try this year to put a complete stop to hounding in the Adirondacks? Appear before the Legislature, I mean. I wish to see the [Boone and Crockett] Club do something.

Madison Grant was a new member of the club in whom Roosevelt saw much promise. His faith in Grant was soon justified. Grant went to work immediately and, in the next session of the legislature, bills were introduced that would have outlawed both jacklighting and hounding. But representatives from the Adirondack counties defeated them as they had earlier conservation bills. In the same session, however, a law was enacted that authorized the appointment of a Fisheries, Game and Forest Commission, one of the first such agencies in the United States.

One of the champions of the deer, who was enlisted by Madison Grant, was Martin Van Buren Ives of St. Lawrence County. Ives knew that if the sportsmen-conservationists were to realize their objectives of outlawing unsportsmanlike hunting methods, they would have to accept some compromise and attack the problem in stages. Most of the Adirondack deer hunters favored the generous game laws, and they were joined by the North Woods guides and hotel proprietors who profited from the annual influx of sportsmen. Ives introduced a new bill that retained the open season but limited the use of hounds and jacklights to the first fifteen days of October. The bill passed after a bitter floor fight and was signed into law. For the conservationists, it was a minor victory, but it was a step forward. Ives's strategy was working.

In 1897, Senator William Cary Sanger joined Ives in introducing identical bills absolutely prohibiting the hounding and jacking of deer for a period of five years. The five-year limitation was intended as another compromise, but the Ives Law wrote the obituary for the abuses against which it had been aimed. By the time the five years expired, the sportsmen of New York State had come to regard the use of dogs and lights as unethical, and the practices never again were legalized in New York State.

The Ives Law provided a model for other states, and most of the eastern states that still had huntable populations of white-tailed deer promptly adopted similar legislation. Night hunting, except for a few nocturnal species, such as raccoons, is now universally prohibited, and the use of dogs for deer hunting is tolerated only in parts of some southern states where cover conditions are such that it is the only practical way to hunt deer.

It is interesting to note that, while these New York bills were being debated, proponents had cited an "excessive" annual deer kill approaching five thousand animals a year. In recent years, the forests and woodlands of New York State have supported an average annual take approaching fifty thousand head.

Between 1865 and 1900, game-administration machinery was set up in one state after another, and the few that had been established in the early years of this period grew in manpower and complexity. Some of these agencies were outgrowths of older citizen-sportsmen's groups. The state governments merely made the officers of the sportsmen's clubs official commissioners. In others, existing state fishery commissions were expanded to handle wildlife affairs. The Massachusetts Commission of Fisheries and Game was created as early as 1865. In New Hampshire, the state legislature handed responsibility for wildlife to its Fisheries Commission and expanded its title to the Commission on Fisheries and Game; its first annual report, issued in 1880, devoted two paragraphs to wildlife and the rest to fish. In South Dakota, wildlife administration had its genesis in 1887, when the legislature empowered the district judges to appoint attorneys to prosecute game-law violators. Thus, in the various states, official agencies of one kind or another were set up to provide at least nominal protection for the wildlife resources.

These early agencies were feeble organizations with minuscule appropriations and little power. Some states appointed only a single salaried commissioner or state game warden whose responsibility was to coordinate the activities of the locally elected or appointed enforcement officers, over whom the state officials had little or no actual control. Particularly in those states having strong sportsmen's organizations, however, the powers and responsibilities of these little state agencies were gradually expanded. Most, in the beginning, were concerned only with the enforcement of laws. Then predator control assumed importance in some areas, and the successful introduction of the ring-necked pheasant into Oregon brought demands for introduction of the hardy Oriental game bird in other states; state game farms were required to meet the demand. Gradually, around the little nuclei that had been established, the beginnings of real wildlife administrative agencies formed.

All of the early state wildlife agencies were financed entirely by appropriations from the general treasuries. But in 1895, North Dakota passed a law requiring all hunters to purchase licenses from the state. This innovation was adopted by many other states, although as late as 1922, there were still fourteen that required no licenses of their resident hunters.

In nearly all states that had some form of central wildlife administrative agency, turnover of personnel was rapid, and the spoils system prevailed. The game warden who arrested a politically influential citizen usually found himself looking for other employment the next day. Fish hatcheries and game farms were used as political tools to favor districts supporting the administration in power and thus buy votes, while game wardens sometimes were used to harass citizens of opposing political views.

Except for its important role in protecting the buffalo and other threatened wildlife in the national parks, the federal government took little part in wildlife conservation throughout the 1800s. There were no federal laws to protect wild birds, mammals, and fish of any kind, and no federal agency to enforce them if they had existed. Even the national parks, nominally under the jurisdiction of the Department of the Interior, were still protected and supervised by the United States Army.

On March 3, 1885, Congress authorized the use of funds by the Department of Agriculture for studies in entomology, ornithology, and mammalogy as the result of a resolution adopted at the annual meeting of the American Ornithologists Union in New York City. Understandably, because of its origin, the little agency concerned itself at first almost entirely with birds and their relationships with agriculture. Dr. Clinton Hart Merriam, a doctor of medicine and a self-taught zoologist, was selected to head the Division of Economic Ornithology and Mammalogy, as the office was known.

Merriam was one of the earliest advocates of bird protection, and, in spite of limited funds and manpower, his office turned out hundreds of leaflets, pamphlets, and booklets on the value of birds in insect and weed control, life-history studies, and methods of attracting beneficial birds. With the object lesson of the passenger pigeon fresh in the public mind, these efforts received public attention and appreciation.

Merriam and his staff, like the conservation-minded public, were much concerned about the activities of the plume hunters. These were outlaw market hunters operating primarily in the South who were slaughtering herons, egrets, and other plume-bearing birds for the millinery market, which was centered in New York City. They operated in the breeding rookeries of the birds, and their activities not only killed nesting birds but destroyed or caused the abandonment of dozens of nests and nestlings for each bird killed. Feather boas and plume-decorated hats were then considered the height of ladies' fashion, and the breast skin and plumes of a single snowy egret brought up to five dollars in New York. Because the birds crowded nest on nest in their rookeries, one man could kill and process a hundred in a day and make more money in a month than contemporary bankers made in a year. As a result, the plume-bearing birds of several dozen species were dwindling rapidly.

The activities of the plume hunters were illegal under the laws of most states where they operated. But enforcement was almost nonexistent, and after he smuggled his take across state lines, the poacher was out of reach of the law.

This was another dilemma for the infant conservation movement to solve and another standard around which its people could rally.

The bison was the dominant form of life on the prairies on North America, and fingers of its range extended eastward almost to the Atlantic. *Credit*: Jim Yoakum.

Acquisition of the horse revolutionized the life style of the buffalo-hunting Indians. *Credit*: Library of Congress.

Near the end of the trail in 1879. The great buffalo slaughter lasted little more than fifteen years. At the end, the untold millions were reduced to remnant bands. *Credit*: The Huffman Pictures, Miles City, Montana.

In the South along the coast were great swamps of bald cypress, their gnarled limbs festooned with Spanish moss. *Credit*: Rex Gary Schmidt, U. S. Fish and Wildlife Service.

In the Rockies there were lush mountain meadows and peaks perpetually cloaked in snow. *Credit*: Photo by Hileman, Glacier National Park.

On the Pacific slope was the most stately forest of all. *Credit*: Save the Redwoods League.

Unchecked natural fires and those deliberately set by Indians had profound effects on the prevailing vegetation before the coming of the whites. Above, Custer's expedition to the Black Hills of South Dakota in the summer of 1873. Note the extensive stands of aspen, brushlands, and grasslands—abundant forage for deer, elk, and mountain sheep. *Credit*: South Dakota Historical Society.

Custer's old campsite as it looked a century later in 1973. Note the dense stands of yellow pine on the hills and the general scarcity of aspen and the paucity of grassy clearings. *Credit*: South Dakota State University, Agriculture Experiment Station.

The spring and autumn flights of waterfowl were awe-inspiring sights to the first explorers. *Credit*: Peter J. Van Huizen, U. S. Fish and Wildlife Service.

Other than man, the beaver is the only animal capable of altering the prevailing habitat to meet his ecological needs. Through their dam building, beavers create habitat for a wide range of wild animals. *Credit*: Utah Cooperative Wildlife Research Unit.

The mountain men, in their quest for fur, were the advance scouts of civilization in the American West. *Credit: Free Trappers*, oil by C. M. Russell in the Mackay Collection, courtesy Montana Historical Society.

The beaver—an animal that shaped American history. Huge fortunes were made in the fur trade before the collapse of the beaver market in the 1830s. *Credit*: U. S. Fish and Wildlife Service.

Thomas Morton's fraternization with the Indians—and his monopolization of the fur trade—brought down the wrath of the Pilgrims on his followers at Merry Mount. *Credit*: Library of Congress.

The sinkbox, a deadly method of taking waterfowl, first appeared on Long Island Sound in the early 1820s. *Credit*: Library of Congress.

The dense flocks of the passenger pigeon made it highly vulnerable to netting by market hunters. *Credit*: Library of Congress.

In the mid-1800s wealthy sportsmen from Albany and New York City "discovered" the Adirondacks, which harbored one of the few remaining deer herds in the East. The above is an oil painting by Arthur Fitzwilliam Tait entitled *Still Hunting on First Snow—a Second Shot*. Painting in 1855, Tait depicted himself drawing a bead on a magnificent buck from the cover of a windfall. His companion, believed to be pioneer photographer Mathew Brady, had already dropped a fat doe with his single-shot muzzleloader. *Credit*: The Adirondack Museum.

Demands for laws to protect game birds during their breeding season first came from eastern sportsmen in the early 1800s. *Credit*: Library of Congress.

Exploitive logging that stripped the land of its timber was followed by disastrous wild fires . . . *Credit*: U. S. Forest Service.

. . . that brought death to everything in their paths. *Credit*: U. S. Forest Service.

Timber was "mined" with little or no consideration for future productivity. This great "clean cut" was only beginning to develop tree cover, fifteen years after it was logged in 1920. *Credit*: U. S. Forest Service.

Until 1897, there were virtually no restrictions on the methods by which deer could be taken in New York State. Jacklighting, as recorded in the above sketch by Arthur Fitzwilliam Tait around 1865, was a popular sport. *Credit*: The Adirondack Museum.

The spectacular success of the introduced Chinese ring-necked pheasant brought demands for the construction of game farms by the early state wildlife agencies across the nation. *Credit*: Wildlife Management Institute.

Part 3

A Turn of the Tide

Chapter 10

Breakthrough: the Roosevelt-Pinchot Years

At the close of the nineteenth century, the United States had the rudiments of a national conservation program. It still lacked a name, and it could scarcely have been called a movement. It was more of a drifting trend born of the awakening realization by a few thinking Americans that the nation's natural resources were finite. For more than a century the United States had squandered its natural wealth in the belief that its forests, soils, waters, minerals, and wildlife were inexhaustible. But in the face of galloping economic, industrial, and population growth, demand on all resources was increasing annually at an accelerating rate with visible and alarming impacts on the existing supplies.

Since the conclusion of the Civil War, there had been progress toward husbanding the nation's natural resources, but the effort had been fragmented and lacked central direction. Forest conservation, under the prodding of the American Forestry Association, had made significant strides forward. But the forest reserves that had been set aside lacked realistic management plans. Four national parks had been created. But there was no central agency to administer them. A number of the states and territories had small, poorly financed fish and wildlife agencies, only a few of which could be dignified by the name "departments." At the federal level, Dr. C. Hart Merriam's little Division of Biological Survey in the Department of Agriculture was engaged solely in scientific research and educational programs, and it lacked any vestige of police power. No one was doing much about soil and water conservation except on the local level.

There had been progress, but it was like that of a man moving a wagon with the wheels removed and the team unhitched. Before there could be significant unified forward movement, someone had to put the parts together and gather up the reins. Theodore Roosevelt did that for conservation. Few if any men of his time were better equipped for the task.

Roosevelt's interest in and concern for the nation's natural resources long predated his rise to the Presidency. A dedicated naturalist and avid reader since early childhood, he had steeped himself in the writings of the leading authorities of the times. Through the membership of his Boone and Crockett Club and through other personal contacts and correspondence, he had associated himself directly or indirectly with the most prominent theorists, scientists, and philosophers in natural-resource management. His experiences in the West had been a post-graduate course in natural-resource problems.

Many, if not most, of the Vice-Presidents of the United States, obscure in the shadows of the chief executives, have been virtually unknown to the general public. Not Roosevelt. His championship of the working man against the political bosses and industrial giants had made his name a household word across America while he was still governor of New York. His widely publicized exploits with his Rough Riders in the recently concluded Spanish-American War had made him a national hero. On his rise to the Presidency in 1901, he enjoyed more popular recognition and support than any previous Chief Executive in decades. Moreover, as an astute politician, he commanded the votes of powerful groups in both Houses of Congress. The influence of his equally powerful political adversaries was more than neutralized by the solid support of a broad segment of the voting public.

In his views toward natural-resource use, Roosevelt stood somewhere around midpoint between the pragmatism of Gifford Pinchot and the appreciative, nonconsumptive stance of John Muir. In his early years, he had leaned heavily toward protectionism. Although he was an enthusiastic big-game hunter, he had felt that the national forest reserves should be declared inviolate wildlife refuges and protected from all exploitive use. He had been a strong supporter of the establishment of the Adirondack Forest Preserve, which set the early precedent for the National Wilderness System. He had fought for the enactment of the Yellowstone Park Protection Act.

Before Pinchot arrived on the scene with his new philosophy of sustained-yield forestry, there appeared to be no middle ground between total protection of renewable natural resources and their destruction by exploitation. Roosevelt was quick to grasp Pinchot's teachings that forests, under properly controlled use, could return crops of timber indefinitely with dividends in watershed protection, wildlife habitat, recreation, and other public values. This was a major turning point in the development of a national conservation policy— not only as it affected forest management but the management of wildlife and all other renewable natural resources as well.

Pinchot became Roosevelt's principal advisor on natural-resource matters, but Roosevelt was also a man with well-defined ideas of his own. The views of other associates and past personal experience also influenced his thought and action as Chief Executive. Before he be-came President, he and George Bird Grinnell had co-authored a num-ber of articles ranging from the need for forest protection to that for stronger game laws. The retiring author/publisher/scientist was a frequent visitor at the White House. Like Roosevelt, Grinnell, with his keen perception and broad personal knowledge of natural-resource problems, saw the logic of Pinchot's forest-conservation theory and supported its implementation. But Grinnell did not share Pinchot's utilitarian impatience with the idea of nature preservation for esthetic appreciation alone.

After his rise to the Presidency, TR sought out and camped in May, 1903, with John Muir in the Yosemite National Park and was highly impressed by the experience.

The result of these varied influences and stimuli was presidential leadership that produced a federal natural-resource program well bal-anced between economic development and esthetic preservation. It also produced, in seven years, more progress in natural-resource man-agement, protection, and restoration than the nation had seen in a century.

One of Roosevelt's earlier moves as President of the United States had no direct reference to wildlife conservation. Because of the influ-ences of his move on more than a third of the American landscape, however, its eventual impact on wildlife was enormous. This was his endorsement and enthusiastic implementation of the Reclamation Act of 1902. Although the bill that became the Reclamation Act was sponsored by Senator Newlands of Nevada, Roosevelt was the prime mover in pushing the bill through Congress in the face of heavy op-position from western livestock interests and a states'-rights bloc that considered the development of the western rivers a prerogative reserved for the states.

Before 1900, most of the land between the Great Plains and the crest of the Cascades was generally considered worthless except for grazing livestock. Between 1875 and 1900, millions of cattle and sheep replaced the millions of bison that once had roamed the prairies and foothills. The typical livestock ranch was little more than an ag-gregation of buildings and corrals that served as the focal point for a grazing operation that often embraced several hundred square miles of publicly owned rangeland. As in the days of the Spanish *rancheros,* most of the ranchers ran their flocks and herds on unfenced open range with minimal human control between roundups. The key to the success of each of these operations was a reliable source of water, and water rights—acquired legitimately through claims under the Homestead Laws, or by purchase, or simply appropriated and held by force—were the livestock owners' most treasured and jealously guarded possession.

The potential of the American West as an agricultural region had been recognized soon after the Civil War by Major John Wesley Powell. The one-armed veteran of the Union Army had made natural-history surveys of the western plains and Rocky Mountains in 1867 and 1868 and, under the auspices of the Smithsonian Institution, had completed a dramatic 900-mile exploratory expedition through the Grand Canyon of the Colorado.

Additional trips to the West in the early 1870s and subsequent writings brought him national recognition. In 1875, he was placed in charge of the United States geological and geographic surveys in the Rocky Mountain region. His *Report on the Lands of the Arid Region of the United States,* published in 1878, based on his observations and scientific research, contended that most of the soils of the West were fertile; all that was needed to make the deserts bloom was water. In this and later writings, he strongly advocated the use of federal funds to build dams and irrigation canals on all of the major water courses west of the 98th Meridian. On his explorations, he had identified many of the better damsites on the public lands and he urged the government to protect them for future development. With his appointment as director of the Geological Survey in 1880, his advocacy of a federal-irrigation program gathered greater public and political support. In 1888, Congress authorized the establishment of an Irrigation Survey, which was charged with the task of selecting the best reservoir sites in the West.

But Powell was dealing with a region of the nation where the cowboy and the miner, in terms of political power, ruled supreme. Neither took kindly to the thought of turning the river valleys of the West over to the "soddies." Opposition from western politicians was so strong that the Irrigation Survey was killed in 1890, two years after its creation, and Powell was forced to resign from his directorship of the Geological Survey in 1894. He remained in federal service as director of the United States Bureau of Ethnology, a post he held until his death in 1902, just as his dreams were beginning to reach fruition.

Roosevelt and Pinchot had both become converts to Powell's teachings, and Roosevelt had the votes needed to drive the Newlands Bill through Congress. The Reclamation Act of 1902 realized many of the recommendations for which Powell had worked so long and so hard. Before Roosevelt left office in 1909, Congress had authorized and work had begun on thirty reservoir projects capable of irrigating three million acres. Federal funds expended in this development were at least partially recoverable from the sale of lands, irrigation water, and mineral rights. The law limited the size of farms on the irrigated lands to 160 acres for each family. This was about the maximum acreage a single family could manage under the agricultural technology of the day. It also prevented opportunists from amassing huge private holdings, as many had done through abuse of the Homestead Laws.

The Reclamation Act virtually rearranged much of the wildlife habitat of the West. Reservoirs inundated many traditional wintering grounds of mule deer, elk, and bighorn sheep. But newly created water supplies converted other areas, that previously had been unable to support significant wild populations, into useful wildlife habitat. Development of canal systems, stock tanks, and reservoirs favored increases in waterfowl and upland birds. Irrigated grainfields proved especially attractive to many native birds and to the ring-necked pheasant, which, in the early 1900s, was just beginning its prairie-fire invasion of central North America.

Apart from its influence on the geography of the West, irrigated farming brought significant changes in western attitudes. The miners and ranchers who had dominated the West for at least fifty years were, for the most part, independent, self-sufficient loners whose concept of the law often was colored by expediency and personal needs. This was especially true of their attitudes toward game laws. Although some of the western states and territories had game-law codes as progressive as any in the East, enforcement effort was so diluted in the West's wide-open spaces as to be practically nonexistent. The miner, cowhand, or shepherd killed game whenever he needed meat, with little if any thought of legal consequences or personal guilt.

The irrigation farmers, although newcomers to the West, soon put down roots deeper than the semi-nomadic miners and livestock men who had been in the region for decades. They established permanent homes and communities in which respect for the law was a basic tenet. Where most of the miners and stockmen were unabashed exploiters, the farmer was a builder, carefully nurturing his crops and husbanding his allotted acreage of soil and water.

Although the change was gradual and subtle, the imposition of an agrarian culture on what had been a pioneer society radically altered the social, economic, and physical character of the West. Ranchers who had cursed the homesteaders for fencing their lands against trespass by livestock adopted fencing as a means of controlling and managing their cattle, sheep, and horses, and maintaining the soil, water, and vegetation as self-sustaining resources.

By 1902, the old frontier was just about gone. The effect on wildlife would be profound.

Roosevelt, soon after attaining the Presidency, set about the task of strengthening the weak federal wildlife program. A foundation for governmental action already existed in the Lacey Game and Wild Birds Preservation and Disposition Act of 1900. This law, unimplemented and on the books only fifteen months before Roosevelt's inauguration, was—apart from the Yellowstone Park Protection Act— the first to bring the federal government into the wildlife-conservation picture. It made the interstate shipment of wild birds and mammals and their products taken in violation of state laws a federal offense and regulated the importation of foreign species.

But passing a law and implementing it are two different things. Before the Lacey Act could become effective, Congress had to appropriate funds with which to build a specialized enforcement staff. Customs inspectors could control the importation of foreign wildlife with little additional effort. But only special federal agents could enforce the provisions applying to the interstate shipment of illegally acquired native wildlife. By an Act of April 25, 1896, Congress had created a Division of Biological Survey in the Department of Agriculture through a minor expansion and reorganization of the Division of Economic Ornithology and Mammalogy, but its small staff consisted primarily of taxonomists, food-habits researchers, and other scientists with little talent for any major law-enforcement effort. But Dr. C. Hart Merriam and his assistant, Dr. A. K. Fisher, had proved themselves capable administrators, and their little agency was an existing platform on which an action organization could be constructed. Roosevelt sought the funds with which to build it.

On March 14, 1903, Roosevelt issued an executive order setting aside Pelican Island as a federal bird reservation. This was the first unit in the National Wildlife Refuge System that eventually would encompass nearly 40 million acres.

Pelican Island, in size, was a relatively insignificant bit of real estate lying in the Indian River near Sebastian, Florida. But its mangrove thickets were crowded with the nests of brown pelicans, egrets, great blue herons, and roseate spoonbills. All of these species were targets of poachers exploiting the millinery feather trade in violation of a state law, enacted in 1901, that accorded full legal protection to nongame birds. Commercial fishermen, convinced that the pelicans were competing with them for fish, often visited the island to break their eggs or club their nestlings and fledglings.

Frank Chapman, one of the nation's leading ornithologists, had visited the island on several occasions and recognized its importance as a nesting ground for species that elsewhere were declining rapidly. In 1900, he was accompanied by Frank Bond, an employee of the U. S. General Land Office and an enthusiastic amateur naturalist. Bond's investigation on his return to Washington showed that the island belonged to the federal government, which opened the possibility of its being made a federal reservation. Bond's proposal moved through channels to the desk of the President of the United States.

More cautious chief executives would have hesitated. There was no real precedent for the use of presidential powers in establishing a federal wildlife refuge. The single possible exception was the Afognak Forest and Fish Culture Reserve in Alaska, which had been created by President Harrison in 1892 at the request of Secretary of the Interior Noble. In 1889, Congress had directed the Commissioner of Fisheries to investigate the Alaskan salmon fisheries. A four-man committee dispatched to Alaska to carry out the field work recommended that the President set aside Afognak Island as a salmon-spawning reservation, under powers granted him by the Forest Reservation Creative Act of March 3, 1891.

Marine mammals, at the time, were being ruthlessly exploited by sealers and ivory hunters of many nations, and the rapid decline of several species had become a matter of concern to mammalogists. Grinnell and a number of his scientist friends saw in the proposal an opportunity to obtain a refuge for walruses, sea lions, seals, sea otters, and marine birds, merely by extending the boundaries of the proposed reservation to include some of the outlying islets and rocks. On April 23 and 30 and May 21, 1891, *Forest and Stream* ran a series of articles by prominent scientists endorsing such action. On December 24, 1892, Harrison signed an Executive Order creating the Afognak Forest and Fish Culture Reserve, "including its adjacent bays and rocks and territorial waters, including among others the Sea Lion and Sea Otter Islands." Although the act created a wildlife refuge in fact, neither its title nor text made direct reference to wildlife other than fish, which played second billing to forests.

The Creative Act, under which Harrison had established the first forest reservations, including the Afognak Reserve, was still in force during Roosevelt's Presidency. It stated:

> The President of the United States may . . . set apart and reserve, in any State or Territory having lands bearing forests, in any part of the

public lands wholly or in part covered with timber or undergrowth, whether of commercial value or not, as public reservations. . . .

When the Pelican Island proposal reached his desk, Roosevelt asked few questions. Was there any timber on the island? Well . . . there were a lot of mangroves and palmettos. Undergrowth! Bully! Roosevelt's order directed that Pelican Island was "hereby reserved and set apart for the use of the Department of Agriculture as a preserve and breeding-grounds for native birds."

Roosevelt's establishment of a national bird sanctuary with the stroke of a pen sent the state Audubon Societies that were coming into existence across the nation scrambling in search of other federally owned lands with potentials as bird sanctuaries. On October 4, 1904, at the request of the Louisiana Audubon Society, TR proclaimed 25-square-mile Breton Island and a number of adjacent smaller islets off the coast of the Pelican State a second federal bird reservation. By the close of his first term of office in 1904, the naturalist President, by executive decree, had created fifty-one wildlife refuges in seventeen states and the Territories of Alaska, Hawaii, and Puerto Rico.

Roosevelt also applied his presidential prerogatives in setting aside and preserving for public benefit a number of scientific, historical, and scenic sites—among them the Petrified Forest of Arizona and the Natural Bridge of Utah.

Roosevelt's free-wheeling use of presidential power to establish bird reservations and to protect virtually treeless scenery under a law designed by Congress to save forests caused congressional grumbling. Most of this ended with the election of 1904. TR's landslide victory over Alton B. Parker gave him a resounding popular mandate and swept from office most of the untraconservatives who had sought to obstruct his actions. Never the shrinking violet, TR plunged into his second term with cock-sure fervor.

One almost immediate effect was the realization of Gifford Pinchot's dream of a national forest system administered by professional foresters. The Transfer Act of February 1, 1905, removed the forest reserves from the jurisdiction of the Department of the Interior and placed them under the administration of the Secretary of Agriculture. A quickly passed followup Act of March 3, 1905, authorized "all persons employed in the Forest Service of the United States" to make arrests for violations of laws and regulations relating to the "national forests."

With Roosevelt's enthusiastic support, Pinchot built up a staff to administer and manage the 56 million acres that then constituted the National Forest System of the United States. Most of the recruits were youngsters fresh from newly created schools of forestry at land-grant colleges across the nation. In 1890, the only trained foresters in America had been a handful of men who, like Pinchot, had been trained in European forestry schools. Cornell University, in 1898, had begun offering courses in forestry based largely upon European concepts. In 1900, when Roosevelt was governor of New York, Yale University had established a full-fledged School of Forestry, the first in the nation. By 1903, similar schools had come into existence at the Universities of Maine, Michigan, and Minnesota, and at Michigan State College. Few of their early graduates lacked employment opportunities.

Under Pinchot's almost evangelical leadership a crew of nearly eight hundred foresters went to work inventorying the resources of the national forests and identifying areas for special management under Pinchot's multiple-use concept. Among them were refuge areas with special value for wildlife. After years of direct exploitation and competition with domestic livestock, most of the larger mammals of the nation were at dangerously low levels. The national forests played an important role in sheltering breeding stocks of deer, elk, antelope, and other large mammals until more intensive restoration efforts could get under way.

In 1906, Congress confirmed and extended the, until then, somewhat questionable authority of the President to set aside public lands, other than forest lands, for special purposes. The Antiquities Act of June 8, 1906, authorized the President of the United States to establish as national monuments areas of historical, archeological, or outstanding scenic interest. Then, on June 28, 1906, Congress adopted another law making it illegal to disturb birds on any federal lands "set aside as breeding-grounds for birds by law, proclamation, or Executive Order." In a round-about way, this latter act gave clear congressional endorsement to Roosevelt's earlier action in creating the Pelican Island, Breton Island, and other federal bird reservations.

With these congressional mandates behind him, Roosevelt signed proclamation after proclamation designed to protect scenic vistas, wildlife ranges, fossil sites, cliff dwellings, and other Indian artifacts in eighteen areas. He proclaimed Lassen Volcano a national monument in 1907 and did the same for Grand Canyon in 1908. Congress not only concurred but elevated both of these areas to full national-park status a few years later. In 1908, Roosevelt created additional wildlife reserves in Alaska, Florida, Oregon, and Nebraska. At least two of these are still keystones of the National Wildlife Refuge System. One is Malheur Lake in Oregon, the other Lower Klamath on the Oregon-California border. These were among the first national refuges set aside specifically for the benefit of migratory waterfowl. Both are major wintering and breeding grounds for ducks, geese, swans, and shorebirds along the Pacific Flyway.

One of Roosevelt's great gifts was an ability to act coolly, decisively, and with the speed of a frontier gunfighter in emergency situations. In 1908, he received word that a politically influential speculator was planning to lay claim to the rims of the Grand Canyon, an area that TR had recommended to Congress for national-park status. Within hours after receiving that disturbing intelligence, using powers accorded him by the Antiquities Act, he signed an executive order reserving the area as a national monument.

In the previous year, a coalition of western senators had managed to attach to an important appropriations bill a rider calling for the repeal of the Forest Reservation Creative Act of 1891 as it applied to the states of Idaho, Montana, Oregon, Washington, and Wyoming. With the unsigned bill on his desk, Roosevelt and Pinchot hastily outlined on maps scattered around the President's office the choicer forested areas of the designated states. At the end of the day, they had added 16 million acres to the National Forest System through executive order. Then TR signed the appropriations bill with the rider that repealed his own authority to take such action in the five northwestern states. During TR's administration the cumulative area of the National Forest System increased from 42 million acres in 1902 to 172 million acres in 1909.

Pinchot, through Roosevelt, also brought many reforms to public-land management. Applying the logical premise—rather than a specific law—that users of publicly owned resources should pay for their privileges, the chief forester imposed fees on livestock operators running cattle, sheep, and other livestock on national forest rangelands. He initiated timber sales that were regulated and supervised by his forest rangers. He identified and reserved for future federal development the key power sites on sixteen western rivers in accordance with the earlier recommendation of John Wesley Powell. The rights to 75 million acres of coal and phosphate deposits were placed in public trust, although most of the surface rights were later opened to entry as farms and ranches. Pinchot's farsightedness in this matter did not become fully apparent until the energy crisis of the 1970s.

The word "conservation" as it applies to natural resources did not come into the English language until 1907. In his autobiography, *Breaking New Ground*, Pinchot wrote that, while riding in Rock Creek Park in Washington, D.C., the thought occurred to him that there was no single word to describe the interrelationship and sustained-yield use of forests, soils, waters, fish, wildlife, minerals, and all other natural resources. "Protection" and "preservation," then in common use by contemporary authorities on natural-resource matters, implied non-use—a locking up of resources—a concept that grated on Pinchot's practical sensibilities. He discussed this gap in the vocabulary with a number of friends, among them Overton Price, an associate in the Forest Service. In this discussion, either he or Price came up with the word "conservation." The word apparently was derived from "conservator," the title of an office in colonial India under the British Civil Service. When Pinchot discussed the newly coined term with Roosevelt, the President adopted it immediately and, from that point on, "conservation" became the keynote of the Roosevelt Administration.

Conservation also was the theme of the White House Conference of Governors called by Roosevelt for May 12–15, 1908. It was this meeting that put the new meaning into the dictionaries. As used by Pinchot and Roosevelt, conservation meant prudent use without waste of natural resources, tempered by reason and consideration for the basic supply. It implied the restoration or expansion of the bases of renewable natural resources and the protection of reserves as a hedge against unprecedented demands.

Roosevelt and Pinchot used the Conference of Governors to hammer home their theme—that the states must join the federal government in inventorying, managing, and husbanding their respective natural resources. The waste of the past must stop.

To implement his recommendations, Roosevelt on June 8, 1908, appointed a 49-member National Conservation Commission with Pinchot as chairman. The commission was charged with making a detailed inventory of the nation's supplies of water, forests, lands, and minerals and staging a conference to discuss methods of improving natural-resource management at state and federal levels. The Joint Conservation Conference, attended by all Cabinet members, delegates from all states and territories, and representatives of all federal agencies and private institutions and societies, convened in Washington, D.C., in the following December.

As a result of this conference, an organization known as the National Conservation Association was established with offices in Washington, D.C. With Thomas R. Shipp as its executive secretary, it set as its goals the sponsorship of conservation legislation and the promotion of conservation programs at state and national levels. Using the base already formed by the Joint Conservation Conference, the NCA formulated plans for a similar national meeting to be held on an annual basis. The first congress of the National Conservation Association convened in Seattle, Washington, on August 26–28, 1909.

The second, held in Saint Paul, Minnesota, in 1910, was addressed by newly installed President William Howard Taft and former President Theodore Roosevelt. It attracted fifteen thousand people.

Although wildlife played a secondary role in most of these activities and programs, the programs' effects on wildlife were profound. Roosevelt and Pinchot's constant hammering on the conservation theme captured the national imagination and spurred the states and municipalities into action. State park and forest systems were established or expanded and tree-planting bees became popular civic and social events. Counties and rural communities organized volunteer forest-fire fighting companies. State wildlife agencies received broader public support.

Important as these material gains might have been, the most significant heritage of the Roosevelt-Pinchot team was the building and launching of the conservation movement that they represented. TR and his chief forester had gathered fragmented parts into a solid structure and launched it with momentum enough to carry it forward for centuries. America's wildlife would be one of its major beneficiaries.

Chapter 11

Plume Birds and Bison

A foundation for active federal involvement in wildlife conservation came into being a year before Theodore Roosevelt entered the White House. The Lacey Act of 1900 was designed primarily to curb the illicit traffic in wildlife products, especially the plumes and feathers used in the millinery trade. It applied equally, however, to poachers who were killing game for meat and hides in states where wildlife was protected and smuggling them for sale to states without protective laws. Because of its scope, it enjoyed united support of the organized sportsmen and the increasing number of bird protectionists who were organizing across the nation.

In the two decades that spanned the turn of the century, high fashion dictated that bird plumage be worn on ladies' hats to the extent that church gatherings and other social events often resembled aviaries. Herons, egrets, ibises, and other wading birds bore the brunt of the slaughter that fed this fad, but no attractively plumaged bird was immune. Some hats were essentially mobile habitat groups, festooned with mounted warblers, cardinals, or bluebirds arranged in lifelike poses. The snowy breast feathers of the terns were considered especially stylish. Raids by the plume and feather collectors wiped out dozens of coastal rookeries and nesting colonies and brought a number of marine and wading species close to extinction.

A campaign against this destruction of bird life opened on October 1, 1884, with a speech by William Brewster at a meeting of the American Ornithologists Union in New York City. Brewster was head of the Department of Mammals and Birds at the Cambridge (Massachusetts) Museum of Comparative Zoology and, in the previous year, one of the founders of the AOU. His address moved the members to create a committee on bird protection consisting of J. A. Allen, Frank Chapman, William Dutcher, and George B. Sennett. This committee immediately launched an intensive campaign to enlist public support for bird protective laws and drafted a model law for consideration by state legislatures. New York State was the first to adopt an amended version of the law.

Grinnell, another charter member of the AOU, adopted a different approach through the pages of his *Forest and Stream* weekly. In February, 1886, he announced the formation of an "Audubon Society," named in honor of the husband of his boyhood mentor, Mrs. John James Audubon. Male members were required to pledge that they would refrain from "killing, wounding, or capturing any wild bird not used for food." Female applicants gave their word to eschew the use of nongame plumage for decorative purposes. The response overwhelmed the comparatively small staff of the magazine. In the next three years it processed and acknowledged more than fifty thousand pledges. The program became prohibitively expensive, and Grinnell reluctantly abandoned it in January, 1889. But in the meantime it had built strong popular support for the objectives of the AOU Committee on Bird Protection and sparked a movement that soon would become national in scope.

In an editorial published in *Forest and Stream* in 1894, Grinnell added another dimension to the fight to save America's beleaguered wildlife:

> The game supply which makes possible the general indulgence in field sports is of incalculable advantage to individuals and the nation; but a game supply which makes possible the traffic in game as a luxury has no such importance. If this is granted, public policy demands that the traffic in game be abolished. . . . We suggest this declaration, *The sale of game should be forbidden at all seasons*, as a plank in the platform of that vast body of men scattered in hosts over the country, interested in preserving the game of the continent. . . .

Until that time it had been an accepted practice for sportsmen who wished to dispose of their surplus bags by sale and for market hunters, so long as they respected the closed seasons and other regulations, to ply their ancient trade. But with the practical extinction of the buffalo, the reduction of the passenger pigeon to scattered remnants, and the decimation of the plume birds and songbirds, the market hunter was losing his social acceptability. In response to the blandishments of the AOU Committee on Bird Protection, *Forest and*

Stream, and the organized campaigns of state sportsmen's groups and bird clubs, a number of states, like New York, adopted laws prohibiting the sale of wildlife products either totally or during established closed seasons.

Many of these laws, however, had gaping loopholes, kept open through the lobbying of the market hunters, milliners, game dealers, restauranteurs, and others who profited from the trade in wildlife products. The law adopted by New York, for example, although based on the AOU model, applied only to mammals and birds resident in the state. Woodcock or grouse killed in New Jersey or terns killed in Massachusetts, even in violation of the laws of their state of origin, could be marketed legally at any season. The dealer needed only documentary proof in the form of a receipt. Since a Massachusetts roseate tern is indistinguishable from a New York roseate tern, and since receipts are easy to forge, many of the "Massachusetts" terns that found their way to the New York millinery market were killed on Fire Island. The only solution to this scofflaw problem was an effective federal law or a total ban on the sale of wildlife products by the state.

Supporters of a federal law sought out Congressman John F. Lacey, who had already demonstrated his interest in conservation. On July 1, 1897, Lacey, a close friend of Grinnell, introduced a bill that would have made the interstate shipment of wildlife products taken in violation of state laws a federal offense and made the possession of wildlife or their products subject to the laws of the states or territories into which they were transported. The bill failed to pass.

In 1900, Lacey tried again. This time his bill sailed through Congress to the desk of President McKinley, who signed it into law on May 25. In addition to prohibiting the interstate shipment of illegally killed wildlife, it imposed restrictions on the importation of foreign wildlife and an iron-clad ban on the importation of mongooses. The English or house sparrow and the European starling had become major pests in the United States after their introduction in the last half of the nineteenth century, and the mongoose had become a major predator wherever it had been introduced. Administration of the law was vested in the Secretary of Agriculture.

One major difference between the climate in 1897—when Lacey's first unsuccessful bill was introduced—and 1900 was a great upsurge of public support for bird protection. The educational work of the American Ornithologist's Union had taken root. A number of the states had adopted the AOU's model bird law, and local bird clubs had come into existence in nearly every state. Strong popular support for bird protection had marshaled under the banners of several state Audubon Societies. The first of these had been organized in Massachusetts in 1895 by William Brewster, whose speech eleven years before had sparked the drive for bird protection. In 1896, Brewster had become president of the AOU and was a member of the board of directors of the Massachusetts Game and Fish Protective Association, an organization of sport hunters and anglers that had made the Bay State an early leader in wildlife conservation.

Organizations patterned after the Massachusetts Audubon Society for the Protection of Birds came into being in Rhode Island in 1897 and in Connecticut and Indiana in 1898.

The fish and game protective associations that existed in nearly all states by 1900 were unified in support of the Lacey Bill. The numerically small, but highly influential Boone and Crockett Club, of which Lacey was a member and whose membership included many of the nation's leading ornithologists and mammalogists, solidly supported its enactment.

Support for the Lacey Act expanded still further with the establishment on January 18, 1898, of the League of American Sportsmen by George Oliver Shields, editor and publisher of *Recreation* magazine. The major objectives of the League, as defined by its bylaws, were:

> . . . protecting game and game-fish, the song, insectivorous and other interesting birds not classed as game birds. Its prime object is to enforce game-laws where such exist and to secure such laws which are not now existent. It aims to promote good fellowship among sportsmen; foster love for nature; encourage propagation of game and game-fish; restock game fields and public waters; to oppose excess killing and the sale of game and fish; and work for reasonable bags and gun license laws.

From a nucleus charter membership of 140 sportsmen in seventeen states, the League of American Sportsmen grew to a nationwide force of thousands within a few years.

Shields, through his magazine, had a major influence on most state game and fish codes, especially as they applied to the imposition of reasonable daily bag and creel limits. It was he who put the terms "game hog" and "fish hog" into the American lexicon. In doing so, he used ridicule like a broadsword. After portable cameras compact and simple enough for amateur use came into general use, successful hunters and fishermen customarily sent pictures of themselves with outstanding catches or game bags to local newspapers and, if the take was really spectacular, to one of the national sportsmen's journals. The typical picture showed one or two hunters or anglers posed woodenly beside long strings of dead ducks, quail, geese, and other game birds or racks of trout. The editor usually published it with a banal caption indicating mild praise, and the clipping went into the proud "sportsman's" scrapbook.

Those who sent such photographs to Shields received a jolting awakening. Shields published the pictures with names and addresses but he captioned them: "These men are hogs!" Later he ran a picture in each issue of *Recreation*, featuring the "game hog" or "fish hog of the month." He spared no one, and some of the subjects of his ridicule were among the prominent social and economic leaders of the nation. Although state bag and creel limits were highly generous where they existed at all, sportsmen, through Shield's wrath, became consciously aware of the limits of taste. Most found themselves supporting limitations on the numbers of fish and game to which the individual was entitled in a day. These limits soon found their way into the game codes of the states.

All of these forces—from the scientists represented by the AOU to the lay nature enthusiasts and sportsmen represented by the state Audubon Societies, local bird clubs, the League of American Sportsmen, and the state game and fish protective associations—solidly endorsed the enactment of the Lacey Act in 1900.

One obstacle in the path of implementation of the Lacey Act after its enactment was that many states had only rudimentary wildlife protective laws. In others law enforcement was virtually nonexistent. But the presence of the federal law provided a strong incentive for sportsmen and bird protectionists in all states to unite in campaigns to adopt realistic state wildlife protective laws.

One of the most energetic and persuasive fighters for reform was T. Gilbert Pearson, a youthful biology instructor at Guilford College in North Carolina. The barrier islands on North Carolina's coast with their rich nesting colonies of terns, gulls, and black skimmers were concentration points for market hunters plying the millinery feather trade. The state had only the most rudimentary of game laws, enacted at the county level and largely ignored both by the shooters and the authorities. Robins, meadowlarks, and other songbirds were sold for food in the butcher shops along with quail, snipe, and waterfowl. Shooting nighthawks at dusk was a favorite rural pastime.

Appalled at this slaughter of birds at all seasons, Pearson launched a one-man campaign for protection of nongame birds and a sensible, centralized state game code. As part of this effort, he wrote a book, *Stories of Bird Life*, which attracted the attention of William Dutcher, who had recently become chairman of the Bird Protection Committee of the American Ornithologist's Union. Dutcher wrote to Pearson congratulating him on his newly achieved authorship and suggesting, incidentally, that he consider forming an Audubon Society in the Tarheel State.

Although Pearson was somewhat disenchanted with the extremist propaganda in some of the supporting literature that Dutcher sent him, he recognized that the organizational route was the only clear avenue to his objectives. On March 12, 1902, he addressed an audience of two hundred in the college chapel at Greensboro. At the close of the meeting, he collected dues or pledges from two-thirds of his audience as charter members of the North Carolina Audubon Society.

Through lectures, writings, and personal persuasion, Pearson soon expanded his organization into a political force to be reckoned with. Much of his support came from the sportsmen of the state. "Gentlemen hunters," he wrote in his memoirs, "were my main supporters. They loved the out-of-doors and wanted market-shooting and plume-hunting brought to an end; while men who did not hunt seemed to take no interest in laws to protect wildlife."

Ten days after the founding of the North Carolina Audubon Society, Pearson became a charter member and vice-president of the North Carolina Academy of Science, a position that gave his views ready exposure to the state's scientific community.

Although Pearson had been working tirelessly for the enactment of game laws and full protection for nongame species in his state, he recognized that, without enforcement, laws were meaningless. North Carolina, still digging itself out of the morass in which the Civil War had left it, was a poverty-stricken state. In 1901, the state legislature had been able to appropriate no more than $100,000 for public education—barely enough to keep the public schools open for four months. The likelihood of obtaining even a pittance for wildlife law enforcement was a vain hope.

With able legal help, Pearson drafted a model state game law that contained some unique provisions. It proposed to replace the patchwork of ineffective county game laws with a unified state game code, and provide full legal protection for most nongame species. It would impose a ten-dollar license fee on all nonresident hunters, the proceeds to be earmarked for use of the state Audubon Society, which would assume full responsibility for game law enforcement.

Hunting licenses, especially for nonresidents, were not unheard of in the United States at that time, although only a handful of states required any licenses at all. But the idea of making a private organization a quasi-state agency with full police powers raised legal eyebrows.

Pearson's proposal ran into a hornet's nest of opposition from the market and plume hunters and from guides, hotel proprietors, and resort owners who feared that the licensing feature would discourage visits from their out-of-state customers. North Carolina was a popular hunting ground for many wealthy northern sportsmen. Some of the more affluent owned or leased extensive quail-shooting preserves. Others made their hunting headquarters at hotels and lodges catering to their special interests. Revenue from these sources was an important item in the state's flagging economy.

On the other hand, if there were going to be game laws and game-law enforcement, Pearson's plan offered advantages to a financially depressed state like North Carolina; it could be implemented without costing the taxpayers of the state a single cent.

Although competent legal authorities advised him that his proposal had no chance of acceptance by the State General Assembly, they underestimated Pearson's powers of persuasion. He elicited promises from several prominent legislators to introduce or support his bill. Governor Charles B. Aycock responded to Pearson's personal appeal by recommending the bill's enactment in an address to the General Assembly. It became law on March 6, 1903.

As a result of a resounding and almost single-handed victory in a state that until then had demonstrated little or no conservation interest, Pearson became a celebrity in wildlife conservation circles. In April, 1902, Dutcher had formed the National Committee of Audubon Societies, a loosely knit organization of the officers of the state Audubon groups, who met annually to exchange information and to coordinate their activities in the national arena. As president of the North Carolina Audubon Society, Pearson automatically became a member of the committee.

In November, 1904, Dutcher sent Pearson an urgent plea to meet him in New York City on a matter of great importance. On Pearson's arrival on November 25, Dutcher informed him that a wealthy New Yorker, Albert Wilcox, had become interested in wildlife conservation and was considering donating money to the National Committee for the advancement of its cause. Pearson immediately visited Wilcox. At the close of their discussion, the New Yorker offered to contribute to the committee $3,000 a year for at least two years and to provide it a legacy of $100,000 in his will. His conditions were that the committee be incorporated as a national action organization, that Pearson devote at least half his time to its work, and that the scope of its program encompass useful mammals as well as birds. Dutcher, with Pearson's concurrence, enthusiastically agreed.

On January 30, 1905, the board of directors of the National Association of Audubon Societies for the Protection of Wild Birds and Animals (later, through a name change, the National Audubon Society) met in New York City to sign the papers of incorporation and to elect officers. They were William Dutcher, president; John E.

Thayer, first vice-president; Theodore S. Palmer, second vice-president; T. Gilbert Pearson, secretary; and Frank M. Chapman, treasurer. Wilcox died on August 13, 1906. His bequest to the association was $320,000—at least two million dollars in terms of modern purchasing power.

Largely through the energetic missionary work of Pearson, the association rapidly built its membership and financial support. Pearson toured the country, helping to organize state and regional affiliates, marshaling support for realistic state game laws, and developing opposition to the millinery feather trade. Twenty-three state legislatures adopted the Model Bird Law, responsibility for whose promotion the association had acquired from the AOU.

Because of Wilcox's generous support, the fledgling society was able to undertake activities that otherwise would have been impossible. It was able, among other things, to establish a special fund to provide physical protection for some of the more vulnerable nesting colonies of egrets, herons, terns, and other birds favored by the millinery trade and the poachers who fed it, and to assume from the American Ornithologists Union the expenses of providing patrol for the federal bird reservations. When Pelican Island was declared a bird reservation the AOU had agreed to pay the salary and expenses of an officer to protect it. Through an order signed on April 4, 1903, by Secretary of Agriculture James Wilson, Paul Kreugl, a resident of the nearby mainland, had become the nation's second federal wildlife law-enforcement officer; a few years earlier, Charles J. "Buffalo" Jones had been sworn in as a federal game warden for the Yellowstone National Park. To supplement the action of the AOU, the Florida Audubon Society purchased a naptha-powered motor launch to facilitate Kreugl's patrol work. Similar protection was later accorded to Breton Island and other federal bird reservations by the AOU and the National Association of Audubon Societies until the Bureau of Biological Survey obtained adequate appropriations to field its own enforcement personnel.

The work of the early bird wardens was difficult and dangerous. The outlaws against whom they were pitted were always armed, and most worked in teams. They were most active in areas remote from human habitation, where help for the law-enforcement officer in trouble was unlikely and detection of murder improbable. The National Association of Audubon Societies had barely assumed responsibility for this activity when, on July 8, 1905, one of its wardens, Guy Bradley, was shot and killed by plume hunters raiding an egret rookery on Lake Cuthbert in Florida. His brutal murder, widely publicized, built further public support for the cause of bird protection.

Under the leadership of Dutcher and Pearson, the National Association of Audubon Societies grew rapidly in strength and political influence. On May 7, 1910, it achieved a major breakthrough in its long campaign against the slaughter of birds for their decorative plumage when New York Governor Charles Evans Hughes signed the Baynes Audubon Plumage Bill outlawing all traffic in wild bird plumage in the state. The fight had been uphill all the way against formidable odds, but the victory had significance extending far beyond the limits of the state. New York City was the center of the American fashion world and of dozens of the high-style millinery shops that it supported. It was the principal port of entry of foreign bird skins shipped to North America and the destination of those of native species taken legally and illegally in every state in the Union.

For nearly two months before the passage of the plumage bill, Pearson practically lived in Albany, unabashedly lobbying for the protective law. Pitted against him was a powerful coalition of industrial interests, from the milliners, who claimed that a business employing twenty thousand people was at stake, to the railroad and steamship interests that profited from the traffic in plumage. The fight against the bill was led in the legislature by Alfred E. Smith, later a candidate for the Presidency of the United States, and the New York *Times*, backing its editorial opinion with caustic cartoons, branded the Audubon bill "Piffling Legislation."

The enactment of the Audubon Plumage Law did not kill the feather trade outright, but it wounded it so critically that it died a lingering death. It set the stage for the full legal protection of nongame migratory birds that would be realized in the following decade.

In this and other campaigns, Pearson sought and received the active support of the organized sportsmen of New York and the nation. He was elected an associate member of the Boone and Crockett Club, and, through his novel arrangement with the North Carolina State Legislature which made him a de facto head of the state's wildlife agency, he became active in the affairs of the National Association of Game Wardens and Commissioners to the extent that he became its president in 1910.

The National Association of Game Wardens and Commissioners—now, through a broadening of scope, the International Association of Game, Fish and Conservation Commissioners—originated at a meeting of the heads of the state wildlife agencies in Yellowstone National Park on July 7, 1902, as a vehicle for comparing notes, upgrading national and state conservation programs, and developing interstate cooperation in problems of mutual interest. Its membership represented the leading authorities on fish and wildlife administration in the nation, with ready access to the governors and legislatures to whom they were responsible. As such, it soon became a leading force in promoting the wildlife conservation movement.

One major beneficiary of the strengthening conservation movement in the early 1900s was the bison, which had become a symbol of America's depleted wildlife resources. At the turn of the century, the species was in a precarious state. Although the Lacey Yellowstone Park Protection Act and, after 1900, the laws of Montana and Wyoming provided full legal protection for the park buffalo, the population in the park continued to decline until 1902, when officials in their annual count could find only twenty-three head. These were the only wild, free-roaming survivors of the species left in the United States.

The situation in Canada was somewhat brighter. In 1893, the Winnipeg *Free Press* reported the discovery of a "lost herd" of wood bison ranging near the Great Slave Lake in the Northwest Territories. The first inkling of its existence came when a Manitoba businessman found twenty heads and robes in a fur trader's warehouse in Edmonton, Alberta, and forwarded the intelligence to his hometown newspaper. The trader had informed him that he had purchased the trophies from Indians, who had told the trader that they had killed more than two hundred of the animals in the previous season. The survivors of this band formed the nucleus of the herd of sixteen thousand that now roams the vast Wood Buffalo National Park of western Canada.

Soon after Theodore Roosevelt moved into the White House, emphasis shifted from protection of the tiny bands in Yellowstone National Park to an active program of restoration. Under the aggressive leadership of W. F. Scott, chief game warden of Montana and the first president of the National Association of Game Wardens and Commissioners, poaching by miners operating along the borders of the park was brought to a virtual halt. In 1902, Congress appropriated $15,000 with which to rebuild the Yellowstone herd.

Although the bison was nearly extinct as a wild species, there were, scattered here and there across the nation, bands of captive animals. In 1884, Michael Pablo, a Mexican-Indian halfblood, had purchased ten buffalo from Walking Coyote, a Pend d'Oreille Indian who had developed a private herd from a nucleus of four calves that he had captured in southern Alberta in 1873. Pablo released his animals on the Flathead Indian Reservation north of Missoula, Montana. In 1874, C. B. Alloway, a Canadian fur trapper, had captured five calves in Saskatchewan. Offspring of these became the nuclei of the herd in Banff National Park and the Charles Allard herd in Kalispell, Montana.

Around 1886, Colonel Charles J. Jones, a former buffalo hunter turned rancher, roped some calves from the remnant southern herd in Texas and began experimental crossbreeding of bison and domestic cattle on his ranch near Garden City, Kansas, in an effort to produce a tractable hybrid with superior meat qualities. "Buffalo" Jones's "cattalo" project failed financially, but it gave the colorful frontiersman more expertise in handling buffalo in captivity than any other man in the world.

Toward the close of the nineteenth century, fenced game parks had become popular hobbies with wealthy easterners, and the more elaborate featured herds of bison. Austin Corbin, the developer of New York's Manhattan Beach and Coney Island, through purchases of a nucleus breeding stock from Jones, established a herd on his sprawling park in Croyden, New Hampshire, a herd that eventually numbered nearly one hundred purebred plains bison. This and other captive herds assumed great importance when the bison-restoration program attained momentum.

The idea for a national organization to promote a buffalo-restoration program initiated with Ernest Harold Baynes, a mild-mannered young naturalist who had conducted a study of the buffalo on Corbin's Park. On January 18, 1905, he addressed the Boston Society of Natural History on the subject "The American Buffalo—A Plea for Its Preservation," illustrated with stereopticon slides. At the close of the lecture he suggested that the Boston society organize a popular movement to promote and finance a buffalo-restoration program. His suggestion was rejected offhand.

In the audience in Boston that evening, however, was T. Gilbert Pearson. Although he found the young naturalist's presentation ineffective and his slides of poor quality, he recognized Baynes's sincerity and the worthiness of his cause. Buttonholing the speaker at the conclusion of the meeting, he suggested that Baynes carry his case to the New York Zoological Society where, Pearson assured him, his idea would receive a warmer reception.

The advice was sound. The New York Zoological Society and the Boone and Crockett Club had already combined forces in a campaign to aid the buffalo. One week after Baynes's Boston address, President Roosevelt, on January 24, 1905, signed into law a bill authorizing the President of the United States to set aside areas in the Wichita National Forest Reserve in Oklahoma "for the protection of game animals and birds and be recognized as a breeding place thereof." This law had been promoted largely by the two New York-based organizations. The area designated in the law had been selected by them on the basis of its potential value as bison range.

Less than five months later, on June 2, 1905, Roosevelt signed an executive order that renamed the Wichita National Forest Reserve in Oklahoma as the Wichita National Game Reserve—now the Wichita Mountains National Wildlife Refuge. In testimony favoring the enactment of the game-reserve law, representatives of the New York Zoological Society had promised to donate to the government fifteen bison from its collection in the New York Zoological Park as a nucleus breeding stock. In contrast to the remnant herd of mountain buffalo in Yellowstone, these were purebred plains bison whose ancestors had been part of the great southern herd that had roamed the prairies of Kansas, Nebraska, Oklahoma, and eastern Texas. In 1903, W. C. Whitney, who had purchased ten buffalo from Jones, had abandoned his family game park in western Massachusetts and presented his twenty-six buffalo to the New York Zoological Park, which already owned seven animals that it had bought from Jones and Charles Goodnight of Clarendon, Texas.

The offer of the New York Zoological Society was contingent upon the condition that the government, before accepting the proffered animals, fence part of the refuge as a precaution against loss by wandering, predation, and poaching. President Roosevelt and Secretary of Agriculture Wilson quickly obtained congressional approval of a bill appropriating $14,000 for enclosing fourteen square miles of the protected range. The fifteen buffalo from the East arrived at their future home in specially reinforced cattle cars.

With this major undertaking already under way, the New York Zoological Society received Baynes's suggestions for a popular organization to promote and expand the bison-restoration work with undisguised enthusiasm. On December 8, 1905, the American Bison Society was incorporated with Dr. William T. Hornaday, director of the New York Zoological Park, as president and Martin S. Garretson as secretary and executive officer. Under the leadership of Garretson and Hornaday the new organization immediately launched a campaign publicizing the plight of the bison and designed to raise funds that could be used to restore the species to other appropriate refuge areas as they became available.

The American Bison Society scored its first major success on May 23, 1908, when Congress enacted a bill establishing the National Bison Range near the confluence of the Jocko and Pend d'Oreille rivers on the Flathead Indian Reservation north of Missoula, Montana. This Act of Congress authorized the President to set aside 12,800 acres and appropriated funds to enable the Secretary of Agriculture to reimburse the confederated tribes of the Flathead, Kootenai, and Upper Pend d'Oreille, who occupied the reservation; to fence the area; and to construct buildings and corrals needed to care for a nucleus herd of buffalo promised the government by the American

Bison Society. Through public subscription, including the nickels and dimes of school children, the Society had raised $10,000 with which to purchase breeding stock. A follow-up Act of Congress on March 4, 1909, authorized the expansion of the reservation up to twenty thousand acres, and on the following October 17, the first of thirty-four bison purchased by the Society were turned loose on the fenced range. Most of these animals were locally bred northern plains buffalo from the Conrad Herd, which had been built from Pablo-Allard stock on a ranch near Kalispell. At least one animal, however, came from the Corbin Herd in the faraway hills of New Hampshire's Sullivan County.

On August 10, 1912, Congress created the Wind Cave National Game Preserve in Wind Cave National Park, which had been established in South Dakota in 1903. The Wind Park Game Preserve Law authorized an expenditure of $26,000 for fencing, sheds, and buildings on:

> . . . a permanent national range for a herd of buffalo to be presented to the United States by the American Bison Society, and for such other game animals as may be placed therein. . . .

As soon as the structural improvements had been made, the American Bison Society stocked the refuge with fourteen bison.

Meanwhile, the federal government had initiated an intensive management program for the surviving wild buffalo in Yellowstone National Park. In 1902, Congress appropriated $15,000 with which to establish a "buffalo ranch" within the park where the animals could be protected and propagated under controlled conditions. The fenced ranch, south of Mammoth, was stocked with eighteen cows from the Pablo-Allard Herd, three bulls from the Goodnight Herd, and a few calves captured from the wild herd roaming the park outside the fence. As the captive herd prospered and multiplied, a larger and more elaborate ranch was established in the Lamar Valley in 1907. Until 1952, when the National Park Service abandoned the last vestiges of artificial propagation, the captive animals were subjected to all of the approved cattle-raising techniques of the time—artificial feeding, culling and selective castration "to improve the breed," and regular examination by veterinarians. The annual buffalo roundup for many years was a popular tourist attraction in Yellowstone Park. Hundreds thronged the areas outside the corrals to watch and photograph the spectacle of buffaloes being driven by cowboys through the chutes and into holding pens for their annual inspection and ministration.

Although the artificiality of the buffalo ranching jarred the sensibilities of naturalists, it was effective and undoubtedly hastened the day when the animal could be permitted to range the parks and refuges with only nominal and incidental interference by man. In 1902, including the still-wild remnant bands, bison in Yellowstone numbered around forty-six head; in 1907, there were 107, enough to insure some safety from inbreeding. By 1915, their numbers had more than doubled to 239, and in the early 1950s, before a severe winter in 1955–56 cut back the swollen herds, the population within the park soared to nearly fifteen hundred, in spite of an annual reduction of around ten percent annually through sales and transfer of animals to unoccupied habitat on other federal and state refuge areas.

Nationally, the increase in buffalo numbers kept pace with that in Yellowstone. In 1905, a national census conducted by the Bureau of Biological Survey found 970 animals in wild herds, private collections, and zoological parks. In 1933, there were nearly 22,000. The American Bison Society, its objectives attained, quietly closed its books.

Today the national bison population in federal, state, and privately owned herds is stabilized at around 25,000 head. Another sixteen thousand roam Canada's 11-million-acre Wood Buffalo National Park.

The segments of the continental population are dispersed widely enough to assure the survival of the species even though individual herds may become threatened.

Theoretically, there would be enough bison today to restore the species to the vast numbers that existed in the early 1800s. But, practically, this could be accomplished only by evacuating most of the domestic livestock and the works of man from substantial areas of the West.

Chapter 12

The Treaty and the Statute

Civilization's relentless march across North America in the 1800s drastically altered the composition and distribution of the continent's wildlife population at a very early date. One class of birds, however, for many years, seemed relatively unaffected by the avalanche of human progress. These were the waterfowl. Each autumn they swept southward in waves and clouds of thousands to winter in the ice-free marshes, bays, sloughs, and bayous of the South as they had in the early days of white settlement.

Many of these ducks, geese, and swans nested in portions of the continent that were lightly touched by man. Nearly all of the geese and a substantial proportion of the ducks nested almost exclusively in the vast tundra and taiga belts that spanned the northern half of the continent. Although the coastal fringes of these huge breeding grounds were familiar to thousands of sealers and whalers, their interior was known to only a handful of whites.

The most productive duck nesting grounds of all—an area that often produced twenty or more broods to the square mile—were the glaciated grasslands of the northern Great Plains, studded with pot-holes, sloughs, and shallow marshes that made ideal habitat for mallards, pintails, canvasbacks, and other ducks of more than a dozen species. Even after the railroads began to cut the northern prairies into segments, and settlers, attracted by the rich, treeless soils, began to pour into the region, their presence had only a minor impact on the waterfowl. With his horse-drawn equipment, the pioneer farmer accepted the presence of wetlands on his property and ploughed around them. His introduction of small grains and corn to the prairies brought a rich supplement to the diets of the resident waterfowl that more than offset the effects of his subsistence hunting.

Even along the bustling coasts, civilization had bypassed most of the wintering grounds of the waterfowl. Locally, industrial and municipal pollution and filling had destroyed some coastal riparian marshes. Boston's Back Bay—now a teeming residential and business district—was, at the time of the Revolution, a broad shallow bay that wintered hundreds of thousands of ducks and geese. But most of the natural wetlands inland and along the coast remained unaffected by the tide of human activity that welled around them.

In spite of the general health of its habitat base, the waterfowl population entered a noticeable decline in the late 1880s. One species of waterfowl was extinct and two or three others seemed on the way to oblivion. The last known Labrador duck was shot on Long Island Sound on December 12, 1872. The reasons for its demise as a species can only be guessed. But like the great auk, it occupied a restricted breeding area that was highly vulnerable to exploitation by New England and Canadian bird-down hunters who raided the nesting grounds of the northern sea birds during the eighteenth and early nineteenth centuries to obtain the materials for featherbeds. The down of the eiders, old-squaw, and other northern waterfowl was prized for its high insulation value in the frigid climate of Canada and the northern United States. The Labrador duck was so rare, even in the days of Audubon, that the great naturalist-painter never saw a live specimen but painted the portrait of the bird from a pair killed by Daniel Webster on Martha's Vineyard. Once the species had been reduced to remnants by commercial exploitation, the customary subsistence hunting and egg gathering by Eskimos, with whom it shared its habitat, and incidental shooting on its wintering grounds along the northeastern coast of the United States apparently eliminated it as a species.

The trumpeter swan, North America's largest waterfowl, also suffered heavily from commercial exploitation as the demand for its plumage soared during the early 1800s. Between 1853 and 1877, the Hudson's Bay Company purchased 17,671 swan skins, nearly all of which came from the trumpeter. The majority of these skins were taken by Indians incidental to fur-trapping operations that centered in the heart of the great white bird's nesting grounds. The smaller whistling swan nested primarily along the coast of the Arctic Ocean and migrated almost nonstop to its wintering grounds in the southern United States. By contrast, the trumpeter was relatively sedentary, migrating southward only until it found open water even though it was a stretch of river rapids or an ice-bound thermal spring. These habits made it vulnerable at all seasons to Indians seeking a salable commodity. At a later date, the trumpeter was subjected to heavy subsistence hunting along the southern portions of its range in Canada and the United States by settlers, miners and prospectors. A trumpeter swan cygnet weighs around twenty pounds and can furnish a full meal, with leftovers, for a relatively large family.

Another species for which early concern was felt by ornithologists was the strikingly plumaged wood duck. The wood duck was the first species of waterfowl to feel the full impact of settlement along the Atlantic Coast. Its range coincided with the great eastern hardwood forests which the early colonists felled with enthusiasm in developing their fields and farms. In early times the abundance of the wood duck depended in large measure upon the beaver, as nearly every well-established beaver pond had its complement of wood ducks. Large standing snag trees killed by the flooding behind beaver dams provided many of its essential nesting cavities, and the still, shallow waters of the ponds provided ideal rearing ground for the broods of young.

The elimination of the beaver and the clearing of the eastern forests greatly reduced the wood duck population. During the 1800s it was found primarily along timbered flood plains and riparian swamps that had escaped the feller's axe. It found some compensation for the loss of its earlier habitat in the wooded backwaters of the mill ponds and reservoirs that existed near almost every eastern community.

There were enough of these areas to support a substantial population of wood ducks. But unlike the geese and most other species of waterfowl, the wood duck lived year around in close proximity to man. Because it frequented small water areas ringed with brush that provided ideal concealment for gunners, it was especially vulnerable to pot and market shooting at all seasons of the year. Although the wood duck received full legal protection in Massachusetts and several other states by 1900, law enforcement was still a hit-or-miss proposition, and the laws were easily circumvented by any determined poacher. In most states, waterfowl hunting seasons opened in early September and closed in March, April, or May with no restrictions on individual bags or methods of hunting. Even where the closed season was rigidly enforced or strictly observed, it provided no more than nominal protection for wood ducks. The result of this attrition was that by 1900, Edward Howe Forbush, Massachusetts's state ornithologist, considered the wood duck an early candidate for extermination.

In capsule, the story of the wood duck was that of waterfowl in general around the turn of the century. Beginning in the early 1880s, market hunters and sportsmen invaded the prairies of Canada and the American Great Plains in droves. In 1884, Burr Polk, a correspondent to *Forest and Stream* wrote:

> The gunners [on sandbars on the Platte River in Nebraska] have so increased in the last three years that the weary goose, coming down from the North, or in from the fields to rest and slake its thirst, can hardly find a place out of the range of some one's gun. Blinds line the bars in the stream for one hundred miles so thickly as to preclude all chance of a fair bag.

With the development of the transcontinental railways in the United States and Canada, towns and villages mushroomed within the heart of the most productive waterfowl breeding grounds on the continent. The rails made possible the shipment of the gunners' kills to markets in the East and along the Pacific Coast. They also brought in hundreds of sportsmen whose cumulative effect on the waterfowl was as great or greater than the pressure exerted by the comparatively few who shot for profit.

Since the close of the Civil War, the efficiency of the waterfowler had increased phenomenally through improvements in firearms. By 1875 breech-loading firearms using self-contained cartridges had superceded the awkward and less reliable muzzleloader. The new shotgun barrels were choked—with a slight restriction at the muzzle —which controlled the spread of the shot charge and nearly doubled the effective killing range of guns charged with given loads of powder and shot. By 1890, comparatively reliable repeating shotguns, recharged from tubular magazines beneath the barrels by a hand-activated slide pump, were in production. The tubular magazine permitted the shooter to get off five to seven shots without reloading. An expert could empty such a gun at a flock of waterfowl with almost machinegun rapidity. Repeating shotguns were especially favored by the market hunters who used them with great execution against flocks of ducks and geese concentrated on the water.

The devastating effect of spring shooting on woodcock, quail, and other upland game birds had been recognized as early as the 1850s by Henry William Herbert, but it was not until the 1880s that its equally destructive effect on waterfowl was recognized, and then only by a comparative few.

One of the major difficulties in the path of any movement to bar spring shooting was that few states, even those that had progressive laws for the protection of resident game species, felt any proprietary interest in the migratory fowl that were only temporary and transient visitors to their borders. The general feeling was that if the hunters in their state didn't kill their share, those in the next state would.

As the Canadians pushed their own rail lines across the Great Plains in Alberta, Saskatchewan, and Manitoba, paralleling those of the Great Northern which bisected the Dakotas, the heartland of North American waterfowl production was thrown open to virtually unrestricted shooting. Market hunters swarmed out from the railheads and set up their blinds along the streams and at the edges of the sloughs and potholes. Thousands of affluent sportsmen—Canadian, American, and European—flocked to the region each autumn and spring to take advantage of the spectacular shooting provided by the massed flocks. Some of these sportsmen operated from rented parlor cars offered and conveniently side tracked by the railway companies while others, including members of the British nobility, leased or purchased choice segments of marsh for private use and operated from plush lodges built for the exclusive use of themselves and their guests.

The result of this concentrated gunning pressure on the breeding grounds was devastating since it was concentrated on the production base of the continental resource. Modern waterfowl research has shown that female waterfowl have a natural affinity for their natal marshes. Banded and color-marked hens have been found to return to nest year after year in the same acre or two of northern marshland after wintering on the coast of the Gulf of Mexico. Quite obviously, gunning pressure that removes a substantial number of breeding hens can seriously reduce the future productivity of a given breeding marsh. Spring shooting in the South, although its effect was less specific on given areas, was equally destructive. Ducks are now known to pair on the wintering grounds and return north ready to enter the annual business of raising young. Geese and swans pair for life and take a new mate only after the death of an original partner. The killing of one member of a pair in early spring almost invariably meant one less brood produced before summer.

Coupled with this disruption and destruction of breeders was an equally destructive attrition on the young of the year occasioned by the early opening of the autumn hunting season. Young birds just trying their wings were easy marks for gunners and could be lured into range by the crudest of decoys. Many of those killed were females that, with adequate protection, would have returned to the same area in spring to produce new broods.

George Bird Grinnell was among the first to recognize the devastating effect of spring shooting on waterfowl. As early as 1880, through his *Forest and Stream*, he had castigated the practice in dozens of editorials, but at the time he received almost no support. The waterfowl resource seemed limitless, and the need for conservation appeared satisfied by the laws already on the books.

By 1890, Grinnell and a few other pioneer conservationists who foresaw the destruction of the waterfowl resource gained converts in their effort to curb spring shooting. Sportsmen throughout the country were becoming alarmed over the steady decline of the autumn flights. Some rationalized that the birds had changed their flight patterns. But when they, like many of the gunners who had ravaged the goose flights along the Platte, moved to other areas that promised better shooting, the story was the same. In 1894, Grinnell issued his call for the prohibition of the sale of game at all times. The idea was adopted immediately by the American Ornithologist's Union, which until then had concerned itself primarily with nongame species, and by many of the state game protective associations. Through the pressure of these groups, several state legislatures adopted laws outlawing the sale of waterfowl and other game birds.

But the tradition of spring shooting took longer to die. Gunners in a number of states contended that the only good shooting they enjoyed came during the spring migration. And the old argument that "if we don't get them, hunters in the next state will" still prevailed. The dominant attitude in most state legislatures, even in those that had taken decisive steps to protect resident species, was that their own hunting constituents should not be deprived of shooting privileges so long as neighboring states permitted unrestricted hunting of the same birds. The result was a grim competition to see which state could kill the greatest number before the migrating flocks passed from the range of its hunters' guns. For the most part, the half-hearted legislation designed to bar market hunting and spring shooting that had been enacted in a few states were ignored by most of the shooters and often by the law enforcement officers themselves.

In 1899, waterfowl flights plummeted to an all-time low as a searing drought spread across the breeding grounds. It suddenly became apparent that if duck and goose shooting were to be preserved as traditional American sports, drastic steps were needed. Since the states refused to work together toward this end, the only recourse was through federal legislation.

The first attempt to put waterfowl hunting regulations on a realistic basis by bringing all migratory game birds under federal control was made by Congressman George Shiras III of Pennsylvania through a bill introduced on December 3, 1904. Shiras was not a professional politician but a nationally recognized naturalist and outdoorsman. He had pioneered in the night photography of wildlife, especially deer and other big game, and the Shiras moose of the Rocky Mountains had been named in his honor. His entry into politics was merely an accommodation to his political party and he gave notice, on his election in 1903, that he planned to serve but one term.

Shiras was assigned to a congressional committee involved with the problem of water pollution in interstate waters. The thought occurred to him that if the federal government could use its police powers to destroy bacteria detrimental to human health in adjacent states, it could use the same powers to regulate the taking of migratory birds.

On December 5, 1904, he introduced H. R. 15601, "A Bill to Protect the Migratory Birds of the United States." Although at Shiras's request no hearings were held on this bill, it opened an entirely new dimension to wildlife conservation, and it was almost prophetic in its wording. Its principal shortcoming was that, from the standpoint of public acceptance, it was a decade ahead of its time. The bill states, in part:

> Whereas, experience has shown that laws passed by the States and Territories of the United States to protect game birds within their respective limits have proved insufficient to protect those kinds and classes of said birds which are migratory in their habits. . . .
>
> And whereas the absence of uniform and effective laws and regulations in such cases has resulted in the wholesale destruction and the threatened extermination of many valuable species of said game birds. . . .
>
> Be it enacted in Congress assembled.
>
> That all wild geese and wild swans, brant, wild ducks, snipe, plover, woodcock, rail, wild pigeons, and all other migratory game birds which do not remain permanently the entire year within the borders of any State or Territory shall hereafter be deemed to be within the custody and protection of the Government of the United States. . . .
>
> That the Department of Agriculture is hereby authorized to adopt suitable regulations to give effect to the previous section by prescribing and fixing closed seasons, having due regard to the zones of temperature, breeding habits, and times and line of migratory flight, thereby enabling the Department to select and designate suitable districts for different portions of the country within said closed seasons it shall not be lawful to shoot . . . kill or seize and capture migratory waterfowl within the protection of this law.

Shiras made no attempt to press for enactment of his bill. His stated purpose was to circulate the printed document among the various state game commissioners, sportsmen's groups, and naturalists as a basis for discussion and debate. Shiras himself seemed to recognize the shaky constitutional grounds on which he had based his bill.

The bill was a revolutionary concept that caught parliamentarians off stride. The regulation of interstate commerce in game, embodied in the Lacey Act of 1900, was a simple extension of a recognized federal prerogative. But the idea of living, wild migratory waterfowl and other birds as a federal rather than as a state resource had no precedent in law. The regulation of hunting, by common law and by custom, always had been a matter for the several states.

Even Congressman John F. Lacey, the "father of conservation legislation," had personal doubts. In a letter of February 5, 1905, to Judge D. C. Beaman of Denver, Lacey wrote:

> The thought that interstate commerce has anything to do with the proposition, I think, is too remote to form a basis for Federal legislation. In my judgment there is only one ground on which legislation along this line could be defended in Congress. . . . I suggested it to Mr. Shiras and drew a section for him to incorporate in the bill and suggested to him to introduce it. . . . Under Section 8 of the Constitution, Congress has power to provide for the "general welfare" of the United States. . . . This question presents a new phase of the "General Welfare Clause" of the Constitution. But so have other questions [that have] come up from time to time as necessity has arisen.

Like Lacey, most congressmen were of the belief that Shiras's bill was a violation of states' rights, and the bill died with the adjournment of the 57th Congress.

The idea behind it, however, remained very much alive, and, with the continued decline of the waterfowl flights, it received increased support from the organized sportsmen, the American Ornithologist's Union, and state and national Audubon groups. This support was greatly expanded in 1906 when on November 24, *Forest and Stream* ran an extensive brief defending the constitutionality of the measure. Authored by Shiras, himself, it occupied thirty columns of type and contained 20,600 words.

In 1908, Congressman John W. Weeks of Massachusetts reintroduced a bill that, except for details, was identical to the original Shiras Bill—to the extent in fact that it was still popularly called the "Shiras Bill." Although the original Weeks Bill received more attention from Congress than Shiras's effort, it failed to pass.

In 1911, the drive for federal regulation of waterfowl hunting received support from a surprising source. T. Gilbert Pearson was approached by a representative of the Winchester Repeating Firearms Company which had become disturbed by the decline in game birds and mammals and which recognized that "as the game declines, our business grows less." Pearson was invited to meet with H. S. Leonard of Winchester, who offered him a position as head of a new organization dedicated to the preservation of game birds and mammals. Pearson suggested that if the preservation of game was in the best interests of Winchester, it was equally in the best interests of the other members of the sporting firearms and ammunition industry and that Leonard obtain support for his proposed organization from a coalition of the interested companies. He also suggested that, rather than form a new group, he provide the tendered financial support to the Audubon Association to finance a department of game conservation within the existing organization.

Soon after this meeting, Leonard wrote to Pearson stating that he had received pledges of financial support from most of the prominent members of the sporting arms and ammunition manufacturers. The letter offered Pearson presidency of the new organization, which would be incorporated as soon as Pearson's acceptance was received or, alternatively, the funds subscribed would be donated to the National Association of Audubon Societies specifically for game-conservation work.

Under the leadership of Dutcher and Pearson, the Audubon Association had become a highly effective conservation organization on its own. Although the offer of the arms companies would double the annual budget of the association, and the prospective donors pledged that they would do nothing to try to control the activities of the association, the association's directors, in special meeting and after much debate, declined the offer with thanks. Although many of the directors favored acceptance, others felt that accepting the offer would tend to move the policy of the organization off its central purpose of working for the improved protection of all forms of wildlife.

On September 25, 1911, a new organization, the American Game Protective and Propagation Association was incorporated in New York City. Its president was John B. Burnham, chief game warden of New York State, a former staff member of *Forest and Stream*, a widely traveled sportsman, and a man of integrity and organizational ability.

The avowed purpose of the new organization was to promote wildlife restoration on a national and international scale. One of its first announced goals was the enactment of legislation based on the principles of the Weeks Bill, which was then dormant in Congress.

Its efforts soon breathed new life into the effort to place a migratory bird law on the federal statute books. Early in 1912 no fewer than three bills were introduced in Congress to achieve this purpose —a new bill by Weeks, a second by Congressman Daniel Reed Anthony of Kansas, and a third, identical to the Weeks Bill, by Senator George P. McLean. On March 12, 1912, the House Committee on Agriculture conducted a hearing on the Weeks Bill but declined to pass it to the floor.

On September 18, 1912, a group of supporters of the bill gathered at a dinner meeting in New York City. Among the fifteen people present were John B. Burnham and William S. Haskell of the American Game Protective and Propagation Association; Dr. William T. Hornaday, Madison Grant, and Professor Henry Fairfield Osborn of the New York Zoological Society; Edmund and Julius Seymour of the Camp Fire Club; T. Gilbert Pearson of the National Association of Audubon Societies; and George Bird Grinnell and Charles Stewart Davison, representing the Boone and Crockett Club. At the meeting, Pearson suggested that the McLean Bill be broadened to include all migratory birds, regardless of their status as game. Before the meeting adjourned, the participants had rewritten the bill to include all species of insectivorous and songbirds that crossed national and state borders in migration. In this form it was promptly reintroduced by its author and by Weeks in the House.

Including these species proved to be a shrewd political move apart from its logic and demonstrated need. The Bureau of Biological Survey, for many years, had been conducting a strong publicity campaign designed to prove the value of birds to agriculture. While some of its claims of the effectiveness of birds in weed and insect control were biased and inflated, this flood of propaganda greatly benefited the supporters of the expanded Weeks-McLean Bill. Farmers' representatives in Congress who had been apathetic about saving waterfowl were not to be caught voting against "the farmer's feathered friends" and destroyers of weeds and insects. It also brought the powerful support of protectionists like Henry Ford, who, on January 13, 1913, assigned Glenn Buck, a member of his advertising staff, as a full-time lobbyist in support of the bill.

As a result of this drive, both bills slipped through congressional committee hearings that rang with praise for the proposed law. The Senate passed the McLean Bill without a single dissenting vote and appended it as a rider to the Agricultural Appropriations Bill. It was this bill that reached the desk of President Taft on March 4, 1913.

William Howard Taft signed the Weeks-McLean Bill in a last-minute flurry of activity before leaving the White House for the last time, although he was unaware of the fact until days later. In the rush to wind up his official affairs he had overlooked completely the obscure rider on the Agricultural Appropriations Bill. Later, in New Haven, Connecticut, when a sportsman friend, Louis Welch, praised him for giving the country a federal law to protect migratory birds, Taft replied in his bluff, forthright manner, that he would have vetoed the entire Appropriations Bill if he had known that such a rider was attached to it: He regarded the entire proposal as fundamentally unconstitutional and had specifically warned Congress that he would veto any bill carrying a rider dealing with basic legislation. It was only by the slenderest margin of chance that the nation obtained a federal migratory-bird law as early as it did, nearly ten years after George Shiras first made the proposal in Congress.

The Weeks-McLean Migratory Bird Act had far-reaching effects. It dealt a body blow to the institution of market and plume hunting and made legal spring shooting of migratory game birds a matter of history. It conferred on the Secretary of Agriculture powers to fix closed seasons during which time it would be illegal to kill or capture migratory birds, and it closed the season entirely on nearly all nongame species.

The federal regulations seem to have been observed almost unanimously by the sportsmen of the nation, who had been among the leading proponents of federal regulations since the early days of the Shiras Bill. But there remained a hard core of diehards who refused to accept the proposition of federal authority over hunting. In this they had the support of competent legal counsel. The 1915 report of the Game Conservation Committee of the Boone and Crockett Club stated:

> Able lawyers disagree on the constitutionality of this law. A case to test it is already before the Supreme Court, and may be argued in the spring. The Attorney General will welcome briefs to show that the law is constitutional. The American Game Protective and Propagation Association is soliciting such briefs, and all members of the Club should assist in any way possible.

In the meantime, the Bureau of Biological Survey had been entrusted with the enforcement of the new law, and imperfections in the early regulations were being ironed out with the assistance of a nongovernmental Advisory Board whose members included Grinnell, Shiras, Lacey, and Hornaday, with Burnham as chairman. T. Gilbert Pearson was later appointed a member of the Advisory Board.

The Weeks-McLean Law, in spite of its demonstrated value, stood on shaky legal foundations. As soon as it passed, Congressman Frank W. Mondell of Wyoming, an implacable advocate of states' rights, introduced a bill for its repeal. Moreover, the odds appeared heavily in favor of an adverse decision by the Supreme Court when that august body reached it in its order of business. The expected unfavorable decision would have turned back the clock at least ten years in migratory-bird conservation.

On January 14, 1913, slightly less than seven weeks before the passage of the Weeks-McLean Law, Senator Elihu Root, formerly Secretary of State under Theodore Roosevelt, a recent winner of the Nobel

Peace Prize, and one of the most respected members of the Senate, had quietly introduced a Senate resolution authorizing the President of the United States to enter into international conventions for the protection of migratory birds. In the last-minute drive to push the Weeks-McLean Bill over the line before the adjournment of Congress, Root's action received slight notice from either the supporters or the opponents of the bill in question. Later, as the Weeks-McLean Law came under the inevitable heavy attack from disgruntled market hunters and advocates of spring shooting, Root's approach assumed increasing importance.

Root's resolution, although it was introduced too near the closing hours of the congressional session for action, provided an entirely fresh approach to the whole problem. Root, himself, was among those who questioned the constitutionality of the Weeks-McLean Law, and his active opposition would have killed it. Root, however, recognized the need for the law even though he disagreed with its approach. Rather than oppose it, he suggested the treaty route as a method of achieving its purposes through an avenue that would be unassailable on constitutional grounds.

On April 7, 1913, Senator McLean, with the law that bore his name under heavy attack, introduced a new version of the Root resolution. It passed on July 7, five weeks before Congressman Mondell introduced his bill to repeal the Weeks-McLean Law.

The draft of the treaty, prepared by the State Department and Department of Agriculture (principally by Dr. T. S. Palmer with the aid of John Burnham and William Haskell of the American Game Protective and Propagation Association) began its long and tedious trip toward confirmation. But the treaty had scarcely been drafted when the world burst into flames as German troops poured into Belgium and the British Empire became confronted with problems more pressing than protection of birds. In spite of delays caused by World War I, however, Dr. C. Gordon Hewitt and James White of the Canadian Department of Conservation were able to keep the treaty moving forward in Dominion circles; John Burnham made at least two trips to Ottawa to assist them. Meanwhile, Dr. E. W. Nelson was steering and pushing the treaty draft through winding governmental channels in the United States.

Finally, on August 16, 1916, the Treaty Between the United States and Great Britain for the Protection of Migratory Birds in the United States and Canada was formally signed for Canada. Two days later the Treaty was signed by President Woodrow Wilson. Signed ratifications were exchanged on December 7, 1916.

Without an enabling act of Congress, however, the Migratory Bird Treaty was little more than a gesture. Simultaneously on January 13,

1917, bills to provide congressional approval were introduced in both Houses of Congress and two more on April 10. Appropriately, in view of his sustained effort on behalf of the treaty, it was a bill written by Senator McLean that passed the Senate on July 30, 1917. A similar act was adopted by Canada's House of Parliament on August 29.

Even at this late date an attempt was made to kill the treaty by defeating the enabling bill in the House of Representatives. In the face of the unified support of organized sportsmen, bird protection groups, and farmers' organizations, however, these attempts proved futile. On June 6, 1918, the House approved the enabling act by a vote of 237 to 48, and on July 3, President Woodrow Wilson affixed his signature to the document that made the Migratory Bird Treaty the law of the land everywhere in North America north of the Mexican border.

In the meantime, opponents of the Weeks-McLean Law, under which the Bureau of Biological Survey had been attempting to curb the unrestricted killing of birds while the treaty was being perfected, had been waiting eagerly for a decision on their test case before the Supreme Court. The decision never came, since the adoption of the enabling act for the Migratory Bird Treaty made the Weeks-McLean Law a dead issue.

The enemies of federal regulation, however, were not ready to give up without one last try. Much of the opposition stemmed from market hunters and large duck clubs in the Middle West, especially in Missouri. An opportunity to test the constitutionality of the treaty came when Attorney General Frank McAllister of Missouri was arrested by Ray P. Holland, a federal game warden. The landmark case of *Missouri vs. Holland* ended when Associate Justice Oliver Wendell Holmes read the resounding decision of the Supreme Court:

> But for the treaty and the statute, there soon might be no birds for any powers to deal with. We see nothing in the Constitution that compels the government to sit by while a food supply is being cut off and the protectors of our forests and crops are destroyed. It is not sufficient to rely upon the States. The reliance is vain, and were it otherwise, the question is whether the United States is forbidden to act. We are of the opinion that the treaty and the statute must be upheld.

The Court's decision in *Missouri vs. Holland* decisively ended all doubt concerning the constitutionality of the Migratory Bird Treaty Act. Under regulations promulgated by the Secretary of Agriculture through the Bureau of Biological Survey and their Canadian counterparts, most of the more destructive abuses of migratory-bird exploitation were eliminated. The sale of game birds covered by the treaty was prohibited at all times, spring shooting and night shooting were abolished, and the plume birds and those classified as song and insectivorous species were accorded full legal protection. Daily bag limits—extremely generous by modern standards but still drastic by the standards of the time—were imposed on all migratory birds classified as game. A hunter, for example, could take no more than eight geese and twenty-five ducks of all kinds in any one day. In recognition of their threatened status, closed seasons were imposed on the hunting of wood ducks, swans, and all species of shorebirds except snipe and woodcock; shooting sandpipers, plovers, yellowlegs, and other shorebirds had been a traditional spring sport for a century or more. Hunters were restricted to the use of shotguns of ten-gauge or less, effectively eliminating the huge puntguns that had been instruments of mass slaughter in the hands of the market gunners.

After the decision of the Supreme Court in *Missouri vs. Holland* cleared the air, the states, with few exceptions, accepted the Migratory Bird Treaty Act for what it was—the undisputed law of the land. The Act provided that states electing to do so could make regulations more restrictive—but not more liberal—than those provided by federal law. Many did so. The majority of the state legislatures also adopted laws that made their own regulations applying to migratory birds parallel to those issued by the federal government. Since the relatively few federal law-enforcement agents numbered less than one to each state and territory, this opened the door for federal-state cooperation through the far more numerous state game wardens scattered across the nation, and poised a double-edged sword over the heads of prospective violators. The state game warden, faced with flagrant violations of the migratory-bird game laws that local justices of the peace and judges of state courts took lightly, could contact the federal game warden and bring the weight of the federal courts down on the heads of the culprits.

The effect on the depleted flights of waterfowl and other species covered by the Migratory Bird Treaty was salutory. Within two years after the implementation of federal regulations, sportsmen and naturalists noted significant increases in the flocks moving south in autumn. While, at a later date, the regulations first promulgated by the Bureau of Biological Survey would prove inadequate, they were sufficient, in their time, for checking what could have been a disastrous decline of migratory birds in general and the destruction of a dozen or more species.

Chapter 13

A Quest for the Panacea

After a feeble beginning in the late 1800s, state fish and wildlife administration rapidly gained momentum following the turn of the century. Although neither was involved directly with the management of fish and wildlife, Theodore Roosevelt and Gifford Pinchot, through their evangelical espousal of the conservation cause, created the climate in which wildlife conservation could take root and flourish. By 1910, nearly every state had some form of administrative office responsible for protecting its native wildlife and for replenishing its fishery resources. Older agencies, like those in Massachusetts, New York, and Pennsylvania, had developed sizable staffs and long-range programs.

Some of the early state game and fish commissioners were little more than political hacks occupying *sinecure* positions in return for services to the party in power and whose sole qualifications were a personal interest in hunting and fishing. But there were giants among the pygmies. New York State had become the training ground for John B. Burnham before he rose to national and international prominence. Others who left their marks were T. Gilbert Pearson of North Carolina; John Titcomb of Vermont; Carlos Avery, for fourteen years head of the Minnesota State Game Commission; I. T. Quinn, commissioner of game in Alabama and later director of the Virginia Commission of Game and Inland Fisheries; Dr. Joseph Kalbfus, John M. Phillips, Charles Penrose, and Seth Gordon of the Pennsylvania Game Commission; and William F. Scott, game and fish commissioner of Montana, who in 1902 helped found and hosted the first meeting of the National Association of Game Wardens and Commissioners at Mammoth Hot Springs in Yellowstone National Park. The biennial and later annual meetings of this organization, the foundation of the present International Association of Game, Fish, and Conservation Commissioners, provide a vehicle through which state and federal conservation administrators could compare notes on program enhancement and, through resolutions, support or oppose pending federal legislation and administrative action affecting fish and wildlife resources.

The majority of these early leading administrators, although not all, were independently wealthy; many served in their official capacity without compensation and some helped defray organizational costs and payroll deficiencies from their own pockets.

A number were farsighted beyond their time. In 1900, Theodore Roosevelt, as governor of New York State, appointed Major W. Austin Wadsworth, president of the Boone and Crockett Club, to the presidency of the New York Forest, Fish and Game Commission, forerunner of the present New York Department of Environmental Conservation.

In the Sixth Annual Report of the Commission, Wadsworth recommended the enactment of laws to protect the forests from fire, to outlaw spring waterfowl shooting, and to protect female deer as a method of increasing the state's depleted deer herds. All of these measures were adopted during his tenure of office. Wadsworth was among the first to recognize the need for water-pollution abatement, long before most other Americans gave the matter more than passing notice.

In 1901, he wrote in his report for the Commission:

> It is not necessary to destroy or hamper any industry in order to prevent the pollution of water courses. What is really needed is to check the criminal selfishness of those who would rather poison their fellow citizens with their offal than to spend a few dollars to take care of it.

Even in states that were fortunate enough to find competent administrators, however, wildlife-conservation programs were woefully underfinanced. Nearly all depended entirely upon the whim of the state legislature in appropriating funds on a year-to-year basis. In a few states, such as Pennsylvania, the legislatures authorized the earmarking of portions of fines imposed for infractions of the game laws for the use of the state game commission. This, in many states, provided a fairly substantial supplement to funds obtained through legislative appropriations, but in others, the judges and justices of the peace before whom game-law violators were brought looked lightly upon the game laws and imposed commensurate nominal fines, if any at all. Income derived from fines, also, could not be relied upon absolutely by the early wildlife administrators; in 1907, Pennsylvania's State Treasurer arbitrarily reverted all game-law fines collected to the General Fund, in spite of a law authorizing their use by the Game Commission.

In an effort to obtain a steady and more reliable source of funds, a number of state wildlife agencies, early in the 1900s, adopted the mechanism of the hunting and fishing license. In the belief that users of publicly owned resources should pay for their privileges, the concept was supported by most of the organized sportsmen's groups of the nation. As in North Carolina and Pennsylvania, the legislatures were quick to adopt the idea—but only as it applied to nonresidents of the state. With an eye toward a potential backlash at the polls, few state lawmakers were willing to risk levying special taxes on any specific class of resident citizens. There was even reluctance on the part of some state wildlife administrators to seek such licenses. Dr. Joseph Kalbfus, secretary of the Pennsylvania Game Commission, favored appropriations by the state legislature over a special tax on the grounds that much of the Commission's program involved the protection of nongame species that were as much the concern of the nonhunter as they were the sportsman. This was also true in North Carolina, where the state Audubon Society had assumed responsibility for wildlife law enforcement under the unique arrangement worked out by T. Gilbert Pearson.

As a result of political opposition and the inertia of the legislative process, many state wildlife agencies received little direct financial support from the sportsmen until the 1920s when the resident hunting and fishing license came into more general use. Pennsylvania was among the first states to adopt a plan for licensing its resident hunters. The idea was first suggested as a means for financing wildlife restoration programs as early as 1895 when the Pennsylvania Game Commission was created. Despite the fact that the idea was supported by most of the state's sportsmen, individually and through their organizations, it took eighteen years and the personal endorsement of the bill by former President Roosevelt before Governor John K. Tener was able to sign into law the Resident Hunters' License Act of April 17, 1913.

The Pennsylvania law was typical of those that were under consideration by most state legislatures in the early 1900s. It required all resident hunters, except those hunting on their own property, to purchase a one-dollar license with receipts earmarked for the use of the wildlife agency. To the discomfiture and confusion of the game protectors who had to enforce the law, however, it exempted from the license requirement those who wished to hunt foxes, crows, and other species not then covered by the game laws. Although it had obvious weaknesses and loopholes, the Pennsylvania license law brought in $305,028 in its first year, a sum that far exceeded the niggardly and uncertain appropriations that had been doled out in prior years by the state legislature for wildlife protection and restoration. Following the example set by Pennsylvania, other states quickly adopted similar methods of financing their wildlife-restoration efforts.

Major emphasis in the early state fish and wildlife agencies was on law enforcement. The early game wardens were a mixed lot from a wide range of social backgrounds. Even in the more progressive states, the pay was atrociously low. The salary of a game protector in Pennsylvania in 1909 was fifty dollars a month. Since there was little or no precedent on which to draw job specifications, the game commissions in hiring law-enforcement officers often looked first for physical strength and skills in woodsmanship and secondarily for tact and intelligence. Few of the game wardens had any knowledge of court procedures or police methodology. On the theory that "it takes one to catch one," some wildlife agencies recruited their field officers from the ranks of former poachers and market hunters who had come on hard times with public resistance to the sale of game. Some of these men were hard-fisted toughs who stalked the trails and rode the back roads in buckboards of Model Ts and through their presence alone instilled fear of the law into the hearts of potential violators. They did little for the public image of the early wildlife agencies. But scattered among them were others, mostly young men, with higher principles and a clearer concept of their public responsibilities. Later, as states like New York and Pennsylvania led the way in bringing the wardens under civil-service requirements and raising job standards, most of the old "woods cops" were weeded out and men with higher professional standards were retained.

The early twentieth century was a period of trial and error for fish and wildlife administrators who were feeling in the dark for meaningful and productive programs. There was practically no scientific research on which to base programs, and little prior experience in the field into which they had ventured. If one state administration tried a method or program that seemed to work, others were prompt to adopt it, even though conditions varied widely from one state to the next.

Among the earliest and most successful projects—at least in the northern states—was the establishment of the ring-necked pheasant, which, by 1900, occupied an expanding bridgehead in the Pacific Northwest. Changing land-use patterns, especially in the central plains, were greatly reducing the natural grassland habitat available to the native prairie grouse and creating an entirely new type of habitat that consisted predominantly of cornfields and small grains. This, together with the interspersed brush, sedge, and grass cover around marshes, potholes, and outcroppings that resisted the plow, produced ideal habitat for the big gaudy bird from the Orient.

The *blitzkrieg* invasion of the Northwest by the Chinese pheasant after 1881 captured the imagination of early wildlife administrators and contemporary sportsmen. Farmers and trappers in Washington and Oregon soon developed a lucrative business by shipping live-trapped birds to the Middle West and East. Little was known of the bird's habitat requirements, and thousands were wasted after being dumped unceremoniously into woodlands and sterile wastelands and in states with climates untenable to the species. But where the pheasants were released in suitable cover, especially in the corn- and grain-producing northern states and southern Canada, the response was spectacular.

The insatiable demand for live pheasants soon opened new avenues of endeavor to the state wildlife agencies. Artificial propagation of trout and other fish had succeeded in reshuffling the distribution of North America's fishes, and many of the state agencies had inherited fish hatcheries from the earlier fish commissions. It was a logical extension of this principle to apply it to pheasants and other game birds. In 1911, the State of Oregon leased Gene Simpson's commercial pheasant farm near Corvallis and, under Simpson's experienced supervision, produced so many birds that it was able to supply the needs of nearly all states that wished to experiment with propagation, over and above its domestic stocking requirements. By World War I, nearly every state within the habitable range of the pheasant was producing birds for stocking through artificial propagation.

Since the state wildlife agencies lacked adequate funds and manpower, pheasant chicks freshly hatched on the game farms usually were placed in the care of farmers, Boy Scouts, and sportsmen who raised them until they were ready for release in the wild. Most of the agencies offered modest incentive payments to cooperators, although the sportsmen and civic groups usually accepted the responsibility as a public contribution and refused any proffered compensation. Many of the birds released through these efforts were too young to survive. Others succumbed quickly to the ravages of foxes, dogs, and house cats, and many were freed in habitat totally unsuited to their survival. But the saturation releases of thousands of birds found good habitat as well as bad, and within a decade or two after the stocking began, the pheasant had become one of the most abundant and most popular farm game birds in the northern states.

The ring-necked pheasant was a happy accident. Under the circumstances under which it was introduced to America, it could have proved a threat to agriculture and a competitor with native species. Some prominent ornithologists, such as Massachusetts's Edward Howe Forbush, opposed its introduction because of justified suspicions on both grounds. Fortunately, their fears proved ungrounded. The pheasant adapted itself to a manmade ecological niche in which native quail and grouse could not thrive. It brought with it to America no new diseases or parasites to threaten native wildlife. Its principal foods proved to be waste grains and weed seeds. Its large size and long legs permitted it to dig for food through snows that were lethal to bobwhite quail. It proved to be an outstanding game bird, wary, swift of leg and wing, and holding well to trained bird dogs. Its white flesh made it a choice table bird. It was as prolific as it was hardy, the hens producing a dozen or more eggs in a clutch. Because the bird was polygamous with one cock serving a dozen or more hens, the loss of surplus males to hunting could not check its population increase. The sexes were readily distinguishable in the field, and most states soon enacted laws or regulations protecting the hens and permitted the shooting of cocks only during brief open seasons.

Success with the pheasant brought a demand for the introduction of other promising foreign game birds and the expansion of state game farms to propagate native species. Early efforts with exotics centered on the European gray, or Hungarian partridge. Like the pheasant, it was subjected to heavy stocking in nearly every state and Canadian province; it found its American niche only along the northern fringes of the Canadian-United States grain belt that was already occupied by the pheasant.

Both the pheasant and European partridge reproduced readily in captivity and retained most of their innate wildness. Success with these species led to demands for replenishing native wild populations through the same methods. To assist state propagation programs, the American Game Protective and Propagation Association established an experimental and demonstration game farm near Carver, Massachusetts, where it perfected techniques for propagating bobwhite quail and pheasants but failed in its experiments with prairie chickens, ruffed grouse, and wild turkeys. The grouse produced some fertile eggs, but the resultant chicks were tamer than barnyard chickens and totally unsuitable for release in the wild. The "wild" turkeys also bred readily, but those released usually wandered into the nearest farmyard and ended up in the farmer's pot. The breeding stock for these birds was of doubtful origin. The blood of most was infused with that of Mexican stock that had been domesticated since the days of the Aztecs. Cortes had taken birds raised by Montezuma's people back to Spain in the early 1500s. Turkeys were common table birds in Europe long before the Pilgrims landed on Plymouth Rock, but the eastern wild turkey defied all attempts at domestication.

Early state wildlife agencies and sportsmen's groups also tried to pen-raise cottontail rabbits and snowshoe hares, but both refused to breed in captivity.

With the failure of these efforts, the early wildlife administrators turned their attention to the pheasant and quail, which had proved their adaptability to confinement. Each spring and summer, thousands of young birds were released into the coverts by agents of the wildlife agencies and cooperating farmers and sportsmen in the belief that they were doing much to increase the local wildlife populations. After the initial years of the stocking program, however, the coverts were fully occupied with wild-reared birds with which the bewildered newcomers could not compete. It was not until several decades, after modern wildlife research entered the picture, that the futility of these well-intended efforts was demonstrated.

Predator control was another shibboleth of the early wildlife authorities. Generations of frontier survival had conditioned Americans to categorize wild animals as "good" or "bad." The epitome of evil was the wolf, which had been marked for extermination since earliest colonial times as a destroyer of livestock and game. The bounty, a price placed on the heads of wolves as an incentive for their destruction, dated back to the earliest history of the law-making process in America. At later dates, bounties were paid by states, counties, and local organizations for nearly every species of wildlife known or suspected of killing livestock, poultry, game, and beneficial nongame species in nearly every state. Massachusetts, until recent years, paid five dollars each for the scalps of seals that sometimes tore up fishing nets and preyed on commercial fishes. The wolf bounty was extended to cougars in all states where cougars occurred, and the laws of the northern New England States considered the black bear a bountiable species. The killing of foxes, coyotes, bobcats, and the larger hawks and owls was at one time or another subject to cash rewards in nearly every political subdivision in which they occurred. In some jurisdictions, bounties also were paid for robins, blackbirds, bobolinks, gray and red squirrels, chipmunks, English sparrows, and kingfishers and other fish-eating birds. Alaska paid bounties on bald eagles for nineteen years after the Bald Eagle Protection Act of June 8, 1940, accorded federal protection to the eagle in the lower 48 states.

Most of these bounties long antedated the creation of official wildlife agencies. But with the establishment of these agencies, state legislatures almost invariably assigned to them responsibility for administering the state bounty laws. At a time when the rural vote dominated all state legislatures, the pioneer state wildlife agencies had to accept these responsibilities, whether they wanted them or not, or face oblivion. Most of the bounty laws applied to animals considered injurious to livestock and crops rather than to other forms of wildlife, and the bounties were imposed and retained at the insistence of the livestock and agricultural lobbies. The Pennsylvania Game Commission obtained the needed rural support for its resident hunting license in 1913 only by agreeing to accept a clause authorizing and financing a bounty of four dollars for each bobcat, two dollars for each gray fox or weasel, and fifty cents for each goshawk, Cooper's hawk or great horned owl. In a number of states, raccoons, foxes, and black bears, on which bounties were paid, were regarded as important game animals by many sportsmen, who, through the license law, were being forced to pay for the elimination of animals that they considered the basis for their sport.

Not all of the early wildlife administrators and sportsmen accepted the burden of predator control and the bounty system reluctantly. Little was known of natural function of predation or of predator-prey relationships. Since wolves ate deer and moose, it was a logical argument that the way to increase moose and deer was to kill wolves. Foxes and some of the hawks and owls ate rabbits, quail, and songbirds. Kill the foxes and avian predators and there would be more of the "desirable" species. This philosophy was supported by some of the best biologists and naturalists of the time. Dr. William T. Hornaday listed the peregrine falcon—now an endangered species—among those that should be shot on sight. Although Edward Howe Forbush deplored the indiscriminate slaughter of nearly all hawks and owls, he excluded the accipiter and great horned owl from his blessings.

Predator control was a time-honored game-management practice in Europe. Since the United States had no wildlife-management experts of its own, some state wildlife agencies imported foreign advisors to assist in their programs. Most of these experts were English and Scot game keepers. The difference between the minicured private game preserves of Great Britain and the hunting fields of America were not apparent, and shooting "vermin" as a means of increasing native wildlife, as advocated by the game keepers, appeared a logical solution to the problem of wildlife scarcity.

Even where bounty laws were not in force, sportsmen were urged by state and federal government publications and by the leading sportsmen's journals to kill predators on all occasions. Sportsmen's clubs, farm organizations and civic groups offered rewards to school boys for crows' feet, woodchuck tails, fox scalps, and similar trophies from other predators and crop pests. Organized campaigns against vermin became popular projects for sportsmen's clubs. It was a time when the carcasses of "chicken hawks"—more often than not beneficial buteos, like the red-tailed—were festooned on barbed-wire fences or displayed crucified on barn doors. The devastatingly unselective pole trap set by farmers accounted for many of these birds.

The federal government threw its weight into the campaign against predators on July 1, 1915, when the Bureau of Biological Survey, with a congressional appropriation of $125,000, entered the fray. An Act of Congress signed on June 30, 1914, authorized the Department of Agriculture to spend money for "experiments and demonstration in destroying wolves, prairie dogs, and other animals injurious to agriculture and animal husbandry." This program was quickly expanded to include cougars, coyotes, bobcats, eagles, and all other species deemed detrimental to the farmer and rancher. The scope of federal programs and the contemporary philosophy of wildlife administrators as it applied to predators are exemplified by an extract from an address of Dr. E. W. Nelson, chief of the Bureau of Biological Survey before a meeting of the International Association of Game, Fish and Conservation Commissioners on August 28, 1917. In reporting the first two years of the federal program, Nelson proudly proclaimed:

> The Biological Survey is engaged in another activity that is helpful to game. This is the destruction of predatory animals, particulary in the West. . . . The western States are divided into districts, including one or two States, with an inspector in charge of each, who has a corps of expert hunters and trappers continuously hunting and poisoning predatory animals. We have from 175 to 300 of these hunters, the number varying with the season. As a result, up to the first of August the present season our men had taken the skins of 980 gray wolves, over 34,000 coyotes, about 110 bob-cats besides several stock-killing silver-tipped grizzly bears. . . . Everyone is aware that mountain lions, wolves, coyotes and other beasts of prey destroy vast numbers of game animals. For this reason, the destruction of the predatory animals, while primarily to protect live stock, at the same time is helping increase the amount of game. . . . There is little question that in five years we can destroy most of the gray wolves and greatly reduce the numbers of other predatory animals. In New Mexico we have destroyed more than fifty per cent of the gray wolves and expect to get the other fifty per cent in the next two or three years.

Although most of the early state wildlife commissioners, reflecting the best scientific thinking of the day, considered predator control an essential ingredient of wildlife conservation and welcomed its incorporation into their programs, many of those saddled with the bounty system soon had second thoughts. Under the usual law, animals offered for bounty were presented to town or county clerks, who paid the claimant and in turn were compensated by the state game commission. Plagued by inadequate financing to start with, many had to divert funds from law enforcement and other essential activities to pay the soaring bounty claims.

Many of the wildlife authorities recognized some of the built-in shortcomings of the bounty system from the start. Through the conditioning of the sporting press and contemporary scientific opinion, the quail hunter would shoot every hawk, crow, or fox that blundered within range of his gun, whether a bounty was offered or not. Among the fur trapper's stock in trade were foxes, coyotes, weasels, and other bountiable "vermin." The farmer would have set his pole traps to protect his free-roaming poultry whether he was paid for his catch or not. Thus, many animals turned in for bounty were animals that would have been killed even if no reward had been offered. It was also apparent that no youngster finding a dead fox, crow, or other animal carrying a price on its head would pass up the chance of making fifty cents to five dollars by turning it over to the county clerk.

The bounty system, especially in the West where two- and three-figure rewards were offered for wolves and cougars, inspired some professional trappers and hunters to engage full time in bounty hunting. But these were the exceptions rather than the rule. And the professional hunter operated where predators were most numerous, not where they needed control.

Worse than its inefficiency, the bounty system was an open invitation to racketeers. The differential in bounties adopted by various states played directly into the hands of unscrupulous sharpies. If one state paid two dollars for a fox head and a second ten dollars, trappers in the first state could make more money by bootlegging their catches into the second state than by turning them in locally. If a state paid no bounty at all and a neighboring state did, its trappers could make a tidier profit by selling their catches to crooked buyers along the border than by processing them for fur.

The practice of giving justices of the peace and town and county clerks or commissioners responsibility for identifying and tallying animals presented for bounty contributed to this fraud. Most of these officials were town or city bred and lacked all but the rudiments of biological training. Few could distinguish a fox scalp from that of a woodchuck, and the latter often were passed off as foxes by unscrupulous bounty hunters. Some bounty claimants, with good insight into human psychology, presented for payment sacks of chicken heads well ripened in the sun, topped off with a few hawk heads. When one of these characters arrived at the county courthouse with his smelly trophies and offered to dump them for tally, the clerk almost invariably accepted the claim eagerly and paid promptly without examining the evidence.

Most of these transactions involved penny-ante swindles amounting to only a few dollars. But cumulatively they were a severe drain on the limited finances of the wildlife agencies, and some of the more ambitious swindlers tried for higher stakes. In 1915, Dr. Kalbfus of the Pennsylvania Game Commission obtained legislative approval to have all bounty claims processed by his state game protectors rather than the county officials. Subsequent investigations uncovered a mess more odoriferous than the sacks of specimens that had been presented for bounty.

Game Commission investigators apprehended one man who had purchased two thousand weasel skins rejected by furriers in New York and imported them to Pennsylvania for bounty. They successfully prosecuted a justice of the peace who had knowingly solicited trappers to turn in raccoon skins as those of foxes in exchange for a split in the bounty. Other officials were found to be kiting claims so that they received ten times the money they had paid out. One man claimed to have killed 102 goshawks in four days in summer and to have trapped 347 weasels in two months within short range of a large city. The official to whom he presented a putrid mass of feathers and hide testified on the witness stand that he had paid the claim without question after turning the mess over with a stick, simply to get the nauseous evidence out of his office as quickly as possible. State game protectors also testified to finding in a search of the defendant's basement a tub containing a bushel of heads from rabbits, squirrels, turkeys, and chickens. Their suspicions had been aroused by the fact that goshawks were winter migrants to Pennsylvania and not found there in summer. They also recognized that the probability of one trapper taking 347 weasels from a small geographic area in a few months added up to a near impossibility. The claimant went to jail.

These and similar cases helped to clean up the flagrant abuses in Pennsylvania, but its Game Commission, like those in most other states, remained saddled with the wasteful bounty system at the insistence of rural legislators seeking subsidies for their constituents.

The state wildlife agencies that came into being or gathered momentum in the late 1800s and early 1900s centered their attention largely on the management of small game birds and mammals; there was little big game left to manage. Except for mule deer in the Rocky Mountains, which remained common enough to warrant limited hunting, most of the other species of big game had been so reduced in numbers that little could be done except try to protect the survivors.

Ironically, not long before 1910, only the bison, secure on national parks and federal refuges, seemed assured of future survival. South of Canada the bighorn sheep had been reduced to scattered bands by market hunters who had turned their attention to lesser species after eliminating the great herds of buffalo. In 1908, Dr. T. S. Palmer of the Bureau of Biological Survey undertook a census of the pronghorn antelope in North America. His results indicated a population of seventeen thousand in the United States and three thousand in Canada. Most of these were on private lands and protected from poachers by cattle ranchers seeking to retain some living reminder of the past.

Moose, south of Canada, had been reduced to scattered bands in the northern Rockies, northern Minnesota, and northern Maine. Woodland caribou disappeared from northern New England around 1900 after the loggers invaded the last virgin forests in the Northeast. The species persisted south of the Canadian border only in tiny depleted groups that roamed the bogs of northern Minnesota and the Selkirk Mountains in northernmost Idaho.

There seemed to be more hope for the elk, or wapiti, which, under protection in Yellowstone National Park, was increasing in numbers and extending its range into the surrounding national forests in Wyoming, Montana, and Idaho.

If there was one bright shining spot in the big-game picture for the early wildlife administrators, it was in the suddenly improved status of the white-tailed deer in the northeastern states. Well before the turn of the century, deer had been eliminated from all of New England except northern Maine and southeastern Massachusetts, where a small herd numbering less than a thousand had persisted on Cape Cod and adjacent Plymouth County since early colonial times. A few thousand ranged the wilder portions of New York's Adirondacks and Catskills. Maryland, New Jersey, Ohio, Pennsylvania, and all midwestern states south of the Great Lakes had virtually none. Scattered remnant populations found refuge in the Ozarks and in the dense swamps of the lower Mississippi Valley, Gulf Coast, and the Middle Atlantic States south of Maryland. This, in broad strokes, was the status of the white-tailed deer east of the Great Plains in 1890. Total numbers did not exceed 500,000 and may have been as low as 350,000 head.

Coinciding with the growth of public interest in conservation that produced the state fish and wildlife agencies there had been a major change in the dominant habitat types in the Northeast. The abandonment of marginal and submarginal farms had begun before the Civil War and accelerated throughout the last half of the nineteenth century. Farmers, whose families had worked the rocky hills of New England, New York, and Pennsylvania for generations, could not compete economically with those who had moved to the western prairies. Centuries of overgrazing and erosion had depleted the soil, and the glitter of the cities with their factory jobs siphoned off most of the young people and the laborers. Some of the younger farmers joined the movement to the level, fertile lands that were being opened to farming in the West. Others took jobs in town. Those fortunate enough to have farms located on more productive soils increasingly specialized in products, such as eggs, poultry and dairy products, that found a ready and lucrative market in the nearby cities and towns. Most of the livestock growers raised some of their own feed, but increasingly it became more economical to buy that produced in the sprawling grainfields of the Midwest.

The opening of the West and improvements in transportation brought other dislocations to the northeastern rural economy. New England, since the beginning of industrialization, had been the center for the nation's textile manufacturing industry. Until the Civil War, most of the raw wool that flowed into the mills was produced in the Northeast. Sheep raising was a profitable sideline and nearly every farmer owned a dozen or more. Some woolen manufacturing companies owned or leased extensive acreage on which they ran large herds of sheep that helped supply their demands. The rapid development of the western sheep-raising industry and the phenomenal expansion of steam-powered transportation on land and water after the Civil War ended the reliance of the mills on domestically produced wool. Cheaper wool, first from Texas, the western plains, and the Rocky Mountains, and then from Australia and New Zealand, soon ended the eastern wool bonanza.

These economic changes brought a massive wave of land abandonment to the northeastern states. In 1850, Massachusetts's 5.5 million acres were nearly eighty percent in cropfields, pasture, and orchards; by 1900, farm acreage had shrunk to three million; and by 1960, only 826,000 acres were classified as improved farmlands.

The swift development of the automobile after 1910 retired still more land in the Northeast from agricultural use. Before that time— with the exception of the steam locomotive—nearly all transportation and hauling was done by horses, mules, and oxen to the extent that at one time there were nearly as many draft animals in the United States as there were people. Mules pulled the barges on the East's network of canals. Teams of horses and oxen drew the plows and cultivators and hauled the produce to market. Horses pulled the street cars, carriages, and wagons in the towns. In all cities and towns, livery stables and blacksmith shops were as common as gasoline filling stations and garages today. In 1910, farm horses and mules alone numbered nearly 25 million as opposed to three million in more recent agricultural censuses. In 1910, probably as many horses were used for urban, industrial, and military purposes as were employed on farms. The decline of the horse and mule as a source of power was sharper in the industrialized Northeast than in any other region in the nation.

Each draft animal required about three acres of cropfields and grasslands to provide its feed, pasture, and bedding. Although many acres freed from use by and for horses and mules were used to support growing herds of dairy cattle, many thousands of acres were retired from all agricultural use and permitted to revert to woodland and forest.

Many of the old fields left to the elements were quickly invaded by sun-loving pines and other rapid-growing conifers, whose dense crowns shaded the forest floor and precluded the establishment of any low-growing shrubs and shade-intolerant hardwoods that tried to compete with them.

Around the turn of the century many of the pastures, fields, and entire farms that had been abandoned or retired first were supporting almost pure stands of pine, birch, and other hardwoods of commercial quality. Some landowners began cutting their own timber, but most sold their timber "on the stump" (usually at a fraction of its true value) to itinerant owners of portable sawmills, who swarmed into the forests of the Northeast by the hundreds. The "gyppo" operator, with his steam- or gasoline-powered saw and a crew of cutters, stripped everything of value within—and at times a little beyond—the boundaries of his timber purchase.

The forest that regenerated over extensive areas in the wake of this destructive logging was different from any that had predominated in the Northeast in the past. Within a few years after the conifers were felled, the sites were reclothed in hardwood seedlings and saplings, stump sprouts, fruit-bearing bushes and vines interspersed with scattered conifers, snags, and wolf trees left by the loggers. Most private landholdings in the Northeast were small, rarely exceeding a hundred acres. The hit-and-skip logging by the gyppo sawmill operators left in its wake a patchwork of forest in various stages of succession, from freshly clearcut openings to scattered stands of mature timber. Although the overall effect was appalling to the professional forester, it produced over extensive areas ideal habitat for white-tailed deer and related forest wildlife. Moreover, this development came just as the embryonic state wildlife agencies were beginning to emerge from their cocoons and seek out constructive projects.

Vermont had already shown the way. In 1878, a sportsmen's club in Rutland had purchased seventeen captive deer—ten for the keepers of New York's State Prison in Dannemora—and released them in woodlands closed to hunting by a special state law. By 1898, the deer population had increased enough to warrant limited hunting.

Other northeastern states adopted similar programs as their state wildlife agencies came into existence. Pennsylvania began stocking deer in 1899, when whitetails from Michigan and Maine were released on a few state forests. Later, in 1905, the commission began establishing deer refuges—areas of prime habitat scattered strategically throughout the state, posted, and heavily patrolled against poachers and marauding stray dogs. The earlier releases on the state forests had reproduced so well that no more animals needed to be imported, and natively produced whitetails were used to restock the refuges. As early as 1907, the white-tailed deer had so repopulated the Keystone State that the Game Commission felt warranted in declaring a short open-hunting season, the first in nearly a century. Hunters took two hundred bucks from a state that ten years before had contained no wild deer at all.

The return of the deer to the expanding woodlands and forests of the Northeast was almost as spectacular in other states. As the woody cover returned to the land, remnant populations, like those on Cape Cod and in the Adirondacks, that had persisted since colonial times on the brink of extermination, multiplied in numbers and expanded their ranges. The process of repopulation was sometimes artificially accelerated, as in Pennsylvania, by establishing populations on refuge areas outside range originally occupied. In other areas, as in New Hampshire and Massachusetts, reoccupation came, under protection, from populations spreading outward from adjacent states. By 1920, most of the new woodlands of the Northeast from Maine to the Potomac supported deer herds as large or larger than those that had existed in primitive times.

The restoration of the deer to the Northeast was the most dramatic achievement of wildlife management in the first decades of the 1900s. Like the establishment of the pheasant in North America, it was a product of luck as much as it was of skill, for without the expanding habitat that attended their efforts, the early wildlife administrators would have failed. But the fact that they succeeded in establishing a new species and reestablishing and restoring a depleted population to the most densely populated region of the United States was proof of improving law enforcement and public acceptance of their efforts. These, more than the introduction of the pheasant and the restoration of the deer herds, were the major gains of the first few years of professional wildlife administration in North America.

Part 4

The Emergence of Wildlife Management

Chapter 14

Dissension in the Ranks

The America of Warren Gamaliel Harding and that of Theodore Roosevelt differed as much as the personalities of their leaders. During the scant two decades that separated their two administrations, the nation and the continent had seen great changes. From a big, distant country-cousin of the British Empire at the turn of the century, the United States of America had emerged from World War I as a rich, self-confident giant whose strength commanded respect around the globe. Between 1900 and 1920 its population had grown from 76 million to 106 million, the increase equal to the entire national population at the time of the Grant Administration. During the same twenty years, the genius of Thomas Alva Edison and Henry Ford had transformed the face of the nation and the lives of its people.

Americans in 1920 enjoyed more personal mobility than any previous generation in history in any nation on the globe. Ford's assembly lines were spewing out Model Ts by the hundreds of thousands, and mass production had dropped their prices to a figure within reach of all but the poor. In his automobile, the average American could cover more ground in a day than his father could have traveled in a week. A network of paved roads linked town to town and farm to city.

The impact of these social and industrial changes on fish and wildlife and the lands and waters that supported them was great. The automobile industry alone required more oil, iron, rubber, copper, coal, and other raw materials than the total needs of the national economy in 1900. Open-pit mines yawned in the Appalachians, the Lake States, and the Rocky Mountains, as the mining industry struggled to keep pace with the demand. Mine wastes and silt converted hundreds of streams to biological deserts, and industrial and municipal wastes were poisoning rivers, lakes, and estuaries.

But few Americans cared. With the defeat of the Kaiser and his Huns, the world had been made safe for democracy and the United States had entered an era of perpetual peace and unprecedented prosperity. The stock market was booming, wages were soaring, taxes were low, and unless one ventured into the darker slums and rural byways, all Americans were rich and happy. Moreover, for the first time in history, the average working citizen could enjoy the luxury of leisure. The working day and work week had become steadily shorter, and some of the more progressive business firms and industries were beginning to offer their employees paid vacations. Americans in unprecedented numbers turned to hunting, fishing, and other forms of outdoor recreation as escapes from the drudgery of workaday life.

For federal and state administrators responsible for maintaining fish, wildlife, and recreational resources, these changes brought new and massive problems. Population and industrial growth meant less living space for wildlife and increased intrusion of disruptive human activities into the remaining wildlife habitats.

There were, in the early 1920s, an estimated six million licensed sport hunters, double the number in 1910. But their impact on the game resources could not be measured by numbers alone. In Theodore Roosevelt's time, the ordinary citizen who hunted had been able to enjoy his sport only a few days of the year. Few besides the prosperous business and professional man and the gentleman farmer could afford to leave their jobs for a week or two afield. By the time of the Harding Administration, thousands of hunters from the laboring and middle classes were competing with the wealthy sportsmen in the hunting fields.

Although the sportsman at the turn of the century had ready access to comfortable and efficient railway systems, his hunting territory on a day-to-day basis had been limited to the area he could cover on foot, on horseback, or by buckboard.

Unless he ventured into roadless wilderness, the sportsman of 1920 was tied neither to the rails nor the horse. His noisy but efficient touring car or sedan, with its high clearance, could negotiate all but the roughest and muddiest of country roads, ford streams, and even navigate across fields and prairies or through open woods where there were no roads at all. He was no longer a slave to the static travel schedules dictated by railway timetables. A twist of the key and a spin of the crank started him on his way, to the field or homeward at the onset of a whim. If one area failed to produce game, he could be hunting in another twenty-five miles away in less than an hour. His car could carry camping equipment, bird dogs, and a portable boat with room to spare for all the game he could bag.

By 1920, sporting firearms design was attaining a plateau approaching developmental perfection, and mass production had placed fine rifles and shotguns within the financial reach of all. For less than fifty dollars, a hunter could buy a pump gun, autoloading shotgun, or magazine rifle nearly as reliable, effective, and as accurate as those available today.

The presence in the field of thousands of new, well-armed, and highly mobile hunters taxed the ingenuity and resources of the state fish and wildlife agencies that, with limited funds and manpower, were charged with the somewhat contradictory tasks of maintaining optimum wildlife populations and providing enough game to satisfy the needs of a growing army of hunters. Much of the burden fell upon the law-enforcement staffs.

Many of the neophytes to the sport had received little exposure to the traditions of sportsmanship and violated the spirit and bounds of the law. Some sped across fields and prairies in automobiles, shooting any game that flushed. Others discovered that the motor car, with its carbide or electric lights, made an ideal shooting platform for night-hunting deer.

In the eastern industrial states, immigrants from southern Europe posed a particular problem. In Italy and other southern European countries, bird protective laws were virtually nonexistent, and anything that flew was considered fair game. Attracted by the high wages offered by American steel and textile mills, millions of Italian and Hungarian workers immigrated to the United States, many bringing with them a love for hunting and a taste for songbird stew. Several states, including Massachusetts and Pennsylvania, enacted laws forbidding aliens to own firearms or severely restricting their hunting privileges.

On the positive side, however, the increase in the number of hunters and anglers provided the state fish and wildlife agencies with more funds than they had known at any time in the past. Even in those states that did not have licensing requirements for residents, increasing revenues from fines and the sale of nonresident licenses provided fairly substantial funds with which to supplement income from legislative appropriations. Most of the agencies were able to equip their law-enforcement officers with automobiles or motorcycles to match the mobility of potential game-law violators or to reimburse them for the expense of operating personally owned vehicles. During the 1920s state game laws became increasingly complex. Night hunting, except for raccoons and other nocturnal game animals, was almost universally outlawed. Hunting and fishing seasons and daily creel and bag limits were sharply curtailed.

In their efforts to curb law violators and game hogs, the state law-enforcement agents enlisted the support of the organized sportsmen and rural landowners, and the telephone became an important instrument in their campaigns.

Demand for reforms in the game laws, to bring them in line with the realities of the twentieth century, had many supporters, especially among the hunters themselves. The first to call for shorter open seasons and smaller bag limits had been George O. Shields through his League of American Sportsmen and his vitriolic editorials in *Recreation* magazine. Soon after Shields opened his campaign, the state Audubon Societies entered the lists beside the state fish and game protective associations. After 1911, the American Game Protective and Propagation Association, popularly known as the American Game Association, provided a national clearing house for information on state legislative action in the field of wildlife conservation.

Apart from Shields, however, the most vocal individual exponent of reform was the redoubtable Dr. William T. Hornaday. As a personality, William Temple Hornaday was one of the more interesting and complex figures in the field of conservation—a knight in shining armor rising to the defense of wildlife and swinging a mighty sword with such vigor that he often laid open his allies along with his enemies. A reviewer of one of his books, who knew him well, called him "one soldier who is not in step with the army" and observed that Hornaday fully enjoyed that distinction.

In his younger years Hornaday had been an avid hunter, a hobby that led him unerringly into his first profession as a taxidermist. After graduating from Iowa State Agricultural College, he joined the staff of Ward's Natural Science Establishment in Rochester, New York, which supplied mounted specimens for museums throughout the world. In 1882, he was appointed chief taxidermist for the U. S. National Museum in Washington, D.C.

Paradoxically, in the light of his later bitter opposition to hunting, Hornaday, in his official capacity on expeditions around the globe, killed as wide a variety of rare and endangered species as any contemporary American.

Appointed superintendent of the newly formed National Zoological Park in Washington, Hornaday resigned in 1890 after a dispute with his superiors. In 1896, following a stint in private business, he was appointed director of the New York Zoological Park, which was then being developed by the New York Zoological Society. It was in this capacity that he first received national recognition, for the zoological park that he built was considered among the best and most modern in the world. His achievements won him the first of three honorary doctorate degrees conferred on him by the University of Pittsburgh, Yale University, and Iowa State College.

Although a member of many conservation organizations, including the Boone and Crockett Club, Camp Fire Club of America, and National Association of Audubon Societies, Hornaday seemed capable of working closely with none of them. He launched gadfly attacks against the programs of nearly every conservation organization and agency, largely because they did not promise the overnight results he desired.

A man of elegant appearance, with clipped beard and flashing eyes, Hornaday was a forceful speaker and persuasive writer, the ideal crusader type. In his makeup there was no room for compromise, and he regarded any concession, even to logical argument, as a sign of weakness. Hornaday's contribution to the cause of wildlife conservation, especially in the first twenty years of the twentieth century, was real and significant, although he had an unfortunate tendency to claim personal credit for achievements that involved hard effort and sacrifice by many others. At other times he blocked the progress of constructive legislation that would have materially advanced the causes for which he fought. Despite the fact that he was a member of the scientific community, Hornaday was contemptuous of the rudimentary wildlife research effort that was developing throughout his career, although he readily accepted any findings that supported his own prejudices.

Hornaday was born in 1854 and was professionally involved with wildlife during the slaughter of the bison and passenger pigeons. From these examples, he evolved a simplistic theory that hunting, and only hunting, was responsible for the decline in wildlife that he had witnessed. This was first generally evident in his book, *Our Vanishing Wild Life*, which was published and widely distributed by the New York Zoological Society. The book was a hard-hitting indictment of America's casual neglect of its wildlife resources. In 1913, when it first appeared, it was a timely document. Market hunting was still practiced in many states; plume hunting had not been entirely eliminated; spring shooting of waterfowl, shorebirds, and upland game birds was a nearly universal practice; game laws were extremely liberal; and the automobile and rapid social change were beginning to have their first direct and indirect impacts on the wildlife resource. Hornaday predicted the imminent extinction of a dozen or more species if these abuses were not corrected.

In the context of the time, he was probably right. Overexploitation by sportsmen as well as commercial interests was having a depressing effect on many species. But even as Hornaday's book was being published, great changes in public attitudes toward wildlife were bringing legislative and regulatory reforms that would reverse these trends. Hornaday's book—some of which was bold-faced propaganda—played a major role in speeding the process. When the Migratory Bird Treaty Act was under consideration, the New York Zoological Society sent a copy to every member of Congress. The book also brought its author financial independence that permitted him to devote almost full time to his conservation activities, although he retained his post at the New York Zoological Park until 1926.

The concept of a private foundation with resources of $100,000 to combat the "enemies of wildlife" was outlined by Hornaday in his book. The framework for such a foundation had been built in 1911 with rather meager resources. Hornaday later described it as:

> . . . created to forestall the efforts of the enemies of William T. Hornaday to stop his activities by bringing secret pressures on his employers. The power of that menace was felt for the first time when we were loyally trying to induce the New York State Legislature to pass the Zoological Society's own bill against automatic shotguns. It was felt again in 1912 in the fight to save the fur seals, when a scheme was hatched in Washington to "Stop Hornaday."

Soon after Hornaday's book appeared, the assets of the Permanent Wild Life Protection Fund swelled rapidly to $105,490. Henry Ford, George Eastman, Max C. Fleischman, and Andrew Carnegie each subscribed five thousand dollars. But Mrs. Russell Sage, an elderly widow from Louisiana with a deep concern for wildlife, was so moved by Hornaday's writings that she more than matched the combined donations of these multimillionaire philanthropists with a gift of $25,000.

With this substantial support, Hornaday became something of a one-man guerrilla army in the conservation field. He testified before congressional committees, lobbied openly for pet projects before Congress and state legislatures, and badgered the state and federal wildlife administrators. He castigated or ridiculed any who disagreed with his views.

Hornaday sought few allies and gave no quarter. He considered the American Game Protective Association a tool of the sporting arms and ammunition manufacturers and the National Association of Audubon Societies under Pearson as soft and vacillating. Pearson was suspect because he and Burnham collaborated in working through less precipitous routes for many of the same reforms demanded by Hornaday.

Hornaday's demands were a curious mixture of the practical and impractical. He demanded the halving of all hunting seasons and bag limits. He called for a total ban on the manufacture of sporting firearms capable of firing more than three shots at a loading. He insisted that sportsmen be permitted to hunt only every other year; that an immediate five-year closure of hunting be declared for ruffed grouse, prairie chickens, sage grouse, and quail; that the mourning dove and bobwhite quail be universally classified as songbirds; and that gray squirrels and European starlings be accorded perpetual protection. Among naturalists, he was one of few who steadfastly defended the reputation of the introduced starling.

In 1912, some of his demands were justified, although others were based on Hornaday's personal whims. As early as 1907, Pennsylvania had outlawed the use of autoloading firearms for hunting, and in 1912 New Jersey banned the use of all repeating shotguns unless their capacity was reduced to two shots.

Largely through Hornaday's efforts and in one of his few single-handed victories, the Ohio State Legislature placed the bobwhite quail on its songbird list in 1915. This "perpetual protection" was lifted in 1949 after biologists, by comparing quail populations in Ohio with those in adjacent states where the birds were hunted annually, demonstrated that regulated hunting was an insignificant limiting factor in bobwhite numbers.

The passage of the Migratory Bird Treaty Act eliminated market gunning and spring shooting of migratory birds and provided full legal protection for many species. Most of the state wildlife agencies adopted laws or regulations according similar protection to resident game animals during the spring months. Hunting privileges were steadily curtailed through longer closed seasons and smaller bag limits.

Hornaday chose to ignore most of this progress and the people who helped bring it about—except for those who acknowledged his primary role in the reform movement.

Hornaday's last book on wildlife conservation, *Thirty Years War for Wild Life*, which appeared in 1931, was a curious rehash of his 1912 effort, still gloomily forecasting the imminent demise of most of the species whose extinction he had forecast nearly twenty years before:

> I think that [the grouse species] are the next candidates for oblivion, and that the ruffed grouse is nearly there!
> . . . Twenty years from now, look in some museum for the "last sage-hen."
> . . . But let no man be so rash as to conclude . . . that the armies of hunters . . . cannot wipe out all the turkeys that remain. . . . There

are still a very few Florida turkeys in Florida, and traces of Merriam's Turkey in New Mexico, Arizona, and northern Mexico; but they will not last long.

In his list of sixteen "Birds Believed Beyond Saving," he included the woodcock, sharp-tailed grouse, and pinnated grouse, all of which still support substantial hunting effort in various parts of the United States and Canada. Nearly all of the other species on his list of the doomed were never subjected to sport hunting, and only three were officially classified as endangered in 1975.

In spite of Hornaday's poor batting average as a prophet, his impact upon the wildlife movement in the 1920s was significant. His one-track argument that the way to save wildlife was "to prevent its killing" was easier for the nonhunting public to grasp than were the more complex explanations by those who favored hunting in moderation and under strict control. He gave scant recognition to the fact that changes in wildlife habitat brought about by man's use of the land had any bearing on the case or that weather on the breeding grounds could influence autumn waterfowl flights. He shrugged off scientific evidence of cyclic fluctuations in the populations of grouse.

Hornaday's appearance, commanding personality, and caustic statements endeared him to the press, and he received more publicity than any other conservationist of his time. Moreover, his controversial statements and his national reputation as a crusader brought his prolific writings ready acceptance in editorial circles. In most of these writings he downgraded the efforts of others and painted himself as a lone warrior manning the bastions of wildlife conservation against a storming army of opposition. His detraction of the efforts of others had the inevitable effect of dividing the wildlife conservation movement into those who followed Hornaday and those who favored more temperate and more realistic action.

One of the bitterest battles in the conservation movement swirled throughout the 1920s around the question of how best to manage the nation's waterfowl resources. It was a clash of a new policy of "positive production" of wildlife espoused by the American Game Protective Association, the National Association of Audubon Societies, and allied groups against Hornaday's "inflexible law."

By 1920 the Migratory Bird Treaty Act had become an accepted fact. The Bureau of Biological Survey and its counterpart in Canada had set up machinery for implementation, and opposition by most hunters to federal control had subsided to querulous mumblings in the shooting camps of the old timers. Responding to the abolition of spring shooting, market hunting, other reforms achieved through the treaty, and a series of favorable breeding seasons, ducks, geese, and shorebirds were returning to their wintering areas in numbers that had not been seen since the turn of the century.

But to men who possessed a degree of foresight, dark clouds were visible on the horizon. Under the pressures of a growing population and an expanding economy, waterfowl habitat was shrinking. Along the Mississippi and its far-flung tributaries, swamps and marshes were being drained behind a growing system of levees; and burgeoning towns and cities were spewing their wastes into once-pure waters. Back from the rivers, increasingly intensive agriculture was encroaching upon the prime waterfowl-breeding habitat of the Great Plains.

The answer was obvious. If waterfowl were to be saved in any numbers the choicer wetlands had to be preserved through public ownership, not only in the breeding grounds of the North but in the wintering areas of the South with protected resting places in between. The road toward that goal was strewn with hurdles. There were no federal funds available for a land-acquisition program of the magnitude required, and the attitude of most states was that, since the federal government had assumed control of waterfowl hunting it had stripped the states of responsibility for the migratory wildlife resource. Some states—notably Louisiana, California, Minnesota, and Wisconsin—had taken more liberal attitudes and created refuges primarily for waterfowl, but these were too few and too scattered to assure the future of the birds. A few federal refuges, including Malheur and Klamath in Oregon, had been established by President Theodore Roosevelt in 1908, but these were in the West and available only to birds in the Pacific Flyway. Most of the federal refuges were for the protection of large mammals, such as the bison, for sea birds, and marine mammals. Opportunities for creating useful waterfowl refuges by Presidential Order, as Roosevelt had done, were shrinking with the gradual liquidation of the public domain and limited to the far western states. Most of the remaining wetlands east of the Rockies, where the need for habitat protection was most critical, were in private ownership.

East of the Cascades, throughout most of the 1920s, there was only one national wildlife refuge of major importance to breeding waterfowl. This was the Upper Mississippi Wild Life and Fish Refuge, created by Act of Congress with an authorized appropriation of $1,500,000 on June 7, 1924, but in the process of acquisition well into the 1930s. The refuge, protecting three hundred miles of riparian marshes and overflow lands between Rock Island, Illinois, and Wabasha, Minnesota, in the upper stretches of the Mississippi, remains a monument to one man, Will H. Dilg, the Chicago advertising man and outdoorsman who founded the Izaak Walton League of America.

In keeping with his profession, Dilg was a man of great persuasive power. T. Gilbert Pearson called him "a modern Peter the Hermit," while Hornaday, with whom Pearson rarely agreed, dubbed him "a conservation John the Baptist." With Hornaday, Dilg shared traits that evoked great public support while grating on the sensibilities of his fellow conservationists. A dapper, spare, and angular man, he was, like Hornaday, imperious, egotistical, and quixotic, but he was also a master organizer and public relations expert with the fervor of an evangelist. While Hornaday chose to fight alone, Dilg marshaled an army to lead into battle.

In January, 1922, fifty-four sportsmen gathered in the Chicago Athletic Club to discuss ways of increasing the nation's stocks of game animals and fish. Dilg made an impassioned speech urging the creation of a national organization, with members enlisted from the nation's sport hunters and anglers, to spearhead a drive for clean waters and the restoration of fish and wildlife resources. On March 1, 1922, the Izaak Walton League of America opened its offices in Chicago with Dilg as president. With its emphasis on pollution control, it became the pioneer among environmental organizations.

Under Dilg's energetic leadership, the League rapidly gained in strength and numbers, especially in the vast heartland of the United States between the Appalachians and the Rockies where something of a vacuum in conservation organization had existed before. Dilg hired agents to recruit members on a commission basis and to organize state and local clubs. Within five years the League boasted three thousand chapters in forty-three states with an aggregate membership of more than 100,000.

Even before founding the League, Dilg, on a fishing trip on the headwaters of the Mississippi River, had conceived the idea of a vast national refuge designed to protect the breeding habitat of the fish and wildlife that abounded in that area, still largely untouched by the channelization and leveeing that had destroyed much of the fish and wildlife potential of the great river downstream. On assuming the presidency of his new organization, Dilg made his idea a major plank in its program of immediate objectives.

Dilg carried his concept, now crystalized in the draft of a bill written for him by General Jacob M. Dickinson, former Secretary of War in President Taft's cabinet, to Congressman Harry B. Hawes of Missouri, a staunch supporter of conservation issues, an enthusiastic sportsman, and author of a book called *My Friend, the Black Bass*. Hawes introduced the bill in the House on December 23, 1923, and Dilg, with an impressive staff of assistants housed in a suite of rooms at Washington's Willard Hotel, led the drive for enactment. On June 7, 1924, President Calvin Coolidge signed the bill into law. Although the act called for a congressional appropriation of $1.5 million—a hitherto unheard of public commitment to wildlife conservation—Congress appropriated only $400,000 through fiscal year 1926. But it was the first significant step toward saving the more important waterfowl breeding grounds in the central region of the nation.

Even if an adequate waterfowl refuge system had existed, it still would have left unsolved a second problem of concern to sportsmen and wildlife administrators, that of providing hunting space for thousands of new shooters who were joining the ranks of the waterfowl hunters each year. In an attempt to suggest solutions to both problems, the American Game Protective Association, under the presidency of John B. Burnham, had published in its *Bulletin* of July, 1919, a significant editorial:

> If the young men of the next generation are to enjoy from the country's wild life anything like the benefits derived by the present outdoor man, we must be the one to shoulder the burden and see that our thoughtlessness or selfishness does not allow us to squander that which we hold in trust.
> Public shooting grounds must be established for the rank and file of the gunners who cannot afford to belong to exclusive clubs. This is the duty of the state, but the sportsmen must take the initiative. . . . In many places land of little value from a commercial standpoint furnishes the best hunting territory. Why shouldn't such tracts be set aside as public recreation grounds for all times to come? . . . With the public shooting grounds must come more reserves where the birds should have absolute protection, for as the country becomes more settled, shooting would become impossible without them. . . .

This proposal had been inspired by the success of the Reelfoot Lake Public Shooting Ground, which had been established by Tennessee opposite the Big Lake National Wildlife Refuge, across the Mississippi in Arkansas.

Less than a year after this editorial appeared, in April, 1920, the Association devoted a full issue of its magazine to the discussion of the public shooting grounds-refuge proposal with feature articles in its support by E. W. Nelson, chief of the Bureau of Biological Survey; Aldo Leopold; and Colonel Henry S. Graves, chief forester of the United States.

The concept of public hunting grounds was not new; it had been discussed for years at formal and informal meetings of sportsmen who had watched helplessly as their favorite local marshes were drained, filled, or posted. No one, however, had been able to suggest ways of financing a land-acquisition program of the magnitude required without creating administrative machinery so cumbersome that it would devour most of the funds received.

The idea of a federal waterfowl-hunting stamp to finance such a program originated with George A. Lawyer, chief United States game warden, shortly after World War I. Ray P. Holland, the federal warden who had precipitated the test case that had established the validity of the Migratory Bird Treaty Act, had frequently discussed with his chief the shrinking waterfowl habitat and the feasibility of a federal hunting license to help cope with the problem. Holland had left federal service to join the staff of the American Game Protective Association as editor of its *Bulletin*. Inspired by a news release issued by Dr. Nelson pleading for the preservation of wetlands, Lawyer wrote to his former subordinate suggesting that the government issue hunting stamps that could be sold at post offices, eliminating much of the red tape and administrative complications that previously suggested methods would have entailed. "Why not sell them," he asked, "as the government is selling war savings stamps?"

Holland carried the idea to Burnham and it was adopted immediately as a part of the program of the American Game Protective Association. Then, in April, 1921, Frederic C. Walcott, former fish and game commissioner of Connecticut, who had attained international recognition as a member of Herbert Hoover's United States Food Commission, supported the proposal in a strong article entitled "The Necessity of Free Shooting Grounds." It was illustrated with a rough sketch by Belmore Browne of a proposed "U.S. Hunting License Stamp" featuring a Canada goose in flight—the first concrete forerunner of an idea that would receive official sanction thirteen years later.

Walcott had many friends in Congress and his endorsement of the proposal was enough to set the legislative machinery in progress. On May 2 and 5, 1921, respectively, Senator Harry S. New of Indiana and Congressman Dan R. Anthony of Kansas, introduced identical bills that embodied the proposals in Walcott's article.

The New-Anthony Bill was a sweeping piece of legislation. If it had been enacted when first introduced, it might have saved millions of acres of wetlands and altered the future course of the waterfowl conservation movement. It provided for the establishment of a far-flung system of inviolate refuges with adjacent areas open to regulated hunting. Each area would be selected by a Migratory Bird Refuge Commission, consisting of the Secretary of Agriculture, the Attorney General, the Postmaster General, and four members of Congress—two senators selected by the President and two congressmen selected by the Speaker of the House. The commission was to approve the land acquisition, which was to be financed by the sale of a one-dollar federal hunting license required of every waterfowl hunter.

The New-Anthony Bill had the endorsement of the nation's organized sportsmen. Nelson endorsed it for the Department of Agriculture; Pearson testified for its passage on behalf of the National Association of Audubon Societies; Walcott recorded the support of the American Wildlife Protective Association; Charles Sheldon testified in its favor for the Boone and Crockett Club; and Karl T. Frederick for the Camp Fire Club of America. John M. Phillips registered the support of the Pennsylvania Game Commission and the International Association of Game, Fish and Conservation Commissioners. In spite of almost monotonous testimony in its behalf, the bill, after passing the Senate by a vote of 36 to 17, was defeated in the House by a coalition of southern and western states'-rights advocates led by Wyoming's Frank Mondell.

Anthony reintroduced his bill in the opening hours of the 68th Congress, and this time the support seemed overwhelming. At the public hearings in July, 1924, the hearing rooms were crowded with those favoring the proposal. The recently concluded President's Conference on Outdoor Recreation had resolved unanimously in its favor; it was personally endorsed by the Secretary of Agriculture. Support from the press had brought a flood of editorial backing. The influential New York *Times* and *Saturday Evening Post* published editorials urging its passage as did seven of the nation's leading outdoor journals.

All of the organizations and agencies that had testified in favor of the original bill reaffirmed their support for the second. They were joined by the American Fisheries Society; the American Forestry Association; the American Farm Bureau Federation; the American Association for the Advancement of Science; the American Legion; the Council on National Parks, the Forests and Wild Life; the Izaac Walton League of America; the National Association of the Fur Industry; the National Federation of Women's Clubs; the National Grange and hundreds of local Rotary Clubs, the Kiwanis Clubs, chapters of the Order of Maccabees, the Lions Clubs, the Odd Fellows, and similar groups.

With this formidable support the bill passed easily with an affirmative vote of 211, a gain of 76 over the ballot in the 67th Congress. But it failed to come to a vote in the Senate, which adjourned before action could be taken. But public support for the bill now seemed so insuperable that its supporters were looking forward to its enactment in the 69th Congress with optimism that approached certainty.

Sportsmen's organizations in some states began selecting and mapping wetlands that would be suitable for purchase by the government, and the New Mexico Game Protective Association, under the leadership of Aldo Leopold, went so far as to lease tracts of wetlands with options to buy in order to forestall land speculation by local promoters.

All of this optimism faded rapidly with the opening of the 69th Congress. The proponents of the Game Refuge-Public Shooting Grounds Bill had not counted on the formidable opposition of Dr. William T. Hornaday.

Ever since the enactment of the Migratory Bird Treaty Act, Hornaday had been carrying on a relentless campaign against the liberal bag limits and open seasons that had been set by the Bureau of Biological Survey. The feeling that the waterfowl hunting regulations erred on the liberal side was shared by many sportsmen and conservation groups. But even under these generous regulations, flights of ducks and geese were increasing annually. Since there seemed to be no urgent need for precipitous action, most conservationists shared the view of the Bureau of Biological Survey that it would be best to use discretion until the new principle of federal control was more firmly established and effective federal law-enforcement machinery could be built.

A few years earlier, in 1919 when the first federal regulations had been imposed, the wildfowlers had been asked to accept cuts in their hunting privileges deeper than those ever imposed before, and they had done so graciously. But opposition to the law was still very much alive in the early 1920s, especially in the states'-rights circles. Further drastic reduction in bag limits and open seasons in the absence of a demonstrable emergency, as demanded by Hornaday, could have fanned the dying embers of reaction into a blaze that might have consumed the whole machinery of the law.

Adequate safeguards to cope with emergency situations had been built into the Act. The Secretary of Agriculture was authorized to alter the regulations, or to order a complete closure of hunting of any migratory game bird whenever its status appeared threatened. The federal regulations also were outside limits within which any state could set more stringent regulations, and many had already done so. Most conservationists felt that the best course was to accept the *status quo* until a real reason for curtailment appeared, and to use the flexible powers vested in the Secretary of Agriculture if a real emergency arose.

Hornaday, mistrusting the intent of the Bureau of Biological Survey and considering the state fish and wildlife agencies and most organized conservation groups as tools of the firearms and ammunition manufacturers, regarded all of this as vacillation and eyewash. The value of flexible regulations and the vital need for preserving habitat appeared to have been lost on him in his preoccupation with the issue of hunting regulations. He called for Congress to establish by law fixed hunting seasons and bag limits that halved those then permitted by the Bureau. He saw in the proposed waterfowl-refuge system nothing more than a method of concentrating waterfowl in order to give more hunters an opportunity to kill more ducks and geese. The proposed shooting grounds were, in his words, prospective "slaughter pens." He branded all proponents of the game-refuge shooting-grounds bill as tools of "game hogs" and "butchers," including, with remarkable impartiality, some of his own more generous financial supporters. John C. Phillips and Frederic C. Walcott, both among the founders of his Permanent Wild Life Protection Fund, were dedicated wildfowlers and firm supporters of the policies of the Bureau of Biological Survey.

Hornaday used the respite given him by the adjournment of Congress to build his attack. Through the pages of the *People's Home Journal*, one of the more widely circulated family magazines, although one hardly qualified to comment impartially on problems of wildlife management, he had already started his intensive campaign to provide full protection for quail and mourning doves. The magazine came to his editorial support in his one-man battle against the refuge —public hunting bill. He also enlisted the support of leading urban newspapers whose editors and publishers, he knew, were not well informed on the principal issues of the case. To this nucleus of supporters he added many individuals and groups with widely divergent and sometimes devious interests. Some, who misunderstood the purpose of the proposed law, honestly regarded the one-dollar license fee as an infringement on the rights of the average duck hunter, for whose benefit the bill had been written. Others, at the opposite extreme, were representatives of wealthy duck clubs who feared the expropriation of their favorite hunting grounds under the proposed law. States'-rights advocates saw in the law a further reduction of the traditional state control over wildlife resources. All of these diverse forces were allied under Hornaday's banner when, on January 26, 1926, Congressman Anthony and Senator Smith Brookhart of Iowa introduced the bill for the third consecutive time.

This bill, too, was doomed to failure. Under an impassioned attack by a young and rising city-bred New York Congressman, Fiorello LaGuardia, whose opposition had been inspired by Hornaday, the Senate bill was shuffled to the bottom of the committee files, and efforts of its proponents in the House were hampered by the absence from the Congress of Anthony, who had sustained serious injuries in an automobile accident. In the Senate, the united and bitter opposition of states' rights Senators William H. King of Utah, James A. Reed of Missouri, and Clarence C. Dill of Washington State kept the bill from a vote. Failure number four.

The presence of the Missouri delegation in Hornaday's corner was interesting in view of the Show-Me State's record to that time in migratory-bird protection. Missouri had provided the test case that established the validity of the Migratory Bird Treaty and, as late as 1930, in open defiance of the federal statute, allowed its hunters an open season on waterfowl that extended through April 30, nearly four months later than that permitted by federal law.

At the close of the 69th Congress Senator Peter Norbeck of South Dakota had taken a strong personal interest in the bill and, in the opening session of the 70th Congress, he emerged as the sponsor of a bill patterned closely after the earlier unsuccessful measures, while Anthony made another try in the House. On April 18, 1929, after a bitter Senate debate, the federal-licensing and public shooting grounds provisions were stripped away and in this form the Norbeck Bill passed the Senate. Anthony's bill, which still contained the controversial provisions, remained bottled up in committee. On January 23, 1929, young Congressman August T. Andresen of Minnesota tossed into the hopper a new bill that was identical to the amended Norbeck Bill. Both bills now provided for a straight refuge system, without appended public shooting grounds, to be financed through congressional appropriations rather than through direct levies on the sportsmen.

Almost abruptly, proponents and opponents of the earlier bills found themselves on the same side of the fence behind a bill that both could support. Men who had been glaring at each other for years found themselves working shoulder to shoulder to push the refuge bill over the line. Less than two weeks after it was introduced, the Andresen Bill received a unanimous affirmative vote in the House, and the Norbeck Bill was approved by the Senate Committee on Agriculture with a recommendation for immediate passage. On February 18, 1929, the Norbeck-Andresen Migratory Bird Conservation Act, after eight years of dissension, placed on the books a workable waterfowl-refuge law.

A significant by-product of the fight for a refuge-acquisition law was a proposal that originated with a committee appointed by the International Association of Game, Fish and Conservation Commissioners at its annual meeting in 1925. This committee of five, which included Pearson and Burnham, was charged with the task of studying refuge bills then before the Congress in an attempt to find a compromise that would be more acceptable to the opponents. They recommended that the existing ten percent federal excise tax on sporting arms and ammunition be earmarked by Congress to finance the land acquisition as a substitute for the federal hunting license. Before this could be acted upon, Congress made it a dead issue by repealing all excise taxes. The idea remained alive, however, and was revived a decade later to form the basis for the Pittman-Robertson Federal Aid in Wildlife Restoration Act of September 2, 1937, the most productive and far-reaching piece of wildlife legislation enacted in the United States.

In 1926, the IAGFCC committee was enlarged and became the National Committee on Wild Life Legislation. Among its new members were Carlos Avery, who had succeeded Burnham as president of the American Game Protective Association, and John C. Phillips, president of the newly organized American Wild Fowlers. The latter group was largely responsible for effecting the compromise that led to the enactment of the Migratory Bird Conservation Act.

The American Wild Fowlers, an offshoot of the Boone and Crockett Club, functioned with great effectiveness between 1927 and 1931. Its stated objectives were to interest the public in waterfowl conservation, to help preserve the authority of the Bureau of Biological Survey over migratory birds, to cooperate with the state agencies and the Bureau in making waterfowl censuses and enforcing the laws, and to assist in scientific research on waterfowl biology and movements.

In the winter of 1926–27, Dr. Lewis S. Morris, a member of the executive committee of the Boone and Crockett Club, wrote to many of his duck-hunting friends to discuss the waterfowl situation and to sample sentiment among them for forming a private organization to supplement the work of the Bureau of Biological Survey. The response was enthusiastic, and Morris and George Bird Grinnell arranged a dinner meeting in January at which a committee of organization for a "Wild Fowlers League," consisting of Morris, Grinnell, and L. H. Beers, was appointed. The fifteen charter members pledged a sum of $3,650 for three years, and invitations to join were sent to many other waterfowl hunters. But the response was not felt large enough to warrant the creation of a large national membership association. During its brief span of life, the American Wild Fowlers remained a relatively small but highly effective group.

Grinnell and Phillips were among the leading authorities on waterfowl in North America. Phillips's major work, *A Natural History of the Ducks*, in four massive volumes probably has never been equaled in its coverage of the Family Anatidae throughout the world. One of the founders was Charles Sheldon who, as chairman of the Game Preservation Committee of the Boone and Crockett Club, had expounded the philosophy on which the new organization's platform was based.

> Wildlife conservation will best be promoted by the encouragement of legitimate sport; of scientific interest in natural history; and by building up the public opinion to make and enforce wise laws. All are indispensably complementary to this end.
> Laws can be better enforced if made flexible so as to be quickly adapted to changing conditions; that is, by giving discretionary powers to some responsible official or commission to make regulations for the preservation of game as changing conditions may demand.

Sheldon's concepts, penned in 1915, not only established a platform for the American Wild Fowlers and the Boone and Crockett Club but established guidelines for the future course of American wildlife administration.

Sheldon, a powerfully built, clean-shaven man with a boyish face, was a native of Vermont and a graduate of Yale in the Class of 1890. By profession he was an engineer and, except for a passion for the out-of-doors and a love of nature, there was little in his early career to foreshadow his later great contributions to conservation and the biological sciences. After serving as the assistant superintendent of the Lake Shore and Michigan Railroad and manager of a manufacturing firm, he had been selected by New York financier Colonel O. H. Payne to handle his interests in Mexico. From 1898 to 1903 Sheldon lived in Mexico as general manager of the Chihuahua and Pacific Railroad and the Chihuahua and Pacific Exploration Company, directing, during the first years of his sojourn there, the construction of a railway between the mining regions and the capital of the province.

Retiring from business in 1903 when only thirty-six years of age, Sheldon started the first of his explorations and hunting trips that took him from the camps of the then-wild Seri Indians of Baja California to the peak of Mt. McKinley. While planning an early hunting trip to Alaska, he contacted Dr. E. W. Nelson, chief of the Bureau of Biological Survey. The two became fast friends and Nelson carefully nurtured and guided Sheldon's interests, energy, and enthusiasm into productive channels. All of Sheldon's hunting trips, mostly along the Rockies, from Alaska to deep into Mexico, became much more than personal recreation. He became a proficient observer and collector of zoological specimens for the United States Museum of Natural History and the leading authority on the wild sheep of North America.

Theodore Roosevelt, who became his close personal friend, called him "a capital representative of the best hunter-naturalist type today."

The American Wild Fowlers officially came into being on May 25, 1927, with Phillips as president, Sheldon as chairman of its executive committee, and Grinnell as a member of its board of trustees, which also included Nelson, who had recently retired from federal service. The organization engaged Nash Buckingham, one of the nation's most prominent and dynamic outdoor writers, to serve as its field secretary with offices in Washington, D.C. He assumed his duties on March 1, 1928.

One of the admitted weaknesses in the camp of the proponents of the wildlife refuge bills before Congress was a dearth of scientific information on the status and movements of the various segments of the continental waterfowl population. Shortly before the Wild Fowlers was organized, the Bureau of Biological Survey, under Nelson, had done some banding work and had started a primitive annual waterfowl census, but the federal agency was handicapped in its fact-finding efforts by a general lack of funds. To assist the census the Wild Fowlers appropriated $1500 a year and additional amounts for banding operations and other basic research.

One of its first projects, launched in the spring of 1928, was the financing of a field party, headed by Archie Hull of Salt Lake City, Utah, to study crow-waterfowl relationships on the Canadian breeding grounds of Alberta. In an attempt to obtain clues to the movements of the blue goose, the Wild Fowlers, in 1929, financed the first of two studies by Frederick C. Lincoln, a biologist of the Bureau of Biological Survey, on the Paul J. Rainey Sanctuary in coastal Louisiana. Lincoln's attempt to band geese failed although he successfully banded many ducks. In the previous September he had been sent to the ranch of George Slade near Dawson, North Dakota, where he had affixed bands to 1,450 ducks. Three hundred were recovered by hunters that fall, providing the first concrete measure of hunting pressure on waterfowl. The experience also lent weight to Lincoln's theory that the waterfowl of North America break down into relatively distinct populations which move north and south along fairly well defined flyways. This theory, backed by hundreds of thousands of banding returns since that time, now forms a basis for modern migratory game-bird management. Lincoln worked closely with the American Wild Fowlers, throughout its history, collaborating in 1930 with Phillips in writing *American Waterfowl*, which embodied the philosophies of its sponsors.

Buckingham, as field secretary, devoted much of his time to law enforcement in cooperation with federal agents. On a tour of the

Midwest with Colonel H. P. Sheldon, chief of the enforcement branch of the Bureau of Biological Survey, to map a chain of proposed waterfowl refuges, he helped break up a notorious duck-bootlegging ring near Stuttgart, Arkansas.

Hornaday's long campaign to eliminate the discretionary powers of the Secretary of Agriculture and the Bureau of Biological Survey as they applied to migratory bird hunting regulations climaxed with the introduction of identical bills in both Houses of Congress written to meet Hornaday's demands. Each would have established by federal law a daily fixed bag limit of fifteen ducks and four geese. The Senate bill was authored by Senator Charles L. McNary and that in the House by Gilbert N. Haugen of Iowa, a friend and supporter of Hornaday. At the hearing held on the Haugen Bill on January 27–29, 1930, opposition was registered by Paul G. Redington, Nelson's successor as chief of the Bureau of Biological Survey; Pearson, for the National Association of Audubon Societies; and Phillips, for the American Wild Fowlers.

Seth E. Gordon, conservation director of the Izaak Walton League of America, testified in opposition, and Carlos Avery submitted a written statement for the record opposing it for the American Game Protective Association. The bill failed to move out of committee and died with the adjournment of Congress.

After their victory in the fight to block the Haugen Bill and with their primary goal achieved through the enactment of the Norbeck-Andresen Migratory Bird Conservation Act, the founders of the American Wild Fowlers saw the need for a large-membership organization that could expand the programs in which they had pioneered. Many of its subscribers already were contributing to a new organization that had been established by Joseph Knapp in 1930 called More Game Birds in America Foundation, Incorporated. On May 13, 1931, American Wild Fowlers closed its books and turned its files over to the new foundation, which, in 1937, was to be reorganized and expanded as Ducks Unlimited, an organization that has done much to save and restore the waterfowl breeding grounds of Canada.

Hornaday died at the age of eighty-three in 1937, bitter to the end over the rejection of his views and still convinced that the major game birds and mammals could not survive him by more than a few years. He lived long enough to witness the greatest decline in waterfowl flights ever recorded and the imposition of wildfowl-hunting restrictions far more rigid than any he had proposed.

In 1929, while Hornaday and the American Wild Fowlers were jousting over the Haugen Bill, biologists of the Bureau of Biological Survey noticed the first signs of a collapse in the duck flights as drought seared the prairies and wheat and corn crops turned to straw. Although Hornaday lost the Haugen Bill, the hunting regulations promulgated for the 1930-31 hunting season by the Bureau of Biological Survey generally matched Hornaday's recommendations for a bag limit of fifteen ducks and four geese a day. And things were to get much worse before they improved.

Chapter 15

Hard Lessons

Some of the methods for increasing wildlife numbers that had been developed in the first decades of the twentieth century began to break down in the third—a few under the weight of their own success.

When President Theodore Roosevelt established the Grand Canyon National Game Preserve on November 28, 1906, he provided full protection to one of the healthiest remaining deer herds in the United States. The new federal refuge consisted of nearly a million acres of relatively flat tableland atop the Kaibab Plateau on the Colorado River in northwestern Arizona. This great mesa was the home for approximately three thousand Rocky Mountain mule deer, noted for their spectacular size and the massive antler development of the older bucks. To the north and northeast, from the base of the plateau, open sagebrush desert with little potential for supporting deer stretched for nearly thirty miles.

On the south and southeast, the plateau was bounded by steep cliffs dropping to the floors of the Grand and Marble Canyons and on the west by the deep slash of Kanab Canyon. For practical purposes, the Kaibab plateau was a biological island with all of the advantages and disadvantages of an insular environment. The deer had evolved in almost complete genetic isolation.

Before the coming of the whites, the Kaibab had been a traditional hunting ground for the Navahos and Paiutes who gathered there each autumn to collect their winter supplies of deerskins and venison, but it supported no permanent Indian communities. In those days the Kaibab was covered with lush grassy meadows that in summer sparkled with the glow of wildflowers studded with groves of aspen and pine. Here the deer spent the warmer months and reared their young. In late autumn they drifted down the slopes to the east and west to seek shelter from the snows and winds of winter in the piñon-juniper thickets of many small canyons.

Well before 1906, much of the character of the plateau had been changed. As early as 1893, when Kaibab and adjacent lands were set aside as the Grand Canyon National Forest Reserve, at least 200,000 sheep, 20,000 cattle, and an equal number of horses were pastured on the plateau. By the time the area was declared a wildlife refuge, this excessive grazing pressure had been reduced. Most of the sheep were later eliminated by U. S. Forest Service regulations, but permits for more than thirteen thousand cattle and horses were issued in 1906 and increased gradually to more than sixteen thousand in 1913. Actually, these were minimum numbers, as some livestock owners exceeded their permits and half-wild range stock from the adjacent desert often wandered onto the plateau, attracted by the abundant forage.

Early overgrazing had left its mark. Most of the tall, perennial grasses had been eliminated, and gullies scarred the once-picturesque glades. Under usual circumstances, the reduced grazing pressure by domestic livestock would have had little or no effect on the deer. Cattle and horses favor grasses while mule deer depend more heavily on woody vegetation or browse. Kaibab, however, proved to be a special case.

Roosevelt's mandate to the Forest Service in creating the wildlife reserve was to give priority to "the propagation and breeding" of mule deer. The foresters turned to their assigned task with enthusiasm. The area was declared off bounds to hunters, and patrols against illegal hunting were initiated. Patrol was a relatively easy matter since the plateau was readily accessible only at a comparatively few points. A systematic campaign against predators was inaugurated. Between 1906 and 1931, government hunters, using poison, traps, and guns removed 781 cougars, 20 gray wolves, 4,889 coyotes, and 554 bobcats.

In its first few years, the Grand Canyon National Game Preserve seemed an amazing success. The original three thousand deer doubled in less than ten breeding seasons, and two years later, by 1918, they had doubled again. By 1923, official estimates placed their numbers at a conservative thirty thousand while local observers estimated the population to be at least 100,000 head.

Under this mounting pressure the range was beginning to deteriorate. The better range grasses had disappeared and the cattle were feeding on the woody browse in direct competition with the deer. The cliffrose, an important winter deer food, was chewed back to stubs by autumn.

In 1919, E. A. Goldman, the leading biologist in the Bureau of Biological Survey, was dispatched to the Kaibab to begin the first of a number of annual studies of the problem. His reports each year reflected growing alarm. In 1922 he wrote: "Unless the number of deer is controlled, serious damage to the summer range and parts of the winter range is to be expected." Goldman's findings were supported by former Congressman George Shiras III, one of the nation's leading authorities on hooved mammals, who visited the Kaibab in 1923. He reported that "from 30,000 to 40,000 deer are on the verge of starvation." He described the range conditions as "deplorable."

Faced with these depressing reports, Secretary of Agriculture Henry C. Wallace appointed a nongovernmental Kaibab Deer Investigating Committee made up of representatives from the leading conservation organizations. One motivation behind Wallace's action was to resolve an interagency controversy in which his department was deeply involved. In 1919, Congress had created the Grand Canyon National Park, the boundaries of which encompassed the southern fourth of the Kaibab Plateau. When the Forest Service suggested that the deer population be thinned by shooting, Stephen T. Mather, the first director of the National Park Service, exploded in anger. Since the establishment of Yellowstone National Park, hunting and shooting had been prohibited in the national parks. Moreover, Mather was a city-bred businessman with little if any expertise in evaluating range conditions or biological problems.

The Kaibab Deer Committee consisted of Burnham, Pearson, Hayward Cutting of the Boone and Crockett Club, and T. W. Thompson of the American National Livestock Breeders Association. In August, 1923, the committee members, guided by S. B. Locke of the Forest Service and accompanied by Goldman and Richard T. Evans of the Geological Survey, began a ten-day tour of the plateau. They killed several deer for necropsy and found the stomachs of all crammed with fir needles, which deer rarely eat unless on the verge of starvation. They counted more than a hundred deer each day. Pearson reported that the ribs of all were clearly defined, although in late summer they should have been sleek with fat.

All of the choicer winter browse plants—snowberry, serviceberry, and dwarf ceanothus—had been eaten back to coarse stems, and the cliffrose had been browsed to ground level. In one evening they counted 1,028 deer.

In its report to Washington, the committee recommended that the deer population be reduced at the earliest possible date by fifty percent. It recommended that the Forest Service trap deer from the plateau for sale at cost to states with depleted deer range. If these measures proved insufficient, it recommended that sportsmen be permitted to hunt deer under the supervision of forest rangers and kill fifteen thousand deer, half of which were to be does.

In the event that all of these measures proved unacceptable or ineffective, it recommended that, as a last resort, government hunters shoot the first fifteen hundred deer encountered and that the hides be donated to the Indian agencies.

The Forest Service first tried trapping. Only eighteen deer were taken, and most of these died in attempts to escape the traps.

Then sport hunting was tried. The hunters killed 675 animals, but most sportsmen were repelled by the emaciated condition of their quarry and the ease with which the animals could be killed.

The recommendations of the committee brought strong support and stronger opposition. Humanitarians belabored the committee for its "heartless and inhumane" approach. Mather, still unconvinced of the need for bringing the suffering animals down to a level the range could support, took the issue to a sympathetic urban press. To those far removed from the scene, a quick death by a hunter's bullet was unthinkable, while slow death by starvation and malnutrition was acceptable as "nature's way."

Bitterest opposition of all came from Arizona's governor, George Hunt, who had little interest in humanitarianism but who was unalterably opposed to federal control on the issue of states' rights. When the Forest Service announced that hunters would be permitted to kill deer under federal regulation, Hunt ordered his state game wardens to arrest every hunter who left the wildlife reserve with a deer carcass.

People with little knowledge of deer habits conceived the idea of driving several thousand deer off the plateau and into the underpopulated range that existed beyond the natural barriers that surrounded the Kaibab. On paper the idea seemed plausible, although both Burnham and Pearson immediately saw its futility. Congressman Carl Hayden of Arizona tried to enlist the services of the United States cavalry in a massive drive, but the War Department respectfully declined to authorize the use of troops for the purpose.

Novelist Zane Grey, however, pursued the idea. Enlisting the help of neighboring ranches and Indian leaders, he marshaled a force of forty cowboys and more than seventy Navajo Indians. Grey's plan was for his troops to cut off from five thousand to eight thousand deer, drive them down passes to the Colorado River, and there to force them to swim the turbulent stream to brighter pastures on the far side.

At dawn on December 14, 1924, Grey, with a small group of

friends and a number of photographers, stationed themselves at a pass near Saddle Mountain to watch the spectacle of thousands of deer streaming past ahead of the drivers. Far back on the plateau, a long line of mounted drivers was filing into the chaparral. At a signal, the riders turned on a flank, forming an arching line nearly two miles long. Whooping, yipping, and flailing the brush with lariats and quirts, the colorfully clad drivers began their advance, deer flushing ahead of them like frightened calves. Grey's photographers waited with cameras poised to capture the drama on film. But when the long line of riders swept down on their position, there was not one deer ahead of the line. More agile than even the brushwise cow ponies, they had cut back through the drive or sideslipped its ends. In the evening, back on the Kaibab Plateau, more than thirty thousand scrawny deer were nibbling hungrily on the half-dead browse.

Grey made a second attempt two days later before admitting defeat.

That winter the deer began to die in masses. Goldman revisited the plateau in the early spring of 1925 and reported that deaths from starvation and malnutrition had run into the thousands and that "10,000 to 15,000 may not be too high an estimate." He documented the deaths of ninety percent of the fawns of the previous season and noted that the mortality had cut heavily into the number of does, which were unable to compete with the larger bucks for the limited forage still available.

In 1925, William B. Greeley, who had succeeded Graves as chief forester, determined to take action that would forestall the seemingly inevitable destruction of the Kaibab Plateau and the deer that it supported. The government, after a case that reached the Supreme Court of the United States, obtained an injunction against interference by the Governor of Arizona in its deer-reduction program. But reducing the herd by direct killing was still opposed by well-intentioned humanitarians and protectionists in urban centers. As Pearson, who was intimately involved in the controversy, caustically observed: "Many animal-lovers as well as game-killers need to be taught sane principles of wild-life preservation."

The delaying action of the opponents of deer control reduced efforts of the Forest Service to holding operations that did little more than check the deterioration of the range. In the five years between 1925 and 1930, the Forest Service had managed to take and relocate 1,907 fawns and 745 adult deer; 1,124 deer were killed by government agencies; and 11,641 were removed by sportsmen under federal permits. But the removal rate scarcely kept pace with annual reproduction.

In 1930, the government decided to subject the deer herd to another study by a team of experts. The new committee included

George D. Pratt, president of the American Forestry Association;
Mark Anderson of the Izaak Walton League of America; Dr. E. Raymond Hall of the American Society of Mammalogists; K. C. Kartch-
ner of the Arizona Game and Fish Commission; J. C. Macfarlane of
the American National Livestock Association; A. A. Nichol of the
American Game Protective Association; Paul G. Redington, chief of
the Bureau of Biological Survey; and Pearson as chairman.

The committee, on its horseback tour of the range, found the vegetation even nearer depletion than it had been in 1925 and the deer
more emaciated and greatly reduced in numbers. In its report it recommended that the trapping of predators, which had been continued
to benefit the livestock, be ended at once; that efforts be made to
remove all wild horses that still roamed the plateau; and that control
efforts by live-trapping, regulated hunting, and shooting by federal
agents be accelerated until the range had a chance to recover.

By this time, public opposition to control had softened. Governor
Hunt had left the political arena, and Arizona had adopted a nonpolitical commission form of wildlife administration which was more
concerned with the wildlife resource than with the politics of the
issue. Under fresh leadership the Arizona Game and Fish Commission
entered into an active cooperative program with the U. S. Forest Service. Public opposition removed from the scene also had been muted
by the volume of scientific evidence gathered by the Bureau of Biological Survey and the various special committees that clearly demonstrated the need for drastic action.

The Arizona Game and Fish Commission, in one of its first acts,
declared a special any-deer hunting season for the Kaibab. In the
fall of 1929, 3,500 hunters killed four thousand deer. In 1930, the
legal kill rose above five thousand. The Forest Service, on its part,
fenced the plateau to keep out stray livestock, tightened controls over
livestock operators, and built roads to improve hunter access.

By 1931, starvation, disease, malnutrition, and shooting reduced
the herd to less than twenty thousand. Relieved of the intolerable
pressures of the past, the range began to improve. New grass and
herbs reclothed the denuded slopes. In the canyons, cliffroses, juni-
pers, and sage put on spring growth for the first time in years. And
with the recovery of the range, the physical condition and reproductive capacity of the deer also returned.

At first through trial and error and then through scientific research,
the Arizona Game and Fish Commission and the U. S. Forest Service
developed a kit of management tools designed to maintain the deer
population at a level that would assure the health and vigor of the
animals and that of the plants on which they depend. The Kaibab

Plateau today again produces some of the largest and heaviest antlered mule deer in North America.

The Kaibab Plateau was only one of the classrooms for the wildlife
administrators of the 1930s. Nature and human frailty were combining to build a second, two thousand miles to the east in Penn's
Woods.

Pennsylvania, starting from scratch at the turn of the century, had
realized almost unbelievable success in restoring its white-tailed deer
population through protection, restocking, and a system of state deer
refuges. By 1907, less than ten years after the Pennsylvania Game
Commission initiated the restoration program, the deer had become
sufficiently well established to warrant limited hunting. To protect
the reproductive base of the herd, which was still expanding in an
understocked habitat, the Commission decreed that only bucks with
one or more forked antlers could be taken legally. Does and other
antlerless deer or spikehorn bucks were rigorously protected by the
largest and most efficient staff of state game wardens—in Pennsylvania, called "game protectors"—anywhere in the United States. To
minimize its need for law enforcement, it initiated a strong educational program to inform the public, especially the sportsmen, of the
need for protecting does.

Since deer are polygamous with one male capable of serving a
dozen or more females, the removal of even a substantial proportion
of the bucks was known to have a negligible effect on the rate of increase of the herd.

The first hunting season was judged a huge success when slightly
more than two hundred bucks were taken by sportsmen. Acceptance
of the doe-protection regulation was all but universal among the
hunters, and game protectors made only two or three cases in which
inexperienced hunters suffering from "buck fever" mistakenly killed
illegal animals. Deer hunting was soon reestablished as an annual
autumn event in the Keystone State. By 1913, the take by hunters exceeded one thousand bucks, and by 1920, it approached five thousand.

But in the meantime, the Pennsylvania Game Commission was
being confronted with new problems. As early as 1914, farmers and
orchardists had begun to complain of damage to their crops and trees,
and investigations by game protectors indicated that most of these
complaints were valid. In one orchard more than a thousand young
apple trees were found to be severely damaged and many had been
killed.

Since the Commission was still establishing deer refuges and many
counties had deer range that was still lightly stocked, it first tried

live-trapping deer responsible for the damage. But, as on the Kaibab, trapping proved extremely costly and largely ineffective. Although the deer readily entered the traps, the process of removing a dozen or so wild, frightened animals armed with sharp hooves and antlers was a dangerous and harrowing experience. Many of the deer killed or severely injured themselves in their frantic efforts to escape.

The Commission next tried to meet the problem by providing fencing materials to farmers and orchardists suffering proven deer damage. Under the regulation, the landowner was required to erect the fence and supply the posts. But fencing one orchard only forced the deer to the next that was unfenced by an owner who could not afford the time and money needed to participate in the program. Finally, this approach, too, was abandoned, and farmers or orchardists suffering damages verified by a game protector were permitted to kill depredating deer, with carcasses remaining the property of the state for disposal through charitable institutions.

By 1923, the Game Commission realized that the time had come to put the brakes on the mushrooming growth of the deer population. Under the ideal habitat conditions that existed in Pennsylvania during the first two decades of the 1900s the deer population had the capability of doubling every two years. With plenty of nutritious food, a doe can produce her first fawn at one year of age, and twins or even triplets in subsequent breeding seasons. All of the conditions necessary for a population explosion existed in Penn's Woods.

In 1923, the Pennsylvania Game Commission obtained legislative approval for a limited open season on antlerless deer in counties where crop depredation had been most serious and symptoms of overpopulation were becoming evident. It announced plans under which one hundred licensed resident sportsmen who purchased special five-dollar permits would be authorized to kill one antlerless deer each, in two townships of Franklin County.

But to its consternation, the Commission found that it had succeeded too well in its early educational efforts to sanctify the doe. Sportsmen snapped up the hundred permits in the first day they were offered for sale. But most had no intention of using them. Advertisements appeared in the local papers exhorting hunters not to kill antlerless deer, and posters and billboards appeared on country roads proclaiming that anyone who killed a doe was "yellow" and a dastardly coward. Landowners posted their properties with signs that emphasized the public sentiment: "No Doe Hunting on This Land." Although deer were so abundant in the townships involved that even the least proficient hunter could have taken a deer in a few days of hunting, only eight antlerless deer were taken. Pennsylvania's first attempt at deer-population control was a fiasco.

Soon after 1925, the Pennsylvania deer bubble began to show signs of collapse. Game protectors who checked hunters' kills began to notice signs of debility—lower average body weight, poor antler development, and increases in the incidence of parasites. Those who hiked or snowshoed into the swamps and thickets where the deer concentrated in winter found well-defined "browse lines" below which the deer had eaten all palatable browse back to finger-thick nubs. Even more alarming, they began to report finding the emaciated carcasses of the victims of starvation and malnutrition and dozens of pathetic caricatures of deer so weakened by hunger that they could not run more than a few steps before collapsing in the snow. The attrition was particularly severe among the fawns and smaller does which could not compete with the larger bucks for the scant amount of browse available at the browse line, five feet above the ground.

That winter the deer began to die by the thousands, and the following spring and summer crop-damage complaints reached intolerable proportions. Although deer-censusing methods were still in a primitive stage of development, many observers estimated the statewide population at nearly a million white-tailed deer.

With effective action blocked by a strange coalition of hunters and sentimental protectionists who opposed all hunting, the Pennsylvania Commission sought outside help. In answer to an appeal by Ross Leffler, president of the Commission, the Bureau of Biological Survey dispatched Dr. Vernon Bailey, its foremost mammalogist, to the scene to study the problem.

Bailey was appalled by what he found. In four townships, he counted more than a thousand deer carcasses, the depletion of nearly all vegetation within reach of the deer, and the resort of the animals to unpalatable foods that lacked nutritional value for sustaining life.

With the backing of Bailey's authoritative report and faced with the threat of a legislative mandate to reimburse farmers for crop damages, a move that would have bankrupted its game fund, the Commission plunged into the swirling current of public opposition. It announced a complete closure on the hunting of antlered bucks for the 1928 season and an open season on antlerless deer. It established a quota for each county on a ratio of eight permits for each antlered buck taken in the previous season when the statewide take had been 14,374.

The uproar that followed public announcement of this revolutionary step shook the state. Sportsmen, convinced that the new policy would wipe out the deer, again joined forces with the protectionists to overthrow the decision. But Leffler and his commission stood firm. In an impassioned plea before the 15th National Game Conference, he defended the position of the Commission and begged the sportsmen of Pennsylvania to "save the deer herd from extermination." "We need," he concluded, "more scientific game administration and less unwise sentiment."

In spite of the bitter opposition, the Commission, firm in its knowledge of what had to be done to save the deer, refused to back away from its decision. That autumn, hunters removed 25,097 antlerless deer from the swollen population, nearly twice the number of bucks taken by hunters in 1927.

In 1930, hunting for bucks was reinstituted, but in a special antlerless season following the buck season 5,979 more does and antlerless bucks were removed. In the next year a similar dual season produced a harvest of 24,796 bucks and 70,255 antlerless deer—95,051 from a state that a generation earlier had been devoid of white-tailed deer!

Gradually, opposition to the hunting of antlerless deer began to fade as the principles of deer management gained public acceptance and understanding. Deer seen by hikers and sportsmen alike were responding to the policy, gaining weight and antler size, and twin fawns again became the rule rather than the exception. Crop-damage complaints gradually dropped. Many sportsmen, unsuccessful in bagging a buck during the antlered season, now saw in the antlerless-deer season a last-resort opportunity to fill their lockers with venison before Christmas.

Faith in the Commission's wisdom was shaken in 1938 when it reimposed another straight antlerless-deer season and the kill reached a staggering 171,662 animals. Many sportsmen were convinced that this would end deer hunting in Pennsylvania for all time, and the Game Commission was faced with another onslaught against its policies. But the deer harvest held up to average in the combination seasons of 1939 and climbed to an until then all-time high of 186,575 in 1940.

Since that time, the annual take by Pennsylvania hunters has averaged around 100,000 antlered and antlerless deer, which maintains the state herd at a healthy level of around a half million, a level that maintains the individual animals in excellent health and vigor and stays consistent with the carrying capacity of the available habitat and the interests of agriculture and forestry.

A third classroom for wildlife specialists had been built amid the snowy peaks of northwestern Wyoming and southern Montana.

Like most other native large mammals of North America, the wapiti, or elk, as it is erroneously but almost universally known, had been progressively eliminated from much of its formerly extensive range by the encroachment of settlement, agriculture, and competition with domestic livestock, and squeezed into a relatively few islands in

a sea of civilization. In the early 1900s the largest of these islands
was formed by Yellowstone National Park and the adjacent national
forests. Within the park, during the warmer months, the scattered
animals found an abundance of forage and cover in which to rear
their young under the protection of federal authorities. As the storms
and snows of early winter drove down from the North, however, the
elk gathered in large bands that drifted southward and northward out
of the mountains. In the old days, the migrating animals had fanned
out over the open valleys and plains and subsisted during winter on
the dry grasses and browse of the lowlands, fifty, a hundred, or even
two hundred miles from their summer range. This had been the ancestral pattern ever since elk and the climate of the area evolved.

With the rapid settlement of Montana and Wyoming, however, this
ancient cycle was disrupted. The migrating elk found old travel routes
blocked by networks of fences and traditional wintering grounds
usurped by domestic cattle and sheep. In moving from the park, they
ran an ever-tightening gauntlet of lead from poachers. Although protected by hunting closures in Montana and subjected to limited sport
hunting in Wyoming, by the early 1900s thousands were being
slaughtered for their canine teeth alone. Gold-mounted on a watch
fob, the tusk of an elk had become the unofficial badge of the Benev-
olent Protective Order of Elks, whose members numbered in the millions. In a day when the big gold pocket watch and ornate watch fob
were considered high fashion, jewelers capitalized on the demand. The
tooth hunter, blood brother of the old buffalo tongue hunters, operated well into the 1920s before improved law enforcement and the
enlistment of the BPOE by conservation groups in an elk-restoration
project ended the illegal traffic. At the peak of their popularity, elk
tusks were bringing the poachers little more than ten dollars a pair.

In spite of this attrition, the herds continued to increase. During
their winter migration many concentrated on private lands where they
raided hay stacks and depleted forage needed by ranchers to winter
cattle and sheep. The northern Yellowstone herd, part of which had
always wintered within the borders of the park, began to mushroom.
The southern herd, wintering in Jackson Hole, was squeezed into a
greatly restricted wintering range. In the Lamar Valley, where park
officials were painstakingly reconstructing the bison herd, it became
necessary to import hay from outside the park because of competition
between the buffalo and the elk for the available natural forage. The
extirpation of the white-tailed deer and bighorn sheep from the park
at around this time may be attributable to the destruction of their
food supplies by overabundant elk.

The first attempts toward correcting the situation were made in
1911 after a census of the northern Yellowstone and Jackson Hole

herds by the Bureau of Biological Survey and the U. S. Forest Service. Live-trapping and transshipment of surplus elk to unoccupied range or to zoos had started as early as 1892. Beginning in 1911, this activity was accelerated; in 1912, the State of Montana shipped five carloads of elk trapped at Gardiner to various places in the United States. Between 1892 and 1939, elk from the Yellowstone herds were used to reestablish the species in most of the western states, including Arizona, where the Merriam's elk had been eliminated, and in several eastern states. Michigan and Virginia succeeded in reestablishing small but thrifty herds within the range of the extinct eastern race. An elk introduction on the National Bison Range proved so successful that annual reduction programs had to be initiated to eliminate competition with the bison. But the removal of elk from the populations in Yellowstone had little effect on the annual increase of the herds.

The plight of the overabundant animals received much publicity and, under a congressional appropriation of $20,000, an emergency winter feeding program was initiated. This not only failed to solve the problem, but developed new problems that were peculiarly its own. Now, instead of spreading out over what range remained available to them, the elk crowded into restricted feeding yards, increasing the threat from disease and parasites, and denuding all natural foods in the surrounding areas. From an esthetic point of view, the elk, one of America's noblest mammals, was reduced by this program to a semi-wild panhandler. The program became exceedingly expensive with each passing season. But worse, it could not be terminated or drastically reduced without threatening the existence of the animals for whose benefit it had been devised.

A more realistic approach was taken in 1912 and 1913 when Congress appropriated $50,000 to the Bureau of Biological Survey to cope with the elk problem. With these funds, the Bureau purchased 1,760 acres of privately owned land near Jackson, Wyoming, which, with a thousand acres of adjacent public lands, became the nucleus of the National Elk Refuge. Dr. E. W. Nelson launched an immediate campaign to enlarge the sanctuary in an attempt to bring the winter range more nearly within balance with the breeding range. He was supported by Colonel Henry S. Graves, successor to Pinchot as chief forester of the United States. The efforts of these two government officials were largely responsible for the introduction, early in 1916, of a congressional bill written by Congressman Mondell of Wyoming to add twenty to twenty-five sections in Jackson Hole to the Teton National Forest for management as an elk refuge by the State of Wyoming.

Graves's views on wildlife problems were broad for a man of his time. On June 1, 1916, before the Second National Game Conference in New York City, he stated:

As long as wild life administration consists only of protection, state game preserves on national forests are all right, especially in the absence of Federal authority. In a number of instances such action has saved a bad game situation. But we have certainly now reached a point where we can begin to handle the game in an intelligent and constructive way with a view toward using them and enjoying the increase, just as in the case of any other natural resource.

This, in many ways, was a simple extension of the Pinchotian philosophy of wise use without waste, but Graves may have been influenced by an incisive statement of the Game Conservation Committee of the Boone and Crockett Club:

The elk of these herds should have . . . scientific management. The Committee believes that in addition to those killed by sportsmen, several thousand should be killed each year. The number killed must be regulated to establish a correct balance between the food supply and the numbers of elk. The killing must be done by officers under proper regulations. By no other means can the problem of these elk be solved.

This committee, chaired by Charles Sheldon, again demonstrated a keen insight into a critical wildlife problem. A generation later, in 1934, with support from nearly every national conservation organization, the federal government initiated a program almost identical to that suggested by Graves and Sheldon.

As reported by Victor H. Cahalane, chief naturalist of the National Park Service:

In 1934, the National Park Service determined to reduce the size of the northern elk herd. If hunting outside the park boundaries could not remove the surplus elk, the animals would be live-trapped within the park and shipped away for restocking purposes. If these measures proved ineffective, the final step—killing elk in the park—must be taken. The plan to remove 3,000 elk annually until the carrying capacity of the winter range had been reached, received the support of an impressive list of individuals and organizations prominent in the conservation field. . . .

During the intervening years, the elk situation in and around Yellowstone National Park grew to critical proportions. In one bleak winter several hundred carcasses were found scattered along a single fence line near Jackson Hole, and this was only a small portion of the total winter kill. Herds moving from the park to the winter range became so large that their trails down the slopes became sources of erosion, and the elk denuded all palatable vegetation along the line of their march.

In 1919, the Forest Service and Bureau of Biological Survey announced a joint program for the management of the Yellowstone elk herds. Its salient features were designed to maintain the herd at the 1919 level of 40,000 to 45,000. It proposed to use the annual increase to restock other ranges and for hunting outside the park, to eliminate all sheep grazing on elk range in the national forests, and to obtain state legislation that would issue hunting licenses by region in order to spread hunting pressure and eliminate firing lines on the park boundaries. It proposed the extension of the park borders southward to include a greater portion of the winter range, the acquisition of an additional ten thousand acres of private lands in Jackson Valley to enlarge the elk refuge, and a state law requiring hunters to report all elk kills and to make full use of all meat taken. A number of the twenty-two recommendations made by Nelson and Graves were adopted by the federal and state agencies involved, but others failed, largely because of local opposition, particularly from sheepmen whose permits were threatened by the proposed land acquisition.

On January 17, 1920, after Nelson had addressed the Boone and Crockett Club on the Yellowstone elk problem, Frederic C. Walcott passed on to the executive committee a proposal that the club try to obtain a fund of $90,000 for the purchase of ranch lands in Jackson Hole. Although Walcott considered the cost of this project beyond the resources of an organization the size of the Boone and Crockett Club, the enthusiasm of at least some of those present was apparent in an offer of $25,000 that George D. Pratt personally pledged as a start toward the needed sum. Walcott asked John Burnham and Charles Sheldon to take up the matter with national officials of the BPOE and other organizations that would be likely to support such a program. The Izaak Walton League of America had made the elk-refuge program one of its first major projects and was responsible for raising $36,000, sufficient to purchase 1,760 acres of wintering range to be added to the elk refuge. The BPOE appointed a committee that obtained additional support from its lodges throughout the nation.

In spite of winter feeding, the expansion of wintering areas, and the live-trapping and transshipment of elk to unoccupied range, none of these approaches could be effective until the basic cause of the problem was attacked, and this, as Graves had stated in 1916, was that there were too many elk for the range. Both Nelson and Graves, however, had erred, in the light of hindsight, in suggesting that the

Yellowstone area could carry forty thousand elk through a severe winter. Elk, like all members of the deer family, are remarkably prolific under ideal breeding conditions such as those that existed in Yellowstone Park, and a minimum calf crop of ten thousand additional elk could be expected from a population of this size, even in unfavorable breeding seasons. Terrible winter losses occurred after every hard winter, and the range continued to deteriorate. The areas around the feeding yards became virtual deserts; and scabies, necrotic stomatitis, and other diseases associated with malnutrition became rampant. In 1926, as a sidelight to the President's Committee on Outdoor Recreation that President Calvin Coolidge convened in Washington, D.C., on May 22–24 of that year, a special Elk Commission was formed to conduct a thorough study of the entire problem. Sheldon was appointed chairman and prepared its final report, which was published under the title "The Conservation of Elk of Jackson Hole, Wyoming." The findings of the commission were placed into operation by the agencies principally involved. One recommendation was that certain lands in the public domain be withdrawn to round out the National Elk Refuge. This was applied by the government with such vigor, through a withdrawal order on July 7, 1927, that it went beyond the recommendations of the commission, that it threatened support that hitherto had been given the Elk Commission by the State of Wyoming through its congressional delegation.

Elk reduction, which the commission advocated, did not get under way effectively until 1934. Public opposition based on sentiment rather than reality, a series of mild winters that kept the elk inside the park and safe from hunters, and abnormal rainfall that interfered with live-trapping were all factors in delaying effective action. By 1942 there were as many surplus elk as ever. But in that year, the Park Service, aided by the Montana Game and Fish Commission, applied the recommendations with full force. Their efforts were blessed by early blizzards that forced the elk out of the park in numbers. When the Montana hunting season closed on January 14, 1943, hunters had taken 6,539 elk from the northern Yellowstone herd and rangers had removed another 691 animals from the troublesome non-migratory population inside the park, effecting a full fifty percent reduction of the northern herd in a single season.

When Congress enlarged Grand Teton National Park on February 26, 1929, the boundaries of the new park embraced much of the winter range of the Jackson Hole elk herd. Section 6 of the act provided for a cooperative agreement between the Wyoming Game and Fish Commission and the National Park Service under which selected licensed hunters deputized as park rangers would be permitted to kill elk whenever park officials found that the need warranted such action. This arrangement, unique in the National Park System of the United States, has eliminated many of the problems that plagued early park authorities and refuge managers. Accompanied by the reduction in nonmigratory bands in Yellowstone Park by park rangers, it has eliminated the need for artificial feeding except during the most severe winters, reduced grazing and browsing pressures on the range, and restored the behavior of the elk to a semblance of its ancestral patterns.

The larger mammals were not the only concern of wildlife conservationists in the early 1900s.

In the rosy dawn of March 11, 1932, Dr. Alfred O. Gross, professor of ornithology at Bates College, hunkered in a blind near the edge of a meadow on James Green's farm outside West Tisbury on the island of Martha's Vineyard below the armpit of Massachusetts's Cape Cod. Soon after daybreak his attention was attracted by a furtive movement in the scrub oak thickets nearby. A brown-barred bird the size of a domestic pullet emerged from the cover and strutted slowly to the close-grazed grassy clearing a few yards from the blind.

For a few minutes it squatted, almost motionless, its head turning slowly this way and that. Then it stood erect to its full height, spread its wings and tail, and bowed until its head almost touched the earth. The long spiny feathers along the sides of its neck sprang erect over the bowed head until they resembled the horns of an oryx. The bird's breath came in sucking gasps and great protuberances the size and color of ripe oranges swelled from the sides of its throat. The feathered feet began a strange shuffling dance interspersed with flurries of stamping that Gross could clearly hear. Wingtips dragging, it raced forward and back, right and left, punctuating its rushes with wild pirouettes and abandoned leaps high in the air. Throughout the performance, the orange air sacs alternately swelled and deflated, emitting weird, resonant notes, like the distant tooting of a steam locomotive.

No other bird, male or female, responded to the calls and ritualistic dancing. For the performer was the last of his kind on earth.

Alternating between feverish note-taking and photography with his bulky Graflex, Gross recorded the event for posterity until the exhausted bird finally slipped from sight in the oaks. He was the last known person to see a heath hen alive. In the report of the Massachusetts director of fisheries and game for 1933, officials wrote the final chapter of America's first concerted effort to save an endangered bird: "The last heath hen apparently is dead, and the race *Tympanuchus cupido cupido* extinct."

Ironically, the heath hen had been accorded more legislative and physical protection than any other American bird to that time. Laws to protect it had been adopted almost as soon as Massachusetts became a state, although like most early game laws they were largely unenforced and, under the conditions of the times, unenforceable. But in 1850, after the bird was eliminated from Long Island and the New England mainland, Massachusetts stepped up its efforts to protect the remnant population that persisted on the little island south of Cape Cod. In 1860, the state declared a complete closure of heath hen hunting for an indefinite period of time without the usual local option under which the selectmen of the island towns had been able to set aside state regulations. Little heath hen hunting, except for incidental poaching, took place after that year.

In 1890, Brewster estimated the population of survivors at between one hundred and two hundred birds. But in 1894, a disastrous fire swept most of the island at the height of the breeding season, destroying many clutches of eggs and broods of downy young and wiping out the cover and food supply of adults who escaped the smoke and flames. This was the first of a number of holocausts that helped seal the fate of the heath hen. After the fire a local resident who had taken a personal interest in the fate of the birds combed the island with well-trained bird dogs. He could flush only five birds.

In 1902, in a well-intentioned but potentially disastrous effort to bolster the flagging population, the Commission of Fisheries and Game released three greater prairie chickens in the heath hen coverts on Martha's Vineyard. These western cousins of the heath hen physically are almost indistinguishable from the eastern race of pinnated grouse but had evolved on the semiarid grasslands of the Great Plains. No effort was made to band or otherwise mark these birds to determine their fate, but they probably succumbed quickly in the fogs, wet snows, and driving rains characteristic of Martha's Vineyard's winter climate.

Before their release, the western birds were subjected to the most cursory veterinarian examination, if any at all, and may have brought in new diseases and parasites to complicate efforts to save the native heath hens. And if they survived and interbred with the native grouse, the latter ceased to exist as a pure subspecies from that point on.

In 1907, the Commission of Fisheries and Game, Massachusetts Audubon Society, Federation of Bird Clubs of New England, Massachusetts Fish and Game Protective Association, and National Association of Audubon Societies joined forces in an active heath hen restoration campaign. The idea originated with John E. Howland, a native of the island, who suggested the establishment of a special reservation on which the surviving birds could live and reproduce fully protected from disturbance by man, fire and predators. The state wildlife agency immediately assigned a full-time state game warden to the island while the sponsoring private organizations began a drive to collect funds by public subscription. Within a few months they raised $2,420.

In the meantime, the state legislature enacted a bill placing in custody of the Commissioners on Fisheries and Game all lands acquired by purchase, lease, or gift and authorized the board of commissioners to take, by imminent domain, up to one thousand acres of private lands in the name of the Commonwealth. By 1911, the heath hen reservation occupied a block of two thousand acres. The state forestry agency erected a fire tower nearby with a view that covered the entire island, and it was manned during all but the wettest weather. The reservation was surrounded and crisscrossed by plowed firebreaks, and volunteer fire departments in Tisbury and West Tisbury descended upon every suspicious wisp of smoke as soon as it was spotted. William Day, an experienced gamekeeper, was engaged as a resident caretaker and occupied a small farmhouse at the edge of the refuge.

Day maintained a constant patrol against trespassers, predators, and fire, relentlessly hunting down raccoons, foxes, skunks, and house cats. Winged predators were shot on sight or subjected to lingering deaths in pole traps that studded the area. He initiated an artificial feeding program with chains of grain hoppers available to the birds under pine-bough shelters.

The heath hen responded rapidly to this pampering, and Day counted more in each successive spring. In April, 1916, after visiting the reservation, Edward Howe Forbush, the state's chief ornithologist, estimated the population at a minimum of eight hundred, although Day placed the figure at nearer two thousand. A few were trapped and shipped to Long Island in an attempt to reestablish the bird in its former range in New York State, and John C. Phillips acquired several more to release in his mainland hometown of Wenham, Massachusetts. Both of these transplants, however, failed.

Then, in the following month, another great fire swept all of the interior of Martha's Vineyard, easily leaping the firebreaks and devastating the entire reservation while most of the hens were on their nests. Few who have not witnessed one can imagine the ferocity of a spring forest fire in southeastern Massachusetts. The thickly spaced scrub oaks retain their dry leaves until new spring growth pushes them away. The interspersed pitch pines and white pine groves, after a dry spell, burn with an almost explosive intensity that scatters flaming oak leaves ahead of the fire front like fiery confetti.

While tree stumps still flared and smoke seared his nostrils, Day gloomily probed the ashes of his blackened domain in the wake of the fire. Near the sites of many of the nests that he had been observing he found the charred bones of hens that had been suffocated by the smoke or caught by the flames.

Many birds had escaped the fire by flying to unburned cover around the shores of the island. But the majority of these were males, adding a new dimension to the problems facing restoration efforts. In 1917, the usually placid spring display on the booming grounds erupted in feathery brawls as a dozen or more cocks fought for the attention of a lone hen. Hens that successfully bred were harassed on their nests by unmated cocks still driven by the reproductive urge. Although spring brought a resurgence of new cover and food, few broods were produced in 1917.

To complicate matters still more, the following winter saw the heaviest influx of goshawks to Massachusetts ever recorded. Usually uncommon in southern New England, these largest of the accipiters had evolved on a diet made up heavily of ptarmigan and ruffed grouse, both better adapted to escape its talons than the heath hen. In spite of the pole traps and shooting, the big hawks took a heavy toll. In the next spring, Day could find only one hundred heath hens, again with a sex ratio weighted heavily in favor of males. There is a report that Commissioner of Fisheries and Game William Adams personally led a group of game wardens to the reservation to shoot some of the males in an effort to bring the proportion of cocks and hens more closely in balance. If true, it does not appear in the official records, since Adams was well aware of the furor that such drastic action would have caused if it became known to the press.

Another problem was the development on Martha's Vineyard of turkey-farming enterprises. Even Day kept poultry, ducks, and geese on the reservation. Domesticated turkeys are notorious reservoirs of blackhead, a disease lethal to all members of the grouse family.

Shortly before World War I, Martha's Vineyard, until then inhabited by a relatively small population of commercial fishermen, began to be invaded each summer by hordes of summer vacationers from New York and Boston. They brought with them dogs and house cats, many of which were abandoned on the Vineyard at the end of each summer. Reverting to a feral state, the pets became prime predators on the heath hen.

But under protection, the heath hen again recovered from the successive disasters that had threatened its existence. By 1921, the population had rebuilt to a confirmed 414, but after a nesting season punctuated by driving rains, the annual count in 1922 turned up only 117. Day, along with Forbush, who was following the fluctuations of the birds with scientific intensity, found a number of dead and dying birds that were obvious victims of disease. When Gross began his annual observation in 1925, he saw only three on his first visit to the island. Forbush estimated the population on the island at fifty in 1926, but from that point on the number declined rapidly.

As of April 30, 1925, the State of Massachusetts had spent $56,912 in the nation's first all-out effort to save an endangered bird. All of this money and effort did little more than delay the end.

Each spring, Gross spent a lonely vigil in a blind commanding a view of the heath hen's principal dancing grounds where most of the island's population congregated to carry out their strange mating ritual. In the first few years, the little flock of survivors fluctuated between three and a dozen. But in 1930, only one lone male appeared. In 1931, the bird reappeared to go through its pathetic mating dance, and Gross was aware that he was eyewitness to the death of a zoological race. In 1932, the bird reappeared. In 1933, there was none.

One man who followed the dramas of success and failure of wildlife conservation in the early 1900s with great intensity was Aldo Leopold, by profession a forester but nationally recognized as a leading authority on wildlife. On receiving his Master of Forestry degree from Yale's School of Forestry in 1909, he joined the U. S. Forest Service and was assigned to the Kaibab National Forest as a forest assistant. Promoted to deputy forest supervisor and then supervisor of the Carson National Forest in New Mexico, Leopold became active in the affairs of the New Mexico Game and Fish Protective Association and, as its president, attained national recognition for the reforms in the state's wildlife administration that his followers pushed through the state legislature. In this capacity and as assistant district forester for the Service's southwestern district he was chiefly responsible for the creation of the Gila Wilderness Area in New Mexico, the first unit of wilderness set aside by the U. S. Forest Service.

From 1925 to 1927 Leopold was associate director of the Forest Products Laboratory in Wisconsin but resigned from federal service in 1928 to accept a post as consultant to the Sporting Arms and Ammunition Manufacturers Institute. In this capacity, he undertook an intensive study of wildlife populations and problems in the northern Middle West, the first detailed analysis of its kind.

In 1933, the year the heath hen was officially declared extinct, Leopold was appointed professor of game management at the University of Wisconsin, the first such academic post in the United States. In the same year, he published *Game Management*, a book destined to alter the course of wildlife conservation in the United States and the world.

Leopold, a tall, lean, bespectacled man, was a keen observer and avid reader with the probing mind of a scientist. Rather than focusing on narrow issues and problems, as most earlier naturalists and wildlife conservationists had done, he recognized a broad spectrum of interrelationships—of animals to plant communities, of plant communities to climate and soil chemistry, of predators to prey, and, above all, of human influences to natural ecosystems.

He recognized the importance of legal protection for wildlife, but fifty years of protection had not saved the heath hen, while its western counterpart and close relative, the prairie chicken, was holding its own under generous annual hunting seasons. Why did some species that had never been hunted—such as the ivory-billed woodpecker— verge on extinction while the heavily hunted quail and cottontail rabbit thrived?

In seeking the answers to these and other riddles, Leopold developed a set of principles: Every species and subspecies has a clearly defined set of seasonal requirements for food, cover, water, and space that differs in some degree from that of every other. In understocked habitat, each species tends to increase at a degree of rapidity governed by its breeding potential to a ceiling, or carrying capacity, dictated by the availability of its seasonal needs. In temperate climates, there is a great difference between the carrying capacity of spring and early summer and that of late winter. All species, especially the short-lived plant-eaters and insectivorous animals, produce young surplus to the number that can survive to the next breeding season. All of the surplus is eliminated each year by predation, starvation, disease, parasites, accidents, climatic extremes, or stress. If one limiting factor, such as predation on deer in Pennsylvania, is eliminated, another, such as starvation, will take a heavier toll. Hunting, regulated to assure that only game animals surplus to the breeding population are taken, can be substituted for the natural limiting factors, can reduce the effects of these natural factors, can produce economic and recreational values, and can maintain the wild populations at optimum levels consistent with the varied needs of man.

The carrying capacity of any unit of habitat cannot be depicted as a horizontal line on a graph except as the mean of many erratic jogs caused by short-range seasonal weather patterns and other variables. During a series of wild winters or favorable growing seasons a population may build high above normal. When this occurs, populations of grazing and browsing animals have the capacity to impair or destroy their food supplies and depress the future carrying capacity of their own range and that of all other species that depend upon the same habitat before limiting factors take noticeable effect.

But human enterprise can elevate carrying capacities as well as depress them. On hunting trips, Leopold had become increasingly aware that the borders of fields with brushy margins and the edges of forest clearings supported a greater and more diverse wildlife population than the centers of fields or unbroken expanses of forest or brushfields. By cutting and seeding clearings in the forests and lacing large open fields with hedges and clumps of trees, the carrying capacity for wildlife could be doubled or quadrupled. If lack of water was limiting the use of an area for wildlife, the creation of a water hole could correct the situation. If there were no natural nesting cavities in an area, artificial nesting boxes were readily acceptable to wood ducks, chickadees, and bluebirds.

Leopold's principles and teachings are the foundation of many modern wildlife programs. At the time they were first voiced, no state or federal wildlife agency had the funds or the manpower with which to implement them except on a local scale. This would be corrected before the 1930s had run their course.

Chapter 16
The Dirty Thirties

At the close of the 1920s the American economy fell apart like a house of cards. On October 29, 1929, sixteen million shares of stock changed hands on the New York Stock Exchange with a decline in value by the end of the year of $15 billion. Private fortunes deflated like pricked balloons, and millions of workers, jobless, homeless, and destitute, were forced into the streets.

But the collapse of the industrial economy was only part of the picture. America also was facing the worst natural disaster in its history—not by the sudden and passing violence of tornado, hurricane, or tidal wave, but by the slow desiccation of the seemingly eternal drought.

The seeds of the tragedy were sown in the early years of World War I when wheat prices soared under the demands of European nations. The farmers of Europe had been siphoned off by the insatiable demands of the military and many of their farms and fields had been churned to mud by the machines of war. Neutral America, almost literally, became the breadbasket of the world. Spurred by high prices, farmers in the wheat belt ploughed every available acre and drained any wetlands for which they could create an outlet. Prior to harvest, a man could stand on the highest elevation almost anywhere between the Dakotas and the panhandle of Texas and see nothing but a golden sea of wheat broken only by an occasional farm building. Farther to the West, on soils where wheat could not be grown, ranchers increased their flocks and herds on the national forests and public grazing lands. Signs of the damage inflicted by overabundant cattle and sheep can still be seen throughout the West.

At the close of the war, the demand for beef, wool, and grains, especially for wheat, remained high as the European economy struggled back to its feet and America entered a period of unprecedented prosperity. Blessed by excellent growing seasons, American farmers prospered. Since the early days of agriculture, the ability to plough a straight furrow had been the mark of efficiency, and in the rolling-prairie country of the Middle West the furrows ran uphill and down. No one seemed concerned about the bare, yellow blotches of raw subsoil that were appearing on the hillsides as the rains enlarged the higher furrows to rills. No effort was made to restore the fertility of the soil.

But in 1928, there were few rains to cut rills in the hillsides, and winter snows that usually replenished the wells and stock ponds had been light. The wheat crop fell off sharply and dropped even more in 1930. By 1931, farmers found themselves staring into cloudless skies where a relentless sun blazed down from dawn till sunset. The topsoil turned to black powder, and the sprouts of wheat that germinated turned to chaff before they developed heads. Then came the winds, in hot dry blasts that sent the soil flying skyward in choking clouds that grew thicker every day. Farmers watched helplessly as the water levels in their wells and stock ponds, muddied by the flying silt, dropped and finally disappeared. Motorists on the highways in Kansas City and Omaha drove with headlights on at high noon as the all-pervading dust formed windrows along the fencelines and high banks on the lee sides of buildings and idled farm machines. The most prosperous farm region in the world had turned into a desert.

The Dust Bowl was a disaster for the wildlife of the region as well as for human beings, and the greatest impact of all was on the waterfowl. The area of the drought coincided with the most productive duck-breeding territory on the continent—Canada's prairie provinces, western Minnesota, the Dakotas, Iowa, Nebraska, eastern Montana, and Colorado. Nearly all of the prairie-nesting ducks nest in grassy cover some distance from water and lead the downy young to potholes, marshes, and sloughs as soon as they hatch. A decline in the abundance of nesting cover began with the wheat boom when many natural wetlands were drained and farmers tilled the shores of others wherever they could find support for their farm machinery. With the drought, many of the potholes and marshes that had held water for years dried up entirely, and the broods died of thirst, starvation, or predation while the hens frantically led them overland to promising areas farther away. Often, potholes that retained water longer than others became death traps as the hot winds dried them up and turned their bottoms to cracked clay before the young birds could fly.

In the fall of 1929, the drought-stricken flights began to dwindle, and Paul G. Redington cut the bag limit from twenty-five to fifteen ducks a day. But in the hunting season of 1930, duck flights from the north became trickles.

One man who watched this natural tragedy unfold was Frederic C. Walcott, a founder of the American Game Protective Association, who had been elected to the Senate from Connecticut in 1929. In 1930, he and Senator Harry B. Hawes of Missouri, who as a congressman had sponsored the bill for the Upper Mississippi Fish and Wildlife Refuge, introduced a Senate resolution calling for the creation of a special committee for wildlife. The resolution was adopted by the Senate on April 17, 1930. The committee was responsible for enacting some of the most important wildlife-conservation legislation ever written.

In 1931, as the waterfowl picture turned from gray to black, this committee made the waterfowl situation its first order of business. Out of the lengthy debates on the old refuge-public shooting grounds bills, two half-forgotten proposals were recalled and dragged back into the light. The American Game Protective Association had favored the sale of a federal stamp with which to finance a wetlands-acquisition program; More Game Birds in America Foundation had favored a one-cent tax on shotgun shells. At a hearing held by the committee on April 4, 1932, in which more than one hundred witnesses testified, the tax proposal was dropped on the grounds that upland-game hunters should not be taxed to benefit waterfowl.

After the hearing, a group of experts prepared a bill for the committee authorizing the sale of a one-dollar federal stamp with the proceeds earmarked for the purchase, development, and management of waterfowl refuges. The bill was introduced in the Senate by Walcott and in the House by Congressman Richard Kleberg of Texas. The Migratory Bird Hunting Stamp Act became law on March 16, 1934. The artist who designed the first stamp was a political cartoonist called "Ding" who soon would have much to do with administering the law.

Franklin Delano Roosevelt was sworn into office on March 4, 1933, bringing with him a whole package of sweeping social, fiscal, and legislative reforms that would touch the lives of every American and alter the face of the land.

At a meeting with the members of the Special Committee on the Conservation of Wildlife on December 20, 1933, the new President promised to set aside a million dollars in emergency funds for the acquisition of waterfowl breeding and feeding grounds, and to put Civilian Conservation Corps camps on the areas to develop them. Then on January 8, 1934, he appointed a special committee consisting of Jay N. Darling, Leopold, and Thomas Beck to devise a wildlife-conservation program that would dovetail with his submarginal land-elimination program. The fulfillment of FDR's promise, offered in the first warm glow of political victory, did not come as easily as its giving.

Shortly after this special committee had completed its deliberation, Paul G. Redington resigned as chief of the Bureau of Biological Survey, and Jay N. Darling on March 1, 1934, was named as his successor, a choice that amazed no one more than Darling. Except for serving on the Iowa Game and Fish Commission, he possessed little or no experience as an administrator. By profession he was a newspaperman, originally a reporter but more recently a Pulitzer Prize winning political cartoonist who, when occasion demanded, could draw with a barbed pen in acid ink. Moreover, although he was a close friend of Henry A. Wallace, FDR's Secretary of Agriculture, he was a Republican, and much of his recent fame, under the pen-name "Ding," had been built upon searing cartoons aimed at none other than the President himself. He was the most incisive and persistent critic of wildlife programs under the New Deal, and in his appointment Roosevelt may have seen a graceful way to remove a thorn from sensitive political flesh.

If there were doubts about Darling's ability as an administrator upon the announcement of his appointment, they were dispelled immediately. Darling brought to the Bureau an enthusiasm and vigor that had not been seen in years. And, although few were aware of the fact, the new bureau chief also had been a Phi Beta Kappa biology major at Beloit College. In accepting the appointment, he demanded and received from Roosevelt a promise that he would receive a free hand in administering the agency without political interference. He owed no political debts; his integrity was unimpeachable, and a boundless imagination was one of his stocks in trade.

When Darling assumed office, the Biological Survey had a staff of only twenty-four federal game wardens who were sprinkled thinly over the United States and Alaska, presenting a negligible threat to potential lawbreakers. To derive maximum benefits from what seemed an impossible manpower situation, Darling, in one of his first steps, quietly organized newly employed federal agents into highly mobile striking forces that could be thrown into the trouble spots. Duck bootleggers were still operating openly in parts of California and on the Eastern Shore of Maryland, and ever since the passage of the

Migratory Bird Treaty Act, hunters along the Missouri and Illinois river bottoms had been shooting ducks in spring in defiance of federal law.

Ding's "phantom squad," supplemented by local sportsmen and law-enforcement officers commissioned as deputy federal agents, swooped down on the poachers in Illinois in a three-day raid that netted forty-nine convictions. One man who tried to avoid arrest by shooting at an officer was himself severely wounded. Spring shooting rapidly lost its popularity in the Middle West. Similar raids in California and Maryland quickly put the market hunters there out of business and behind bars.

Although Congress still had appropriated no funds to implement the Migratory Bird Conservation Act, Darling began planning a series of refuges extending along the Mississippi Valley from the Canadian border to the Gulf of Mexico as a start for similar chains of refuges in each flyway. But as his plans developed, both Congress and the Administration began to stall and renege and to try to divert duck-stamp funds, amounting to $635,000 in their first year of collection, to unrelated purposes. Darling, many years later, wrote: "I am completely oblivious to anyone's slant on F.D.R.'s contribution to the Duck Restoration Program, but so far as I am concerned he blocked me, and consciously, too, in my every effort to finance the program which he himself had asked me to carry out." Whenever Darling reminded the President of his promise of a million dollars for the refuge program, Roosevelt would laugh, dash off a chit on which he scrawled, "IOU $1,000,000 FDR," and tell Darling to present it to Harry Hopkins, who, recognizing it as a manifestation of his chief's pixyish sense of humor, shunted the harried Darling off to see Interior Secretary Harold L. Ickes or Henry Wallace.

But the new chief of the Bureau of Biological Survey still held three aces. One was an overwhelming support for the waterfowl-restoration program that had been inspired by the Beck-Darling-Leopold Committee, which had written every state wildlife conservation group, gun club, and Izaak Walton League chapter asking for support and recommendation on areas that should be included in the national refuge program. As Darling stated:

> The response was magnetic. The Committee, sitting in a back room in the Agriculture Department at Washington, became swamped with thousands of charts, maps, specifications, and recommendations, each supported by voluminous petitions, which—when added together— amounted to twenty-one million acres. Some were good, and among them were many cheaters, of no value whatsoever, but that nation-wide assemblage of potential waterfowl refuges and nesting areas was a major contribution to the plan for Safety Islands along the four

migratory lanes of the Ducks and Geese. They were ready when I was called to head the emergency duck program of the U. S. Biological Survey.

Response of this magnitude, of course, was backed by a public interest which politicians less astute than Franklin D. Roosevelt could translate into potential votes.

Secondly, Roosevelt's promise of funds for the waterfowl-refuge program had been widely publicized, and Darling was not reticent about letting the public know of the Administration's heel-dragging. He enjoyed a personal popularity that cut cleanly across political lines.

Darling's last ace was Senator Peter Norbeck, co-author of the Norbeck-Andresen Migratory Bird Conservation Act. Norbeck was one of the most popular Senators among his colleagues, and when the duck-stamp appropriations were being debated on the floor, it was common knowledge that he was suffering from terminal cancer. When Norbeck rose and asked in a heavy Scandinavian accent for mutual consent to a rider that specified that the unexpended balance of the previous year's relief funds be appropriated for the acquisition of waterfowl refuges, the proposal passed unanimously. This resulted in the appropriation of not one, but six million dollars, as a start for the Duck Stamp Fund. Darling later wrote that he doubted that the other Senators on the floor understood a word that Norbeck had said but that: "If it had not been for Peter Norbeck's request . . . the whole Duck Restoration Program would have completely collapsed."

In 1935, as waterfowl flights continued to shrink, Darling clamped down with the tightest hunting restrictions to that point in history. The open season was slashed to thirty days, the bag limits were cut back to ten ducks and four geese; bait and live decoys were outlawed; the sinkbox went into limbo; and magazine shotguns capable of holding more than three shots at a loading became illegal. Congressmen representing constituents who objected to these stringent regulations descended on Darling's office, threatening and cajoling. Darling met the assault head on. "The regulations," he told them, "will stay as long as they are needed to bring back the ducks, and if tougher restrictions are needed, we will find some tougher regulations."

The loss of the live decoy was a harder blow for many waterfowlers than the reduced bag limit and other restrictions. This was especially true in southeastern Massachusetts, where the use of goose decoys had been refined to an art. On nearly every one of the hundreds of ponds that dot Cape Cod and adjacent Plymouth County there was at least one and often two goose stands, each representing an investment of a hundred to many thousand dollars.

The typical stand consisted of a slab-board bulwark, head high and from ten to fifty yards long, erected behind a broad white beach and fitted with hinged shooting ports that could be opened with the flip of a latch. The beach itself was often artificially built with sand hauled from coastal dunes. During the hunting season the blind was camouflaged with fresh pine boughs. Set back from the blind and often connected to it by a sunken path or tunnel roofed with camouflage, was a cabin or lodge also festooned with boughs. Off the beach there were rafts of wooden decoys, both duck and goose, with a few "attractors" farther out that were often the size of hogsheads. These were to catch the attention of high-flying flocks and bring them within calling distance of the live decoys. The live goose and drake mallard decoys were tethered to pegs with leather thongs on the beach before the blind, while the hen mallards or English call ducks—usually called "Susies" by the stand shooters—were penned inside the blind. Their incessant calling to the drakes, supplemented by the visual attraction of the wooden decoys, pulled in any passing black duck, which was the staple of the New England wildfowler. Some of the more elaborate stands employed between two hundred and three hundred live decoys and as many or more artificial ones.

Southeastern Massachusetts is off the principal flight lanes of the Canada goose, and the segment of the population that crosses it rarely stops unless forced down by bad weather. The stand shooters therefore killed many more ducks than they did geese.

Between flights, hunters who did not care to wait in the blind stayed in the lodge, playing pinochle or poker by a pot-bellied wood stove while one of their group, or a hired standkeeper, watched for incoming birds. In some of the plusher layouts, he was housed in a heated concrete-block cubicle fitted with glass-paned sighting panels.

When the "watcher" spotted a distant V of geese or flock of ducks, he signalled the hunters in the lodge with a bell or electric buzzer, and the men scurried through the sunken trench to take up positions behind the closed shooting ports, peering out over the water through slots or peepholes.

Often the wild geese continued their flight without breaking formation, but if conditions were right, the leaders, seeing the gigantic attractor decoys first and then the live decoys, massed on the beach, now calling in a cacophony of sound, turned and swung toward the blind. At this point, the watcher pulled a lever to release the "fliers." These were young birds housed in special pens back of the lodge.

When the lever was pulled, the front of the pen opened and the birds flew out, circling over the water, and landing on the beach to join their parents.

This stratagem usually ended any further suspicion in the circling wild flock and the geese drove in, and tumbled down almost vertically until they were fifty feet above the water. Then they set their wings and sailed straight toward the waiting guns.

At a signal from the watcher, each hunter flipped the latch on his shooting port and fired just as the lead birds were touching down. There was a quick barrage of shots, a series of splashes as ten-pound bodies hit water, and the crashing charge of retrievers racing to pick up the downed birds. Then the excitement was over until the next flight appeared.

Certainly no one has invented a more elaborate—or more expensive—method of taking wildlife than the goose stands of Massachusetts. Records of individual stand operators and the reports of the Massachusetts Division of Fisheries and Game indicate a rather small return in geese bagged for the investment expended.

In Maryland, North Carolina, California, and the Mississippi Valley, where geese were more common, such elaborate rigs were unnecessary and five or six live geese tethered before a crude blind were all that were needed to obtain an easy limit of geese.

Raising live decoys was a lucrative business. A good call duck could bring twenty-five dollars or more and gun-trained Canada geese fifty dollars a pair. Some men, especially in Illinois and Massachusetts, specialized in raising decoys, and farmers found the business a profitable sideline.

With the abrupt outlawing of the live decoy, many stand operators and breeders released their birds. Many were shot in the next hunting season. But some joined the wild flocks moving down from the North, while others established local breeding flocks far south of the normal nesting range of the species. The progeny of these displaced, feathered Judases over many goose generations probably outnumbers the total bag of all the stand shooters combined.

Early in his career as a government official, Darling found himself handicapped by an inability to locate an adequate number of qualified men to staff the basic research, management, and administrative positions in his expanding organization. To correct this situation he proposed the extension of training programs that already had proved successful in his home state. In 1931, under Darling's leadership, the organized sportsmen of Iowa had pressed through a state law which removed the conservation department from political influence, the first such law in the United States. The first task that the new non-partisan commission undertook was a complete survey of the recreational and wildlife resources of the state with a view toward establishing a 25-year program for the commission. A prominent member of the survey team was Aldo Leopold, and when it became apparent that the task assigned the survey team could not be carried out without the services of trained technicians, he suggested that a training school in fish and wildlife management be established in Iowa State College at Ames. This project was estimated to cost $9,000 per year. Darling accepted the proposal and offered to pay one third of the cost from his personal funds if the state fish and wildlife commission and the college would share the balance of the expenses in funds or services.

On the basis of three years of successful service from the Ames training school, Darling took an expanded version of his idea to Washington. His proposal for a national program involved the creation of similar wildlife units at nine land-grant colleges with a combined budget of $234,000 for three years. Two-thirds of this amount was pledged by the colleges and the state conservation agencies, but there still remained $81,000 for which no immediate source could be found. Darling's efforts to obtain this sum from the Administration got nowhere.

In his search for funds, Darling invited a group of industrialists to join him in a dinner meeting at the Waldorf-Astoria Hotel in New York City on April 24, 1934, and laid his case before them. As a result of his plea, the duPont Company, Hercules Powder Company, and Remington Arms Company, sparked by the enthusiasm of C. K. Davis, president of Remington, agreed to underwrite the proposed wildlife training courses and to subscribe funds for several other of Darling's pet projects. Out of this single meeting there emerged, directly or indirectly, the Cooperative Wildlife Research Unit Program, the American Wildlife Institute, the North American Wildlife Foundation, the National Wildlife Federation, and the North American Wildlife and Natural Resources Conference.

With this financial backing, Darling and Senator Walcott, on July 16, called a larger meeting at which was founded the American Wildlife Institute, to carry on the expanded public activities of the American Game Protective and Propagation Association, which then became inactive, although it retained its charter and continued its legal entity in order to protect certain endowments. The new Institute came into being officially on August 20, 1935, with Thomas H. Beck as president. Five months later, on February 6, 1936, Beck was succeeded as president by former Senator Walcott.

The Cooperative Wildlife Research Unit Program gathered steam rapidly. Ten land-grant colleges were selected to initiate a research and training program under the supervision of a biologist in the employ of the Bureau of Biological Survey. Each was required to contribute $6,000 in funds, services, or equipment to match equal contributions from the American Wildlife Institute, the Bureau, and the state wildlife agency in which the unit was located. Since that date, this program, expanded to include twenty colleges and universities, has produced an amazing volume of original information on wildlife problems and has developed scores of new techniques in wildlife management while training thousands of young men for professional careers in wildlife work.

At his eventful dinner meeting on April 24, 1934, Darling had suggested that there was a need for a federation of all of the hundreds of local, county, and state organizations that were interested in wildlife conservation. In that year there were more than six thousand sportsmen's and conservation clubs in North America, but their work, as Darling realized, was not effective except in local matters because of the lack of a central coordinating organization on the national scene. The creation of such an organization was one of the first assigned tasks of the newly organized American Wildlife Institute.

In the fall of 1934, while attending a conservation meeting in Chicago, Darling had met C. R. Gutermuth, a young and dynamic banker from Elkhart, Indiana, then director of education of the Indiana Department of Conservation, who had been working successfully for the past year to organize in the Hoosier State, a federation along the lines that Ding proposed. The details of Gutermuth's Indiana plan were transmitted to the chief of the Bureau of Biological Survey at his request in a letter of July 25, 1935:

> The educational Division began operation as such in January, 1934, and a definite program was inaugurated to carry on this work. The state was zoned and a strenuous effort made to organize sportsmen's clubs. This work has been stimulated to the point where we now have 508 active conservation clubs in Indiana. We are unique in this respect and many of the other states are now adopting our plan.
>
> These clubs are local and individual in every respect and each club, in addition to electing its own officers, elects a club delegate. The club delegates from all clubs in each county meet and make up a body known as the County Conservation Council. The county body discusses the problems of interest to their county and to the state as a whole. One person is elected by the county organization to act as a county representative and this representative meets with the county representatives in his conservation district and helps elect a district representative.

As a result of these elections over the state we have sixteen conservation representatives who make up a State Conservation Committee. . . .

Replying to this letter three days later, Darling wrote:

It seems to me you are getting control of conservation in the hands of real sportsmen and conservationists. . . . I would like to see this same plan tried in many other states. . . .

A similar state organization also existed in the New York State Conservation Council, which had been established two years earlier by a group of conservationists headed by Karl T. Frederick.

The plan for a "General Wildlife Federation" that was announced by Darling in an address before the First North American Wildlife Conference was almost identical to the Indiana and New York programs, but it carried the concept a step further to the national level. In its charter meeting the American Wildlife Institute had been charged with fostering the new national group until the proposed federation was able to support its own program from its own resources. This had been made clear in an article published in *American Wildlife* in September, 1935, when the proposal was first made public:

The third task [of the Institute], which is all important, is the task of bringing about a federation of wildlife organizations. This is the work of coordination. . . . The Institute will in no way attempt to dictate the policies' or activities of the federation. It will merely supply the temporary machinery to help bring about such an organization, which will be built from the ground up, starting with the smaller units and not from the top down. Once organized and operating, the federation will be *free* and *independent* of the Institute.

Such was the magic of Darling's appeal that within five months after he announced the plan, twenty-five states reported the mobilization of their conservation clubs under a central state federation. Fifteen already had existing state sportsmen's organizations, and four others were on their way to federation. Darling, who retired as chief of the Bureau of Biological Survey in November, 1935, became the first president of the National Wildlife Federation. To finance its program without taxing the financial resources of the member organizations, he suggested an annual series of wildlife stamps to be offered for sale to the general public. Putting his own talents as an artist to work, he designed the first sheet of stamps. This system of financing is still being used successfully by the National Wildlife Federation.

Darling, before retiring from federal service, hand-picked as his successor Ira N. Gabrielson, a big, vigorous field biologist, whom he had brought to Washington from Oregon to serve as his assistant.

Darling served less than eighteen months as chief of the Bureau of Biological Survey, longer than he had agreed to serve, as he was on leave from his newspaper syndicate. But few public officials achieved more in such a short period of time. When he entered public service, in his own words, wildlife was "the orphan child, without asylum that has subsisted on the crumbs . . . the neighbors sent in." Eighteen months later, the orphan child was eating regularly, was decently housed and putting flesh on its ribs.

Four years after it was created, and after Walcott had retired from the Senate, the Special Committee on the Conservation of Wildlife Resources was increased to seven members under the chairmanship of Key Pittman of Nevada, while the House created a similar committee under the chairmanship of A. Willis Robertson of Virginia. Between them these committees produced the most productive wildlife law ever enacted. To help finance the massive relief programs of the New Deal, Congress had restored the federal excise tax on many items, including sporting firearms and ammunition, restoring new life to an idea that had been considered in the 1920s as a means of financing the wildlife refuge program.

In 1937, Pittman and Robertson introduced identical bills that earmarked the excise tax on sporting arms and ammunition to the state and territorial fish and wildlife agencies for use in wildlife land acquisition, development, and research. Federal allocations were to be matched by state funds on a seventy-five percent federal–twenty-five percent state basis. Since some states had vast areas with small populations and others, especially those in the East, high population densities compressed into relatively small areas, allocations would be made on a formula based fifty percent on the number of licensed hunters and fifty percent on the basis of the area of the state or territory in relation to the entire area of the United States.

One of the most farsighted features was an eligibility requirement that each state pass an enabling act that prohibited the diversion of hunting-license revenues for any purpose other than the administration of its fish and wildlife agency. The Pittman-Robertson Federal Aid in Wildlife Restoration Act became law on September 2, 1937. Forty-three of the forty-eight states passed enabling acts in the first year, and all states became eligible soon thereafter.

This ended the practice, common in many states, of raiding the fish and wildlife agency funds for constructing schools, building roads, and similar activities unrelated to wildlife conservation. In the first year, the excise tax brought in $2,976,019.

With this financial backing and with new authority, the federal and state conservation agencies began the most aggressive and constructive wildlife-restoration program ever known.

President Roosevelt brought to fruition one of Darling's proposals a year after the latter retired from federal office. This was the calling of a national conference on fish and wildlife conservation to bring together all North American agencies, organizations, and interests concerned with wildlife resources and the soils, waters, and forests that supported them. In 1935, Roosevelt issued a call for such a conference.

The conference committee, organized under the chairmanship of F. A. Silcox, chief forester of the United States, included Darling, Ira N. Gabrielson, his successor as chief of the Bureau of Biological Survey, and twenty other federal and state officials and leaders of the more prominent private conservation organizations. Held on February 3–7 in Washington's Mayflower Hotel, the First North American Wildlife Conference was a great success, and its proceedings, published by the government, brought together in one volume more information on the status of North American wildlife and the problems facing wildlife conservation than had ever been produced before.

The North American Wildlife Conference was patterned after the American Game Conference which had been staged annually in New York City by the American Game Protective Association since 1915. Sponsorship of the North American Wildlife Conference as an annual event was resumed in 1937 by the American Wildlife Institute. The conference, now known as the North American Wildlife and Natural Resources Conference, has been sponsored annually since 1946 by the Wildlife Management Institute.

Chapter 17

Wildlife Under the New Deal

The massive social and economic programs that Franklin D. Roosevelt initiated in an effort to bolster the economy of the depression-riddled nation had a tremendous impact on the wildlife habitat of the United States. In the first session of the 67th Congress alone, 110 bills affecting wildlife directly or indirectly were introduced in the Senate and 166 in the House.

Soon after FDR entered the White House, he created the Civilian Conservation Corps to provide employment for the hundreds of thousands of youths who were entering the job market with little prospect of finding work. Enrollment the first year reached 500,000 and, before World War II ended the program, more than three million young men served in the CCC.

Under the supervision of army officers, teams of young workers were dispatched to national and state forests, parks, and wildlife refuges. Housed in tarpaper barracks that they built themselves, they fought wild fires, cleared fire lanes and hiking trails, dug water holes, and created lakes to improve fish and waterfowl habitat. They planted more than two billion trees.

Some of FDR's make-work relief programs were counterproductive of wildlife. While the CCC boys were busily creating waterfowl habitat, hundreds of thousands of other workers under the auspices of the Work Progress Administration were ditching and draining marshes in the name of mosquito control. But overall, the Roosevelt Administration's contribution to wildlife conservation was overwhelmingly on the plus side. They made available for fish, wildlife, and related natural resources more funds and manpower than had ever been expended in the past.

One of FDR's more ambitious projects was to implement the Weeks Act of 1911, sponsored by John W. Weeks of Massachusetts during the Administration of William Howard Taft. Before 1911, all of the national forests were in the West and had been created by withdrawing land from the public domain. In the East, all of the lands suitable for national forests, other than those that had been set aside by the states, were in private ownership. The Weeks Law authorized the U. S. Forest Service to purchase lands east of the Mississippi for national forests to protect the critical watersheds of the region, and to increase the national timber reserves. Although twenty-four national forests had been created by the time FDR entered office, these were little more than outlines on maps in the office of the Chief Forester. A patchwork of five million acres, interspersed with many private holdings, had been acquired, and little development or management had been accomplished on these. Roosevelt allocated more than $37 million of public works money with which to purchase eleven million acres of land to flesh out the eastern units of the National Forest System.

Attention of the Forest Service focused on the Appalachian Mountains, the source of most of the water supplies for the industrial East. Although most of the northern states had done a reasonably good job of protecting their watersheds with state forests, those in the South had not. Most of the forests had been logged off and subjected to repeated wild fires.

The mountains were inhabited by a fiercely independent people, largely of Scotch-Irish descent, whose ancestors had fled to America centuries before to escape religious or political oppression. Isolated in their mountain fastness, they were suspicious of strangers and recognized few manmade laws. In the 1930s many still lived as their ancestors had in the 1730s, in cabins hand-hewn from forest trees, and living off the land. Nearly all kept flocks of sheep for their wool, cattle and goats for meat and milk, horses or mules for transport, and swine for pork and lard. Most of this livestock was permitted to forage for itself in a semi-wild state, the swine to the point where the animals had reverted to fierce shaggy "razorbacks" that had to be hunted down each winter with rifles and packs of hounds.

These thousands of grazing, browsing, and rooting animals and the demands of the people for firewood and other forest products had their inevitable effect on the economy of the region. The mountain soils, thin and fragile even in pristine times, were stripped of cover by overgrazing and burned out by centuries of unrelieved corn production. The southern Appalachians had one of the highest illiteracy rates in the nation, and rickets, hookworm and other afflictions related to malnutrition were rampant.

Attempts of the southern wildlife agencies to restore deer and other species to the Appalachians as had been done in the North quickly aborted in the face of the native mountaineer's Mosaic belief that all wildlife was placed on earth for the use of man. A rifle or shotgun was the ever-present companion of nearly every male, and anything edible was considered fair game. Even if the native's wild-life-conservation attitudes had been more advanced, the competition from livestock would have precluded the success of restoration efforts.

In the mid-1930s there was only one viable deer herd in the southern Appalachians. This was on the Pisgah National Game Preserve high in the mountains of western North Carolina and part of the Pisgah National Forest. The 100,000-acre game preserve was the former property of George Vanderbilt, where Gifford Pinchot had carried out his early experiments in forestry. Vanderbilt had stocked the area with whitetails from Florida and New York's Adirondacks, and by 1916, the area held more than a thousand deer. By 1936, they numbered nearly ten thousand, in spite of heavy hunting of the fringes of the reservation by members of hunting clubs whose holdings surrounded the national forest. This herd became a valuable reservoir of nucleus stock in restoration efforts throughout the East.

Although many of the southern mountaineers resisted relocation, the majority eagerly accepted the government's offer to buy their worn-out acres. Much of the feral livestock and half-wild dogs abandoned by the evacuees was rounded up or shot by forest rangers and state conservation agents. CCC crews immediately were set to work planting trees and improving that area for wildlife.

One of the festering sores left by centuries of neglect of the land was in the Tennessee Valley, a region raped by the last of the timber barons and stripped of its former riches in oil and natural gas. A proposal for the construction of a dam to harness the waters of the Tennessee at Muscle Shoals had originated as early as 1903. Theodore Roosevelt had vetoed a bill that would have permitted the licensing of private interests to develop the choice hydroelectric site. In 1928, Senator George Norris of Nebraska introduced a bill to permit the federal government to construct a dam at Muscle Shoals. It was vetoed by Calvin Coolidge. A similar bill introduced by Norris in 1932 was vetoed by Herbert Hoover as a threat to the private-enterprise system. But FDR saw the proposal in a different light and made federal development of the lower Tennessee a major plank in his campaign platform. Soon after he attained the Presidency, he signed a bill creating the Tennessee Valley Authority, a semi-autonomous regional agency with broad powers to develop not only Muscle Shoals but the entire resources of the Tennessee Valley.

Under the TVA, the entire region was transformed as a series of dams that changed seven hundred miles of the silt-laden Tennessee and its tributaries into vast manmade lakes. CCC crews planted more than 200,000 trees, and local farmers were taught the principles of soil conservation for the first time in their lives. Navigation on the TVA lakes permitted the tapping of rich phosphate deposits, providing abundant jobs for the hitherto impoverished hill people, while new industries were attracted by an abundance of cheap electricity supplied by the hydroelectric dams.

The TVA engaged its own wildlife biologists and, in cooperation with the state wildlife agencies, wildlife habitat was improved, fish stocking was initiated, and deer and wild turkeys were stocked on the newly regenerating forests. From the most depressed rural region in the United States in 1930, the Tennessee Valley emerged from World War II as among the most prosperous in the United States.

The Tennessee was not the only river valley transformed during FDR's long stay in office. Dams were built on most of the major rivers of the nation. The Army Corps of Engineers broke ground for dozens of navigation, hydroelectric, and flood-control projects on the Missouri, Arkansas, and Mississippi, while the Bureau of Reclamation began an intricate system of canals to bring water to California's Central Valley, and erected the gigantic Grand Coulee and Bonneville dams on the Columbia River.

These massive construction efforts had both positive and negative effects on the fish and wildlife resources of the nation. Waterfowl habitat was eliminated by the inundation of marshes, and salmon spawning runs were blocked by dams. Bottomland hardwood overflow lands were eliminated by permanent flooding or leveeing, and thousands of miles of trout habitat were destroyed.

The impact, however, would have been far worse without the influence of another law produced through the efforts of the Special Committee on the Conservation of Wildlife Resources of the U. S. Senate. This was the Fish and Wildlife Coordination Act of March 10, 1934, which required construction agencies of the federal government "to provide that wildlife conservation shall receive equal consideration and be coordinated with other features of water-resource development. . . ." As later amended it required the construction agencies to consult with the U. S. Fish and Wildlife Service and state fish and wildlife agencies in planning water-development projects and to compensate for fish and wildlife habitat destroyed or impaired through construction activities.

Among the first achievements under this act was the installation of fish ladders on the Columbia River dams.

Another significant product of FDR's New Deal from the standpoint of wildlife was the creation, in April, 1935, of the U. S. Soil Conservation Service in the Department of Agriculture. It was headed by Dr. Hugh Hammond Bennett, a big, forthright crusader from the hill country of North Carolina. Bennett was a veteran career government employee, having joined the staff of the Department of Agriculture's Bureau of Soils on his graduation from the University of North Carolina in 1903. A product of the impoverished erosion-ridden clay soils of the South, he dedicated his life to correcting the abuses of the land. While on soil surveys in Virginia in 1904 and 1905 he became aware of the magnitude of the soil-erosion problem. In November, 1928, when called on to testify before an agricultural subcommittee of the House of Representatives, Bennett estimated that the annual cost to the nation in diminished productivity alone was at least $400 billion and that the loss of fisheries alone through siltation would greatly magnify that sum. Alarmed by this testimony, the House voted an appropriation of $160,000 for investigations of soil and water conservation by the Bureau of Chemistry and Soils. Bennett was appointed to head this agency. In September, 1933, Congress established the Soil Erosion Service, and Bennett was named its chief administrator. When Roosevelt attained the Presidency, the Soil Erosion Service was expanded to become the Soil Conservation Service with Bennett as its chief.

Bennett's approach to soil conservation was relatively uncomplicated—anchor the soil and keep the raindrops on the land. Under his evangelical preaching, farmers were urged to abandon their age-old practice of plowing straight furrows. SCS technicians helped farmers lay out patterns of cultivation that followed the contours of the land. They helped develop thousands of farm ponds that improved wildlife habitat, provided stock water, and furnished recreational fishing. Gulley plugs were installed to check existing erosion until permanent vegetation could be developed to anchor the soil in place. Cover crops of legumes that could be plowed under in spring to furnish "green manure" held the soil in place between growing seasons. Where farmers had practiced crop rotation in the past, the common practice was to devote one year to growing corn and the next to hay or soybeans. Bennett convinced most that it was as economical to grow both crops in the same year in alternate strips planted on the contour.

In 1937, Dr. Edward Harrison Graham, who held a Ph.D. in botany from the University of Pittsburgh and who had served for three years as curator of botany at the Carnegie Museum, joined Bennett's staff as biologist and advanced rapidly to chief of the Division of

Biology. Graham's proposals for enhancing wildlife through soil conservation dovetailed perfectly with Bennett's approaches to soil conservation. Each farm, especially those in rolling or hilly country, had areas that, for various reasons, could not be economically tilled. Rock-outcroppings, field borders adjacent to woodlots, lands too wet to plow, and sodded waterways to carry off surplus waters could be devoted to wildlife production by establishing permanent vegetation in trees, shrubs, grasses or legumes. Sterile barbed wire could be replaced by attractive hedgerows of multiflora rose or other shrubs, whose dense, thorny canes would discourage unauthorized trespass and contain cattle and other livestock more effectively than its metal counterpart. The SCS distributed and promoted the use of millions of seedlings of bicolor lespedeza, multiflora rose, kudzu, Russian olive, and similar plants of high value to wildlife as cover or food.

By 1940, with financial assistance from the Agricultural Adjustment Administration and technical help from SCS, nearly six million farmers were engaged in soil conservation programs, adjusting farming practices to include greater acreages of grasses and legumes, applying lime and phosphate fertilizers, planting woodlots and windbreaks, and constructing ponds and reservoirs. Contour farming, strip cropping, and terracing, as recommended by Bennett, had become standard practices and were being carried out on fifty million acres of farmland.

These practices created a greater diversity of wildlife cover than the farming regions of the nation had seen since the passing of the colonial split-rail snake fence. The thorny tangles of the multiflora rose hedges provided ideal nesting cover for dozens of species of song and insectivorous birds and safe travel lanes for rabbits, woodchucks, quail, and similar species. The replacement of 26 million acres of soil-depleting crops with legumes and grasses provided nesting cover for prairie chickens, meadowlarks and a host of other ground-nesting species. The woodlots and shelter belts made the prairies habitable to squirrels, woodpeckers, and deer. Farm ponds and stock tanks created habitat for waterfowl, herons, and kingfishers.

One of the most grandiose projects of the New Deal involved the planting of a 200-mile wide strip of shelterbelts of trees that stretched one thousand miles from the Dakotas through the Texas Panhandle. Chief Forester F. A. Silcox called the Prairie States Forestry Project "the largest project ever undertaken in this country to modify climatic and other agricultural conditions."

Although the project never attained the scope of its original concept, 222 million elms, willows, cottonwoods, sycamores, Russian olive, and honey locusts were planted by CCC and WPA work crews. The principal objectives of the shelterbelt program were to break up the hot southern winds that previously had blown unchecked across the prairies, to provide shade for cattle and other livestock, and to retain moisture in the soil. It also added greatly to the diversity of the wildlife habitat of the Great Plains.

The result of these depression-spawned programs, with the passing of the drought, was the greatest upsurge of wildlife populations the nation had ever seen. Waterfowl, favored by a series of good breeding seasons, returned south each autumn in greatly increased numbers. In 1940, the Bureau of Biological Survey was able to recommend a 45-day hunting season for ducks and geese, fifteen days longer than had been deemed feasible since Darling had clamped on the lid in 1934.

At the end of the 1930s, with trained specialists in wildlife management supplied by graduates from colleges and universities participating in the Cooperative Wildlife Research Units, and with assured funds guaranteed by the Pittman-Robertson Act, the state wildlife agencies were on the verge of launching a massive campaign for restoring the nation's fish and wildlife resources. Most of these plans faded as new black clouds appeared on the horizon. This time it was not dust but the acrid smoke of a second world war.

Chapter 18

In the Wake of War

During World War II, wildlife conservation was reduced largely to a holding action as the insatiable demands of the war effort sapped manpower, funds, and resources from any program not related directly or indirectly to the international struggle.

But with the return of peace after the surrender of Japan on September 2, 1945, progress resumed. Franklin D. Roosevelt had died on April 12 and had been succeeded by Harry S Truman, a forthright, no-nonsense Missourian who continued most of FDR's conservation programs.

The machinery for concerted national effort in fish and wildlife restoration had been built before or in the early years of the global conflict and lay oiled and ready to move forward. At the federal level, the United States Fish and Wildlife Service had been formed in 1940 by combining, under the jurisdiction of the Secretary of the Interior, the Bureau of Fisheries of the Department of Commerce and the Bureau of Biological Survey of the Department of Agriculture. Its first director was Dr. Ira N. Gabrielson, who had succeeded Darling as chief of the Bureau of Biological Survey. Gabrielson was one of the most experienced biologists in the Bureau of Biological Survey, having joined its staff in 1915 and served in field and supervisory positions that involved almost the entire spectrum of the new Service's interests.

There were 159 million acres of national forests under the jurisdiction of the U. S. Forest Service that protected the habitats of thirty-four percent of the nation's larger mammals and a wide range of non-game bird, mammal, and reptilian species. They contained ninety thousand miles of streams and 1.4 million acres of lakes and ponds.

The National Park System provided more than fifteen million acres of inviolate sanctuary for wildlife. When the U. S. Fish and Wildlife Service was formed, it assumed jurisdiction over nearly ten million acres of wildlife habitat in the National Refuge System.

Most of the state wildlife agencies had reorganized along nonpolitical lines to match blueprints drawn by two remarkably prophetic documents. One was the American Game Policy, written by a committee headed by Aldo Leopold and presented at the Seventeenth American Game Conference on December 2, 1930. The second was a model wildlife-administration law drafted in 1934 by a committee chaired by Seth Gordon, then President of the American Game Association, for the National Committee on Wildlife Legislation.

The Model Game Law called for the adoption by each state of a nonpolitical, nonpartisan commission, consisting of from three to six nonsalaried members serving for staggered terms in order to avoid "packing" by the governor or political party in power. The commission was to be charged with powers to set hunting and fishing regulations within broad standards set by the legislature, to establish policy for the fish and wildlife agency, to employ or discharge its director, and to serve as a buffer between the agency and the political arena. The director was to have full authority over the affairs of the agency within limits established by law and the decisions of the commission.

Adoption of versions of the model law in nearly all states eliminated the repeated turnover of administrative personnel every few years and assured continuity of programs. In the earlier days and in states lacking these safeguards, it was not uncommon for the fish and wildlife agencies to lose all of their supervisory personnel after every gubernatorial election, and many constructive programs were aborted before they could produce results.

The enactment of the Pittman-Robertson Federal Aid in Wildlife Restoration Act required each participating state to pass an enabling act that prevented the diversion of funds from state fishing and hunting licenses to purposes unrelated to the programs of the fish and wildlife agencies. In the Pittman-Robertson Fund at the close of the war, there was a backlog of from ten to twelve million dollars in unobligated federal revenues that had accumulated during the conflict and which were available to states for wildlife-restoration work. Under the system of financing state wildlife programs from hunting licenses, increases of millions of dollars in revenues would come automatically as the citizen soldiers, sailors, and marines resumed their interrupted lives.

Before the war, as the universities and colleges began turning out the first trained wildlife managers, technicians, and research specialists, the state agencies had begun intensive research, land acquisition, and habitat development that could be resumed with the return of peace.

Some of the state wildlife agencies had started cooperative arrangements with the U. S. Forest Service under which state biologists worked with forest rangers and supervisors in developing plans for timber harvest and silviculture that would benefit fish and wildlife. One of the more ambitious of these programs had been initiated by the Virginia Commission of Game and Inland Fish on the 1.4 million acres embraced by the Thomas Jefferson and George Washington National Forests in the state. Intensive habitat-restoration work by the state agency, in cooperation with the federal service, was carried out through the sale of a special one-dollar use stamp whose receipts were earmarked for fish- and wildlife-restoration work. Under state law, all hunters and fishermen using the national forests were required to purchase such a stamp in addition to a general state hunting license. In the first seven years after its adoption on June 13, 1938, national-forest use-stamp sales had brought in nearly $100,000. A herd of two hundred elk, originating with animals obtained from Yellowstone National Park, had been established on the Jefferson National Forest. With the removal of the mountaineers and their livestock and dogs, deer, wild turkeys, and many smaller mammals and birds were making a strong comeback.

Following the example set by the University of Wisconsin in 1933, most of the state colleges and universities had created departments of wildlife management, whose professors, as often as not, were products of Leopold's teaching. The ten Cooperative Wildlife Research Units were geared to continue their teaching and research activities. Each unit was headed by a federal biologist in the employ of the Fish and Wildlife Service who conducted long-range research while supervising the research conducted by students. Each unit was financed by the university, the state fish and wildlife agency, and the U. S. Fish and Wildlife Service, with supplementary funds from the American Wildlife Institute. On their return to civilian life, thousands of veterans, under the auspices of the G. I. Bill, took advantage of the opportunity to enter the professions of wildlife management, conservation, and research, while many others who had already entered the field returned to the universities to extend their training in the graduate fields.

There were changes, too, in the private sector. Darling's General Wildlife Federation, by now the National Wildlife Federation, had been launched in 1935 with funds provided by the American Wildlife Institute.

Darling also had envisoned a massive superorganization that would affiliate all groups interested in the conservation of wildlife in a central organization. In addition to the sportsmen's groups, he hoped to affiliate state women's clubs, garden clubs, Boy Scouts, and other youth groups. Under his proposal, the national wildlife and conservation groups—National Audubon Society, Izaak Walton League, American Forestry Association, Ducks Unlimited, and others—would amalgamate into his superorganization. By concerted effort, such a group obviously could have affected the course of any conservation legislation or program.

The weaknesses of this elaborate proposal were apparent to C. R. Gutermuth, who had established the model of Darling's federation on a state scale in Indiana. Each of the existing national organizations had its own sphere of interest and its own history, and none was willing to abandon either. Gutermuth, while supporting the format of the National Wildlife Federation as organized, argued for a small, flexible organization made up of the leaders of all of the conservation organizations who would meet periodically to exchange views and discuss current issues, but take no formal action in the name of the group. Each member organization would be free to take any action it desired on any issue or to take no action at all.

This idea reached fruition in October, 1946, when the Natural Resources Council of America was established at a meeting of the heads of the leading conservation organizations at Mammoth Cave, Kentucky, with Dr. Alfred C. Redfield of the Ecological Society as its first chairman and Gutermuth as secretary.

By 1944, Darling's National Wildlife Federation was in financial difficulty and having problems getting off the ground. Although nearly all of the states had federations affiliated with the national group, they contributed no funds to the parent organization, which was financed entirely by the voluntary sale of wildlife stamps. Darling had retired from the presidency and been replaced by David A. Aylward, president of the Massachusetts Fish and Game Association. Inflation and the stringencies of war had placed it heavily in debt.

The Federation, however, possessed enormous future potential. In 1946, when Gutermuth arrived in Washington as secretary of the American Wildlife Institute, one of his first steps was to dissolve more than $40,000 in debts outstanding against the Federation after printers refused to accept its orders as a poor credit risk. With this boost and under new business leadership, the Federation began moving ahead to become the largest membership conservation organization in North America.

The National Audubon Society also had suffered during the war years. Internecine bickering between state affiliates and the national leadership and between officers and members had dropped its membership to around 3,500 at the outbreak of the war. Its presidency had been assumed in 1934, on the retirement of Pearson, by a blunt, burly giant of a man named John H. Baker. Although he antagonized some of his veteran employees to the point where they resigned, he initiated strong working relationships with the other conservation groups and with the U. S. Fish and Wildlife Service and was largely responsible for rebuilding the National Audubon Society into the strong national conservation organization that it had been in the heyday of T. Gilbert Pearson.

In 1946, the public activities of the American Wildlife Institute were assumed by a new organization known as the Wildlife Management Institute, with offices in Washington, D.C., and a highly trained professional staff. Its president was Ira N. Gabrielson, who resigned his federal position as director of the U. S. Fish and Wildlife Service to accept leadership of the new organization. The old American Wildlife Institute was converted into the North American Wildlife Foundation and was headed by former Senator Frederic C. Walcott, who until then had served as president of the American Wildlife Institute. The purpose of the foundation was "to render moral support and financial assistance to wildlife restoration efforts and conservation in much the same manner as existing foundations are advancing the cause of public health and education." Gutermuth, who had been brought to Washington by Walcott to serve as executive secretary of the American Wildlife Institute, became vice-president of the Wildlife Management Institute and secretary of the North American Wildlife Foundation.

One legacy that both of the new organizations inherited jointly in their dichotomy was a unique facility on the southern shores of Lake Manitoba in Canada. In 1925, James Ford Bell, a Minneapolis industrialist, had acquired a large acreage of the Delta Marsh for use as a private shooting grounds. In 1930, when the drought started and waterfowl flights declined, Bell determined to raise more waterfowl than he shot. On his property he constructed a duck hatchery and engaged Edward Ward, his guide and caretaker, to operate it. Ward searched the marsh for duck nests that were especially vulnerable to predation or to drought, removed the eggs, and hatched them in incubators. When the birds were old enough to fly, they were released to join the wild birds on their flights to the southern wintering grounds. Through this unusual system, thousands of ducks that otherwise would not have hatched or would have succumbed as ducklings were saved.

It soon occurred to Bell that his program could yield scientific information as well as retrieve waterfowl, and in search of advice, he contacted the American Wildlife Institute. In 1938, Professors Leopold of the University of Wisconsin, Miles D. Pirnie of Michigan State College; and William Rowan of the University of Alberta, whom the Institute had recommended as best qualified to provide advice, visited the Delta Marsh and laid out a proposal for a combined research and student-training program under which graduate students working for degrees in wildlife management at Canadian and United States universities could conduct research on waterfowl biology and marsh ecology under the supervision of a qualified director.

In 1938, H. Albert Hochbaum, who held degrees in ornithology from Cornell and wildlife management from the University of Wisconsin, was engaged as director and immediately launched intensive studies of the marsh and its waterfowl. In the following year, a staff of student assistants from several universities was organized. Although Hochbaum continued his research, the student training program was suspended during the war. These activities were financed jointly by Bell and the American Wildlife Institute. After the formation of the Wildlife Management Institute and the North American Wildlife Foundation, Bell ceded his property to the foundation, while management responsibilities were vested in the Institute.

Ducks Unlimited had emerged from the war as a growing entity. It had evolved from the More Game Birds in America Foundation on January 29, 1937, when it was incorporated in New York City. Created at the height of the duck famine, it had set for its goal the restoration and protection of the duck-breeding marshes of Canada, where the federal government of the United States was impotent to act. It was supported through contributions and dues from a membership made up almost exclusively of waterfowl hunters. Its field branch, Ducks Unlimited (Canada), applied funds collected by the foundation to wetland acquisition, construction of impoundments, banding operations, and other research. At the close of the war it boasted forty thousand members who were contributing $400,000 annually and had completed 155 marsh-restoration projects in the prairies of south central Canada.

All of these programs and organizations were waiting and ready when the mightiest war machine in history was dismantled within months and millions of young Americans were released on the fields, forests, lakes, and streams of the United States.

Chapter 19

Bringing Back the Big Ones

At the close of World War II, wildlife administrators braced themselves for an upsurge in hunting and fishing pressure. It was well that they did, for the demobilization process proceeded more rapidly than anyone had believed possible. Many of the millions of young men released from active service at the height of the autumn hunting season in 1945 had been overseas for two or more years. With veterans' bonuses and mustering-out pay in the bank, most were in a position to take a month or two of recreational leave before returning to civilian jobs. Hunting license sales, which had numbered around seven million in each of the years before the war, exceeded eight million in 1945 and zoomed above the twelve million mark in 1947. Fishing license sales increased by nearly half a million between 1945 and 1946.

But on the positive side, there were five hundred young scientists holding bachelor-of-science or doctorate degrees in wildlife management who were again available to resume their careers in state or federal wildlife agencies or in the universities. So were thousands of experienced conservation officers and wildlife technicians, now more mature and with broadened viewpoints of their responsibilities and duties. Many took advantage of the G.I. Bill by returning to college to extend their training and obtain advanced degrees.

Another gain was in the momentum of wildlife-restoration programs that had been initiated between 1937, when the Pittman-Robertson Act became effective, and the outbreak of the war.

When federal funds first became available for concerted wildlife-restoration efforts, much of the attention of the state wildlife agencies concentrated on the larger ungulates, whose ranks had been riddled during the days of the market hunter.

Changing patterns in land use, brought about by Franklin D. Roosevelt's massive reforestation and resettlement programs, had converted millions of acres of worn-out agricultural lands to forest and grassland in the East and Middle West. Much of this potentially productive deer and turkey habitat was devoid of any wildlife larger than jackrabbits. Although the northeastern and Lake States had successfully repopulated most of their available deer ranges by the early 1930s, there were extensive areas in the Middle West and South where vacuums occurred on the distribution maps of the white-tailed deer. Florida, which had maintained one of the largest deer populations in the East during the 1800s and early 1900s, had subjected its deer to ruthless slaughter in the early 1930s in the mistaken belief that the animals were important hosts of the cattle-fever tick.

In the West, similar pockets of unoccupied big-game range existed. The bighorn sheep had been eliminated from much of its former range by market hunters before the turn of the century or by diseases and parasites contracted from domesticated sheep. Ranches with networks of fences, residential development, and highways had usurped much of its wintering range and segregated widely spaced bands of wild sheep in scattered islands of habitat. Wyoming was the only state that permitted hunting, and this under a limited-issue special license.

Considerable progress had been made before the war in restoring elk and pronghorn antelope by live-trapping and transshipment to unoccupied range. Dr. E. W. Nelson's census in 1922–24 had indicated a national population of 26,604 pronghorns. In 1946, thanks largely to prewar transplanting activities, their numbers had been increased to 233,900, with Montana's population alone equal to all of those that had existed in the entire United States in the early 1920s.

With the return of peace, the state wildlife agencies resumed their interrupted restoration work with renewed intensity. In the first ten years of Pittman-Robertson Act programs, between 1938 and 1948, thirty-eight states acquired nearly 900,000 acres of refuges and wildlife-management areas on which millions of tree and shrub seedlings were established. Dams, dikes, and water-diversion projects that benefited the larger hooved species and provided incidental benefits to waterfowl and a host of nongame birds and mammals were constructed to provide reliable water supplies, and dense stands of brush and timber were opened to establish clearings that provided the grasses and legumes essential to the local survival of most species of forest wildlife.

In the Southwest there were many thousands of acres of potential deer, antelope, and desert bighorn sheep habitat that lacked the all-important element of a reliable water supply. Using federal-aid funds, wildlife biologists constructed fan-shaped concrete aprons to catch and concentrate the infrequent desert rainfall. Extensive research was conducted by state biologists and by university students into the habitat needs, food habits, movements and status of the various species of wildlife. Live-trapping techniques that eliminated much of the cost, inefficiency, and hazards—both to the wild subjects and the trappers—of earlier methods were developed, perfected, and put into use. One of the most revolutionary methods for taking larger mammals was through the use of the Cap-Chur gun, developed by Dr. Frank Hayes of the University of Georgia Department of Veterinary Medicine and Jack Crockford, biologist of the Georgia Fish and Game Commission. This gun uses a carbon dioxide-propelled syringe dart to immobilize animals from a distance, either for restocking or to obtain weights, measurements, blood samples, or other research data as well as for restocking purposes. Since its development, this instrument has become an important tool of wildlife research and animal husbandry around the world.

Using these newly developed techniques and research information, the wildlife agencies began massive restocking programs to vacant or newly developed habitat. Between 1939 and 1948, the states transplanted 17,434 deer, 7,162 pronghorns, 1,054 elk, 54 mountain goats, 193 mountain sheep, and 10 bears. The effectiveness of these methods was soon apparent.

The last known native white-tailed deer in Indiana had been killed in Knox County in 1893. In the early 1930s the Indiana Division of Fish and Game began releasing deer obtained from Wisconsin, Michigan, and Pennsylvania on reverting cutover forests and abandoned farmland in the south-central counties of the state. When funds from the Pittman-Robertson Act became available, these efforts were greatly accelerated and expanded. Releases of deer were extended to suitable range east and west of the original stocking area. By 1944, the state held about twelve hundred whitetails, and by 1951, there were nearly five thousand populating nearly all of the southern half of the state. In 1970, hunters took six thousand from a herd of at least fifty thousand.

States in the South and Middle West realized equally dramatic success. Emulating the system developed in Pennsylvania, most used substantial portions of their federal-aid allotments to purchase and develop extensive blocks of forest and brushlands as deer refuges. The Catoosa Game Management Area acquired by Tennessee comprised sixty thousand acres. In Virginia, which before 1930 had only a few hundred deer in several of its coastal counties, the Game and Inland Fisheries Commission purchased and released 1,374 white-tailed deer on prepared release sites. By 1960, the state population exceeded 200,000 and deer hunting was permitted in all except a few predominantly urban counties.

In 1939, there was a single deer on Mississippi's 33,000-acre Leaf River Refuge and fewer than 4,600 in the entire state. In that year, the state released seventy-two whitetails on the refuge, which rapidly became a source of seed stock for transplants to other parts of the state. By 1952, Mississippi had more than fifty thousand deer. Today there are more than a quarter of a million.

The Georgia State Legislature reinstituted deer hunting in November, 1952, after sixty years of closure, and the eleven southern states reported a combined kill of 68,378, double that of ten years earlier. By 1960, as deer herds built up to carrying capacity in nearly every state and signs of overpopulation began to become evident, deer hunting was restored as a pastime in every state.

Problems facing restoration efforts in the West, with its huge masses of public lands, differed sharply from those facing wildlife managers in the East. Unlike the eastern white-tailed deer, the mule deer, elk, and sheep migrate between summer range on the high elevations to winter range in valleys and canyons. As the West became increasingly settled, much of the traditional winter range of the larger animals was taken over by irrigated farming, ranching, and engineering development. Fences, highways, and irrigation ditches became physical barriers across the migration routes, and huge blocks of wintering range were inundated under the waters of irrigation and hydroelectric reservoirs.

Deer, elk, and mountain sheep, whose existence was threatened by the usurpation of their wintering range, were live-trapped and moved to unoccupied or understocked range elsewhere. Idaho obtained fifty elk from Wyoming with which to restock its vacant but hereditary elk range, and Wyoming live-trapped and transplanted 929 elk to protected range within its own borders.

Under protection, elk increased sharply on the headwaters of the Sun River in Montana. But their winter range was occupied by two large ranches, and the animals were causing increasingly severe damage to crops and forage. Faced with the choice of eliminating the elk or buying the ranches, the Montana Game and Fish Commission chose the latter course, acquiring 65,280 acres of prime winter range. Within a few years, the Sun River elk herd, numbering three thousand head, comprised one of the largest herds in the country.

Great areas of brush and desert scrublands were made habitable to big-game animals by installing water catchment devices or by enlarging natural seeps and springs. Twenty million acres of California were supporting low-density deer populations because of the unbroken nature of the chaparral. Research workers found that burning chamise, a dominant plant in the chaparral, followed by heavy deer browsing of the sprout growth and a second burning, was an effective way to create the semipermanent openings in the brushlands essential to the maintenance of mule deer. The creation of these openings tripled the deer population in their vicinity within a few years. The openings also served as firebreaks, and wild fire is a constant hazard, not only to wildlife but to human life and property in much of California. They also greatly increased the amount of water available to deer and the other animals with which they shared the improved habitat.

By creating similar openings in the coastal forests, Washington, Oregon, and California greatly increased the range and numbers of the Columbian black-tailed deer.

Restoration of the wild sheep presented special problems. The California, desert, and Rocky Mountain bighorns had been reduced to fragments of their original abundance by market and subsistence hunting before the turn of the century. Those that survived were riddled by diseases and parasites contracted from domesticated sheep. Loss of habitat, particularly of wintering range, had fragmented the occupied sheep range south of Canada into scattered islands. Sheep had been eliminated from Washington, Oregon, eastern California, Texas, and the Dakotas. Only Alaska, home of the pure-white Dall sheep, had enough to warrant general hunting, although Arizona, Montana, Nevada, and Wyoming permitted limited hunting for bighorn rams under special permits.

In seven years, between 1939 and 1946, Colorado transplanted 241 Rocky Mountain bighorns and, in 1947, traded sixteen from its Tarryall Herd for mountain goats from Montana. North Dakota, which had lost its last native sheep in the early 1900s, restocked its Badlands with California bighorns obtained from British Columbia. The Badlands were the former range of the closely related Audubon bighorn which had become extinct in 1905.

Other states from which wild sheep had been missing for years began restoration work through live-trapping and transplanting with sheep obtained from other states or from Canada. The majority of these transplants were highly successful in dispersing the populations over a wider range and in increasing the overall occupied sheep range. Dispersal also minimized the danger of the population being destroyed by an epizootic or other disaster.

Colorado opened its sheep hunting under limited permit in 1953 when heavy lungworm infestations, symptoms of overpopulation, were found in several herds along the eastern slope of the Rockies. This was the first legal sheep hunt in the state since 1885. Arizona, in January of the same year, reinstated limited-permit sheep hunting for the first time in fifty years. Both of these hunts provided valuable information on the physical condition, food habits, and parasites, as biologists examined all of the kills.

The eight Rocky Mountain goats that Colorado received from Montana prospered in the high peaks along the Continental Divide, even though Colorado was south of the ancestral range of the species. Of all of the larger mammals of North America the mountain goat had been least affected by the influences of man. Occupying the highest mountain peaks between Montana and northern Alaska, it was disturbed only by an occasional hunter, hardier and better conditioned than most who ventured into its craggy haunts. Its range supported none of the lush grasses or fertile soils coveted by livestock growers and agriculturists, and even the miners passed it by. Not long after the first goats were released in Colorado, their numbers increased to several hundred.

Another southern and eastward extension of the Rocky Mountain goat range occurred in South Dakota when a number of goats were accidentally released from a display pen in the Black Hills during a storm.

As a result of these factors, the wild goat may be as abundant as it was in the days of the Indians, and possibly more so.

In the 1940s, in response to protection and improved habitat conditions, moose began to expand their limited range in the states south of Canada. They invaded the Uinta Mountains of northern Utah where historically the species had not been recorded, and extended their occupation of northern Maine. The process was accelerated in Wyoming where the Game and Fish Department live-trapped and relocated moose to unoccupied suitable range. The response of the moose was particularly dramatic in Minnesota, which, in 1922, contained only two thousand of the largest member of the deer family. By the 1950s the population had been rebuilt to eight thousand head and today to more than ten thousand.

As moose increased to the carrying capacity of their ranges, state wildlife agencies in Minnesota and Utah opened limited-permit hunting seasons to correct imbalances in the sex ratios and to relieve browsing pressure on the range.

One of the most dramatic achievements of the Pittman-Robertson Federal Aid in Wildlife Restoration Act was the restoration of the pronghorn antelope from the brink of extinction to relative abundance. In June, 1909, the prestigious New York Zoological Society published an estimate of five thousand as the contemporary prong-horn population of the United States. The first detailed census, however, was not made until 1921 when M. S. Garretson, secretary of the American Bison Society, canvassed every state and Canadian province in the ancestral range of the species. His tally indicated a continental population of 11,749.

In the year that Garretson's report was published, Dr. E. W. Nelson, as chief of the Bureau of Biological Survey, initiated a three-year study of the status of the antelope, using the full resources of his federal agency. The results, published in 1925, showed a population of 30,326 in 286 individual bands in Canada, Mexico, and the United States.

Part of this encouraging increase was due to the protection afforded the animals by the National Wildlife Refuge System. In 1909, the Boone and Crockett Club had purchased antelope for release on the National Bison Range in Montana. The American Bison Society and Hornaday's Permanent Wildlife Protection Fund had combined forces to stock the Wichita National Game Range in Oklahoma. The Permanent Wildlife Fund also contributed money to place nucleus herds in the Grand Canyon of the Colorado and on the Fort Niobrara National Wildlife Refuge in Nebraska. Nevada had established two special antelope refuges aggregating more than five thousand square miles. In 1925, these two refuges held nearly five thousand pronghorns.

The concept of a national wildlife refuge specifically for antelope originated in the late 1920s with E. R. Sans, a predator-control hunter in the employ of the Bureau of Biological Survey who had interested himself in a little band of pronghorns that was eking out a spare existence around a few springs in a great expanse of semi-desert in northwestern Nevada.

In 1928, T. Gilbert Pearson, then president of the National Association of Audubon Societies, visited Nevada to inspect a pelican colony at Anaho Lake. While there, he was buttonholed by Sans who agreed to guide the eastern conservationist on his inspection tour of the pelican colony on the condition that Pearson accompany him on a tour of his proposed antelope refuge. Pearson reluctantly agreed, but returned to New York carrying with him much of Sans's infectious enthusiasm for the antelope-refuge project. He presented the proposal for financial backing to the conservation committee of the Boone and Crockett Club, and it was adopted by resolution at the next meeting of the club's Executive Committee on October 11, 1928. Meanwhile, Pearson had obtained the support of the Board of Directors of the National Association of Audubon Societies to match funds raised by the club.

Charles Sheldon, the Boone and Crockett Club's energetic and constructive conservation committee chairman, had died of a heart attack on September 21, 1928, and it was decided that the proposed refuge should be created as his living memorial. The Sheldon Memorial Sanctuary Committee, under the chairmanship of Childs Frick, had little difficulty in reaching its goal of $10,000, which was promptly matched by the Audubon Association. With this fund nearly five thousand acres around the vital springs were acquired and turned over to the Bureau of Biological Survey for management.

Upon learning of the public-spirited action of the Boone and Crockett Club and the National Association of Audubon Societies, President Herbert Hoover promptly withdrew from entry thirty thousand acres of adjacent public lands and on January 26, 1931, signed an Executive Order officially creating the Charles Sheldon National Antelope Range, totaling 34,325 acres.

President Franklin D. Roosevelt, on December 21, 1936, issued a second Executive Order that created a 549,000-acre game range adjacent to the Sheldon refuge. At the same time, he established the Hart Mountain Refuge in eastern Oregon at the request of the Oregon State Game Commission and Dr. Ira N. Gabrielson, chief of the Bureau of Biological Survey. These refuges complemented one another as range for the Tri-State Antelope Herd, which ranges into Nevada, California, and Oregon. The Sheldon refuge protects its principal wintering grounds while Hart Mountain, during the summer months, produces most of its fawns.

Although these measures assured the survival of the pronghorn as a species, they did little to repopulate hundreds of thousands of acres of available habitat, both on public and private lands. Because antelope do not compete with cattle and are only minor competitors of sheep, ranchers were much more tolerant of these beautiful prairie speedsters than they were of elk and mule deer.

As soon as funds from the Pittman-Robertson Federal Aid in Wildlife Restoration Act became available, the western state wildlife agencies began to correct this situation. Since the antelope does not jump—unlike the deer, which can clear a six-foot fence from a standing start—it can be confined behind a relatively low barrier. Biologists soon developed portable corral traps that could be erected quickly on occupied antelope range. The animals were then herded into the traps by low-flying light planes and trucked or air-shipped to their new homes.

In the first ten years of the federal aid program, eight state wildlife agencies relocated more than seven thousand pronghorns and between 1949 and 1953, ten states moved five thousand more.

One problem that faced wildlife managers in their restoration efforts was the prevalence of fences on much of the antelope range. Antelope must go through or under a fence, and a tight woven-wire fence can prove a deadly barrier. Attaining speeds of more than fifty miles an hour, a frightened band will slam into such a barrier at full speed with resultant injuries and deaths. Biologists sought and received acceptance of fencing design and installation that permitted the passage of antelope while confining domesticated livestock.

These steps were highly effective. In spite of a die-off during the severe winter of 1948–49, Wyoming biologists, in an aerial survey, counted 78,850 pronghorns in the summer of 1950, the largest number recorded in the state to that time. The population today is twice that number. Wyoming and Montana took the lead in reinstituting antelope hunting under special licenses, and most of the other western states had enough to follow suit soon after.

Today the American prairies support nearly one million pronghorns, and bands of antelope have again become a common and stirring sight for travelers in the West.

The beaver was nearly trapped out of existence south of Canada in the heyday of the fur trade, and as recently as the 1930s it was confined largely to the Rocky Mountains and the wilder portions of the Lake States and northern Maine. Because of the known value of beaver ponds to a wide range of fish and wildlife species and for their stabilizing effects on watersheds, fish and wildlife agencies launched beaver-restoration programs as soon as adequate funds became available.

In the first ten years of the Federal Aid in Wildlife Restoration Program, twenty-seven states initiated beaver-research and restocking programs in which 8,470 of the big rodents were moved to a long-vacant habitat. Biologists in Colorado developed an ingenious and spectacular method for restocking the animals in wilderness areas without the time and expense involved in transporting them by pack train. Beavers were packed individually in "clam-shell" crates that self-opened after they were parachuted to earth.

Special priority was accorded to moving beavers that invaded agricultural areas. In spite of its great value as a natural wildlife habitat developer, the beaver can be an infernal nuisance to farmers and road-maintenance crews. It can plug culverts, block irrigation and drainage outlets, and flood out roads, crops, and pasture, and it relishes apple-tree bark with a connoisseur's delight. It considers any tampering with its works as a challenge to rebuild better. Break a beaver dam and it will be repaired the same night. Pull a beaver-installed culvert plug, and it will be replaced tighter than ever within hours.

To compromise the interests of beaver and man, biologists of the New Hampshire Department of Fish and Game hit upon an ingenious device. Where beaver flooding threatened roads, crops, or other developments, and where the presence of beavers was otherwise compatible with the interests of man, they installed long, perforated drain pipes in the dam to maintain the water level in the pond at a noncritical level. None of the furry engineers has been able to solve this riddle.

As a result of these efforts, beaver have been restored to all states in their original range, and annual trapping seasons have been instituted in most states to prevent an overabundance that could lead to damage to crops, forests, or other human interests. Beaver, today, can be found within a few miles of the outskirts of nearly every large metropolitan center in the East and Middle West, after an absence of more than a century.

As recently as the 1930s, the wild turkey was considered a logical candidate for early extermination. And among contemporary authorities, the pessimistic William T. Hornaday was not alone in predicting that fate. Once ranging in abundance throughout the hardwood forests and prairies of the Middle West from southern Maine to Arizona and from South Dakota to Florida, the turkey had been reduced to scattered fragments of its original numbers. It had been eliminated from all of the Lake States and the northern and central Great Plains and all of the Northeast except for the mountains of southern Pennsylvania. Relatively small populations existed in Maryland, West Virginia, Virginia, and the Carolinas. Populations in a few states of the Deep South were still large enough to warrant limited open-hunting seasons, but the numbers in all states were declining, and the future of turkey hunting and even of the turkey itself anywhere in the United States seemed in doubt.

Early efforts to restore the species by raising and releasing pen-reared birds had met with limited success or outright failure. Most of the available breeding stock carried the genes of domesticated turkeys, and the released birds betrayed their lineage by roosting close to farm buildings and by using roads and highways as travel lanes. Even those conditioned to a degree of self-sufficiency in large "hardening pens" lacked much of the innate wariness characteristic of wild-reared turkeys and proved easy quarry for poachers and predators. Live-trapped wild birds refused to breed readily in pens.

When Federal Aid in Wildlife Restoration funds became available, state wildlife agencies within the ancestral range of the wild turkey began intensive research to find solutions to these problems. One of the early approaches was through selective breeding. Semi-wild turkey hens, selected for characteristics that most closely approached the standards of their wild counterparts, were pinioned or brailed and placed in open-topped pens in occupied turkey range. After the confined hens mated with wild gobblers, the resulting eggs were incubated artificially, and any young demonstrating domesticated traits were destroyed. Through this process, a pen-raised bird exhibiting all of the wildness, wariness, color, and configuration of the native wild turkey was eventually produced.

The reestablishment of turkeys on suitable unoccupied range by live-trapping and transplanting of wild birds had been stymied by lack of an effective trapping method. Wild turkeys refused to enter bulky box traps and similar devices and were highly suspicious of the conspicuous drop traps that biologists had used effectively to trap waterfowl and other less wary flocking species.

To overcome this trap-wariness, ingenious bio-inventors developed the cannon trap. When set, the 50-square-foot net, pleated into a compact elongated bundle, was easily camouflaged to allay the suspicions of birds attracted to the site by liberal applications of corn or other bait. A series of mortars was loaded with projectiles attached by lines to the outer edge of the folded net. When a number of feeding turkeys concentrated within range, a biologist, concealed in a distant blind overlooking the trap site, simultaneously fired the mortars, lifting and spreading the net over the birds before they could take wing. With this method, whole flocks could be captured safely and at low cost, either for transshipment to unoccupied habitat or for banding and to obtain weights, blood samples, and other scientific information.

As wild stock for transplants became more readily available, most state wildlife agencies abandoned game-farm operations and concentrated on live-trapping and transshipment to refuge areas especially prepared to receive them by patchcutting the forests and reseeding the cleared areas to grains, grasses, and legumes. Although wild turkeys require large blocks of mature timber, they also must have openings to provide the insect and herbaceous foods required by newly hatched poults.

Through such habitat improvement and leapfrog restocking with live-trapped birds, the Pennsylvania Game Commission rapidly extended the occupied range of the turkeys eastward and westward and moved the population center from its lower tier of counties well north of the midpoint of the state.

By 1954 turkeys from the Keystone State had spread into New York State's Allegany and Steuben counties, and the New York Conservation Department picked up the ball, setting as its goal the release or transplanting of a minimum of 550 birds a year. Meanwhile,

Massachusetts was restocking turkeys on the sprawling reservation that surrounds Quabbin Reservoir in the central part of the state, and New Hampshire, Ohio, and Vermont had all established viable flocks.

In Missouri, where settlement had reduced the original occupied range of the wild turkey by eighty-three percent, the Conservation Commission had spent nearly $100,000 between 1925 and 1944 in a futile attempt to extend the bird's range by releasing nearly fifteen thousand pen-reared turkeys. After shifting the emphasis to the transplanting of live-trapped wild birds, it quickly established flocks on seventy-three areas in fifty-eight counties. Spring gobbler hunting was initiated in 1960 in three counties. In 1970, forty-one counties were open to spring gobbler hunting.

In Ohio, the last known native wild turkey was killed in 1904. In 1952, the Ohio Division of Wildlife instituted a restoration program using releases of wild-trapped birds obtained from other states. Today the wild turkey has been restored to all forested regions of the state.

Through similar techniques, nearly every state east of the Mississippi was able to repopulate at least some of its forests with eastern and Florida wild turkeys, the majority to huntable numbers.

Texas, by live-trapping and transplanting three thousand wild turkeys between 1939 and 1949, soon built its turkey population to more than 500,000 and became a source of wild breeding stock for western states with piñon-oak forests adapted to the needs of its native Rio Grande subspecies.

One of the most dramatic accomplishments of the turkey-restoration program was the establishment of huntable populations of Merriam's wild turkeys in nearly all of the Rocky Mountain and Pacific coastal states where wild turkeys had not occurred in the days of the Indians. In colonial times, the Merriam's turkey was confined primarily to Arizona, New Mexico, and southeastern Colorado. Today there are thriving populations in California, Oregon, North Dakota, Utah, and Wyoming with expanding numbers in Idaho and Washington.

By 1975, the stirring call of the wild gobbler had been restored to the woodlands and thickets of forty-three states and the turkey has been expanding its range and numbers, which nationally exceed 1.5 million. As recently as 1952, official estimates placed the national population at 421,880, which produced a hunting harvest of 47,367. In 1970, hunters took 137,533 wild turkeys in spring and autumn seasons.

Wild turkeys are one of the few game animals that can be hunted in the spring without depressing the overall rate of increase of the population or upsetting the reproductive cycle. The turkey is a polygamous species with each dominant gobbler forming a large harem of hens. All of the subdominant gobblers serve no function in the reproduction process except as standby replacements in the event that a dominant tom is injured or killed. As regulated by law, spring hunting is permitted only after the hens have completed their clutches and are incubating their eggs.

Spring turkey hunting is a sedentary avocation, since a gobbler can detect the least movement by a hunter long before the hunter can see him. To assure success, the hunter must be in position before dawn when the bachelor gobblers are most active. He must be seated immobile against a tree trunk or stump. By accurately imitating the call of a hen, he will, if lucky, coax a gobbler within range of his gun. Most states limit each hunter to one turkey a season, and a success ratio of one in ten is considered high.

As recently as the time of William T. Hornaday, the survival of nearly all of the larger wild animals of North America, beyond the middle of the twentieth century, appeared remote, and even the restoration of the deer to much of the South and Midwest seemed an impossibility. Over most of the United States the beaver and the wild turkey were little more than memories.

That the restoration of these larger animals was carried out in an age of industrial, economic, and technological development and human population pressures beyond the dreams of the early conservationists is the highest tribute to the American system of wildlife management. Moreover, it was accomplished almost entirely with funds derived from hunting-license fees and special taxes on the sportsmen of America, at practically no expense to the general taxpayer.

Chapter 20

The Eisenhower Years

By 1952 the Republican Party had been out of power since the days of Herbert Hoover, and its leaders were hungry for votes. Although the Democrats, led by candidate Adlai Stevenson of Illinois, had lost public favor through Harry Truman's involvement of the nation in an unpopular Korean War, the Grand Old Party decided to assure its chances for victory by nominating a national hero. The choice narrowed down to two five-star generals, the austere, autocratic Douglas A. MacArthur, whom Harry Truman had "martyred" in the eyes of many, by relieving him from command of the armed forces in Korea for insubordination, and Dwight D. Eisenhower, former supreme commander of the Allied Expeditionary Forces in Europe. Eisenhower, big, affable, and with a ready smile, won the toss over the grim, unsmiling hero of the Pacific. He was inaugurated on January 20, 1953.

Although Eisenhower had demonstrated diplomatic skill in a difficult position during World War II, all of his working life had been spent in the military and he was innocent of any exposure to partisan politics. As a result, he abrogated most of the leadership in political matters to professionals who had made the science of politics their life work. The result, for most of the federal conservation programs, was near disaster.

The Republican choice for Secretary of the Interior was Douglas McKay, a wealthy automobile dealer from Oregon whose sole qualification for office was a substantial contribution to the Republican war chest. One of McKay's first steps was to introduce the spoils system to the U. S. Fish and Wildlife Service. Ever since the creation of the Bureau of Biological Survey in 1895, it had been customary under a dozen Administrations to fill the top post in the fish and wildlife agency by promoting career employees from within. The incumbent director, Albert Merrill Day, had joined the service in 1922 and had served as assistant director under Ira N. Gabrielson from 1942 to 1946 when the latter resigned to assume the presidency of the Wildlife Management Institute. McKay promptly fired Day to create a position for John L. Farley, a Republican who had received exposure to fish and wildlife as executive officer of the California Fish and Game Department but whose biological training had been limited. Day promptly joined the staff of the Arctic Institute of North America as director of its wildlife research and subsequently became director of the Oregon and Pennsylvania Fish Commissions before becoming a private conservation consultant.

Among the next to go was Dr. Clarence Cottam, a much-honored and distinguished scientist who had joined the Bureau of Biological Survey in 1927 and worked his way up to the post of assistant director in 1946. He resigned to accept the position of Dean of the College of Biological and Agricultural Sciences at Brigham Young University and in 1955 became director of the Welder Wildlife Foundation in Texas.

Dr. Durward L. Allen, a brilliant young scientist, considered by most Washington observers as second to Cottam in the line of succession to the directorship, also resigned in 1954 as chief of the Branch of Wildlife Research to assume a professorship in wildlife management at Purdue University in which capacity he became one of the leading authorities on timber wolves and predator-prey relationships in the world.

As McKay and his henchmen fired or forced the resignation of leaders and key personnel, morale in the ranks of the U. S. Fish and Wildlife Service fell to the lowest point in its history. Many promising young biologists who had been looking forward to productive careers in public service resigned to accept positions with state wildlife agencies or in private industry. Most of these vacated positions were not refilled.

Ever since the establishment of the national wildlife-refuge system, private interests had coveted the resources enclosed by the blue-goose refuge signs. Most aggressive in their attacks on the system were the oil and gas companies, but successive Secretaries of the Interior since the days of Theodore Roosevelt had resisted these overtures in war and peace. Not "Generous Doug" McKay, as syndicated columnist Drew Pearson dubbed the Oregonian. In eleven years, between August 18, 1942, and August 31, 1953, the Department of the Interior had issued only twenty-two oil- and gas-exploration permits on refuges, mostly on the least productive wildlife range on the larger refuges in Alaska and the Southwest. In three years, between 1953 and 1956, McKay issued sixty-four permits, many on the fragile waterfowl marsh refuges along the Gulf Coast.

McKay justified his action on the grounds that Dr. Gabrielson, as chairman of his Advisory Committee on Conservation, had stated in meetings of the committee that he had no objection to opening the refuges to mineral exploration. Gabrielson countered with an indignant special news release, issued through the Wildlife Management Institute, stating that he not only had vigorously opposed opening the refuges to exploration at meetings of the committee with the Secretary on January 27–28 and December 1–2, 1955, but that he had questioned the legality of McKay's action.

As a result of the Administration's threats to dedicated wildlife lands, Congressman Lee Metcalf of Montana introduced a bill early in 1956 to exempt the national wildlife refuges from oil and gas exploration. Metcalf was joined by Congressman Henry S. Reuss of Wisconsin and Senator Hubert Humphrey of Minnesota, who introduced identical bills to stay McKay's open-handed generosity. These three congressional leaders became the nucleus of a conservation bloc that thwarted the virtual dismantling of the American conservation system under McKay's leadership.

One reason for the low morale in the Fish and Wildlife Service was the fiscal policy of Eisenhower's Bureau of the Budget and McKay's ready compliance with its recommendations. On recommendations of the Bureau of the Budget, the House trimmed $2 million from the already inadequate appropriation to the Service in 1954. McKay promptly made up the deficit by dipping into the unobligated backlog of Duck Stamp funds. In fiscal year 1953, only $3 million was spent on waterfowl land and water acquisition while $36 million was diverted to routine operational, administrative, and maintenance programs in contravention of the intent of the Migratory Bird Hunting Stamp Law.

Throughout much of Eisenhower's Administration, the military was riding high as a result of the Korean War and the ever-present threat of all-out war with China or Russia. During World War II, in response to the urgent need for building an efficient war machine virtually from scratch, the government had opened large segments of the national wildlife-refuge system to military use. Under conditions far less critical than those that had existed during the recent global conflict, the armed forces renewed their efforts to invade the National Wildlife Refuge and Parks System, at times with eyebrow-lifting results.

In 1955, representatives of the United States navy approached McKay and announced that national security demanded that he grant permission for the installation of a top-secret naval station at Cape Hatteras. The Cape Hatteras National Seashore, the first unit of its kind in the national-park system, had been established on Hatteras and Okracoake Islands on the coast of North Carolina in 1937 as a recreational area for the American people. Focal point of the development of the area by the park service was historic Hatteras Light that for nearly a century had protected sailors from the treacherous shoals and currents of the Cape. It was at this point alone, the navy said, that the secret installation so vital to national defense could be built.

Without investigating further, McKay promptly signed an order transferring several acres in the shadow of the light to the navy. Instead of devices to detect approaching intercontinental ballistic missiles or atomic submarines, the navy constructed a prosaic tide-measuring station! Its buildings and structures still clutter the landscape of Hatteras.

Far more dangerous and less frivolous threats to lands entrusted to the Department of the Interior came in 1956 when bills were introduced in Congress to turn the Wichita Mountains National Refuge over to the army as an extension of its Fort Sill artillery and guided-missile range in Oklahoma, and the Desert Game Range in Nevada over to the air force as a bombing range. The effect would have been to wipe out one of the largest remnant herds of buffalo remaining in the United States and one of the few thriving herds of desert bighorn sheep.

The air force also was applying heavy political pressure to obtain permission to use the Cabeza Prieta Game Range and adjacent Organ Pipe Cactus National Monument in Arizona as a bombing range as it had done in World War II. These areas also supported thriving bands of desert bighorns and most of the remaining protected range of the Sonoran pronghorn antelope, the smallest race of the species. Only fifty were known to survive.

In the case of the 59,000-acre Wichita Mountains National Refuge, McKay redeemed himself partly, at least, in the eyes of conservationists by refusing, in a firm letter to Secretary of the Army Wilber M. Brucker, to turn the refuge over to the army through administrative order. Some of this sudden stiffening of backbone may have been caused by a recent public furor attending an attempt by the air force to use the Aransas National Wildlife Refuge and nearby Matagordo Island in Texas as a photo-flood bombing range. These areas represented the sole wintering grounds of the endangered whooping crane. Bitter public and congressional reaction had forced the airmen to beat a hasty retreat.

The arrogance of the military toward natural-resources programs at this time is epitomized by the action of General P. W. Rutledge, commanding officer of Fort Bliss in Texas. Rutledge, early in 1956, signed an order authorizing the soldiers under his command to hunt on the fort's 400,000-acre target range in adjacent New Mexico without benefit of New Mexico hunting licenses. The general received a resounding lesson in the principles of states' rights when indignant conservationists, joined by all members of New Mexico's congressional delegation, descended on the Pentagon.

Conservationists, generally, breathed a collective sigh of relief when, in late 1956, President Eisenhower accepted the resignation of Douglas McKay and appointed in his stead a brilliant newspaper publisher from Nebraska who had demonstrated a keen interest in the welfare of the nation's natural resources. As Secretary of the Interior Frederick A. Steaton sought the advice of the national conservation community and proved as approachable to its members as his predecessor had been distant. One of his first steps was to rebuild the shaky morale of the U. S. Fish and Wildlife Service. In December, 1956, he established two nine-man expert panels made up of the top administrators and biologists within the Service to study and make recommendations for policy and program priorities. He also reinstituted the policy of promoting career personnel within the Service to top administrative posts by appointing Daniel A. Janzen, a career biologist, as director.

Shortly before Seaton assumed office, the Congress had passed the Fish and Wildlife Reorganization Act of 1956. This, in a sense, was a compromise arising from an attempt by commercial fishing interests to divorce themselves from the U. S. Fish and Wildlife Service. In May, 1956, there was introduced in the Senate a bill to create a separate U. S. Fisheries Commission, consisting of representatives of the commercial fishing industry with its chairman to have the rank of Assistant Secretary of the Interior. The proposal immediately received the endorsement of thirty-five Senators, and a companion bill was introduced in the House by Representative Don Magnuson of Washington. Although strongly supported by the fishing industry, it was bitterly opposed by most conservation interests.

In order to resolve this conflict, Herbert C. Bonner, chairman of the House Merchant Marine and Fisheries Committee, introduced a bill that he hoped would satisfy the demands of the commercial fisheries while maintaining the integrity of the U. S. Fish and Wildlife Service.

It called for the division of the Service into two agencies, the Bureau of Sport Fisheries and Wildlife and the Bureau of Commercial Fisheries, each with its own director serving under a single commissioner who, in turn, was to be responsible to the Assistant Secretary of the Interior for fisheries and wildlife. A companion bill, sponsored by Senator Warren G. Magnuson of Washington, was introduced in the Senate. The Bonner-Magnuson Bill elevating fish and wildlife interests to subcabinet status became law in July, 1956.

Ross L. Leffler, who had retired as executive vice-president of the Carnegie Steel Corporation and who had served as a member and president of the Pennsylvania Game Commission between 1927 and 1944, became the nation's first assistant Interior secretary for fish and wildlife. Arnie J. Suomela was promoted from the ranks of the Service's commercial fisheries experts to serve as the first commissioner.

One of Leffler's first steps after assuming office was to try to resolve the controversy with the army over the Wichita National Wildlife Refuge. In February, 1957, after studying the issue, he led a delegation consisting of Suomela, J. Clark Salyer, chief of refuges, and representatives of the national conservation organizations to the office of Charles C. Finucane, Under Secretary of the Army. As a result of this meeting, the army agreed that it could meet its needs with a buffer zone for its target areas only 3,600 feet wide along the southern part of the refuge. Finucane agreed to this proposal and to the relocation, at the army's expense, of two public campgrounds that the Service had developed in the buffer zone.

This compromise was entirely acceptable to Leffler and his lieutenants, who otherwise were in danger of losing the entire refuge. It was less acceptable to army officers on the scene. In August, Major General Thomas de Shazo, commanding officer of Fort Sill, reopened a personal drive for full army control of the refuge. The Leffler-Finucane solution, although made before witnesses, had not been formalized in writing. On September 6, Leffler and Finucane again met and drew up a formal agreement that was signed by both parties and distributed to the press, with a special copy going to de Shazo. The bills pending in Congress that would have turned the refuge over to the military were quietly pigeonholed and died with the adjournment of Congress.

With this long-standing controversy behind him, Seaton began tidying up some of the loose ends left by his predecessor. Early in 1958, he signed orders making oil and gas exploration on the national wildlife refuges subject to the direct approval of the Secretary of the Interior. He expanded the Kodiak Island National Wildlife Refuge by 379,000 acres by closing a one-mile border strip to grazing and other entry to protect the huge Kodiak brown bear from persecution by grazing permittees. He eliminated a threat to Tule Lake National Wildlife Refuge by issuing orders regulating and controlling home-steading operations by World War II veterans that had been permit-ted on the refuge. When his powers were challenged in September, 1958, by congressmen representing the district, he obtained the In-terior Solicitor's decision reaffirming his authority. Through a special order, he restored water flow to Topock Marsh, an important water-fowl wintering area between Needles, California, and Topock, Cali-fornia, that was threatened by a channelization project of the Bureau of Reclamation.

During this period, the Natural Resources Council of America that C. R. Gutermuth had been instrumental in organizing in 1946 be-came an important medium for interorganizational cooperation in the advancement of national conservation programs. Its members con-sisted of the executive officers of all of the major national conserva-tion organizations whose interest and cumulative expertise in natural resources were little short of encyclopedic. Most, although not all, were headquartered in the nation's capital, which facilitated frequent informal meetings for the interchange of information.

Among the more active Washington-based members, in addition to Gutermuth, then its secretary, were Henry Clepper, executive sec-retary of the Society of American Foresters; Dr. Edward H. Graham, chief biologist of the Soil Conservation Service but representing the Soil Conservation Society of America on the Council; Joseph W. Pen-fold, conservation director of the Izaak Walton League of America; Charles H. Callison, conservation director of the National Wildlife Federation; Howard C. Zahniser, executive secretary of the Wilder-ness Society; and Carl D. Shoemaker, former conservation director and then conservation consultant to the National Wildlife Federation.

Shoemaker's long tenure of office as secretary of the Senate Special Committee on the Conservation of Fish and Wildlife gave him an in-sight into the vagaries of the legislative process and a first-name familiarity with more congressional leaders than anyone else in the conservation community. He edited the Council's *Legislative News Service*, which provided a valuable medium for keeping the members informed on the progress of conservation legislation in Congress.

This close working relationship and communication among the scientific, professional, and lay conservation organizations permitted a show of strength on legislative matters and administrative policy that otherwise would have been fragmented and ineffectual. By the mid-1950s the National Wildlife Federation, after a slow start, had begun to realize some of the ambitions that Jay N. Darling, its foun-der, had set for it. It boasted active affiliates in nearly all states, and

was fiscally solvent and realizing a substantial income from its wildlife stamp sales. Under the leadership of John H. Baker, the National
Audubon Society, as the National Association of Audubon Societies
was rechristened in 1950, had been restored with an effective and
growing membership in all states. The Izaak Walton League of America had chapters in nearly all states. The Wildlife Management Institute, with its close relationships with the professional sector, could
draw quick support from the administrators of state fish and wildlife
agencies. Similarly, on matters directly or indirectly affecting forestry
or soil conservation, the Society of American Foresters and the Soil
Conservation Society could marshal a flood of letters and editorials
from their professional constituents in support of or in opposition to
various measures.

The effectiveness of this approach was demonstrated during the
1950s when the Bureau of Reclamation sought to invade Dinosaur
National Monument with a massive dam that would have flooded one
hundred miles of scenic canyons at a cost of $417 million. Although
only minor forestry and wildlife values were involved, the variegated
conservation organizations closed ranks in opposition. The threat was
not only to one of the most scenic canyon areas in the West but to
the entire National Park System.

The sanctity of the national parks had been violated once before
by a water-storage structure. In 1900, when the City of San Francisco
was looking for supplementary hydroelectric power and domestic
water supplies, the eyes of its engineers focused on the Hetch
Hetchy Valley on the Tuolumne River in Yosemite National Park.
Although the valley was among the most scenic in the park, it also
provided the most promising damsite. Furthermore, since the park
was public property, cost to the taxpayers of San Francisco would be
nothing, providing permission could be obtained to develop it. Bills
authorizing the construction of the dam were introduced in seven
consecutive Congresses.

Gifford Pinchot, who considered nonutilization of natural resources
"sentimental nonsense," strongly supported the project. The fight
against it was led by John Muir and his Sierra Club, and the coolness
that already existed between these two conservation leaders turned
into a monumental iceberg. For nearly thirteen years, Muir and his
followers managed to stave off the attacks. But in 1913, the Hetch
Hetchy Dam Act was signed into law, and lovely Tuolumne Yosemite
was gone forever.

Dinosaur Monument had been set aside in 1915 to preserve an
eighty-acre deposit of fossilized dinosaur remains in northeastern
Utah. In 1938, it had been enlarged to include 206,000 acres of super-
latively scenic canyons cut by the Yampa and Green rivers.

Without consulting the National Park Service, the Bureau of Reclamation, in the mid-1940s by publication in the Federal Register, staked claim to two reservoir sites in Dinosaur National Monument. There were also nearly thirty other damsites in national parks and monuments coveted by the Bureau of Reclamation and the Army Corps of Engineers.

Construction of the dams was favored by incumbent Secretary of the Interior, Oscar L. Chapman, and a powerful bloc of western congressmen and senators. Although alternative damsites outside the national monument existed, the Bureau of Reclamation shrugged them off as unacceptable because of expected evaporation losses. One of the damsites in the monument was rejected, even by supporters of the Bureau of Reclamation, because of an unfavorable cost/benefit ratio. But in June, 1954, a bill authorizing the construction of Glen Park Dam as a part of the Upper Colorado River Storage Project was passed by committee to the floor of the House.

Member organizations of the Natural Resources Council of America immediately launched their counterattack. Combining resources, they prepared and published a hard-hitting leaflet that was distributed to their combined membership and the news media. Featured in the report were facts and figures derived from a report by the prestigious Engineers Joint Council that questioned the economic feasibility of the proposed project and the reliability of the data that the Bureau of Reclamation had developed to justify its invasion of the National Park System. On July 3, 1954, Leslie A. Miller, former governor of Wyoming, testifying at hearings on the Upper Colorado River Storage Project before the Senate Subcommittee on Irrigation and Reclamation, singled out Glen Park Dam for condemnation on behalf of the Water Resources and Power Task Force of the Hoover Commission on Reorganization of the Executive Branch of the Government. Then on August 9, 1954, Senator Hubert Humphrey launched a stinging floor attack on the entire Upper Colorado River Storage Project.

Stung by this bitter criticism, the Bureau of Reclamation backed off, revising downward its estimate of evaporation losses at alternative sites—not once but twice.

But in 1955, a bill authorizing construction of Glen Park Dam as part of the Upper Colorado River Storage Project was reintroduced in the House with the sponsorship of eleven western congressmen. It was publicly endorsed by President Eisenhower and Interior Secretary Douglas McKay, by the Corps of Engineers and by the Federal Power Commission.

By this time, however, the united opposition of the conservation organizations had built such a storm of public protest over the impending invasion of the National Park System that it threatened the passage of the entire Upper Colorado River Storage Project. Faced with this prospect, the Bureau of Reclamation and the sponsors of the bill quietly consented to the elimination of the Glen Park Dam proposal and the substitution of a damsite less objectionable to conservationists. Dinosaur Monument was saved for the American people. Since that time, no bill proposing an intrusion of the National Park System with engineering structures has advanced in Congress.

The united conservationists affiliated with the Natural Resources Council of America made their strength evident in another sector involving public lands in the 1950s. Although the national forests were created originally to protect critical watersheds and a national reserve of timber, grazing had always been accepted as an appropriate use of the national forests under Pinchot's philosophy of multiple use. The first chief forester had initiated a permit system to regulate livestock use of the lands in the early days of the Forest Service.

Through an Act of Congress of April 24, 1950 the process for issuing grazing permits was redefined and local advisory boards were established. Under the law the advisory boards were authorized to make recommendations to the Secretary of Agriculture relative to quotas of permits for each grazing unit consistent with the maintenance of other values and uses of the forests. The advisory boards were made up of from three to twelve representatives of the local grazing permittees and a representative of the state fish and wildlife agency. There were, at the time, approximately seventeen thousand grazing permittees using the national forests. At the same time in 1953, the U. S. Forest Service had tallied 35,400,000 recreational visits to the national forests—three million for hunting and seven million for fishing. From the standpoint of big-game animals the national forests constituted the most important classification of land in the United States.

In 1954, the American Association of Livestock Growers led a drive to grant the grazing permittees practically full control over the national forest lands on which they ran their stock. A bill was passed by the Senate that permitted grazing permittees to appeal administrative decisions of the Forest Service to local courts, to authorize the permittees to purchase perpetual grazing permits from the federal government, and to authorize permittees to sell their grazing permits without interference from the government. Further, it would have authorized the permittees to construct fences and other improvements on the public forests. In December, a House version of this bill was appended as a rider to the farm subsidy bill.

Again the conservationists took up the cudgel. Editorials denouncing the federal "give-away" appeared in newspapers and magazines across America. The heads of thirty state affiliates of the National

Wildlife Federation representing more than a million individuals wired their congressmen and senators in response to an appeal from the parent organization. Although passed by both Houses of Congress the offending rider was stripped from the bill in Conference. In January, 1956, the stockmen tried again, this time by trying to have the grazing lands on the national forests turned over to the states, which would have been more responsive to their demands. This proposal got nowhere in the Congress.

One important achievement during the Eisenhower Administration was the creation of the Outdoor Recreation Resources Review Committee, which was charged with inventorying all of the nation's recreational resources and making recommendations with a view toward guiding the future course of national policy toward parks, wildlife refuges, and forests at local, state, and national levels. Created in 1958, the ORRRC consisted of four members from each House of Congress and seven civilians appointed by the White House.

On September 25, 1958, Laurence S. Rockefeller, president and director of Rockefeller Brothers, was sworn in as chairman of the new commission. The members under him were Samuel T. Dana, president emeritus of the University of Michigan School of Forestry; Mrs. Katherine Jackson Lee of New Hampshire, a director of the American Forestry Association; Bernard Orell, president of the Weyerhaeuser Timber Corporation; Joseph W. Penfold, conservation director of the Izaak Walton League of America; M. Fred Smith, vicepresident of the Prudential Insurance Company; and Chester S. Wilson, former director of the Minnesota Conservation Commission.

This committee, between 1959 and 1962, produced an amazing volume of information and recommendations affecting wildlife and outdoor recreation. Their implementation would have to await other Administrations and other Congresses.

Between 1875 and 1900, millions of sheep and cattle replaced the millions of antelope and bison on the western plains. *Credit*: U. S. Forest Service.

President Theodore Roosevelt's proclamation of 1902, establishing Pelican Island as a sanctuary for brown pelicans and wading birds, formed the foundation of the multimillion-acre National Wildlife Refuge System. *Credit*: Luther C. Goldman, U. S. Fish and Wildlife Service.

The dictates of ladies' fashion almost doomed several species of egrets and other plume-bearing birds in the early 1900s. *Credit*: S. A. Grimes, U. S. Fish and Wildlife Service.

The artificiality of early buffalo-restoration programs bothered naturalists, but they were effective in restoring the species to safe population levels in the United States and Canada. *Credit*: Wildlife Management Institute.

In the early 1900s bounties were paid on nearly all animals that ate meat, and predator hunters like this one worked full time at their craft. *Credit*: Wildlife Management Institute.

The fencing of the western prairies and competition from domestic livestock contributed to the decline of the pronghorn to dangerously low population levels in the early twentieth century. *Credit*: Winston E. Banko, U. S. Fish and Wildlife Service.

The advent of the automobile presented new and difficult challenges for the early wildlife administrators. *Credit*: Devils Lake (N.D.) Chamber of Commerce.

Dr. William T. Hornaday (right) with guide and pioneer photographer L. A. Huffman on an expedition in eastern Montana in which he collected specimens of the now extinct Audubon bighorn sheep. Note heap of bison horns on cabin roof behind guide at left. *Credit*: The Huffman Pictures.

By the 1920s, wildlife administrators faced the unexpected problem of over-abundance rather than scarcity in deer and other plant-eating species. Starvation and disease took heavy tolls each winter. *Credit*: Gardiner Bump.

Attempts to meet the problem of overpopulation in Yellowstone elk herds by artificial feeding led to undesirable results. *Credit*: U. S. Fish and Wildlife Service.

The last of its kind! The sole surviving heath hen as photographed by Dr. Alfred O. Gross in 1932. In 1933, the bird was officially declared extinct. *Credit*: Dr. Alfred O. Gross.

The first federal Duck Stamp, designed by Jay N. "Ding" Darling, a mechanism that eventually brought millions of acres of wetlands under federal protection. *Credit*: U. S. Fish and Wildlife Service.

Jay N. "Ding" Darling, Pulitzer Prize-winning political cartoonist, founder of the National Wildlife Federation, and dynamic administrator of the Bureau of Biological Survey under Franklin D. Roosevelt.

President Franklin D. Roosevelt gave his support to the newly organized National Wildlife Federation. Here he receives the first issue of the Federation's wildlife stamps, designed by Darling. *Credit*: Underwood and Underwood.

One of F. D. R.'s great contributions to conservation was his mobilization of the nation's jobless youth in the Civilian Conservation Corps. *Credit*: U. S. Forest Service.

Of the New Deal's many contributions to wildlife conservation, none had more sweeping impact than the Resettlement Act under which thousands of marginal backwoods farmers were relocated on more productive acreage. Their abandoned farms were incorporated into national and state parks and forests and soon developed ideal wildlife habitat. *Credit*: George Washington National Forest.

Hugh Bennett's Soil Conservation Service restored millions of wornout farms to productivity. The creation of wildlife habitat was a major feature of the SCS program. *Credit*: Soil Conservation Service.

The beautiful pronghorn was an early and responsive subject of state wildlife restoration programs after World War II. *Credit*: U. S. Fish and Wildlife Service.

The peregrine falcon, along with the southern bald eagle and brown pelican, declined rapidly after 1950 as a result of DDT contamination. *Credit*: U. S. Fish and Wildlife Service.

The Isle Royale wolf study headed by Dr. Durward L. Allen of Purdue University cast new light on predator-prey relationships. In the remarkable photo above, a cow moose watches helplessly as wolves devour her calf. *Credit*: Dr. Durward L. Allen.

Whales and other marine mammals have been subject to heavy exploitation since early colonial times. *Credit*: Library of Congress.

The Endangered Species Act of 1973 committed the federal government to the management and restoration of endangered and threatened species like the whooping crane. *Credit*: U. S. Fish and Wildlife Service.

Contrary to popular belief, regulated sport hunting endangers no species of wildlife. To eliminate sport hunting, as advocated by some extremists, would be to undermine the principal financial support for the most effective wildlife conservation system in the world. *Credit*: U. S. Fish and Wildlife Service.

Part 5

The Environmental Age

Chapter 21

Catalysts for Action

After the close of World War II the United States entered a period of unprecedented technological development and population growth. The population growth that demographers had expected to stabilize at around 150 million in 1950 did not even slow down as the calendar passed the mid-century point. In 1960, there were nearly 180 million Americans in the fifty states; in 1970, census takers tallied 203,235,000.

Each of these unexpected new Americans, through his demands for food, water, clothing, shelter, and transportation, reduced to some degree the natural-resource base and the habitat available to wildlife. Farming became increasingly intensive and increasingly dedicated to monocultures of wheat, corn, cotton, or other cash crops. With his diesel-powered tractor, plow, combine, mower, baler, and picker, a single farmer with a helper or two could cultivate more acreage than a hundred men at the turn of the century. Between 1930 and 1969, the farm population dropped from 30.5 million to slightly more than ten million while the average size of the farm increased from 137 acres to more than 388 acres. Most of the farm hands and other rural workers displaced by this agricultural revolution gravitated to the cities. As the cities became increasingly crowded and centers of racial unrest and crime, millions of city-dwellers retreated to the suburbs to live while retaining jobs in the city to which they commuted daily. Prior to World War II, the "bedroom town" had been a rare phenomenon, and the transition between the urban and rural sectors was abrupt. Each town and city had been ringed with dairy, poultry, and truck farms that supplied its daily needs and the country estates of wealthy industrialists and businessmen.

With the return of peace after 1945, land speculators and developers, quick to recognize the social and economic trends, began buying and subdividing the peripheral farms. Few rural communities and counties had effective zoning laws to regulate development, and those that did welcomed development as an expansion of their tax bases. As speculation drove up land prices and taxes, the owners of most of the suburban country estates were forced to sell.

Few developers made much effort to preserve existing natural values. Their bulldozers knocked down forests and hardwoods hundreds of years old and pushed them into windrows for burning. In grading, they scraped away centuries of accumulation of rich topsoil and exposed the raw, erosible subsoil to the elements. Most of the postwar single-family homes were built on lots of a quarter of an acre or less, and many were without access to trunk sewer lines and were dependent upon septic tanks for waste disposal. Many houses were built on steep slopes subject to sliding and others on the flood plains of streams.

The result of these developments for local wildlife was disaster. The destruction of the forests eliminated the homes of squirrels, raccoons, and songbirds. Siltation and pollution from overloaded septic tanks polluted streams and made them untenable to fish and wildlife. Moreover, development completely upset the hydrology of the streams as permeable and absorbent forest duff and grasslands were replaced by concrete and asphalt. Roofs, parking lots, and roads served as catchment devices that concentrated rainwater into torrents that rushed to the streams, at times with disastrous effects for downstream residents, especially those who had bought property on or adjacent to the flood plain.

The impact on farm wildlife of the intensified farming that accompanied the postwar suburban housing boom was equally detrimental. The trend toward the use of heavier and larger farm machines and toward specialization in single crops by individual farmers destroyed the diversity that had made the American farmscape so productive of a wide variety of wildlife. Thousands of miles of hedgerows and hedges planted under the auspices of Hugh Bennett's Soil Conservation Service in the 1930s and early 1940s were bulldozed and burned. Potholes and small marshes whose cattails and sedges had provided winter cover for pheasants and songbirds were drained or filled to support the weight of the diesel-powered behemoths. Woodlots and shelterbelts were felled and replaced with wheat, soybeans, or corn. It became common practice to plow fields after the harvest and to leave the soil unplanted and fallow until the next growing season.

Most American farmers seemed to have forgotten the lessons of the 1930s.

One of the reasons for the amazing efficiency of the American farm in the postwar years was the heavy application of new and highly effective synthetic pesticides for controlling weeds and insect pests. DDT (dichloro-diphenyl-trichloroethane) was developed as a delousing agent in World War II and effectively freed the Allied infantrymen of the body louse or "cootie" which had been the scourge of the foot soldier in every war since the days of Hannibal. It also helped free civilian populations of the threat of typhus, malaria, and other insect-transmitted diseases, which had ravaged war-torn nations in every preceding conflict.

Hailed as the ultimate utopia of pesticides, DDT was released for public use long before any adequate research on its effects on the environment was initiated. Farmers quickly adopted the substance as a cureall for the ravages of crop-destroying insects, from cornborers to boll weevils. Foresters found it the answer to their prayers for an effective weapon against the gypsy moth, tussock moth, and spruce budworm. Public-health officials and resort owners found DDT ideal for controlling mosquitos, black flies, midges, and other biting pests.

In answer to this demand, the chemical factories turned out hundreds of thousands of tons, which were promptly applied to the forests, fields, and wetlands by thousands of war-trained pilots who applied their combat skills to jobs as crop dusters. DDT, at first, seemed to live up to its billing. In the wake of the dusting or spraying planes, insects showered down like rain.

Biologists watched this activity with growing concern. DDT was nonselective; many of the insects that it killed were predators on the crop and forest pests, and it was equally lethal to crustacea, such as crayfish and crabs, which have high economic value and importance in the food webs of many desirable species. As early as 1946, Leo K. Couch, a biologist of the U. S. Fish and Wildlife Service, after observing the effects of an aerial application of DDT on forested lands along the Mississippi River in 1945, issued a guarded warning against overreliance on its use before the Eleventh North American Wildlife Conference. But other biologists saw it as a potentially useful repellent of crop-damaging pheasants.

One aspect of the insect problem that was foreseen neither by the entomologists nor the applicators of DDT was a genetic response of the target species to the poison. Although after spraying, the kill of insects appeared total, some, more resistant to the insecticide than the others, invariably escaped. With the rapid turnover of the insect population and its enormously high breeding potential, this soon led to the development of a race of "superbugs" almost impervious to DDT.

This phenomenon first became apparent in Florida, where annual applications of DDT, even heavier than usual, failed to knock back the swarms of mosquitos that poured out of the marshes to harass cottage dwellers and sunbathers.

When DDT lost some of its initial effectiveness, chemists turned out new substances that promised effective control. Chlordane, dieldrin, aldrin, and methoxychlor were developed in rapid succession and placed on the market.

By this time, biologists were thoroughly alarmed. Unlike most chemicals, the chlorinated hydrocarbons from which the pesticides were derived refused to break down after application, but accumulated in the soil and water. Although most of them did not kill earthworms outright, they were absorbed by the worms' organs and passed on to birds and other vermivorous animals in whose tissues DDT metabolized into another substance known as DDE. Through the process of biological magnification, DDT-DDE passes up through the food chain from lower to higher organisms.

One of the first effects of this process was noticed by Dr. Joseph J. Hickey, professor of wildlife management at the University of Wisconsin, who found robins and other songbirds dying in convulsions on the campus. Hickey put teams of students to work combing the shrubbery and thickets around the campus for dead and dying birds. On analysis, the tissues of all showed heavy doses of the metabolite DDE. Hickey became an implacable critic of the chemical industry and of Department of Agriculture policies.

Another unprecedented phenomenon related to pesticides first appeared in nesting colonies of brown pelicans on the Channel Islands off the coast of California. Tracing the cause of a perceptible decline in the number of nesting birds on the islands, biologists discovered that many of the pelicans were laying eggs with shells so thin that they broke under the weight of the incubating mother. All of the eggs collected showed heavy infestation with DDE. Brown pelicans along the Gulf Coast of Louisiana and Texas began exhibiting a similar decline, and by the 1960s had nearly disappeared from the Gulf of Mexico, which receives the runoff—and water-borne pollutants—of nearly a third of the continent.

Then biologists and naturalists began to notice sharp declines in the numbers of bald eagles and peregrine falcons, and less dramatic drops in the number of ospreys. Again investigators found the telltale eggshell thinning in these species and the presence of the poisonous DDE in unhatched eggs.

In 1957, a bill written by Senator Lee Metcalf of Montana authorizing the Department of the Interior to investigate the effects of pesticides on wildlife was passed by the Congress. In response to this law, the U. S. Fish and Wildlife Service assigned a team of experts under the direction of Dr. Lucille Stickel to conduct intensive research into the problem at the Patuxent Wildlife Research Center in Laurel, Maryland. Birds of many species were deliberately fed prepared dosages of various levels of the more commonly used chlorinated hydrocarbon pesticides. Those that survived to reproduce showed the same symptoms that had been found in their wild counterparts.

In 1962, a rather small book hit the book stands of America with the impact of a blockbuster. It was written by a quiet but highly articulate former aquatic biologist who had resigned from the U. S. Fish and Wildlife Service as its editor-in-chief in 1952 to devote her life to writing. In her book she quietly and calmly ripped the lid from the trade in chemical pesticides by documenting the enormous damage that the substances were causing to the environment. She called for alternative methods of pest control and for research into methods and substances that could be applied safely without threats to fish, wildlife, and livestock. As soon as the book appeared, the chemical industry threw into the controversy its highest paid public relations experts in an effort to refute her. In the eyes of the public, they never succeeded. Rachel Louise Carson's *Silent Spring* did more to arouse the American people to the critical needs of their environment than anything published before or since.

The concept of protecting segments of unspoiled America in their natural state had been around for a long time. The idea had originated with Thoreau in the mid-nineteenth century and had been espoused by John Muir before 1900. It reached first fruition in the early 1920s when the U. S. Department of Agriculture, through the influence of Aldo Leopold and his associates in the New Mexico Game and Fish Protective Association, created the Gila Wilderness Area.

In 1935, Leopold and Robert Marshall were among the founders of the Wilderness Society, a citizen's group dedicated to the establishment of a national system of lands from which the works and influences of man would be excluded. Like Leopold, Bob Marshall was a forester, and in 1927, he became chief of the Division of Recreation and Lands of the U. S. Forest Service. In this capacity he was largely responsible for advancing the Service's public recreation and wilderness programs.

Building on the base created by the Gila Wilderness Area, subsequent Secretaries of Agriculture dedicated extensive areas of the western national forests as primitive or wild areas. In 1934, President Roosevelt appointed a President's Quetico-Superior Committee to study a proposal to create a roadless canoe area in the Superior National Forest in Minnesota adjacent to Canada's Quetico National

Forest. The leadership in this campaign came largely from Ernest C. Oberholtzer, a writer and lecturer who had made many early exploratory trips through the area and who became the first president of the President's Quetico-Superior Committee. Subsequently, President Franklin D. Roosevelt established the Boundary Waters Canoe Area, which is among the few strongholds of the timber wolf in the lower forty-eight states. Oberholtzer was among the founders and later honorary vice-president of the Wilderness Society.

In 1964, the national forest wilderness system consisted of seventeen wilderness areas, thirty-two wild areas, and the Boundary Waters Canoe Area aggregating 8,609,659 acres. Additionally there were thirty-six primitive areas comprising more than six million additional acres. But nearly all of these areas had been established by administrative action and were subject to elimination by the same process.

In the 1950s, the Wilderness Society, under the leadership of its executive director, Howard C. Zahniser, began a concerted drive to obtain congressional recognition of the wilderness system. Although bills to achieve this purpose were introduced in successive sessions of Congress, they were consistently blocked in the House by the Committee on Interior and Insular Affairs under the chairmanship of Wayne N. Aspinall of Colorado. The wilderness proposal was bitterly opposed by a coalition of western commercial interests, including the mining companies, timber corporations, and livestock associations.

Support in the Senate, however, remained strong. In 1961, the vote on the Senate floor in favor of the bill was 78 to 8, and in 1963, 73 to 12.

Under pressure from constituents and associates, Aspinall gradually softened his stand. In a speech before the American Bar Association in August, 1963, he stated:

> I can see no reason why Congress cannot immediately give statutory protection for the preservation of wilderness of the eight million acres of land in the national forests that are now classified as wilderness, wild, and canoe, continuing those uses not inconsistent with wilderness preservation and other presently authorized uses for a reasonable time.

In late August, 1963, Congressman John P. Saylor of Pennsylvania introduced in the House a new bill designed to meet the objectives of Aspinall and other key members of the Committee on Interior and Insular Affairs, who had stalled action on a comparable bill introduced in the Senate by Senator Clinton P. Anderson of New Mexico. It called for placing the wilderness, wild, and canoe areas on the national forests directly into a National Wilderness System and making the thirty-six primitive areas subject to further review. The President was authorized to make specific recommendations for congressional action on each area. Primitive areas were to continue under existing administration pending review and recommendation. Other national-forest areas suitable for wilderness classification could be elevated to full wilderness status by congressional action.

This bill proved acceptable both to the House Committee on Interior and Insular Affairs and to the conservation community, nearly all of its members having given full support to the wilderness bills since the beginning of the campaign. On September 3, 1964, President Lyndon B. Johnson signed into law the Wilderness Act. In addition to creating wilderness areas in the national forests it called for the Secretary of the Interior to review every roadless area of five thousand contiguous acres or more in the national parks, monuments, and wildlife refuges with a view toward incorporating them into the National Wilderness Preservation System "for the use and enjoyment of the American people in such a manner as will leave them unimpaired for future use and enjoyment as wilderness, and so as to provide for the protection of these areas. . . ."

A corollary of the Wilderness Act was the establishment by Act of Congress on October 2, 1968, of a system of wild and scenic rivers. The Wild and Scenic Rivers Act set aside segments of seven major rivers in their free-flowing state for recreational and other conservation purposes and authorized the Secretary of the Interior to submit recommendations for including other still-unspoiled streams in the system, as had been recommended by the Outdoor Recreation Resources Review Committee. Like the Wilderness Act, it assured the preservation of large blocks of fish and wildlife habitat that otherwise would have been subject to loss through development.

The recommendations of the Outdoor Recreation Resources Review Committee, which had been formed under President Eisenhower, served as a blueprint for the Administrations of John F. Kennedy and Lyndon B. Johnson in their approach to recreational and environmental matters.

One recommendation of ORRRC that was adopted by Kennedy was the establishment of a Land and Water Conservation Fund that could be used to acquire in federal ownership tracts of privately owned lands and waters with outstanding scenic, recreational, and other public values. After acquisition, the areas were to be incorporated into existing national, state, or local park systems, wildlife-management areas, or recreational programs.

The Land and Water Conservation Act became a law on September 3, 1964, and the Bureau of Outdoor Recreation was authorized to administer it. Established in 1962, its first director was Edward C. Crafts, former chief of the Division of Forest Economics Research of the U. S. Forest Service.

The new law inaugurated a number of important actions. It authorized all federal land-management agencies with holdings open to the public to charge entrance fees for recreational entry, congressional appropriations for the fund of up to $300 million annually, and the earmarking of federal taxes on motor boat fuels. Annual allocations of funds to the states under a matching system were patterned loosely after those already used effectively in the Pittman-Robertson Federal Aid in Wildlife Restoration Act and the Dingell-Johnson Federal Aid in Fisheries Restoration Act. The Act contains a clause providing special authorization for using part of the funds for the benefit of endangered species, and the natural areas acquired by the states and federal government benefited a wide range of fish and wildlife.

Although the Land and Water Conservation Act has played an important role in wildlife conservation, it has failed to meet the full potential foreseen for it by the fish and wildlife conservationists who had supported it. One reason has been the interpretation by successive Offices of Management and Budget and administrative leaders that the principal purpose of the fund was to build city skating rinks, playgrounds, and similar installations rather than to preserve suburban open space convenient to city dwellers, and to expand park and wildlife management and refuge systems. Although Congress was already appropriating funds for such urban installations through the open-space program of the Department of Housing and Urban Development, budget-minded officials and politicians increasingly diverted Land and Water Conservation Fund appropriations to inner-city use while virtually eliminating the HUD open-space funds.

Part of this was a spinoff of the White House Conference on Natural Beauty, called by President Johnson in Washington, D. C., on May 24 and 25, 1965, which, although embracing everything from billboard control and roadside beautification to wilderness preservation, focused on the critical problems of the inner cities. As a result of this meeting, Johnson, by an Executive Order signed on May 4, 1966, established a President's Council on Recreation and Natural Beauty consisting of six cabinet members, the chairmen of the Federal Power Commission and the Tennessee Valley Authority, and the Administrator of General Services, under the chairmanship of Vice-President Hubert H. Humphrey. Edward C. Crafts became chairman. To assist the Council, Johnson also appointed a blue-ribbon Advisory Board consisting of ten prominent citizens under the chairmanship of Laurence S. Rockefeller. The report of this committee was a major influence in reshaping and broadening national conservation policy.

Another citizens' committee whose deliberations affected the course of wildlife-conservation programs in the 1960s and beyond was the

Special Advisory Board on Wildlife Management for the Secretary of the Interior. Chaired by Dr. A. Starker Leopold, son of Aldo Leopold and professor of zoology at the University of California in Berkeley, its members were Dr. Stanley A. Cain, chairman of the School of Natural Resources at the University of Michigan; Dr. Clarence Cottam, director of the Welder Wildlife Foundation in Texas; Dr. Ira N. Gabrielson, president of the Wildlife Management Institute; and Thomas L. Kimball, executive director of the National Wildlife Federation. After Cain was appointed Assistant Secretary of the Interior for Fish and Wildlife and Parks, his place on the committee was taken by Ian McTaggart Cowan, professor of zoology at the University of British Columbia.

During its existence between 1962 and 1968, this expert committee, appointed by Secretary of the Interior Stewart L. Udall, produced three major study reports with recommendations for improving park and wildlife administration. The first, dealing with wildlife problems in the national parks, was submitted to the Secretary on March 4, 1963. Although recognizing that it would be impossible to restore any national park or other natural area to its pristine state, it called for every effort by the National Park Service to move as far as possible in that direction. It called for the phasing out of extraneous development—golf courses, ski lifts, and motorboat marinas—that conflicted with the fundamental purposes of the parks. It recommended the removal and exclusion, wherever feasible, of exotic plants and animals and the encouragement of native species. It opposed public hunting in the parks but recognized the need for controlling populations of grazing and browsing animals and those threatening human safety. The committee further recommended the restoration, wherever possible, of natural predator-prey relationships by reintroducing cougars, wolves, and other large predators where this could be done without conflict with neighboring livestock production.

One recommendation was particularly important. Tracing the ecological history of the parks, it contrasted the present vegetation with that described, painted, or photographed by early explorers. In many places grasslands that, in early times, supported bison and antelope have been replaced by thickets of pines and brush with little value for wildlife. The reason, they recognized, was the traditional policy of the Park Service to exclude fire from its holdings, a policy that dated back to the early years of Yellowstone National Park.

Not only had this invasion of former grasslands and parklands by woody vegetation eliminated species of plants and animals that the parks were established to protect, but it compounded the potential damage of future fires by building up dangerous accumulations of combustible plant debris. As a result of this recommendation the National Park Service engaged Dr. Bruce Kilgore to conduct studies on controlled or prescribed burning in Kings Canyon National Park. Kilgore's studies resulted in substantial changes in Park Service policy relative to fire, and even the U. S. Forest Service, patron of Smokey the Bear, altered its stand on the use of fire as a tool of forestry and wildlife management. Lightning-set fires, which once brought in smoke-jumping fire-fighters at the first wisp of smoke, are now often permitted to burn unchecked, as long as they do not threaten human life and property or other natural values of the forest. In other places and in other situations, foresters are now deliberately setting the torch to woodlands and forests to reduce fire hazards and to encourage the germination of tree seeds that become viable only under intense heat. Incidental benefits to bighorn sheep, deer, elk, and a host of lesser forms of wildlife are substantial.

Before it closed its books with the return of Stewart Udall to private life, the Special Advisory Board on Wildlife Management for the Secretary of the Interior completed two more significant documents. One, submitted in 1968, dealt with the management of the National Wildlife Refuge System; the other, presented to the Secretary on March 4, 1964, delved into the thorny problem of predator and rodent control in the United States.

Chapter 22
The Meat Eaters

Predator-control policy is one of the most controversial issues involving North American wildlife. This was not always the case. Until very recently, public opinion almost universally held that "the only good varmint is a dead one." This concept was shared, not only by farmers, ranchers, and sportsmen, but by some of the leading natural scientists in the country. As late as 1931, Hornaday listed as "pest birds, to be kept shot down to a low point," the horned, barred, and screech owls; the duck hawk (peregrine falcon); goshawk, sharp-shinned and Cooper's hawks; crow; blue jay; purple grackle; magpie; white-headed (bald) eagle in Alaska; and golden eagle. "The gray wolf should always be killed. No danger of his extermination."

This attitude was a legacy from a recent past when farmers and ranchers were trying to carve homes from an untamed wilderness. Their cattle, sheep, horses, and poultry, vital to their prosperity if not to their survival, were vulnerable to a host of predators. The fact that wolves, coyotes, bears, and other predators turned to stock killing because of a reduction by settlement of their natural prey, and that sheep and cattle were easier to kill than deer and bison, is beside the point. The frontiersmen hated predators with a burning passion.

In the 1800s bounty systems aimed at exterminating predators were almost universal. Individual ranchers, livestock associations, states, and counties paid cash rewards for the tails or scalps of any animal that ate meat. Some ranchers employed predator hunters full time, while other trappers or hunters made their living by hunting for the bounties.

The most popular instrument of destruction used by the predator hunters in the late 1800s was strychnine, a highly toxic alkaloid derivative of seeds from the West Indian nux vomica tree. Steel traps, especially those used for taking wolves and bears, are heavy and bulky and take only a single animal at a time. A single packhorse could carry more than a hundred pounds of strychnine, enough to saturate thousands of baits consisting of chunks of meat or whole carcasses of deer, antelope, rabbits, or other range animals, each capable of killing from one to a dozen or more coyotes, wolves, and other meat-eating animals in a night. Individual strings of poisoned baits often extended for many miles across the prairies.

When the federal government, at the behest of livestock interests, entered the predator-control picture in 1915, the Bureau of Biological Survey was selected as the logical agency to "conduct experiments and demonstrations in destroying wolves, prairie dogs, and other animals injurious to animal husbandry" as stipulated in the authorization act of June 30, 1914. With an appropriation of $125,000 the Bureau hired professional trappers and hunters to carry out field operations, and organized the western livestock ranges into control districts, each with a staff of field personnel under a qualified district supervisor.

In the face of this organization the prairie wolves dwindled rapidly. Grizzly bears and cougars, never abundant, were greatly reduced in numbers, and their range became restricted almost entirely to the more mountainous areas of the West. By 1950, the wolf south of Canada had become reduced to remnant populations in northern Minnesota and Wisconsin, Michigan's Upper Peninsula, and a few localities in the Rocky Mountains. The range of the red wolf shrank to a few swamps and thickets in Arkansas, Louisiana, and Texas. Poison and traps eliminated many of these scattered packs by 1960, and the Bureau's predator-control experts shifted their emphasis to lesser meat eaters, such as coyotes and foxes, and rodents, especially prairie dogs, which competed with domesticated cattle and sheep for grass, and whose concentrated burrows posed threats to horses and cattle. Hundreds of prairie-dog towns were systematically poisoned or gassed with cyanide fumes.

Until around 1930, few people questioned the necessity or value of these programs, although some naturalists and sportsmen's groups expressed alarm over their effects on nontarget species, especially the bears, eagles, and other flesh eaters that were poisoned or trapped incidentally to wolf control. The program was accepted generally as one essential to the livestock industry and important to the national economy. Conditioned since early childhood to consider the wolf as a slavering, snarling menace and the fox and coyote as thievish villains, most of the American public could have cared less if the whole lot were exterminated.

Public attitudes changed rapidly after World War II. Conservationists, including some staff members and officials of the Fish and Wildlife Service, began to question the necessity for such a broad-scale program. The need for some control, especially of individual stock-killing animals, was recognized, but the government hunters and poisoners frequently plied their trade in areas far from the livestock ranges. Local government hunters were increasingly accused, often justifiably, of "drumming up trade" by visiting ranchers and convincing them of the need for predator control on their lands even though the ranchers themselves had not recognized the necessity before.

This early opposition hardened and broadened after World War II. During the war a particularly lethal poison was developed as a rodenticide. Compound 1080, sodium monofluoroacetate, is a white powder resembling powdered sugar, completely soluble in water, tasteless and odorless. A teaspoonful sprinkled on a chunk of meat can kill the largest predator. The trouble with 1080, unlike strychnine and other common poisons used before the war, is that it is absorbed and remains as effective as ever in the tissues of any animal ingesting it. The carcass of a coyote killed by 1080 becomes a death trap for any scavenger—skunk, fox, vulture, or eagle—feeding upon it. Deaths of several of the extremely rare California condors were attributed to 1080 poisoning before its use was finally banned.

Conservation groups really rebelled when government agents and ranchers began broadcasting 1080 baits over the ranges from aircraft. As a result of this opposition, the distribution of 1080 was brought under rigid federal control, its private use was banned, and later its manufacture and importation were prohibited.

Attending these developments was a rapidly changing public attitude toward predators. Before World War II, attitudes toward the wolf had been molded largely by literature dating from the time of Aesop that depicted the big wild dog as a vicious killer, if not a man-eater. After World War II, with the development of television and color motion picture film, Walt Disney Studios began releasing nature films, beautifully photographed and skillfully edited, that showed wildlife in a more or less natural state—predators rarely caught up with their prey and usually went hungry. Although heavily laced with anthropomorphism, Disney's films gave the American public a new insight into the characteristics of wild animals they never had before. Through the magic of the lens and film, the early public image of the wolf—confirmed by visits to zoos, where glassy-eyed, unhappy specimens paced endlessly on concrete floors behind bars—was transformed from an ugly brute to a beautiful, interesting, and at times playful creature. The sleek beauty of the hunting cougar, the comical antics of the otter, and the flowing grace of the running coyote or fox were captured on film and piped into American living rooms.

Disney's success prompted other film and TV producers to enter the nature market, each with his own style ranging from cloying sentimentality to factual, highly authentic presentations of life in the wild.

Others, exploiting the children's market, produced serialized stories in which trained wild animal characters played leading roles. In many situations, the protagonist animals exhibited much more intelligence than their human co-actors whom they constantly rescued from highly improbable, hazardous situations. In search of a villain, many of the Hollywood and Greenwich Village writers cast the sport hunter as the ultimate enemy of the wild hero and his furry and feathered friends. Few television programs have given more than passing notice to the fact that without the efforts and money contributed by America's sportsmen over many years, many of the animals so intriguingly depicted probably would have been extinct or reduced to captive remnants in zoos.

The most flagrant distortion of wildlife management came in January, 1971, when the National Broadcasting Company released to its network stations a one-hour special film called *Say Goodbye*. Purporting to be designed to call public attention to the fate of America's endangered species, it emerged as a violent diatribe against hunting. No mention was made of the fact that shooting was a factor in the decline of only a few of the American species on the endangered list or that habitat deficiencies are the major problems facing all endangered species.

Say Goodbye was especially effective as a public-opinion molder because of its heavy-handed use of shock effect. In one scene, a prairie dog literally exploded under the impact of a high-powered rifle bullet. The death of a second was dragged out interminably by the use of ultra-slow-motion filming.

A key scene showed a helicopter swooping down on a mother polar bear and her cub in Arctic Alaska. As the animals cowered in fright, hunters with rifles emerged from the aircraft. One aimed a telescope-sighted rifle at the mother bear as she sought to shield her offspring. Then there was a shot and the big bear writhed in agony, lurched, and dropped bleeding to the ice. The cub, with pathetic back glances at the body of its dead mother, ran away, presumably to perish in the icy fastness of the North. Say good-bye!

This brief emotion-charged sequence did more to convince Americans that hunters were slaughtering the nation's wildlife than any other footage ever filmed. But it raised eyebrows among conservationists who had access to facts not known to the general public. The use of helicopters in hunting and the shooting of bears with cubs are both prohibited by Alaskan game laws. If the sequence depicted fact, the only conclusion was that Wolper Productions, the producers of the film, had deliberately broken both regulations in an effort to get some dramatic coverage.

After seeing the television show, Dr. Daniel A. Poole, president of the Wildlife Management Institute, wrote to James W. Brooks, commissioner of the Alaska Board of Fish and Game, to demand an explanation. As it turned out, Wolper's representatives had approached the Alaska Board of Fish and Game to borrow footage depicting polar bears and other Arctic marine mammals. Among those loaned to Wolper was a sequence showing helicopter-borne state biologists in a routine bear-tagging operation using a tranquilizer gun to immobilize polar bears. Minutes after the mother bear fell, she was back on her feet, unharmed and had rejoined her youngster. By skillful cutting and splicing this with footage of a male bear killed in a hunt outside the United States, Wolper's film editors had converted the record of an unspectacular biological operation designed to save polar bears into a heart-wringing scene of lawlessness, tragedy, and death.

As a result of this misrepresentation and complaints to the Federal Communications Commission by the International Association of Game, Fish and Conservation Commissioners, the House Committee on Interstate and Foreign Commerce subpoenaed Wolper Productions and NBC, and the Federal Communications Commission ordered all television wildlife film producers to append disclaimers to their films indicating that some of the scenes could be simulated.

Recognizing the sweeping change—if not reversal—of public attitudes toward predators that had taken place in America, Secretary of the Interior Udall directed his Special Advisory Board on Wildlife Management, under A. Starker Leopold, to conduct a full-scale investigation of the program and procedures of the Division of Predator and Rodent Control of the U. S. Fish and Wildlife Service. In its reports, submitted to the Secretary on March 9, 1964, the board recommended broad changes in the direction and application of federal animal control efforts. It recommended that federal control activities be minimized and restricted solely to the removal of proven stock-killing predators, and that the use of thallium, 1080, and other persistent poisons be terminated both for killing predators and as rodenticides. It noted that dead and dying prairie dogs, field mice, and other rodents were fed upon by a wide range of desirable forms of wildlife, including eagles and hawks, which were in turn killed by the poison. It recommended that the name of the division be changed to reflect a broadened viewpoint and public responsibility. Most of these recommendations were accepted and implemented by Udall. The Division of Predator and Rodent Control was consolidated with other bureau functions within the Fish and Wildlife Service and renamed the Division of Wildlife Services.

This ended many of the abuses that had been perpetrated under the old division. Trained biologists were employed to replace the old government hunters whose hard-line views about predators had perpetuated many of the destructive practices of the past. Jack Berryman, a highly competent biologist, was named to head the new agency.

But the nagging question remained: Was there any justifiable reason why the government should be in the predator control business at all? Nearly all of the state fish and wildlife agencies had phased out their own predator control activities long ago after dozens of research projects had shown that natural predation had little if any effect on established wildlife populations. To help farmers with real problems with predators, several states, notably Missouri and Kansas, had reduced their operations to extension services designed to teach them how to trap individual offending animals.

The Bureau of Biological Survey had not asked for responsibilities in predator and rodent control when these were handed to it in 1915. The job was forced on the Bureau by Congress because of the pressures of livestock interests, particularly those in the western plains and Rocky Mountain States, whose senators or representatives held powerful positions on congressional committees. The only justification for federal participation was a lame one. Since many of the western livestock men were running their flocks and herds on public lands, it was said, the public had an obligation to protect them from loss. This overlooked the fact that federal predator control was a public subsidy for an industry that was already being heavily subsidized by permitting it to use federally owned grazing lands at prices far below those demanded by private landowners.

The controversy did not end with the implementation of the Leopold Committee report. If anything, it intensified.

Between 1964 and 1971 four major investigations of the federal role in predator and rodent control were made with all of them critical of existing policies while noting significant progress toward the correction of deficiencies. In addition to the Leopold Committee Report, Congressman John D. Dingell of Michigan, chairman of the House Subcommittee on Fisheries and Wildlife of the Interior and Insular

Affairs Committee, conducted public hearings on the issue in 1966. In 1970, the National Academy of Sciences conducted an in-depth study of the extent of animal damage in the United States.

In April, 1971, the President's Council on Environmental Quality and the Department of the Interior agreed to sponsor a joint study by an expert committee of the entire predator control situation at state and federal levels. The panel selected to do the research and develop recommendations contained some of the leading authorities on predatory animals in the nation. Its chairman was Dr. Stanley A. Cain, former Assistant Secretary of the Interior for Fish and Wildlife and Parks, with John A. Kadlec as deputy chairman. Its members included A. Starker Leopold, chairman of the earlier advisory committee; Durward L. Allen of Purdue University, who had conducted intensive studies of wolf-moose relationships on Isle Royale National Park; Maurice G. Hornocker, the leading authority on cougars and other large cats; Richard A. Cooley and Frederick H. Wagner, both authorities on coyotes and predator-prey relationships.

In the course of its investigations, this panel contacted every organization, state and federal agency, and livestock group remotely concerned with the issue for its views and supporting information. Although it found remaining deficiencies in state and federal programs, it also found considerable progress toward a balanced program of predator control that gave hope for saving most of the larger predators in viable populations. Florida had given complete protection to its remnant population of Florida panthers that hunted in and around Everglades National Park. Arizona, California, Idaho, Nevada, New Mexico, Oregon, Utah, and Washington had classified the cougar as a game animal, making its hunting subject to strict state control. Except in a few jurisdictions where livestock interests dominated the legislatures, the bounty system had become a memory. Colorado, Maine, New Hampshire, Pennsylvania, Vermont, Wisconsin, and Wyoming, most of which once paid bounties on bears, had placed the black bear on the game lists and substituted a system of reimbursing livestock owners for proven damages by bears. Grizzly bears that turned stock killers were increasingly being live-trapped and moved to wilderness areas instead of being destroyed.

The panel found that considerable research was being conducted into more humane methods of predator control, such as the use of tranquilizer tabs in relation to steel traps, chemosterilants that inhibited reproduction, and devices that were more selective in taking offending animals. The "coyote getter," which shoots a dose of cyanide into the mouths of animals tugging on a bait, although dangerous to any large meat-eater, including dogs, was a vast improvement over the broadcast distribution of poisonous baits.

Recommendations of the Cain Panel were that federal and state participation in predator-control research be continued on a cooperative basis with funds in their support coming from appropriations from Congress and the state legislatures. Elimination of federal participation, it felt, could lead to a return to unrestricted poisoning by untrained employees of private livestock associations. In 1971, just before the report of the Cain Panel was made public, the Colorado Game, Fish and Parks Commission voted to withhold $45,000 in state cooperative funds unless the U. S. Fish and Wildlife Service agreed to curtail the use of poison in the state.

The Cain Panel recommended the removal of all existing toxic chemicals from registration and use for operational predator control, a continued professionalization of the field force of the Division of Wildlife Services, and the adoption by all states of a cooperative trapper-training extension program that would permit landowners and livestock operators to control individual predators on private land. Some of the worst abuses of poisons had been perpetrated by private operators with little or no biological training or knowledge of ecological relationships.

Although it considered estimates by the sheep-growing industry of losses of lambs at between $4 million and $20 million a year to be inflated, the Cain Panel recognized some justification in claims that predation, especially by coyotes, threatened the economic survival of individual sheepmen and depressed the income of the entire livestock industry. It recommended that Congress initiate an insurance program to relieve livestock owners suffering proven losses.

The Cain Panel recommended that permits and leases for grazing livestock on public lands be subject to revocation if the lessee or permittee violated federal regulations pertaining to predator control. It also advocated the elimination of all predator control on statutory wilderness areas. Under the terms of the Wilderness Act, the grazing of livestock established prior to the effective date of the Act was permitted to continue, subject to regulations deemed necessary by the Secretary of Agriculture. This questionable clause had been written into the Wilderness Act by proponents of the livestock industry in Congress as a qualification for their support of the bill. Although government-control operations had been stopped on the wilderness areas, private-control operations by individual permittees had continued.

Several recommendations dealt with broadening research programs that would cover the gamut of ecological problems associated with predators. These included the effects of predator control on the incidence of rabies and other epizootics. Proponents of predator control, both in the East and West, had used the threat of rabies to justify extensive predator-control programs. Although transmissible to all mammals, including man, the most common carriers of the dread disease are skunks and bats. Of all of North America's animals, the one most feared by pioneers was the rabid striped skunk, which would quietly slip up on a sleeping traveler and inoculate him with the virus of one of the most horrible diseases known to man. Local outbreaks among foxes, raccoons, and other small predators occur with varying frequency in the Middle Atlantic States as well as in the South and West. The reaction of health officials almost invariably is to call in trappers, poisoners, and other control agents to eliminate or reduce the number of carriers.

Biologists have long questioned this approach as useless and, at times, self-defeating. Rabies is almost invariably lethal to the animal infected by it. In an overcrowded population, the transmission of the disease from one animal to another is rapid, leading to a crash decline in the populations of the carriers. The incidence of rabies in wild populations is rarely evident until the crash begins. By thinning the population, massive trapping and poisoning campaigns merely delay the decline and sometimes extend the duration of the epizootic.

Two recommendations of the Cain Panel dealt with the use of aircraft in controlling predators. In the postwar years, shooting from aircraft had become a common method of controlling foxes and coyotes in the Dakotas and wolves in Alaska. In the same states, shooting predators from aircraft had developed into a minor "sport." Although frowned upon by nearly all sportsmen and prohibited by law in most states, the practice was condoned by some.

On the other hand, aerial gunning, of all control methods, is the most selective and effective in controlling coyotes in open country where control is necessary. The Cain Panel recommended that shooting of all wild animals from aircraft be universally banned except under exceptional circumstances, and that necessary control be done only by authorized wildlife biologists of state and federal agencies. It also recommended that the license of any pilot permitting the use of his plane for unauthorized shooting or the distribution of poison be revoked.

The reaction to the report of the Cain Panel was immediate. President Richard Nixon issued an Executive Order prohibiting the use of all chemical poisons on all public lands of the United States. Congressman John D. Dingell prepared legislation carrying out the recommendations dealing with the use of aircraft in predator control which promptly passed both Houses of Congress and was signed by the President. The Federal Aviation Authority wrote tight regulations that called for the revocation of the licenses of any pilots convicted of using their aircraft for illegal purposes. The Environmental Protection

Agency withdrew from certification 1080, thallium, and other persistent poisons. The Division of Wildlife Services greatly reduced the extent of its control efforts and concentrated its activities on individual animals known to be causing livestock losses.

The complexity of predator management is best exemplified by the controversy that swirled around the timber wolf in the early 1970s.

By 1970, the eastern timber wolf south of Canada was reduced to a population of between 500 and 750 in northern Minnesota, a pack of four or five that roamed Michigan's Upper Peninsula, and possibly a few in northern Wisconsin. There were about twenty in Isle Royale National Park, the progeny of a few animals that had reached the island by crossing on the ice of Lake Superior about 1949 to prey on moose which had reached the island early in the century. These animals were subjects of intensive research by teams of student biologists from Purdue University led by Dr. Durward L. Allen. Since the Isle Royale moose and wolves were fully protected from hunting, the island provided an ideal outdoor laboratory in which to study predator-prey relationships and the social behavior of wolves in the absence of human interference. Allen's long-range studies provided new insight into the effects of predators on prey species and into the dynamics of predator populations. Although female wolves are capable of producing litters of a half-dozen young each year, and wolves have few natural enemies other than parasites, the population tended to remain relatively stable for several years at a time.

By 1960, Michigan had repealed its bounty on wolves and accorded the species some form of protection. Classification of the eastern timber wolf as an endangered species under the Endangered Species Preservation Act of 1966, coupled with increased public sympathy for predators generated by television and motion pictures, brought mounting public demands for action by public officials to save the wolf in the lower United States from extinction. Several citizens' groups in Canada and the United States, recruiting their members primarily from youthful environmentalists in colleges and universities, were formed for the specific purpose of promoting wolf conservation. These ranged from the well-informed and realistic North American Wolf Society to small groups whose approach to all wildlife problems can best be characterized as near-hysteria.

Established conservation organizations, such as the National Audubon Society, National Wildlife Federation, and Wildlife Management Institute had been working for years for the repeal of bounties and for reforms in predator control, and had realized considerable success in achieving their aims. They were joined in the 1970s by two humane associations with little exposure to biological reality, the Fund for Animals, under the leadership of Cleveland Amory, a journalist and television critic, and Friends of Animals, Inc., under the presidency of Alice Herrington of New York City, who had expanded her worthy program for neutering surplus city cats and dogs into the field of wildlife protection. While established conservation groups otherwise might have welcomed these new allies, the entry of the Fund for Animals and Friends of Animals into the conservation lists was like that of a squadron of massed tanks running down its own infantry to reach the enemy. Instead of joining the older organizations, they began a systematic campaign to undermine them and to destroy ongoing institutions and programs that offered the only promise of salvation of the animals in which they claimed interest.

The entry of the ultraprotectionist into the folds of the conservation movement confused the public if it did nothing else. On some issues the newcomers allied themselves with the older organizations, but their opposition to wildlife management or population control in any form made it difficult if not impossible for any group with experience and scientific knowledge to work with them. The combined efforts of the established conservation organizations had already led to major reforms in federal rodent- and predator-control programs and had all but eliminated the wasteful bounty system. They had led to the Federal Bald and Golden Eagle Protection Acts of June 8, 1940, and October 24, 1962, and the adoption by nearly all states of the Audubon Society's Model Predatory Bird Protection Law, which placed hawks and owls under full protection. They had successfully obtained reclassification, by most states within its range, of the mountain lion or cougar from a pest to be poisoned or shot on sight to a game animal subject to management and protection from overhunting.

The wolves in northern Minnesota escaped extinction at the hands of government predator hunters and poisoners during the first half of the twentieth century only because they occupied a huge forested area with little or no livestock industry. Their principal prey is the white-tailed deer, although other hooved animals and beavers vary their fare. Many hunters in the northern Lake States still harbor attitudes toward wolves that are holdovers from pioneer times when the wolf was almost universally considered a cruel, blood-thirsty killer. Wolves are not dainty eaters, and the view of a man who has found a game animal torn to pieces is likely to differ from that of a New Yorker whose impression is formed by a television show with Cleveland Amory fondling and cuddling a docile and lovable Jethro. The perspective from a Minnesota dairy farm in the shadow of the wolf woods is different from that from the campus dormitory or a Boston penthouse.

Minnesota repealed its bounty law in 1965 after an educational campaign by the Minnesota Natural Resources Department and state and national conservation groups. The bounty had been in effect continuously since the early 1800s and in its last years an average of 188 wolves were turned in for the $35 reward at an average cost to the state of $80,000 a year. In 1965, in response to political pressure from farmers and hunters in the northern counties, the Minnesota State Legislature passed a bill authorizing the reinstitution of a bounty system. The bill was vetoed by Governor Karl F. Rolvaag. In 1967, proponents of a bounty law tried again. The State Legislature passed the bill, but Governor Harold LeVander returned it because of a technicality, and it died with adjournment.

Changing public attitudes were reflected in the fate of another bill introduced in 1969. The first version, calling for an outright restoration of wolf bounties, was defeated in both houses. Proponents of the bounty system, however, succeeded in pushing through a modified version that placed a bounty on "brush wolves," or coyotes, and contained a provision leaving its implementation as it applied to timber wolves at the discretion of the Conservation Commissioner.

In 1969, Congress passed the Endangered Species Conservation Act. This Act authorized the Secretary of the Interior to cooperate with the states to protect and restore endangered species and directed all federal agencies to take steps to protect any endangered species on lands under their jurisdiction. The eastern timber wolf was listed as an endangered species.

On October 16, 1970, Craig Rupp, forest supervisor of the Superior National Forest in northern Minnesota, issued an order closing all of the national forest to wolf hunting and trapping as an interim measure until the state adopted a suitable and effective wolf-management program. The price of wolf pelts had soared in a few years from around ten dollars a skin to between sixty and one hundred dollars in 1970. To a trapper, a hundred dollars is a lot of money. Trapping pressure mounted sharply. Snowmobiles and four-wheel-drive offroad vehicles permitted trappers who had formerly plodded traplines on snowshoes to run lines hundreds of miles long. Trappers were taking from two hundred to three hundred wolves a year from a population variously estimated at between three hundred and seven hundred animals. The intensive trapping activity also was interfering seriously with research activities being conducted on the forest by Dr. L. David Mech, who was studying the wolf through the use of radio telemetric tracking. One of his radio-equipped animals was shot by a trapper even though it was conspicuously marked with a red collar. Mech had to pay one hundred dollars from his own pocket to recover another radio-equipped wolf from a trapper, who had taken it alive. Mech had obtained his doctorate degree in wildlife ecology from Purdue University where he had worked with Dr. Durward L. Allen in his intensive study of the timber wolves on Isle Royale.

In the meantime, the Minnesota Natural Resources Department had no authority to set up a management or protection program for the wolf since the species, under Minnesota law, was neither a game animal nor a fur bearer. When the controversy first arose, incumbent Commissioner of Conservation, Jarle Leirfallom, resisted attempts to obtain game status for the wolf, but his director of fish and game, Richard Wettersten strongly favored the proposal. On November 9, 1970, Leirfallom and Wettersten and his assistants met with Rupp in an effort to work out a mutually acceptable plan. Although the closure of the Superior National Forest created what was essentially an inviolate wolf sanctuary, it included only part of the range of the wolf in Minnesota. Also, interspersed throughout the forest were privately owned inholdings where Rupp's order did not apply. Under existing conditions, landowners in and around the forest were at liberty to trap or shoot any wolf they saw, or to permit the use of their property for those purposes.

The agreement reached on December 2, 1970, between the Forest Service and Natural Resources Department in consultation with the Regional Office of the U. S. Bureau of Sport Fisheries and Wildlife, called for zoning the state by establishing an endangered-species zone comprising 2,350 miles. On this area wolves would be fully protected from hunting and trapping. The only exceptions were to be in situations in which the animals were in direct conflict with man; when wolf predation was found to be endangering another endangered species; and for capture and release in scientific research projects. Around the sanctuary zone, serving as a buffer between the wilderness in the north and the agricultural communities with their livestock in the south, there was to be a smaller-use zone on which sport hunting and trapping were to be allowed under state regulations. A statewide closure of hunting between April 1 and September 14 and of trapping between April 1 and October 14 would become effective as soon as the plan was approved by the State Legislature. Resident license holders would be able to take no more than ten wolves in a season and nonresidents would be limited to three. After between 150 and 200 wolves were taken, depending upon the current population status, the hunting and trapping seasons would automatically terminate. All wolves taken would have to be reported to a state conservation officer, and the state conservation department agreed to undertake intensive habitat improvement to increase the food supply—and the numbers—of wolves. The plan called for the creation of an advisory committee with representatives from the State Stockmen's Association, conservation organizations, the Trappers Association, the

Minnesota Natural Resources Department, the Bureau of Sport Fisheries and Wildlife, the U. S. Forest Service, and the University of Minnesota, to advise the Conservation Department on regulations.

In drafting the plan, the participants had the counsel of three of the leading experts on wolves in the world—Mech, Dr. Victor Van Ballenberge, and Milton Stenlund, who had been studying the Minnesota wolves for years. The plan had their endorsement, and copies of it were distributed for comment to the leaders of national conservation groups. Except for changes in wording it met almost universal approval. With this support, Commissioner Robert Herbst, who had replaced Leirfallom, prepared to present the plan to the State Legisture for approval.

On November 28, 1972, however, Lewis Regenstein, national director of the Fund for Animals, issued a news release that totally distorted the intent and objectives of the plan. It was headlined: "Extinction of Eastern Timber Wolf Threatened by Government Project."

> The Fund for Animals revealed today that the U. S. Department of the Interior, U. S. Forest Service, and the State of Minnesota had agreed on a plan to virtually destroy the last remaining Eastern Timber Wolf population remaining in the United States. Unless this project can be defeated or amended and prompt protective measures adopted, these animals will be threatened with extinction.

The news release stated that: "Even if this [plan] does not bring about the extinction of Minnesota's wolves, the plan will virtually destroy the packs by breaking down their social organization, and the evolution of the species will be adversely affected in ways impossible to predict." Exactly why this would happen when a full century of unrestricted killing had not brought it about was not clear. Moreover, the wolf population had maintained itself at relatively stable numbers for nearly a decade in spite of intensified persecution, either by recruitment from Canada or by increased survival of pups.

Regenstein's news release stated that the plan would "throw open the Superior National Forest to wolf hunting" and that outside the sanctuary and use zone "wolves may be killed year around without limit. . . ." Actually, the plan called for the imposition of the bag limit and six-month closure of hunting and trapping on a statewide basis. Regenstein sent a copy of his news release to Craig Rupp, who had taken the first official action to save the wolves by closing Superior National Forest. Rupp, who had moved to Washington as staff assistant in the U. S. Forest Service, replied on January 10, 1973, with a four-page single-spaced letter that called attention to the many errors in fact in Regenstein's release.

An important point to remember is that when we closed the Superior National Forest lands, I publicly stated that the closure was an interim measure to remain in effect until we could develop a suitable plan for management and protection of the wolf. We did so because we recognized that the wolf would not benefit in the long run from complete protection. Complete protection of a predator which had an unjustified but nonetheless bad reputation could result in a social-political situation that would force actions and cause reactions detrimental to the wolf. We also recognized the wolf did occasionally kill some domestic livestock and was, in the eyes of many, competing directly with the sportsman for deer and moose.

Regenstein's misleading news release was widely circulated among the urban newspapers and was published by many. HOWL (Help Our Wolves Live), a private organization dedicated to wolf conservation, and Friends of Animals helped generate a barrage of emotional mail to the Department of the Interior and to congressmen and senators attacking the plan. Nathaniel Reed, Assistant Secretary of the Interior for Fish and Wildlife and Parks, responded to this pressure on December 12, 1972, by branding it unacceptable to the Department of the Interior. Reed called for a moratorium on the taking of wolves "until a nationwide recovery plan for the wolf is completed."

The major problem involved in the restoration of any large predator, whether wolf, grizzly bear, or cougar, is in finding habitat in which to develop populations that do not conflict with the economic interests of man. Wolves are never going to be restored on a nationwide basis without moving a lot of people and a lot of livestock. Wolf packs hunt over large territories often embracing several hundred square miles. Unlike deer, you don't raise wolves in farm woodlots. In the East, with the exception of the North Woods of Maine, Minnesota, and Michigan, there are few spots where wolves could be reintroduced without danger to dairy cattle, sheep, and swine. And public acceptance of these projects by the local people is essential to their success.

Opportunities for reintroduction are far brighter in the West, especially since the establishment of the Wilderness System. The Rocky Mountain timber wolf has reinvaded Glacier and Yellowstone National Parks after being wiped out by predator hunters and poisoners early in the century. In the parks, with an abundance of prey and under full protection, the small populations now found should increase and prosper as a welcome addition to the fauna and as a natural control on inflated populations of elk.

But the eastern timber wolf presents a different problem. Suitable range is fragmented by development and even the larger blocks are surrounded by dairy farms and other livestock ventures. Populations of wolves, like those of any other animal, tend to rise to the carrying capacity of their habitat. In a comparatively small area, like that occupied by the Minnesota wolves, this can happen in a very short period of time. Wolf litters average around seven pups a year, and, in underoccupied habitat, reproduction probably occurs each year. Once the habitat becomes filled, natural population checks come into play. Reproduction falls off, and any surplus pups are likely to have a high mortality rate. On Isle Royale, in a decade of intensive study, Allen and students often found an amazing consistency in their wolf counts from year to year. Since Isle Royale is separated from mainland Michigan by a broad expanse of water, any surplus wolves probably died as they had nowhere to go outside the island range.

But northern Minnesota and other areas with potential as wolf habitat are not islands. As the habitat becomes saturated, some surplus wolves are almost certain to be driven from established pack territories into civilization where their only food will be dairy cattle and other livestock. Once this occurs, wolf-conservation efforts will receive a severe setback, certain to be attended by congressional demands to repeal the Endangered Species Act or at least to remove the wolf from legal protection. At best, farmers in the areas at the edge of the wolf range almost surely will take the law into their own hands to protect their livestock. And it is unlikely that a rural jury could be selected that would convict them. Moreover, it would reduce the possibility of other states with unoccupied habitat putting out the welcome mat for wolves.

Wolf-restoration efforts face hurdles high enough as it is without having the public image of the wolf again tarnished as a threat to livestock. In the summer of 1967, in an incredible coincidence, two girls were killed in their sleeping bags almost simultaneously by grizzly bears at widely separated points in Glacier National Park. Although deaths from grizzly bear attacks have been extremely rare in the history of the National Park Service, the incident brought demands, not only in the popular press but in scientific journals, for the elimination of the bears from all of the national parks.

It was to minimize the chances of renegade wolves wandering from their wilderness range into civilization that the drafters of the Minnesota plan wrote into it provisions for peripheral control that would prevent incidents that could cause popular overreaction.

As this is written, wolf populations in Minnesota are nearing the saturation point. The wolf population is spreading and, in some lakeshore areas, the population has reached a density of one wolf to each six miles, the highest ever recorded anywhere in North America, including Canada, where the eastern timber wolf is considered far from endangered. The status of the eastern timber wolf is under official review. This could lead to its being reclassified as no longer endangered or, more probably, to a threatened category. In the former case, it would no longer be a matter of federal concern. In the latter, it would be subject to limited taking under state regulations approved by the Secretary of the Interior. The Minnesota Department of Natural Resources has drafted a more conservative version of its original management plan, and it is likely that this will be approved.

Meanwhile, much more educational effort must be expended, not on urban populations that are only emotionally involved, but on the people living within and on the edges of occupied wolf range or in and near habitat that has the potential for reintroduction. This was borne out by an attempt to reestablish wolves from Minnesota on Michigan's Upper Peninsula.

In a project funded jointly by the National Audubon Society, Huron Mountain Wildlife Foundation, and Northern Michigan University, four wolves—two males and two females—were live-trapped near International Falls, Minnesota, in January, 1974. In March, the animals, fitted with radio tags to trace their movements, were released in Upper Michigan. In July, one of the males was found shot and the other was killed by an automobile. A female was caught in a trap and shot by the trapper in the belief he had taken a coyote. To his credit, after realizing his mistake, he immediately reported the case to the Department of Natural Resources. The fourth was found shot in December, 1974. Efforts to reintroduce the wolf to Michigan will continue and, in spite of these setbacks, there are possibilities of future success.

In the meantime, if wolves are to survive in Minnesota in anything near their present numbers, steps must be taken to expand the deer and other wolf prey populations by habitat manipulation. Many northern forest stands, under intensive protection from fire and limited timber harvest, are becoming too mature to support the primary prey species of the wolf. In much of the North, dense stands of spruce and fir have replaced the aspens, birches, and other hardwoods that provided forage for hares, deer, and moose. Habitat improvement can be done by well-designed commercial logging, by prescribed burning, or by crushing, chaining, or bulldozing. An extensive program of this kind could easily double Minnesota's wolf population without conflict with man. Simply passing a law to protect the wolf cannot assure its safety as a part of America's fauna.

As the North American Wolf Society observes:

"To preserve the wolf, we must also preserve the elk, the moose or deer, and the habitat which supports these inter-related members of the wilderness."

Chapter 23

The Threatened and Endangered

Although greatly intensified by improved communications in recent years, public concern for endangered wildlife is nothing new. Efforts to save the remnant bands of bison that escaped the slaughter of the 1870s began soon after the probable fate of the survivors became apparent. Attempts to maintain the heath hen as a part of America's fauna predated the Civil War. Aransas National Wildlife Refuge, near Corpus Christi, Texas, was established in 1937 to protect the wintering grounds of the whooping crane. But these and similar programs were handled on a case-by-case basis with no overall program or central guidance. Steps toward correcting this situation were taken in 1966 when Congress enacted the Endangered Species Preservation Act. This law recognized a national obligation for the government to act on behalf of native wild species threatened with extinction. It required the Secretary of the Interior to determine what animals were threatened and those that were not, and to publish a list of rare and endangered species in the Federal Register. It authorized the Secretary to conduct research on the animals and to use limited amounts of money up to a total of $15 million from the Land and Water Conservation Fund over a six-year period to acquire habitat for them.

The Endangered Species Conservation Act of 1969, signed on December 5, broadened the scope of the national effort by extending coverage to all vertebrates, mollusks, and crustaceans. It permitted the consideration of subspecies as well as species, authorized the acquisition of water as well as land as sanctuaries for endangered species, and increased the amounts available from the Land and Water Conservation Fund to $5 million per year. It also authorized the Secretary of the Interior to take steps to protect endangered species of foreign wildlife. It substituted the terms "threatened and endangered" for "rare and endangered."

Neither of these Acts extended the authority of the federal government to regulate the taking and possession of wildlife beyond the regulatory powers already vested in it through the Migratory Bird Treaty Act, Fur Seal Treaty, Bald Eagle Act, and the Lacey Act of 1900. It did, however, encourage the states to adopt laws and programs for the preservation of endangered species within their borders. Until 1966, Maryland had permitted hunting of the Delmarva fox squirrel, locally common on its Eastern Shore but restricted to a limited and declining acreage of mature hardwoods centered around three national wildlife refuges.

The Endangered Species Act of 1973, which became effective on December 28 of that year and which Congress substituted for the Act of 1969, contained more teeth. It authorized the federal government through the Secretary of the Interior to intervene in state affairs whenever it felt that state programs were inadequate to protect an endangered species. The new law embraced the entire animal kingdom and included plants as well as animal life. It defined "species" to include subspecies, and "any smaller taxonomic unit of plant or animal, and also any viable population segment thereof." It eliminated all commercial traffic in live, dead, parts or products of any endangered species except under special permit for scientific or propagatory purposes or in cases of demonstrated severe economic hardship. The new law, like the law of 1969, also divided the species covered into two categories—"endangered," those in immediate danger of extinction, and "threatened," those likely to become endangered in the immediate future. For administrative purposes, the Office of Endangered Species in the U. S. Fish and Wildlife Service classified all threatened and endangered species as "endangered" subject to administrative review of their true status. A threatened species, under terms of the Act, may be subject to management and limited taking under state regulations approved by the Secretary of the Interior.

Someone has called the Endangered Species Act an attorney's dream. Parts of it are as confusing to the people charged with its administration as they are to the lay public. Under a strict interpretation of the law, a state conservation officer finding a whooping crane with a broken wing could not legally hold the bird to nurse it back to health without first obtaining a special permit from the Secretary of the Interior, application for which must be published in the Federal Register and subjected to a thirty-day review period. Even federal biologists charged with administering recovery programs for endangered species must go through this cumbersome process.

The inclusion of subspecies and population segments within the definition of species is especially confusing to the public. A species, in the zoological sense, is a group of animals with common characteristics that are passed on to young capable of reproducing fertile young within their own group. Within each species there may be from two to a dozen or more subspecies or races, each of which developed in genetic isolation from the others. Subspecies may differ from one another sharply in size, color, or bone structure. The Key white-tailed deer weighs little more than fifty pounds. A northern whitetail buck from Maine or New Brunswick may tip the scales at more than three hundred. The coat of the Delmarva fox squirrel is a beautiful silver gray while that of the common variety in the Middle West is reddish brown to black. Among other species the differences are so minute that only a trained zoologist can distinguish one subspecies from another.

To compound the confusion, taxonomists—zoologists, ichthyologists, herpetologists, and ornithologists who make the classifications—do not always agree with one another as to what constitutes a species or subspecies. There is a constant conflict between the "lumpers," those who favor ignoring minor variations in color or size, and the "splitters," who see any deviation from the norm in a specimen as an indication of full specific or subspecific rank. Dr. C. Hart Merriam, who did much of the early taxonomic classification for the Smithsonian Institution, was a great splitter. By the time he finished with the grizzly bear, he had named eighty-six separate species of the genus *Ursus*. Modern taxonomists have the classification of the grizzly under review, and tighter consolidation is more than probable. Many now believe all grizzly bears and the Kodiak brown bear to be races of the same species.

Similarly, taxonomists have classified thirty subspecies or races of the white-tailed deer. Two of these, the Key deer of Florida and the Columbian white-tailed deer, are endangered "species." If we apply the definition in the Endangered Species Act, modern wildlife management could claim the restoration to abundance of nearly twenty-eight "species" of white-tailed deer.

On analysis, the record of the American people in saving its warm-blooded wildlife is not as bleak as bald statistics would indicate. In 1975, the endangered species list contained thirty-one fishes, four amphibians, two reptiles, fifty-six birds and sixteen mammals native to the United States and its territories. Of the seventy-two birds and mammals, nearly half, or thirty-four, are found only on Puerto Rico and the Hawaiian Islands. Insular species are particularly vulnerable because they have evolved in fragile ecosystems that are upset or destroyed by any intrusion of man and his works. Violent changes in the Hawaiian ecosystem began with Captain James Cook's discovery of the islands in 1778. The introduction of swine and goats took place at that time or soon thereafter to provide a source of meat for passing mariners. European rats, which infested nearly every sailing ship, probably arrived with Cook and his crew. Later, mongooses and house cats were introduced to control the rats. Evolving, as they had in the absence of mammalian predators, most of the native birds lacked any defense against the meat-eating species. Feral goats and hogs destroyed much of the native vegetation through their foraging and rooting, and the hogs fed on the eggs and young of the ground-nesting species.

Later, as white settlers and tourists swarmed to the islands, they brought with them domestic poultry, dogs and other pets, and disease-bearing mosquitos. In a misguided effort to improve the quality of life, they imported and released dozens of foreign species from Axis deer to Asiatic doves and starlings, which competed for food and cover with the native species. Many of the domesticated and exotic wild birds carried parasites and diseases to which the native wildlife lacked immunity. As a result of these factors, forty percent of the birds native to Hawaii have been wiped out and another forty percent are endangered.

Of the twenty-three endangered birds and fifteen endangered mammals native to the continental United States, only seven birds and four mammals are true species in the zoological sense of the term. Most of the remainder are represented elsewhere by closely related subspecies whose populations range from substantial to abundant. Although the Morro Bay kangaroo rat, *Dipodomys heermanni morroensis*, is on the endangered species list, there are eleven other closely related subspecies in California alone.

The purpose of this discussion is not to minimize the national effort to restore our endangered animals or the public interest that supports that effort but to put into perspective some terms and statistics that are loosely used in the news media and popular press. Since 1768, when the Russians in Alaska slaughtered the last of the sea cows, the North American continent has lost eight unique forms of mammals and six kinds of birds. The record is a sad one. But considering the staggering changes that have taken place in the face of America in that same time, it is surprising that it is not worse.

There are few common denominators in the problems facing the 109 species and subspecies of fish, reptiles, amphibians, birds, and mammals that are threatened with extinction in the United States. Many were not abundant even in precolonial times, and most occupied highly restricted ranges or specialized habitat that have shrunk under the onslaught of civilization. The Florida Everglades kite feeds almost exclusively on a single species of snail that is found only in fresh-water marshes in Florida. Many thousands of acres of marsh-land have been drained in Florida and others have become clogged with water hyacinths, a tropical plant pest introduced from South America before 1900. Periodic drought followed by fire is a constant threat to the kite's food supply. Slightly more than one hundred of the snail kites remain.

The southern bald eagle, like the brown pelican, is threatened by pesticides and a host of other environmental factors. The proliferation of outboard motorboats, private aircraft, and off-road recreational vehicles in the past ten years has left few of the eagle's nesting sites free from human intrusion and the roar of internal combustion machines. Many of the huge snag trees that it prefers as platforms for its nests have been felled in timber-stand improvement or resort-development programs. Some of the big birds also have been electrocuted, especially in the plains states where hunting perches are few and where high-tension power lines provide manmade substitutes for the crags and tall trees they use in other areas. Although protected by state and federal laws, eagles, like most predators, have been persecuted since early times. Some are killed each year by irresponsible shooters, especially by sheepmen who, in spite of evidence to the contrary, still regard the eagle as a major predator on lambs.

In spite of the magnitude and complexity of the problem, some progress—in a few cases, dramatic—has been made in restoring endangered species, if not to abundance, at least to population levels at which their future safety seems assured. In 1935, there were fewer than one hundred trumpeter swans south of Canada, centered around Red Rock Lakes in southeastern Montana. Although still relatively secure in British Columbia and Alaska, these were the only representatives of the species in the contiguous United States. In 1935, the Bureau of Biological Survey created the Red Rock Lakes Migratory Bird Refuge to protect the habitat of the survivors from poaching and other human disturbance. Under protection, the big birds began increasing in numbers at a rate of approximately ten percent a year, from 97 in 1934 to 279 in 1944, to 642 in 1954. In the meantime, breeding flocks were established by transplanting to Yellowstone National Park, the National Elk Refuge in Jackson, Wyoming, Malheur National Wildlife Refuge in Oregon, Ruby Lake National Wildlife Refuge in Nevada, and Lacreek National Wildlife Refuge in South Dakota. Several flocks have reached the carrying capacity of the range while others are still expanding in numbers. In 1955, six birds were transferred under federal permit from the Red Rock Lakes Refuge to the Delta Waterfowl Research Station in Manitoba. After some experimentation, biologists there produced the first trumpeter swan cygnets ever raised in captivity. As a result of releases, the trumpeter swan was restored as a breeding resident of the Delta Marshes from which it had long been absent. There are today approximately one thousand trumpeter swans in the northwestern states dispersed in widely spaced breeding flocks that preclude the extermination of the species by an epizootic or other cataclysmic catastrophe.

Soon after Jay N. "Ding" Darling became chief of the Bureau of Biological Survey, he began an exhaustive search for suitable wetlands that could be acquired as refuges for the nation's hard-pressed waterfowl. The quest carried him from the marshes of Oregon and Washington to the mangrove thickets of the Florida Keys. While cruising along the latter islands in a motor launch in 1934, his attention was attracted to a column of white smoke rising from one of the islets. On approaching the shore, he found a scene of desolation. Charred skeletons of pines towered above the still-smouldering stubble of once-lush palmettos; the white coral sands were blackened with ash. There was no life.

Curious as to how fire managed to start on an uninhabited island, he was told that Cuban fishermen frequently visited the Keys to obtain fresh meat. Their common practice was to set fire to the vegetation to drive the deer to water, where they could be easily shot or clubbed.

Horrified at this callous lawlessness by foreign invaders and outraged as a conservationist, Darling proceeded to sketch a cartoon that, more eloquently than words, reflected his sentiments. This drawing, done on a lap board on a commercial fisherman's boat, later played an important role in enlisting public sympathy for the Key deer.

Upon his return to the mainland, Darling reported the incident to Florida officials, but the Keys were far off the beaten track. More urgent matters kept the state law-enforcement officers fully occupied, and law enforcement on the islands was confined largely to that conducted by federal officers on the Great White Heron National Wildlife Refuge, which included only a fringe of Key deer range. As a federal official, Darling's responsibilities were confined largely to migratory birds. Little more could be done until a more favorable conservation climate existed in the Sunshine State.

After Darling, the first public official to show interest in the plight of the Key deer was James Silver, southeastern regional director of the U. S. Fish and Wildlife Service, who, shortly after the close of World War II, began to mention the deer in his reports to Washing-

ton, suggesting that federal action might be desirable to save a remnant population. Although outside the usual interest of the Service at
that time, a nonmigratory species could be protected by federal action
under the Service's Organic Act if it was found to be endangered.

The Key deer represented the smallest and palest race (*Odocoileus
virginianus clavium*) of the white-tailed deer, which had adapted itself
to the semi-aquatic habitat of the Florida Keys. By the time Silver
began to interest himself in its future, its population had dwindled to
around twenty-five head and its already restricted range was being
threatened by encroaching residential and commercial development
centered on Big Pine Key. Losses to poaching were continuing, and
traffic on the Overseas Highway to Key West, which bisected the
little deer's range, was taking an increasingly heavy toll. The Florida
Game and Fresh Water Fish Commission closed the Keys to all deer
hunting but was unable to spare more than a single conservation officer to patrol the Islands.

Silver's enthusiasm gradually radiated out through conservation
circles. It gained impetus when Bud Jackson, field representative of
the National Wildlife Federation, after visiting the regional director,
enlisted the aid of the Florida Wildlife Federation in working to secure a sanctuary for the deer. At Jackson's suggestion, Silver prepared
a brochure outlining the plight of the animals and explaining the need
for the proposed refuge. Congressman Charles E. Bennett of Florida
on March 2, 1950, introduced in the 81st Congress a bill calling for
a federal Key deer refuge. Although supported by the Florida Wildlife Federation, National Audubon Society, National Wildlife Federation, and Wildlife Management Institute, it failed to pass by a single
dissenting vote.

Jackson's superior in the Washington office of the National Wildlife Federation at that time was Executive Director Richard Borden,
chairman of the Conservation Committee of the Boone and Crockett
Club. At the next meeting of the club, he included in his report a plea
that the club provide stopgap protection for the Key deer until permanent protection could be assumed by the state or federal government.

During the discussion of this proposal, C. R. Gutermuth, vice-
president of the Wildlife Management Institute, secretary of the North
American Wildlife Foundation, and one of the most capable infighters
in the conservation movement, supported Borden's proposal and offered, on behalf of the Institute, a sum of $5,000 toward a fund for
the protection of the Key deer. Noting that federal protection could
not be provided for at least six months and that the situation was so
critical that even in that short period of time, the Key deer could pass

the point of no return, the club authorized Borden, as its representative, "to obtain, without delay, the services of a competent warden, suitably equipped," to protect the deer, and authorized the treasurer of the club to advance a sum of up to $5,000 for that purpose.

Borden had already discussed the proposal with Dr. Clarence Cottam, assistant director of the U. S. Fish and Wildlife Service. Within a week after the club's resolution passed, Cottam dispatched his assistant chief of the Branch of Game Management, Charles H. Lawrence, to Atlanta to discuss the proposal with Silver and obtained a promise of full state cooperation from Coleman Newman, director of the Florida Game and Fresh Water Fish Commission. Lawrence, in his report to Cottam, recommended the immediate employment of a warden who would be deputized to enforce both state and federal laws. On April 21, 1951, Cottam reported to Borden that Jack Watson would start operating from Marathon, Florida, as soon as a work plan was formally approved by the Boone and Crockett Club and the State of Florida. He noted, however, that at least $100,000 would be needed to acquire a refuge large enough to assure the survival of the Key deer.

Jack C. Watson, the husky young biologist employed by the Boone and Crockett Club as temporary custodian of the proposed refuge, threw himself into his task, digging out hitherto unknown facts on the habits, numbers, mortality factors, and needs of the deer. By August, he was able to report that constant patrol had proved effective in discouraging poachers and had diminished the threat of fire. He had been joined by John Dickson, a University of Florida biologist who was beginning a full ecological study of the Key deer. At the end of the year Watson reported substantial population increases.

In the meantime, a second Key Deer Refuge Bill, sponsored by Congressman Bill Lantaff of Florida, was winding through congressional channels. Public sympathy for the Key deer, spurred by the widespread distribution of Darling's cartoon, was increasing rapidly. Through Borden, the National Wildlife Federation agreed to try to raise a special fund to carry on the work started by the Boone and Crockett Club. "Save the Key Deer" became the theme for the Federation-sponsored National Wildlife Week of 1952. But opposition from developers in the Keys who feared loss of their holdings through land condemnation proved strong enough to block passage of the Lantaff Bill.

Direct participation by the Boone and Crockett Club ended on June 30, 1952, and the National Wildlife Federation, by prior agreement, assumed the cost of the project through June 30, 1953. Soon after this arrangement ended, the Interior Appropriations Bill for fiscal year 1954 was signed by President Eisenhower. It contained a clause authorizing the Fish and Wildlife Service to lease lands within the range of the Key deer for refuge purposes. A major weakness, however, was a clause that permitted local landowners to cancel leases on ninety-day notice, whenever they wished to sell or use the land for other purposes.

In the fifth and last of his progress reports on the Key deer, Silver, on January 28, 1954, just before his retirement, reported that the number of deer had trebled in less than three years, landowners were offering their lands for lease on a dollar-a-year basis, and, with the exception of a few diehards, most of the residents of the Keys were supporting the refuge project enthusiastically. But he added, "Somewhere, somehow . . . a small area of land must be acquired under some form of ownership that will guarantee permanent and safe use by the Key deer for all time to come."

Throughout this time, the interest of C. R. Gutermuth in the project remained high. On March 8, 1954, at the annual meeting of the North American Wildlife Foundation in Chicago, he proposed that the Foundation appropriate $10,000 to purchase the nucleus of a Key deer refuge, the lands to be transferred to the federal government as they were acquired.

Soon after this meeting, Gutermuth visited Big Pine Key with officials from the regional office of the Fish and Wildlife Service and selected a 17.5-acre waterfront tract for the headquarters of the proposed refuge. While trying to reach the owners of the property, he became acquainted with Radford R. Crane of Miami Beach who, by the time their initial conference ended, became among the most enthusiastic supporters of the refuge project. Crane agreed to urge the Raymond E. and Ellen F. Crane Foundation to donate the needed land to the North American Wildlife Foundation. In April, 1955, the Crane Foundation presented the deed to the area to the Wildlife Foundation for transfer to the U. S. Fish and Wildlife Service.

Although it provided a site for headquarters buildings, the initial plot was too small to provide more than a minute fraction of the needs of the deer. But it was a significant start, a fulcrum against which a lever could be applied. It offered adequate proof to Congress that the conservationists were seeking more than a federal handout and that there was serious national and local interest in the project. This resulted immediately in the introduction in Congress of a bill by Congressman Bennett to acquire one thousand acres of additional lands by purchase, donation, or exchange and authorized the expenditure of funds in the amount of $35,000 for land acquisition. Power of condemnation was vested in the Secretary of the Interior, although islands crossed by U. S. Route 1, which included Big Pine Key, were excluded from this provision. The bill passed the House on July 1,

1957, the Senate in August, and was signed into law by President Eisenhower a few days later.

While this bill authorized the establishment of the National Key Deer Refuge and the expenditure of federal funds, it appropriated no funds for land acquisition. With his goal so close to realization, Gutermuth intensified his drive to obtain the needed refuge lands. Consulting again with Radford Crane, he obtained a commitment for approximately $100,000 worth of additional land, on the stipulation that the conservationists raise a sum of $40,000 to purchase at fair market price the remaining private holdings that were needed to block out the refuge. Because it was bisected by the Overseas Highway, Big Pine Key already had been impaired as a refuge area. But separated from it by a narrow strait lay Howe Key, virtually undeveloped and isolated from the disturbing influence of civilization; approximately five hundred of its 727 acres were owned by the Crane Foundation. Moreover, it was directly opposite the headquarters site that had already been acquired.

At the next meeting of the Boone and Crockett Club, Gutermuth reported this progress. The Wilderness Club of Philadelphia, which had worked closely with the Boone and Crockett Club, was represented at this meeting by its vice-president, Thomas Dolan, IV. Dolan reported that, in response to Gutermuth's plea, the Wilderness Club had agreed to raise a minimum of $10,000 as a contribution to the cause. The Boone and Crockett Club, on its part, agreed to guarantee the North American Wildlife Foundation a donation of $10,000 toward a fund for purchasing the lands needed for the refuge.

The deed for the last 167 acres needed for the refuge on Howe Key was transferred by the North American Wildlife Foundation to the federal government. This, with later acquisitions by the U. S. Fish and Wildlife Service, virtually assured the perpetuation of the smallest representative of the white-tailed deer, whose extinction seemed imminent in 1950. The population now numbers nearly 300.

Wildlife management, of which protection is a part, achieved other significant successes that predated the enactment of endangered-species laws. While they were unable to restore the species involved to anything approaching abundance, they were at least able to carry nucleus breeding stocks of three distinct species of birds into an age when the climate for serious restoration activities is better than at any time in the past.

In 1937, the population of the whooping crane was only sixteen birds, which plied migration routes 2,500 miles long across the prairies from breeding grounds near Great Slave Lake in the Northwest Territories of Canada to wintering grounds on the Gulf Coast of South

Texas. Although questionable observations by early naturalists place wintering or migrating whooping cranes in Florida and as far off their beaten track as Massachusetts, the original range probably was not much different than that today, and, compared to the more adaptable sandhill crane, their numbers were probably few even in early times. Their breeding grounds were so remote from civilization that they were unknown until the 1950s when Robert Allen, a biologist in the employ of the National Audubon Society, succeeded in locating a nesting colony in the Mackenzie District of the Northwest Territories. Fortuitously, this area had been set aside earlier by the Canadian Government as a refuge for the wood bison. This had eliminated the subsistence hunting and egg stealing by Indians which, before the creation of Wood Buffalo National Park, may have been a reason for the original decline.

With the enactment of the Migratory Bird Treaty Act in 1918, whooping cranes were placed under rigid federal protection on both sides of the border. In 1937, Congress established the Aransas National Wildlife Refuge near Corpus Christi, Texas, and the establishment of waterfowl refuges in the Dakotas, Nebraska, Oklahoma, Kansas, and other states along the migration routes provided protected stopover sanctuaries where the big birds could feed and rest in safety. The National Audubon Society and other national conservation organizations joined the state wildlife agencies in a massive educational program in an effort to eliminate the promiscuous shooting of cranes that had taken a small but serious toll of the migrating birds each year. Federal and state courts, recognizing the urgency of the situation, imposed heavy fines or jail sentences on deliberate violators.

In the meantime, intensive habitat management was initiated on the Aransas refuge. A series of impoundments stocked with marine organisms was created to provide needed animal foods, and large areas, fenced against deer, cattle, and other grazing animals that would compete with the cranes for forage, were planted with grains favored by the birds.

With this encouragement, the crane population began a slow but definite increase broken by occasional unexplained setbacks. In 1972, it reached a modern high of fifty-six but only forty-seven returned in the following autumn and forty-nine were counted in 1974.

In the meantime, the U. S. Fish and Wildlife Service, in cooperation with the Canadian Wildlife Service, began a new phase of whooping crane restoration activity. In compliance with the Endangered Species Preservation Act of 1966, the U. S. Fish and Wildlife Service had established an endangered-species laboratory under the supervision of Dr. Ray Erickson at its Patuxent Wildlife Research Station.

Research had determined that the female whooping crane produces only two eggs a year. But the probability of both eggs producing chicks is remote. If two young crane chicks were produced, the first to hatch usually killed its nestmate. This characteristic offered possibilities to Erickson. If one egg could be removed from each nest and incubated artificially, a captive population could be built up as a reserve against the eventuality of the loss of the wild population to a hurricane or oil spill on its wintering grounds, a fire on the breeding grounds, or some other cataclysmic occurrence.

Whooping cranes adapt well to captivity, but those confined in pens had produced no viable eggs. In an effort to refine methods of crane culture, Erickson and his biologists first developed a captive flock of sandhill cranes, closely related to the whooping crane but still abundant in most of the prairie states and provinces. These were used to develop techniques of incubation, brooding, and handling that could be applied to the endangered whoopers, if and when their eggs became available.

In May, 1967, Erickson, accompanied by Canadian biologists, flew to Wood Buffalo National Park where they collected six eggs. On the same day, through the miracle of modern jet transportation, the eggs, cradled in Erickson's lap, were flown to Maryland and placed in incubators before nightfall. Five of them hatched. To prevent "imprinting,"—the tendency of wild birds to accept as "Mother" the first living thing they see after emerging from their eggs—biologists tending the brooders wore white coveralls and masks that gave them an appearance approaching as closely as humanly possible that of wild whooping cranes.

Although this system was initially opposed by some conservation organizations, including the National Audubon Society, it has provided a captive population of whooping cranes that can be used in future years to bolster the naturally maintained continental population. Opportunities for expanding the protected wintering refuges of the species came in late 1974 when the U. S. Air Force abandoned its bombing range on Matagorda Island only a few miles from Aransas National Wildlife Refuge. Since the island is already in public ownership, it would seem that the most appropriate use of the island would be as an expanded wintering range for the whooping crane, an extension of the effort at Aransas. In recent years, Matagorda Island already had been retired from use under a voluntary agreement with the air force, as a bombing range during the winter months when the cranes were present in the area. Acquisition of the island by the U. S. Fish and Wildlife Service would permit its intensive development to meet the needs of the cranes.

The whooping crane is far from secure as a species. But hopes for its survival into the twenty-first century are now better than they have seemed for years.

The fallacy of believing that you can save an endangered species merely by passing a law to protect it and then leaving it alone, as some protectionists advocate, is best illustrated by the case of the Kirtland's warbler. Tiny, inconspicuous, and probably rare even in primitive times, it is one of those species that, except for the alertness of a few ornithologists and naturalists, might have slipped unnoticed into oblivion.

The Kirtland's warbler nests in a few counties in northcentral Michigan. In its autumn migration it flies almost nonstop to the Bahamas where it winters. The Kirtland's warbler probably reached its greatest abundance in the 1920s when the forests of Michigan were beginning to recover from the devastating logging and fires of the late 1800s. The species is unique in that to nest successfully it requires open stands of jack pines between five and fifteen feet in height with low, brushy undergrowth. In early times, stands of this kind were prevalent owing to the woods-burning operations of the Indians and the prevalence of lightning-set fires. With the settlement of northern Michigan by whites, the frontier farmers continued the practice of spring burning to expand their pasturage and croplands.

With the development of scientific forestry after 1900, fire suppression received top priority. Volunteer forest-fire fighting companies, under federal subsidies, were organized in every community and rushed to every fire at the first wisp of smoke.

While desirable from the standpoint of forest conservation, forest-fire suppression militated against the survival of the Kirtland's warbler. As the pines within its range grew higher and thicker, its nesting range dwindled. Noting this alarming decline of an already rare bird, the Michigan Audubon Society appealed to the regional offices of the U. S. Forest Service, which responded by setting aside 4,010 acres of jack pines for intensive management as a Kirtland's warbler sanctuary. The larger trees were logged off and sections of the area were subjected to prescribed burning each year to maintain the pines at a height useful to the warblers.

Nurseries maintained by the Department of Natural Resources and the Forest Service provided jackpine seedlings to the Michigan Audubon Society, which recruited volunteer planting crews from among its members to reforest denuded areas where the trees were not seeding in naturally. In the meantime, the Michigan Department of Natural Resources began developing similar warbler-management areas, each four square miles in area, on state forest lands.

These programs were just beginning to show results when the forested area was invaded by an unprecedented number of cowbirds. The cowbird is a parasitic nester. The bird does not build a nest or raise its own young. It avoids all parental responsibility by laying its eggs in the nest of a smaller bird, usually a sparrow or warbler. Since a cowbird nestling is more than twice as large as a newly hatched warbler, it is able to grab all of the food brought to the nest by its bewildered foster parents. The result, almost inevitably, is ejection from the nest and death by starvation of the young warblers.

Dr. Nicholas Cuthbert of the Michigan Audubon Society, after a study of the seriousness of the problem, recommended and was given authority to conduct intensive cowbird-control programs. In most situations, cowbird parasitism is only a minor depressant on populations of the host species. But in Michigan, the Kirtland's warbler was so reduced in numbers that its small, isolated population was in danger of being swamped by a species that occurs in abundance over much of the North American continent.

As a result of this management, the Kirtland's warbler population has increased from a few dozens to nearly five hundred breeding pairs. Little is known of the problems that may face it on its wintering grounds in the Bahama Islands. The Michigan Audubon Society has been working through Bahamian bird groups to have some of its scrub forest wintering habitat set aside as a sanctuary. While the little yellowish warbler with the black face mask is not safe from extinction, more is known today of its habitat needs than at any earlier time in history. In the application of that knowledge is the hope for its salvation as a species.

Near the opposite end of the weight scale among endangered bird species is the California condor, as large as a good-sized turkey gobbler and with a wing-span of more than nine feet. In early times it scoured the western mountains from the Columbia River to Baja California, in search of carrion. It probably fed heavily on dead, spawned-out salmon that formerly littered the shores of the rivers of the Pacific Northwest. Elsewhere and at other times it gleaned a living from the carcasses of wild animals and domesticated livestock.

The condor is especially sensitive to human disturbance, and the first threat to its existence came with the Gold Rush and the resultant swarming over the mountains of hundreds of miners and prospectors. Then, towns, ranches, and irrigation reservoirs encroached on much of its former habitat and dams cut off the salmon spawning runs on many of the streams. The condor was especially vulnerable to poisoning during the days of unrestricted predator control. Eventually, the nesting range of the largest of North American vultures was squeezed into a restricted area in the Sierra Nevada foothills and the southern coast range of California. Another small population had been reliably reported in Mexico's Baja California. The population in the United States in recent years has fluctuated at around forty birds, dropping as low as twenty-eight in 1970.

The decline of the condor has been a matter of concern to ornithologists for many years. The U. S. Forest Service, in response to this concern, established two extensive condor sanctuaries on the Los Padres National Forest on which it prohibited the use of poisons and the carrying of firearms on and around these areas. Entry into these areas except by authorized personnel was forbidden. To protect and study the needs of the birds, full-time biologists were employed by the California Department of Fish and Game and the National Audubon Society, and the California State Legislature enacted a law making the killing or molestation of condors subject to fines up to $1,000 and/or a year in prison.

These measures may or may not save the California condor as a living museum piece from the Pleistocene Age. The intrusion of skiing resorts and other developments into the mountain ranges dims hopes for expanding its occupied nesting range. And its low breeding potential—an average of one young every other year—precludes the rapid buildup of population that is possible with most other species.

In suburban Maryland, fifteen miles north of Washington, D.C., in a secluded section of the Patuxent Wildlife Research Station lies a unique "game farm." Its inhabitants are among the rarest animals on earth. This is the Endangered Species Laboratory of the U. S. Fish and Wildlife Service. In roomy pens, screened and barricaded against predators, more than twenty whooping cranes—nearly half as many as there are in the wild—preen and strut and sometimes engage in a comical gangling dance. All are offspring of wild birds artificially hatched from eggs gathered from nests in faraway Wood Buffalo National Park in northwestern Canada.

In similar pens nearby are more than one hundred Aleutian Canada geese, representatives of the smallest and darkest race of the species. Unlike the crane, this dwarf goose breeds readily in captivity, averaging six eggs to each breeding pair. All of those at Patuxent are descendants of sixteen live-trapped on Buldir Island in the Aleutian Islands in 1963. In 1971, the Fish and Wildlife Service began releasing birds from this captive flock, specially conditioned for survival in the wild, to their former range.

Hope for success of these reintroductions appears good. The original sharp population decline was caused by introduction to the islands of blue and silver foxes whose offspring were permitted to fare for themselves until large enough for trapping. The geese and their eggs provided the foxes with staple foods. With the systematic removal of the foxes, the one major check on their increase appears to have been eliminated. The remoteness and barrenness of their nesting habitat preclude the disturbance by human intrusion that threatens the existence of other species in other parts of the world. There is every reason to believe that the Aleutian Canada goose, at least, can be restored to some semblance of its original abundance.

In other pens are flocks of the colorful masked bobwhite quail from the desert Southwest, resembling the common bobwhite in configuration but with brick-red breasts and black instead of white markings on their faces and upper bodies. The enemies of the masked bobwhite are cattle and sheep rather than man. Overgrazing destroyed or damaged its grassland habitat to the extent that it was eliminated from Arizona, the only part of the United States in which it was found. Small populations, however, persisted in Mexico's State of Sonora, which provided a source for a nucleus captive breeding population at the Patuxent Laboratory.

Like the Aleutian Canada goose and the common eastern bobwhite, the masked bobwhite propagates readily in captivity, and a flock of nearly one thousand was quickly built up at Patuxent. Periodic releases of these birds have been made over the past several years on areas in Arizona selected for their suitability to maintain wild population. Most of these grasslands, however, are privately owned lands over which the government has little or no control. Although a number of landowners have proved cooperative, the future of the masked bobwhite as a wild bird will depend upon how much land the U. S. Fish and Wildlife Service and the Arizona Game and Fish Department acquire and manage for its use.

There are no California condors at the Patuxent Endangered Species Laboratory. The species rests on such a knife's edge of precariousness that any attempts to capture breeding specimens would threaten its survival. The laboratory, however, does contain a number of Andean condors, larger and more numerous cousins of the California species. These are being used, like the sandhill cranes in the whooping crane project, as stand-ins for research into methods for raising and handling condors in captivity. Information gathered will be used as a last resort if and when the wild population of California condors appears on the verge of immediate extinction. Similarly, domesticated ferrets are being used to develop techniques for raising the endangered black-footed ferret if such a move becomes necessary to save the species from extinction.

The Endangered Species Act calls for the development of a recovery plan for each of the endangered species in the United States. For some, like the Aleutian Canada goose, the problem is relatively simple. For others, it is extremely complex. Birds like the brown pelican, southern bald eagle, and peregrine falcon, which are threatened by pesticide-poisoning, will be especially difficult to save unless immediate steps are taken to clean up the environment and find safer methods of controlling forest and crop pests. Some progress has been made in that direction. DDT has been withdrawn from general use, although in 1974, the U. S. Forest Service obtained a special exemption in its use over extensive areas in the Northwest to combat an outbreak of the tussock moth. But the elimination of the use of DDT and some related compounds over most of the United States gives hope that after the residues left by earlier blanket sprayings finally dissipate, these birds will resume normal reproduction patterns.

The National Audubon Society maintains a number of extensive eagle sanctuaries to supplement the eagle range in the national Wildlife Refuge System. The National Wildlife Federation, on December 19, 1974, donated a thousand acres of land in South Dakota and Nebraska to the U. S. Fish and Wildlife Service as an eagle sanctuary. Money for this project came from a special fund-raising campaign developed by the Seven-Eleven Food Stores of the Southland Corporation of Dallas, Texas. Although America's national bird may never become as abundant as it was before the days of DDT, there is hope that it can be restored again to safe breeding levels in many parts of its former range.

Population trends of some endangered species can be reversed by simple protection. In the late 1960s poachers operating at night were slaughtering hundreds of alligators for their valuable hides, in open defiance of state laws. Some were operating on national wildlife refuges and even in Everglades National Park. Their apprehension was difficult, and penalties imposed by rural courts on those who were caught rarely exceeded the profits of a night's work. Under this pressure, the alligator was undergoing a sharp decline.

The Lacey Act of 1900, which prohibited the interstate shipment of wildlife and wildlife products taken in violation of state law, applied only to birds and mammals and not to reptiles.

After Congress corrected this oversight by amending the Lacey Act to bring the alligator and other reptiles under its shelter the effect was dramatic. Most of the illegally taken raw alligator hides had found their way to processors in New York City and foreign cities where they were converted into shoes, wallets, and handbags. This lucrative business ended abruptly when the federal government entered the picture and New York State enacted its Mason Endangered Species Act prohibiting the importation of any product of an endangered species into the state. These laws, instead of trying to penalize the elusive poacher, zeroed in on the dealers and processors who supported him. Those who tried to circumvent the law faced stern-faced federal or state judges instead of sympathetic rural justices of the peace, and a few stiff fines and jail sentences discouraged others who were considering entering the illicit trade. With their source of income cut off, most of the poachers returned to their crawdad fishing and muskrat trapping to reminisce about the good old days when a night of "gator" gigging could bring in $200.

Further federal protection for the alligator came when the saurian was declared endangered under the Endangered Species Act of 1973, although by that time the cause for its decline had been virtually eliminated. Inclusion of the species under this Act made it illegal for the states to use legal hunting seasons as a method of controlling population expansion.

Response of the alligator population to protection was quite spectacular. A female alligator produces from fifteen to eighty-five eggs each year. Although many of the young are lost to predators, including other alligators, the population in understocked habitat can easily double or triple in a single year.

Substantial increases in alligator populations soon became apparent in Florida, Louisiana, North Carolina, and South Carolina. In North Carolina, where the status of the species appeared critical in the 1960s biologists tallied 88,400 in 1973. In 1971–72, the Florida Game and Fresh Water Fish Commission estimated the state's alligator population at 250,000, a 53-percent increase over previous counts. Its officers had responded to 4,873 complaints of alligators killing dogs, threatening children, and even invading swimming pools. State wildlife officers had captured and moved 1,680 offending alligators to new homes removed from human habitation, but the problem still persisted. In Cameron County, Louisiana, alligators became so abundant that they threatened the lucrative fur industry. (In view of this, it is interesting to note that neither the mountain caribou, which numbers around twenty in northern Idaho, nor the swift fox, which is so rare that some authorities considered it extinct until a few specimens turned up in South Dakota recently, are on the endangered-species list as of early 1975.)

Early efforts by the states to obtain permission to open problem areas to regulated alligator hunting were blocked by the Department of the Interior on the grounds that it could open the doors to a resumption of poaching. In late 1974, however, after the southern state wildlife agencies released details of a proposal that involved a virtually fraud-proof licensing and tagging system, the U. S. Fish and Wildlife Service agreed to consider reclassification of the alligator either to a nonendangered species or to a threatened species, either of which would permit the states to bring the populations under control through legalized harvest. This would give residents of the alligator country an incentive for protecting the animals instead of resenting their existence.

The most perplexing problem facing wildlife managers involves saving and restoring the red wolf. Originally this small cousin of the timber wolf hunted the swamps, canebrakes, and thickets of eastern Texas and the lower Mississippi Valley. With the advent of settlement, much of its original habitat was destroyed and replaced with open pastures and cropfields that were untenable to wolves but ideal habitat for coyotes. Like all wild canids, the wolf was heavily persecuted with trap, poison, and gun and reduced to fragments of its original numbers.

In earlier times the coyote and the red wolf had evolved in genetic isolation. But as the preferred habitat of the wolf diminished, contact between the two species became more frequent. Although as recently as the 1950s scientists had thought that there were several thousand red wolves, zoologists who examined wild-trapped or road-killed specimens found that nearly all were crosses between wolves and coyotes, and the red wolf was in danger of genetic swamping. Biologists, however, had discovered a population of about three hundred purebred red wolves on the coastal prairie marshes of the Texas Gulf Coast. If coyotes can be kept away from these animals, there is hope for the perpetuation of the red wolf as a species. The problem is complicated by the fact that anything that will kill coyotes will also kill red wolves. Biologists, however, have developed a trapping technique that is highly effective and takes the animals unharmed. This involves the use of a tranquilizer tab used in conjunction with a padded leg-hold trap. As soon as the captured animal instinctively bites at the trap in an effort to escape, the tranquilizer puts it to sleep until the trapper makes his rounds. If the animal captured is a purebred red wolf, it can be released unharmed. Federal agents are now running traplines in a buffer strip around the ranges of known populations of red wolves in an effort to forestall the invasion of coyotes.

By 1975, most of the state fish and wildlife agencies, in compliance with the Endangered Species Act, had developed continuing programs for the benefit of nongame species, with special reference to endangered and threatened species. In a number of states, notably California and New York, efforts along these lines long predated enactment of the federal law.

Existing state fish and wildlife programs, of course, already produce substantial benefits to both endangered and other nongame species. From the standpoint of law enforcement, the distinction between game and nongame is purely artificial. Many more species of birds and mammals receive full protection under state and federal law than those that are hunted for sport or trapped for commercial use. Every conservation officer is as obligated by duty to apprehend someone shooting robins as he is to run down deer poachers. Habitat restoration and preservation for game birds and mammals provides living space for dozens of ecologically related nongame species. Impoundments created for waterfowl attract hundreds of species of songbirds, wading birds, and aquatic mammals of no immediate interest to the sportsmen as game.

But full-scale management programs that will assure the survival of presently endangered species and minimize the chances of others becoming endangered or extinct will cost more money than conservation agencies have now. In a survey conducted by the Wildlife Management Institute for the U. S. Department of the Interior and the Council on Environmental Quality in 1975, it was found that these needs, above and beyond those now available, approximated $40 million. At the present time, state fish and wildlife agencies are supported almost exclusively by hunting- and fishing-license fees and special taxes on hunting and fishing equipment. With the inflationary spiral in recent years, state fish and wildlife agencies are facing difficulties in maintaining existing programs, let alone expanding into new areas of endeavor.

Both Congress and the state legislatures have shown more willingness to authorize constructive fish and wildlife programs than they have been to appropriate actual funds to carry them out. For this reason, reliance on legislative appropriations to bolster existing fish and wildlife agency budgets to benefit nongame and endangered species seems a rather vain hope. But if the public wants an expanded program, the public is going to have to find some way to pay the bill. This may take the form of an excise tax on certain items of luxury equipment related to the outdoor experience, such as binoculars, cameras, or camping equipment. Fortunately, the expertise and techniques for restoration of most endangered species and the maintenance of other nongame species have already been developed. The wildlife-management profession contains a large backlog of well-trained biologists, research workers, and wildlife managers whose skills are now being wasted in unrelated jobs. All that is needed to start things rolling is a substantial inoculation of money.

Chapter 24

Wildlife of the Seas

With the exception of the American bison, few animals have been subjected to more ruthless economic exploitation than the whales and seals. Whaling ranks next to mining and codfishing as the earliest American industry, predating permanent settlement on the East Coast by nearly a century. In early times, most of the whaling was done from shore bases, the whales chased, harpooned, and lanced from small boats, and towed to shore to try out the oil from their blubber. In the meantime, fleets of British, French, and Basque whalers were exploiting the whale "fisheries" of the North Atlantic to the extent that some of the more productive whaling grounds were completely depopulated. By the time of the American Revolution, stocks of right and humpback whales that supported the coastal whaling operations had declined to such a low point that the practice of shore whaling was no longer economically feasible except as a sideline.

But in the meantime, beginning in 1712, when a ship from Nantucket blundered into a pod of sperm whales far out to sea, pelagic whaling from American ports had begun in earnest. By 1800, dozens of ships, especially built and fitted for the trade, from New Bedford, Nantucket, Mystic, and other ports were combing the seas searching for the flash of black flukes or the telltale geyser of white spray that signaled the presence of a surfacing whale. In a time when the petroleum that seeped from the earth here and there was considered only of medicinal value, whale oil, other than beeswax and bayberry candles, was the only practical source of light. Ambergris, a substance formed in the intestines of some specimens of sperm whale, was highly prized as a base for perfumes, and brought exceedingly high prices in Paris and other centers of the perfume industry. Sperm whale teeth consist of a high-grade ivory. In the sperm whale fishery, however, it was the spermaceti, a milky substance with the consistency of molten wax, that was the primary product. Prized for its smokeless qualities and high light intensity when burned, it was a favorite ingredient for candlemakers and for industrial lubricants. A reservoir in the head of a sperm whale may contain a full ton of spermaceti.

The baleen whales—blue, gray, humpback, bowhead, and right—which were the staples of much of the whaling industry, produced several byproducts in addition to the massive quantities of oil in their blubber. One of these was the "whalebone," a strong, elastic structure which was ideal for use as corset stays, cores for buggy whips, and for umbrella frames.

As whales within easy cruising range of the shore points disappeared, the whalers ventured farther and farther from home, deep into the Arctic and Antarctic, and often circumnavigated the world in rambling cruises that sometimes occupied three years or more. By the end of the War of 1812, the whaling ship had become refined for her task. Built for storage capacity and seaworthiness rather than speed, the whaler—whether ship-, bark-, or barkentine-rigged—was broad of beam, plodding, and sluggish in comparison with the swift, racy clippers and packets that left her in their wakes. But between 1800 and 1860, hundreds of ships like these sailed every ocean and every sea in the world in a restless search for oil.

Their crews were incredibly tough and incredibly young. The average age of the officers was less than thirty years and that of the seamen under twenty. In addition to the usual hazards facing all seafaring men in those days—shipwreck, fire, being washed overboard in a gale, or falling from the rigging—they risked life and limb in every encounter with their quarry. Their motto was "A dead whale or a stove boat." The whaleboat was a narrow-beamed, double-ended boat, no more than twenty feet in length, propelled by from four to six oarsmen. The other members of her crew were a helmsman who steered the boat with a tiller and the harpooner who occupied the bow.

The harpoon was not used to kill the whale. Its purpose was to attach a stout line a thousand yards or more long to the whale's body. The head of the harpoon, or lily iron, was hinged so that, after it was driven into the blubber of the whale and brought under tension it turned perpendicular to the shaft locking itself securely into the tissues of the great mammal. There was not much danger in the harpooning itself as the whale usually was unaware of the presence of the boat, and the pain inflicted on such a large creature by the entry of the lily iron was probably little more than a pinprick. The real danger came while the boat crew fought the whale to tire it, as an angler fights a trout. The sperm whale can dive to depths of nearly three-quarters of a mile with incredible speed, and charge back up from those depths like a giant torpedo. Great care had to be applied in laying the harpoon line in the tub before the fight and while it was in progress. The oarsmen fought the whale by playing out and hauling in the line, which was belayed around a snubbing post, as circumstances demanded. When the whale was sounding, the friction of rope against wood sometimes caused the snubbing post to smoke. A snarl or kink could cause disaster by pulling the entire boat under or by snaring the leg or arm of a crew member.

The first strategy of the whale in its attempts to escape was usually a long, steep dive to great depths where it sulked and rested a quarter mile or more beneath the boat. A sperm whale can remain submerged for an hour and a half.

But eventually, as the oxygen in its great lungs was exhausted, it had to surface. For the whalers, this was the most critical moment of all. By this time the whale was fully aware of its tormentors and its strength was little diminished. A sperm whale carries death on either end. Its ten-foot-long jaws with great conical teeth six to eight inches long were evolved to crush giant squids as long or longer than a whale boat. A flip of its tail could send the boat and its crew skyward or smash it to splinters. On November 20, 1820, a male sperm whale charged the Nantucket whaler *Essex* with such force that the 238-ton vessel was sent to the bottom. The collision obviously was deliberate, since the attack was repeated until the seams in the ship opened.

Once the whale surfaced, the crew hauled on the rope until the bow of the boat almost touched the massive head, and the harpooner plunged a long-handled lance deep into its vitals. If it struck the heart, the fight was soon over. But if the wound was not immediately mortal, the result was usually a "Nantucket sleighride" with the whale racing along the surface towing the frail boat in its wake. In the Seamen's Bethel, immortalized by Herman Melville in the opening sequence of *Moby Dick*, there are dozens of wall plaques erected to the memory of New Bedford whalers whose end came when they were "towed out to sea by a whale."

Once the kill was made, all romance associated with whaling ended. Processing the carcass on shipboard was a bloody, smelly business. Once the kill was secured by the mother ship, grappling hooks attached to lines running through blocks and tackle on the mainmast top were fastened to the massive carcass. Then, with flensing irons— long-handled, spade-shaped knives—the whalers sliced through the thick blubber, peeling it away in broad sheets much as one peels an orange. Flensing was also a dangerous operation, as some men had to work on the slippery floating carcass which, in most waters, attracted hordes of ravenous sharks that swirled in feeding frenzies around it.

After the blubber was removed it was cooked in huge pots on brick stoves to try out the oil. The oil was skimmed off with gargantuan ladles and stored in casks. The same ladles were used to spoon the spermaceti from the heads of sperm whales. What little was left of the whale after this process was consigned to the sharks and the sea.

In the heyday of the whaling industry, in 1847, more than seven hundred American whaling ships were operating on every ocean in the world. Officers and crew members of the whalers were paid in shares based on the rank and importance of each. Some ordinary seamen made more money on single cruises than they could otherwise have expected to make in a lifetime, and some ship owners amassed enormous fortunes.

The drain of the resource, however, was staggering, and by the time petroleum was discovered in 1859, many of the whales were nearly extinct.

The whaling industry that Herman Melville had known went into a long, steep decline. The fleets of sail-driven whalers were replaced by a comparatively few but much more efficient steam- or diesel-powered ships armed with harpoon guns.

As the whale stocks declined sharply during the mid-1800s the only species that managed to thrive were those too swift or wary to be overtaken by rowboats. The blue and fin whales, although prized for their oil and baleen, presented special challenges. In 1864, Captain Sven Foyn, a Norwegian whaling captain, developed a small cannon that, mounted on the bow of a ship or boat, could be used to propel the harpoon deep into the vitals of the whale. As a refinement, he added a timed explosive charge to the head of the harpoon that, on penetration, exploded and shredded the lungs and heart of the quarry while the line carried by the harpoon secured the dead or dying whale to the boat. A refined and improved model of the Foyn gun was marketed by W. W. Greener, the famous British gunsmith, during the late 1800s and early 1900s.

In the meantime, diesel fuel and steam were rapidly replacing sail in the whaling fleets. Coupled with the harpoon gun, this made the romantic and dangerous occupation of whaling as prosaic and as safe a trade as stamping beer cans.

Although Greener's improved harpoon gun in 1890 seemed to have about as much future as a refined buggy whip would have had in 1920, the whaling industry was far from dead. Although the electric light was replacing the whale oil lamp, the demand for whale products by industry remained high. Around 1900, explorers probing the bays and inlets of the Antarctic Continent found them teeming with whales. The remaining whalers, now virtually all converted to power and armed with harpoon guns, converged on this concentration to share in the slaughter while the whaling companies of Scotland, England, Denmark, Germany, and the United States hastily placed orders for new and improved whaling ships and established whaling stations on islands convenient to the whaling grounds where the kills could be butchered and processed. Whale kills mounted annually.

In 1924, the first of the factory whaling ships was launched and dozens of others were nearing completion on their ships. The factory ship, often approaching a thousand tons, was the ultimate in deadly efficiency and mechanical ingenuity. It was attended by fleets of killer or catcher boats, each armed with a harpoon gun and capable of operating in safety hundreds of miles from the mother factory ship. As the whales were towed to the factory ship, a huge port or slipway was opened in its stern. Through this the entire body of the whale was drawn inside. Then the machinery went to work, cutting, slicing, grinding, and stewing until the carcass, in little over an hour, was reduced to vats of segregated products—meat for humans or pets, oil for industry, bone for fertilizer—and little returned to the sea except streams of blood.

The ultimate refinement of the whaling operation came after the close of World War II when sonar and radar, designed to track enemy submarines, became available for civilian use. The whalers were quick to adopt these instruments. Now there was no escape for any whale that came within the range of the catcher boats. Sonar could pick up and pinpoint the calls and sounds of whales thousands of feet below the surface, day or night, and be waiting with harpoon guns charged and aimed as soon as one of them surfaced. The take of whales reached a peak in 1962, when the carcasses of 66,090 whales were run through the slipways of the factory ships. No living resource with such a low breeding potential could withstand such pressure.

The right and bowhead whales had already been reduced to remnants of their former abundance, and the great blue whale declined abruptly after the factory ships entered the Antarctic Ocean. In the season of 1930–31, nearly thirty thousand blue whales were killed. In 1964, fewer than four hundred were found by the catcher boats.

Some attempt to slow the slaughter of the whales was made as early as 1931, when an international treaty was drawn at Geneva and ratified as the International Convention for the Regulation of Whaling, in 1935. This treaty provided protection to female whales accompanied by calves and full protection for the surviving right and bowhead whales.

After World War II, in 1946, the International Whaling Commission, with representatives of all whaling nations, was formed as an international body to regulate the whaling industry. Among the participants was the Soviet Union, which, with little or no tradition for whaling in the prewar days, had developed some of the largest and most efficient factory ships after the return of peace. Japan in the postwar years also had greatly accelerated its whaling efforts in response to problems of overpopulation and a decline of domestic stocks of protein.

The intent behind the International Whaling Commission was good, but its achievements as a conservation body have been slim. Dominated by whaling interests, it has expended more effort toward perpetuating the dying whaling industry than in rebuilding and sustaining the resources on which it is based.

Much of the problem stems from the rules under which the IWC functions. Before quotas or closures on the taking of threatened species of whales can be imposed, three-fourths of the members must vote in favor of the proposal. Moreover, the rules give each member virtual veto power over the enforcement of any regulation adopted by the Commission as a whole.

Among the twelve member nations, Japan has taken the lead in opposing every move to adopt constructive conservation actions. Denmark, Iceland, Norway, South Africa, and the Soviet Union almost consistently support Japan. On the other side, the United States, usually supported by Argentina, Canada, France, Great Britain, and Mexico, has taken the lead in attempting to develop an effective international conservation program that will rebuild the whale populations to a point where they can be harvested under a sustained-yield quota system. As a first step toward this goal, the conservation bloc in the IWC has been pushing for a ten-year moratorium on the taking of all whales. It has received some support from Brazil and Panama. But the stalemate in the IWC precludes any action along these lines until the unlikely eventuality that the IWC revises its ground rules. Most of the nations in the conservation bloc in IWC, including the United States, have abandoned whaling as an economically moribund enterprise. The last whaling company in the United States closed its doors in 1972 when Secretary of the Interior Walter J. Hickel placed the great whales on the endangered-species list, effectively shutting off importations of whale products into the United States and exerting some economic pressure on the remaining whaling nations. In the wake of this action, both houses of Congress adopted resolutions supporting a ten-year moratorium on all whaling and an amendment to the Fishermen's Protection Act authorized the President to apply sanctions against any nation that refuses to abide by international agreement. This amendment was aimed primarily at Japan, the most adamant opponent of conservation measures and the most vulnerable to economic sanctions. Japan buys more than $200 million in seafood products alone from the United States. The United States supplies most of the minerals and wood products used in Japanese industry. Unfortunately, as an economic weapon, sanctions have shortcomings as their full application would harm the United States economy as much as it would that of Japan, which could turn to other nations for its raw materials and for ready outlets for its products.

In an effort to force Japan to change its attitude toward whale conservation, the National Audubon Society and the National Wildlife Federation, in 1974, took the lead of twenty-one conservation, environmental, and humane groups in calling for an embargo on all Japanese goods.

Unless these steps prove effective, or Japan and Russia radically change their views, the only hope for most of the whales surviving to the twenty-first century is that the whaling industry will become economically defunct before the last of the leviathans is killed. Japanese thinking apparently is based more upon returning the investment in its existing whaling fleet than it is in the products produced. Whale stocks are so low worldwide that the replacement of the complex and costly factory ships could not be justified. As the existing ships wear out, the whales will receive some surcease from the present pressure. Whether or not this will come soon enough for some species remains to be seen.

Paradoxically, while the federal government of the United States fights in international meetings to curtail whaling, it still permits a particularly destructive and wasteful form of whaling within its own territorial waters. And the whale species involved is one of the most seriously endangered.

For centuries Eskimos on the northern coast of Alaska have hunted the bowhead whales that migrate back and forth in the icy waters offshore. In early days the Eskimo hunters ventured from shore with ivory-tipped harpoons and stone lances in *umiaks*, skin boats capable of carrying a dozen paddlers. Today the Eskimo hunter uses a high-powered rifle, and his *umiak* is propelled by a 75-horsepower outboard motor. Reliable observers estimate that from four to five mortally wounded whales are lost for every one recovered. While the seasonal kill is numerically small, it represents a significant proportion of the population of bowheads left in the world. The species is so rare that it has been protected continuously by international agreement under the whaling convention since that treaty became effective in 1935. Fewer than one thousand are believed to remain alive.

The problem is a complicated one. Eskimos, Indians, and other aborigines have been exempted from the conditions of nearly all conservation laws and treaties because of the dependence of some of their tribes and villages on wild meat and products. Many early treaties between Indians and whites exempted the natives from the application of manmade fish and game laws. The problem is further complicated by the fact that some Eskimo villages still have a real need for harvesting whales, walruses, and other forms of wild meats for subsistence purposes. In others, wild meats and products of wild animals are no more essential to the existence of the native than they are to a Sioux Indian in Fargo, North Dakota.

Eskimos and their proponents defend their continued whaling operations, even from villages where most of the men draw wages and salaries from oil companies and shop in community stores, on the grounds that it is part of their culture and should be preserved as such. But perhaps the preservation of Eskimo culture and the cause of whale conservation in such cases could best be served if the Eskimo laid aside his rifle and outboard motor and resumed the use of the hunting implements of his ancestors.

Concern for the porpoises and dolphins is of relatively recent origin. Although a few species of porpoises and dolphins have been subjected to limited commercial exploitation, none has been accorded the ruthless persecution visited upon the great whales. In the days of the sailing ships and later, schools of porpoises playing in the shadows of the ships' bowsprits were considered good omens by the mariners. Where the great whales were the enemy, the porpoise was the sailor's friend.

Although porpoises often accompanied ships and boats into harbors and frolicked close inshore along the coasts, the animals were little known to the landsman until the 1950s. After World War II aquariums, zoos, and private entrepreneurs with access to salt water, began developing marine exhibits that featured trained dolphins, porpoises, and other small marine mammals. The animals were taught to leap in unison in aerial ballets, to play water polo, and to serve as aquatic steeds for bikini-clad riders. Marineland of the Pacific in California, and the Theater of the Sea and Marineland in Florida were among the first of dozens of such establishments that have proliferated around the coasts of North America. Many have become among the prime tourist attractions in their respective states.

The ability of such displays to mold public attitudes toward wildlife is best demonstrated by the case of Namu, a killer whale captured in 1965 off the coast of British Columbia and acquired by Marineland of the Pacific in San Diego, California. For centuries, sailors and fishermen had considered the killer whale as the scourge of the sea, second perhaps only to the great white shark. In the North, where the shark rarely ventured and the killer whale was common, the sight of the great black triangular fin of an approaching killer whale chilled the heart of the Grand Banks dory fisherman and the Eskimo seal hunter. Weighing five tons or more, it could flip any small boat in a single rush, and its jaws were adapted to crushing and swallowing a hundred-pound seal at a single gulp. Until Namu and his tankmates, this was the image of the killer whale almost universally pictured in romantic literature and in the folklore of the sea.

The tourists who visited Marineland of the Pacific saw an entirely different side of the personality of the killer whale. Here, instead of a menacing, dreadful monster, was a big, beautiful black-and-white animal that tolerated human riders as readily as the dolphins, and who leaped and frolicked in response to human commands. Disney Studios promptly featured Namu in a film, further bolstering the public impression of killer whales as semi-human, lovable friends of man.

Public familiarity with and views toward marine mammals were further molded by technically and scientifically sound television shows, like *The Undersea World of Jacques Cousteau*, and by the sentimental romanticism in *Flipper*, a serialized children's show featuring trained porpoises. Through the television medium, millions of Americans, who might otherwise not have known that such things as porpoises, dolphins, and killer whales even existed, came to love them.

After World War II, the yellowfin tuna fisheries developed new techniques to replace the inefficient handlining methods they had used in the past. The new system consisted of playing out a huge net suspended from floats around a school of tuna until the fish were encircled and then closing the bottom with a line. From the shape of the closed net came the term "purse-seining." The new method greatly increased the number of tuna taken both by individual boats and by the fishery as a whole.

For many years, tuna fishermen had known that the sight of a school of porpoises almost invariably meant a school of tuna below. In early times, the hook-and-line fishing that they had used had no effect on the porpoises. But, with the near-universal adoption of the purse seine, porpoises almost invariably were entrapped with the tuna. When the net was hauled in, the mammals became entangled in the meshes and, unable to surface for air, almost invariably suffocated.

When the magnitude of these accidental losses was made public, a people conditioned by television and motion pictures to consider porpoises as their personal friends jumped with both feet on the tuna-fishing industry and demanded federal action to force reforms.

Public demands for federal protection of marine mammals, however, originated, initially and somewhat incongruously, in a controversy involving a species that is no more than a stray in American territorial waters and a situation over which the federal government of the United States has no official control. The harp seal is a migratory species whose population consists of three discrete subgroups. Two of these migrate eastward along the northern coast of Europe but the third moves westward to breeding grounds off the coasts of Greenland, Labrador, Newfoundland, and Quebec. Large numbers concentrate each winter in the Gulf of the St. Lawrence River. The young are born shortly before the spring breakup of the ice.

For a century or more, Canadian fishermen have supplemented their income at a season when ice and cold made their principal occupation impossible by killing harp seals for their fur and blubber. They are joined by ship-borne sealers from Norway.

Most of the pressure is exerted against the new-born cubs, whose soft, fluffy, pure-white furs command high prices in European markets. Animal slaughter of any kind, even under the most humane and sanitized conditions, is a distasteful business and sickening to the sensitive or squeamish. The killing of the harp seals is especially offensive because it is directed against an animal of exquisite beauty and great human appeal. The harp seal pup, a bit of snowy fluff with big, dark, almost-human eyes, is a creature nearer to a living toy than any other created.

The killing is done with clubs, the sealer cracking the skull of the appealing little beast and stripping off its pelt. Almost invariably, death is instantaneous. Even though the club occasionally misses the skull, a blow anywhere on the upper body of such a fragile animal would render it unconscious even if it did not kill it outright. Not many of the sealers miss their mark.

After World War II, Canadian and British humanitarians began a drive to end the slaughter of the harp seal pups. As part of their campaign, they developed color motion-picture films of the sealing operations that captured all of the gore and pathos of the event, mother seals shunted aside while callous sealers bashed in the heads of their pups, the steaming flayed carcasses, and the pools of blood staining the ice. In an effort to bolster their support, some representatives of Canadian and British humane societies toured the United States as lecturers, although the United States had no jurisdiction over the sealing, and its furriers made little use of harp seal pelts.

In the meantime, Canadian conservationists had become concerned for the future of the harp seal as a species. The original population of seals wintering in Canadian waters had dropped from more than four million to less than two million by the early 1960s, and kills of several hundred thousand a year were removing most of the annual reproduction, especially of the "Front" herd that wintered along the Labrador coast. At the instigation of the Canadian Government, Canada and Norway established a Joint Commission of Sealing to regulate the slaughter.

In 1965, quotas were first imposed on the number of seals that could be taken. In 1971, Canadian and Norwegian sealers were each permitted to take 100,000 pups from the Front population but only sixty thousand in 1972. From that point on, the quota for the Front herd was reduced by twenty thousand each year until it was phased out entirely in 1975. The Gulf of St. Lawrence sealing operation was closed to aircraft and ships over sixty-five feet long, although smaller ships with special sealing licenses and landsmen operating from shore were permitted to continue the killing under reduced quotas and strict government control.

Although Americans were not involved in the harp seal slaughter, they were very much involved in another sealing activity on the other side of the continent. The bleak, fog-shrouded Pribilof Islands, two hundred miles northwest of Dutch Harbor in the Aleutian Islands, were the concentration point and summer breeding grounds of the Alaska fur seal and the site of one of the most intensive and successful wildlife-management programs in North America. In the late nineteenth and early twentieth centuries, after whaling began to decline as a profitable enterprise, many of the ships turned to the seals and sea otters whose lustrous pelts brought high prices in the world fur trade. Although the fur seal hauls out on rocky islands in the Pribilofs to breed and give birth to its young in summer, it spends the rest of the year on the high seas of the North Pacific Ocean and Bering Sea. Although the Russians had exploited the seal colonies on the Pribilofs throughout their occupation of Alaska, sealers from the United States, Canada, Japan, and the Soviet Union hunted the seals when the animals were far from land. Pelagic sealing was both destructive and wasteful. The seals usually were taken by shooting or spearing from boats as they broke water to breathe. Under the circumstances, since only the head and upper back of the animal was exposed, the gunner or harpooner had no way to distinguish a pregnant cow from a bull or pup. As soon as a black bulge appeared above the surface, he had to shoot quickly or miss his chance. If not exceptionally heavy with blubber, seals tend to sink rapidly when shot; unless the sealer secured his dead quarry immediately, the loss of his prize was certain. Three or more were lost for every seal recovered. Under this pressure the seal population that returned to breed in the Pribilofs declined rapidly. Although early censuses of fur seals are unreliable because they were only estimates made by observers circumnavigating the islands in boats, the original numbers were probably around 2.5 million. But in 1911, an official census of the Pribilofs showed only 125,900.

The seals on the Pribilofs were accorded some protection as early as 1834 when the Russians first prohibited the killing of female seals on the islands. This protection was continued after 1869 under American ownership when the islands were set aside as a special reservation for the fur seals. Beginning in that year, the U. S. Treasury Department leased exclusive sealing rights to two companies— the Alaska Commercial Company, which held the leases from 1870 to 1889 and the North American Commercial Company, which leased the sealing rights from 1890 to 1909. Contracts with both companies stipulated that no females be killed.

The drastic depletion of the fur seal population through pelagic sealing is best illustrated by the comparative take by each of these companies in the twenty years that each operated in the Pribilofs. The Alaska Commercial Company had taken 1,977,377 skins; the North American Commercial Company only 342,651.

In the early 1900s, Americans opened the first of a number of lengthy negotiations with foreign sealing countries that culminated in the Fur Seal Treaty of 1911 among the United States, Great Britain, Japan, and Imperial Russia. Each signatory power agreed to prohibit pelagic sealing by its nationals and to manage the populations of fur seals within its own territorial waters. Fur seal rookeries existed also in Russia's Commander (Komandorskie) Islands and on Japanese Robben Island. Each nation agreed to regulate the take of fur skins under its territorial jurisdiction to a quota that would assure the survival and increase of the breeding stock and to share the pelts taken with the other nations as a reward for abandoning pelagic sealing. Canada and Japan each were to receive fifteen percent of the skins from the Pribilofs and fifteen percent from those taken by Russia on the Commander Islands. Canada, Russia, and the United States each received ten percent of the pelts from the Robben Island herd. The terms of this treaty appear to have been honored faithfully by all of the signatory powers until the treaty was terminated by Japan on her entry into World War II. From 1942 to 1957, the Pribilof herd was protected under a provisional agreement between Canada and the United States, under which Canada received twenty percent of the skins taken annually. In 1957, another interim North Pacific Fur Seal Convention similar to the treaty of 1911 was concluded by Canada, Japan, Russia, and the United States.

This was followed by the Interim Convention on Conservation of North Pacific Fur Seals, signed at Washington, D.C., on October 8, 1963, which became effective on April 10, 1964. The Fur Seal Act of 1966, passed by Congress on November 2, 1966, was an enabling act implementing the terms of the treaty on the part of the United States Government.

The Act and the treaty called for intensified research by all signatory powers of the fur seals in their territorial waters, including tagging to trace the movements of the animals. It authorized the taking of specified numbers of fur seals on the high seas by authorized biologists in the employ of all signatory powers for research purposes. The Interim Convention on Conservation of North Pacific Fur Seals also established a North Pacific Fur Seal Commission comprised of one member from each of the parties to the Convention. This Commission was to be responsible for formulating and coordinating research programs, studying the data gathered by research teams, and making recommendations for management procedures and harvest quotas.

Apart from the method of killing, the seal-management program in the Pribilofs has no relationship at all with that involving harp seals. The first is a carefully planned and strictly supervised program designed to save the seals from extinction; the second, until brought under regulation by the joint agreement between Norway and Canada, was purely extractive exploitation without plan or regulation.

The social structure of the fur seal herd is almost tailor-made for management. In May, with the opening of the breeding season, the breeding bulls, or "beachmasters," arrive in the Pribilofs to establish their territories. These are huge, broad-shouldered animals, usually at least ten years old with neck muscles thicker than their heads. Each territory, marked by invisible lines known only to its defender, varies in size with the strength and aggressiveness of its owner. Over this line no male seal will venture without being confronted with a savage, bellowing charge and, unless he retreats, a savage attack aimed at the neck and throat. Through this process of challenge and defense, the size of the territory of each male is adjusted to the strength and vigor of its defender. Some of the early arrivals, old beachmasters beyond their peak or young challengers not strong enough or aggressive enough to cut the mustard, may be forced out of the breeding territories entirely or into tiny areas on the periphery with room for only one or two cows.

Next to arrive, beginning in early June, are the cows, those that had bred in the previous season coming to shore to bear their young, with the unbred females entering the territories of selected bulls. With the arrival of the cows, the rookery erupts into a bedlam of seal-to-seal combat, each male charging continually across the rocks to challenge intruders, sometimes crushing newborn pups and bowling over a swarth of cows in an effort to reach the throats of his rivals. Although the fights almost always draw blood, and the hide of a veteran beachmaster consists mostly of scar tissue, the fights are rarely mortal. The beachmaster rules his harem with iron jaws. A female straying from the territory usually finds herself snatched by the scruff of the neck and hurled bodily back into the harem by her 400- to 600-pound lord and master. The mature cow rarely exceeds one hundred pounds in weight. The average size of the harem is between fifty and sixty cows, but a particularly large and aggressive male may control a hundred or more females. Because of the great disparity in the sex ratio within the active breeding territory, the nonbreeding males serve only as standby replacements for the beachmasters in future breeding seasons. In any one breeding season, their presence or absence in the Pribilofs does not affect one way or another the success of the annual reproductive cycle.

After the territories are established and the harems have been gathered by the breeding bulls, the young nonbreeding bachelor bulls, between two and four years old, reach the islands and form colonies on the outskirts of the rookeries, safe from the teeth of the territorial bulls. Here, they play, bask in the sun, and engage in relatively bloodless mock fights that will condition them for the serious combat that each will face in the future. Yearlings and immature females arrive even later, sometimes only weeks before the rookeries break up in November and the seals return to the sea.

This natural segregation of the seal population by sex, age, time, and space on the breeding grounds and the simplicity of distinguishing one segment of its population from another permits a selective harvest of animals by sex and age classes that is impossible in pelagic sealing. Because the seals concentrate in relatively small areas, their populations can be determined with far greater accuracy than those of animals whose populations are dispersed over wide areas.

In late summer, Aleut sealers, under supervision of federal biologists, move onto the hauling grounds where the three- and four-year-old bulls are concentrated. The Pribilof Aleuts are descendants of slaves brought to the islands by Russians nearly two centuries ago, and sealing is their principal source of income.

As the fur harvest begins, lines of Aleuts slowly infiltrate the herd of bachelor bulls to cut off the escape of a selected group—usually several hundred—to the sea. The young bulls are driven slowly to a flat grassy area from several hundred yards to a half mile away.

Small clusters of about ten are then cut out from the pod for killing and driven past the Aleut clubbers, selected for their strength and experience. Each is armed with a six-foot-long hardwood cudgel resembling an elongated baseball bat. As each seal comes within range of the club it is dispatched with a skull-cracking blow on the back of the head. The carcasses are then quickly dragged into rows of ten for skinning. To make doubly sure that the animal is dead before the pelt is removed, the skinner first shoves the point of his knife into the heart.

Although the Pribilof seal herd has maintained a yield of from sixty thousand to 100,000 pelts, annually, its recovery after 1911 was rapid until, by 1950, it was nearly two million, not much below the 2.5 million believed to be the maximum numbers sustained by the islands in early times. When the population reached two million, however, reproduction dropped off, many pups were being crushed under the charges of the breeding bulls, and the incidence of disease and parasites, particularly emphysema and hookworm, became prevalent. The herd is now maintained at around 1.5 million, a population that assures healthy animals and produces an optimum sustained yield of pelts. Approximately sixty thousand bachelor bulls are slaughtered annually and, since 1956, when the need for population control first became apparent, about thirty thousand nonbreeding females also have been killed each year.

American humane groups who had become incensed over the slaughter of the harp seal pups, either deliberately or through lack of knowledge, have consistently confused the Canadian operation with the American-supervised program in the Pribilofs. Advertisements of Friends of Animals, Inc., widely published in American newspapers, have used pictures of harp seal pups over texts objecting to the seal clubbing on the Pribilofs. They charge that the seals are often skinned alive, and these reports have been circulated widely around the world. Alarmed by these rumors, the World Federation for the Protection of Animals, headquartered in Zurich, Switzerland, sent Dr. Elizabeth Simpson, a distinguished British veterinarian, to the Pribilofs in 1967 to make detailed studies of the killing process.

After observing the killing of more than sixteen thousand seals and making post mortem examinations of 1,121 carcasses, Dr. Simpson found that only twenty-one did not have fractured crania and thirty-eight did not have punctured hearts. She observed, however, that the practice of opening the body cavity prior to skinning would lead to almost immediate death by respiratory failure in the unlikely event that the seal survived both clubbing and stabbing. "I found no evidence," she reported, "that any fur seal had been skinned whilst still alive." From the humanitarian standpoint, Dr. Simpson's major criticism was that some of the killing grounds were somewhat too far removed from the hauling grounds, involving unnecessarily long drives of animals selected for killing. She suggested the development, by grading, of manmade killing grounds more convenient to the hauling grounds. As to the clubbing:

> The fact that the skull of the immature seals harvested is relatively thin, in comparison with the enormous bony development of the occipital region of the mature bull, makes clubbing practicable. Of other methods of killing large numbers of animals presently available, for example, the captive bolt pistol, electrical stunning, and CO_2 stunning prior to sticking, I feel that given the situation of the fur seal harvest, and the safeguards presently applied to the method of clubbing, followed by efficient sticking, this method is probably best. Any method involving more handling of the animals, I feel, would be a step in the wrong direction.

These findings were substantiated by a team of veterinarians dispatched to the Pribilofs by the Department of Commerce in 1971 after public criticism stirred up by the humane associations continued. The reaction of the seals to various methods of killing was measured with electrocardiograms. None of the modern methods suggested as alternatives by humanitarians killed more swiftly with less handling of the animals than the stout clubs that the Aleut sealers had been using for centuries.

Because of their objection to the unesthetic method used for killing the seals, some of the more extreme humane groups have tried to force the federal government to abrogate the Fur Seal Treaty and to eliminate the international cost-sharing system that now exists. For the United States to take such unilateral action, however, would certainly bring the resumption of the destructive and wasteful pelagic sealing by Japan and the Soviet Union, which the Fur Seal Treaty was written to eliminate. The killing of the Pribilof seals would not be stopped; it would merely be transferred to the open seas. It would substitute unrestricted and wanton killing of all age classes and both sexes for a system of management controlled with the precision of a beef-production enterprise. The end result would probably be to head the fur seals back toward their extinction, which was narrowly averted in 1911. If anyone believes that Japan and the Soviet Union would curb the slaughter of seals by their nationals in the absence of a treaty, let him look at the record of those nations as it applies to the great whales.

When the Fur Seal Treaty of 1911 was signed, the sea otter was brought under its protection. Many contemporary authorities felt that the action had come too late, as the species seemed to be extinct. In early times, the sea otter was found in a great coastal arc extending from near Morro Hermoso of Mexico's Baja Peninsula, along the Aleutian Chain, to Hokkaido Island in Japan. Unlike the fur seal, the sea otter did not venture far offshore. Its preferred habitat was the dense kelp beds along the Pacific Coast where it fished for clams, crabs, sea urchins, abalones and other shellfish. Its curse was to be the possessor of the densest, most lustrous, and most expensive fur in the world.

Exploitation of the sea otters began soon after 1741, when Vitus Bering, a Danish sea captain in the employ of Russia, was sent to determine the existence of a mythical continent called Gamaland that legend placed somewhere in the North Pacific. On his fruitless return voyage, in November, with a crew weakened by scurvy, his little ship was caught by a tidal wave and driven, a shattered wreck, far up on the shore of one of the Commander Islands that now bears his name. Bering and many of his crew members who survived the initial shipwreck soon died of scurvy, exposure, or from injuries sustained in the wreck.

The survivors, stranded on a barren, treeless island, fought bitter cold and hunger to stay alive. The sea birds that had crowded the island in the warmer months had long gone south. The only wildlife was represented by elusive blue foxes, and by the huge Steller sea cows offshore that, without boats or gear, the survivors were powerless to capture. The men stayed alive only by grubbing up roots from the frozen soil and gnawing on dried herbs and grasses for what little nourishment they contained.

On one of its endless searches for food, a party of the shipwrecked survivors stumbled unexpectedly upon a group of four-foot-long seal-like animals sleeping on the beach. The animals scarcely stirred as the starving men rushed forward with clubs raised. In a few minutes the Russians had killed them all. Although sea otter flesh purportedly is tough, stringy, and tasteless, it must have seemed banquet fare to the stranded seamen.

Their emergency diet of sea otter flesh and the warm clothing fashioned from their pelts were probably all that carried the sailors through the winter. By spring, the men had managed to build boats from the wreckage of their ship and were living well on fish and the beeflike flesh of the sea cow. In the meantime, they continued to kill the sea otters for their pelts as an investment against their rescue and return to civilization.

By autumn of 1742, the 45 survivors managed to fashion a seaworthy 41-foot sloop. Stocking her with smoked and salted sea cow meat, casks of water, and bundles of sea otter pelts, they set sail for their home of Kamchatka. Three weeks later they dropped anchor in Avacha Bay.

No shipwrecked sailors ever returned to civilization more luxuriously or expensively garbed. Their original woolen clothing had rotted in the damp climate of Bering Island and had been replaced almost entirely with trousers, shirts, coats, and mittens fashioned from sea otter pelts, each worth more than its weight in gold. As soon as they landed they were surrounded by hundreds of frantic bidders vying with one another to purchase the pelts, and offering astronomical prices for even a weather-beaten cap or pair of mittens. Each of the men left the wharf a wealthy man.

Word of the discovery of the sea otters in the Commander Islands set off a fur rush like nothing seen before or since. Dozens of boats and ships, hastily built and underprovisioned, set off to cash in on the bonanza. Nearly half never returned. But those that did sailed home with the most profitable cargos ever carried in sailing ships since the days of the conquistadors. One little ship scarcely larger than a fishing sloop sold its furs for more than a half-million dollars.

After this initial rush, special ships with spacious holds reserved entirely for the storage of pelts were built at Kamchatka and other Russian ports to exploit the sea otters. The crews and otter hunters lived and slept on open decks that were crowded with seal-skin kayaks and hunting gear.

Once on the otter hunting grounds, the ship dropped anchor, the hunters launched their kayaks and paddled toward the kelp beds where the otters were resting and feeding. Each sealer was equipped with a stout club, a harpoon, and a gaff. The otters, innocent of any earlier exposure to man, merely stared as the slender craft glided silently into their midst. Then the clubbing and spearing began, continuing until the last otter in the pod was killed. With the inevitable extermination of the otters in the Commander Islands, the Russians pushed eastward along the Aleutian chain, systematically stripping the sea otter populations as they went.

The advance of the *promyshlenniki* was resisted bitterly by the fierce native Aleuts, adding a new dimension to the hazards faced by the otter hunter. Preoccupied with his clubbing, the hunter sometimes found, too late, that the spear-bearing occupant of the adjacent kayak gliding out of the fog was carrying not another Russian but an Aleut warrior hunting him. Many returned from the kelp beds to find their shipmates slaughtered and the ship itself wrecked or burned.

The otter ships swept eastward to the North American mainland and down the coast beyond the site of San Francisco, returning enormous fortunes to the coffers of the Empire but leaving devastation in their wake.

For nearly fifty years, the Russians monopolized the sea otter trade. But in 1778, Captain James Cook, on his exploration of the Pacific Coast of North America, put into Nootka Sound. Here he encountered Indians who offered prime sea otter pelts in exchange for such mundane products as fishhooks, beads, and other baubles. Little recognizing the value of what they had acquired so cheaply, most members of Cook's crew fashioned the pelts into warm jackets against the cold of the North Pacific.

After Cook lost his life in an attack by natives in Hawaii, his officers took the ship back home by way of China. On landing, the crew was almost mobbed by merchants offering to buy their seaworn garments for unbelievable sums. The skins they had bought for trinkets brought $15,000 in Chinese gold.

Serving under Cook were George Dixon, John Ledyard, Nathaniel Portlock, and Midshipman George Vancouver. On their return to England, all immediately took steps to return to Canada to exploit the opportunities for trade that their earlier voyage had uncovered. Dixon and Portlock formed a partnership and returned to Canada with a load of hatchets, fishhooks, beads, and other trade goods. In a few weeks of trading they filled their holds with bales of otter skins and sailed for China. The sale of the pelts brought $55,000.

In 1792, Vancouver, now captain of his own ship, entered the Strait of Juan de Fuca and found the natives willing to trade otter skins for any trifling items the seamen cared to offer. Reports of these lucrative transactions sent ships of every maritime power racing to the Pacific. When Lewis and Clark, on their return to Washington, D. C., reported rich otter-hunting grounds in waters claimed by the United States, American ship owners were quick to exploit the information. Ships from Salem, Boston, and New York were soon plying a triangular trade route, leaving from ports in the eastern United States with trade goods for the aborigine hunters in the Pacific Northwest, carrying otter skins to the Orient, and returning loaded with porcelain, tea, silk, and ivory to their home ports. In the early 1800s there were nearly fifty companies plying this triangular trade.

Under this pressure, the sea otter declined in numbers and range. Vast areas of its once extensive coastal and insular range had been depopulated entirely, and by 1850, the species was commercially extinct, although whalers and seamen who happened upon remnant pods of otters continued to kill them. Many authorities, by 1900, considered the otter physically extinct. A number of the mammalogists who were responsible for having the species brought under the protection of the Fur Seal Treaty of 1911 were not convinced that their action was more than a vain gesture.

But here and there in the Aleutians and along the coast of the Alaska Peninsula, tiny bands of otters still played and fished in scattered kelp beds. Until around 1930, little concrete proof of their existence was available except for occasional pelts confiscated by the Coast Guard or the U. S. Bureau of Fisheries of the U. S. Fish and Wildlife Service, and no one could be sure that these were not from the last sea otters in the world.

In the early 1940s, however, reliable observers began to report small rafts of sea otters in isolated bays and coves of the Aleutians. Their presence was confirmed by scientists employed by the Bureau of Fisheries. In the meantime Russia had discovered other small but thriving populations in the Kuril and Commander Islands. In United States waters, the largest and thriftiest population was at Amchitka, where, by the mid-1940s, it numbered several thousand.

A tiny band of survivors of the southern sea otter also was discovered along the shores of Monterey County, in California. The animals were immediately brought under strict state protection by the California Department of Fish and Game to supplement efforts at the federal level. In 1957, the official census in California counted 638. In 1964, Karl W. Kenyon, the leading federal authority of marine mammals, counted 396 and estimated a total population in California waters at five hundred. By 1969, the census indicated a population more than doubled at twelve hundred, occupying more than one hundred miles of coastline between Point Conception and Monterey. The census in 1973 showed sixteen hundred to eighteen hundred California sea otters.

In Alaska during this period the northern sea otter was showing similar encouraging signs of recovery. Karl Schneider, a biologist in the employ of the Alaska Department of Fish and Game, early in 1970, photographed from the air one group in the Bering Sea north of the Alaska Peninsula that numbered more than a thousand, the largest group ever caught on film.

Aerial surveys in Alaska between 1959 and 1965 indicated that the sea otter population was increasing at a rate of at least five percent each year and expanding its range into areas from which it had long been absent.

In 1969, the Atomic Energy Commission alarmed conservationists by announcing that it planned a series of underground nuclear explosions in tests on Amchitka Island, the center of the most thriving population of sea otters in the world. Although the Atomic Energy Commission tried to allay public fears over environmental effects, no one was certain what effects the explosions and potential leaks of radiation would have on the otter population. This led to suggestions that some of the otters near the test site be transplanted to suitable unoccupied range elsewhere. Attempts by the U. S. Fish and Wildlife Service to transplant sea otters had been made as early as 1955. These had met with little success, but in the meantime, air transportation had improved vastly and much had been learned about handling sea otters in captivity.

Early in 1970, the Washington Department of Game constructed a holding pool at LaPush built to specifications of sea otter experts. On July 17, a four-engine Hercules float plane took off from Kamchatka loaded with thirty sea otters trapped by the Alaska Department of Fish and Game and the Bureau of Sport Fisheries and Wildlife. Seven and a half hours later they were preening themselves in the pool in Washington State. On July 22, they were liberated in the surf at LaPush to set up new homes offshore.

Using the same techniques, biologists reestablished sea otters on the coasts of southeastern Alaska, British Columbia, and Oregon. All of these populations appear to be thriving and increasing in numbers. Both the northern and southern sea otters now appear safe from the extinction that faced them only a few decades ago. Their combined population in 1973 was estimated at 100,000 to 120,000 and still increasing. Techniques for future transplants have been perfected and are available if and when suitable areas can be found to receive them.

Appealing though the sea otter may be—looking for all the world like a grizzled old man floating in a fur coat—it can, like the timber wolf, conflict with economic enterprise. The conflict is already apparent in California, where abalone fishermen resent the sea otter's presence and sometimes kill it in defiance of state and federal law. Although the State of California maintains a marine sanctuary on the Monterey coast, no state or federal law can confine the sea otters to a given geographic area. Actually, part of the recent spread of the range of the southern sea otter is attributable to the depletion or sharp reduction in its food supplies on its sanctuary area. Its affinity for commercially valuable crabs and other shellfish as well as sea urchins precludes its reestablishment in areas where crab fishing is the basis of the local economy. Like many other species, the sea otter has two types of carrying capacity—a biological capacity for the environment to sustain it, and an economic capacity that can be maintained without serious conflict with human interests. Fortunately, however, along the vast arc of its former range, there are long stretches of coastline in which it can be restored without interfering with economic enterprise.

Public concern for the future of the marine mammals was reflected in the fact that no fewer than thirty-six bills and two resolutions calling for federal protection of the marine mammals were introduced in the first session of the 92nd Congress in the House of Representatives alone. The majority called for a moratorium of the taking of all marine mammals—whales, seals, sea otters, porpoises, walruses, and polar bears—for from three to ten years. All preempted the authority of the various coastal states to manage the animals in their territorial waters, although the Pacific coastal states had many excellent ongoing research and management programs for their benefit. Some, like the California sea otter program, had achieved outstanding results in restoring small remnant populations to safe levels. On the other hand, state authority did not extend beyond the three-mile limit, and the states could control the take of animals outside that limit only through their powers to control interstate commerce. At the time of the hearing on the federal marine-mammal legislation the Alaska Department of Fish and Game was issuing around three hundred special permits for taking polar bears on the offshore pack ice. Most of the bears ranged outside the three-mile limit, but the state officials could control the take rigidly since the hunters had to be accompanied by state-licensed guides and pilots whose licenses were subject to revocation if they permitted their clients to violate the law. Females with cubs were protected, and the use of aircraft was prohibited except as basic transportation to the scene of the hunt. All skins and skulls taken were required to be inspected and tagged by a state biologist.

Although the polar bear hunts were objectionable to protectionist groups, biologists studying the polar bear could find no evidence that the limited annual take was affecting the population of the species.

Alaska's game laws also permitted a similar take of trophy walrus by sport hunters under a $100 permit. In 1970, only twenty-three walruses were taken by sport hunters, an infinitesimal proportion of the kill of 1,304 by natives in the same year. But each of those permits probably saved from ten to a dozen walruses. Eskimo walrus hunting, like their bowhead whaling, is extremely wasteful. Hunters in boats slip up on a pod of animals on the ice floes and fire promiscuously into their midst as long as the animals remain within range. Then the carcasses must be grappled or harpooned before they sink, but several, almost invariably, are lost for each recovered. Others, with mortal wounds, swim off to die beneath the floe ice. In some villages, the only parts of the walruses that are put to use are the tusks, which, when carved, bring high prices from collectors and gift shops. Windrows of bloated walrus carcasses wash up on the beaches of northern Alaska during each spring thaw.

By contrast, the white sport hunter who, under Alaska law, was required to engage the services of a native guide and boat crew, was interested in and could take only one male walrus. Since the cost of his hunt averaged around $2,000, most of which went to the boat crew, he was highly selective in picking his trophy and insuring its recovery. On the same hunt, the same native boat crew, without the incentive of profit, might take and lose a dozen calves, cows, and bulls.

The hearings on proposed legislation for the protection of marine mammals before the Subcommittee on Fisheries and Wildlife Conservation of the House Committee on Merchant Marine and Fisheries in September, 1971, became something of a battleground for the ultraprotectionists—represented by Friends of Animals, Inc., and the Fund for Animals—and the established conservation organizations and scientific societies.

As a result of its deliberations, after studying a massive volume of testimony and supporting data submitted by both sides, the House subcommittee, under the chairmanship of Congressman John D. Dingell of Michigan, rejected proposals that would have abrogated the Fur Seal Treaty, and reported out a bill calling for joint federal-state management of the marine-mammal populations. The Marine Mammal Protection Act was signed into law on October 21, 1972.

The new law established an indefinite moratorium on the taking of all species of marine mammals pending review of the status of each by the Secretary of the Interior. It established cooperative state-federal research programs with a system of federal grants to state organizations and universities and called for intensified research into the population status, limiting factors, and general health of all marine-mammal populations. During the moratorium, marine mammals could be taken or held, under special permit, for scientific research. Individuals, business firms, and institutions able to demonstrate that full implementation of the law could cause them economic hardship could also take or possess marine mammals under permit. Eskimos, Aleuts, and Indians were exempted from the taking provisions for the purpose of obtaining meat for subsistence and ivory and hides for the manufacture of genuine native artifacts and clothing. The sale of all raw products of marine mammals was prohibited as was the importation of marine-mammal products from foreign countries. Natives, however, were permitted to sell ivory carvings, clothing, and other bona fide native artifacts made from the products.

A major bone of contention between the protectionist and conservation-scientific interests was the issue of the incidental taking of porpoises by the tuna-fishing fleet. The protectionists wanted a total prohibition of the taking of porpoises, whether accidental or intentional, backed by stiff fines. The conservation and scientific groups recognized the hazards in such an inflexible position. Without an enforcement officer on every tuna-fishing boat, the law would be all but unenforceable unless purse-seining were prohibited entirely, a step that the fishing industry was unprepared to take. Each of its purse seins represented an investment of thousands of dollars and no owner was willing to return to the costly and comparatively inefficient handlining method. Before accepting such a dictate, the owners would simply register under foreign flags, depriving the federal government of any regulatory control over their methods and operations. The price of tuna in the United States market could be expected to rise sharply, and the killing of porpoises would continue unabated.

Under the Marine Mammal Protection Act, as passed, the tuna-fishing industry was given two years in which to develop fishing gear and methods that would minimize the loss of porpoises. The National Marine Fisheries Service of the National Oceanic and Atmospheric Administration, which had become responsible for marine fisheries under the Reorganization Act of October 30, 1970, that transferred the functions of the old Bureau of Commercial Fisheries to the Department of Commerce, was directed to conduct intensive research into the problem with an authorized appropriation of $1 million.

The fishing industry had already demonstrated considerable concern for the deaths of porpoises incidental to their purse-seining. Their concern may not have been entirely altruistic, since they used the animals somewhat as aquatic bird dogs, and it was in their best economic interest to save as many porpoises as possible. But three years before the hearings that led to the Marine Mammal Protection Act, Joe Medina, a California tuna boat captain, had developed a method that greatly reduced the incidence of porpoise deaths.

Medina had observed that porpoises, in their efforts to escape the seine, almost invariably flee from the boat as the net is hauled in and become entangled in the back of the seine. By sewing a panel of small-mesh netting to the back of his nets, Medina prevented the entrapped porpoises from driving their snouts into the interstices, leaving the animals free to surface for air until they could be released from the net. This could usually be effected by "backing off" the net, checking and slackening its progress to the boat, permitting the porpoises to swim or leap over the lowered cork line to safety.

The 1975 regulations issued by the National Marine Fisheries Service required each tuna-fishing craft to station two small boats at the rear of the net to assist in porpoise rescue during the hauling process. Each boat in the tuna fleet was required to have one or more crew members or officers who have successfully completed courses in rescue procedures conducted by the NMFS. Although some porpoises are still killed incidental to purse-seining by the American tuna fishery, the number lost annually has been substantially reduced. Research into auditory, olfactory, or visual repellents; net design; and fishing techniques to further reduce the kill is being conducted. No surefire method has been found. But the research effort should eventually develop one that will reduce porpoise kills to a minimum.

One of the major problems facing the conservation of porpoises and dolphins is the fact that the United States is only one of a number of maritime powers engaged in the yellowfin-tuna fishery. Without the development of simple, relatively inexpensive porpoise-rescue techniques or repellents acceptable to all nations involved in the tuna fishery, unilateral action by the United States will be little more than a gesture.

Chapter 25

Challenges and Confrontations

The 1970s saw the first real confrontation between antihunting protectionists and the professional wildlife workers, the scientific community and their supporters. For several years the two sides had been sniping at one another in the press, on television, and in congressional hearings on endangered species and marine mammals. The battleground was the Great Swamp National Wildlife Refuge in Morris County, New Jersey, less than thirty miles from New York City. Despite its proximity to metropolitan New York, it is one of the finest natural areas remaining in the Northeast. Ornithologists have identified 154 bird species using the area in migration and more than seventy-five as regular nesters. White-tailed deer, mink, otter, red and gray foxes, raccoons, muskrats, and many lesser mammals are found within its confines.

In the early 1960s, Great Swamp was privately owned by several dozen individuals. The New York City Port Authority, operating under sweeping powers of condemnation, had selected it as the ideal site for a new jetport to supplement existing air facilities serving New York City. If these plans had succeeded, its natural marshes and ponds would have been filled and its beautiful hardwood forests replaced with concrete runways.

In an effort to forestall this eventuality, local conservationists appealed to the Department of the Interior to make the area a national wildlife refuge. But the U. S. Fish and Wildlife Service had no funds with which to buy the land, and the limited money available from the Migratory Bird Conservation Fund could be better justified in other

areas of higher value to waterfowl. Local interests appealed next to
the private conservation sector. In the summer of 1960, after an inspection tour of the swamp, C. R. Gutermuth, vice-president of the
Wildlife Management Institute and secretary of the North American
Wildlife Foundation, began contacting landowners in the area to determine their attitudes toward the refuge proposal. Although the refuge would cause some landowners to lose their holdings, all favored
it over the wrenching ecological and social disruption that would
come to the neighborhood with airport development.

With this encouragement, Gutermuth helped organize a Great
Swamp Committee as an affiliate of the North American Wildlife
Foundation to receive donations of land and money. In September,
1960, he announced the transfer of 1,000 acres valued at $200,000 to
the Department of the Interior as the nucleus of a Great Swamp
National Wildlife Refuge. By 1964, the Foundation had collected
nearly $1.5 million from 6,100 persons and 462 organizations, indus-
tries, and foundations located in 289 towns and twenty-nine states.
On May 29, 1964, Secretary of the Interior Stewart L. Udall officially dedicated the Great Swamp National Wildlife Refuge. "The Great
Swamp Committee," he stated, "has performed nobly in saving some
greenery in the greater New York Region" and he pledged to make it
a "national showcase for wildlife education and interpretation."

In 1966, the New York Port Authority reopened its campaign to
acquire Great Swamp as the site for New York's fourth major jetport.
But by then the refuge had been rounded out to more than three
thousand acres, and public opposition to its destruction was far more
consolidated than before. On December 3, 1966, Udall, speaking at a
Great Swamp National Landmark Ceremony, promised that: "The
Department [of the Interior] will fight any new attempt by the Port
Authority to build a jetport in Great Swamp. . . ." With the enactment of the Wilderness Act of 1964, the Bureau of Sport Fisheries
and Wildlife, supported by sportsmen and conservationists, began a
successful drive to have 2,400 acres of the refuge declared a statutory
wilderness area, further reducing the threat to the area by economic
and industrial encroachment.

By the late 1960s, the Great Swamp deer herd was expanding
rapidly toward carrying capacity. Deer were beginning to wander off
the refuge to raid neighboring truck gardens and orchards, and some
were even browsing on ornamental shrubbery in the front yards of
neighboring homeowners. On the refuge itself, telltale signs of overpopulation were becoming evident to the trained eyes of biologists.
State and federal authorities agreed that the time had come to thin
the deer population before the situation became critical and the animals damaged their own food supply and the habitat of other species

with which they shared the refuge. The method selected was that in common use throughout the National Wildlife Refuge System to check overpopulations of browsing and grazing animals—a regulated hunt supervised by state and federal officials, designed to remove a predetermined number of deer in order to restore the balance between range and population. Applicants holding valid New Jersey hunting licenses could apply on a first-come, first-served basis until the allotted 150 permits were exhausted. Because the Great Swamp was surrounded by residential development, hunters participating were to be limited to the use of short-range shotguns loaded with buckshot, muzzleloading firearms of .45-caliber or more, and bows and arrows.

Announcement of the proposed hunt for December 19, 1972, stirred up an immediate storm of emotional protest among humane groups in New York City and northern New Jersey. An *ad hoc* citizens organization calling itself DEER (Deer, Ecology, Environment, Resources) was hurriedly organized to lobby against the management proposal. Friends of Animals, Inc., ran advertisements in New York and New Jersey newspapers in the form of an open letter to Rod Hunter, sports columnist of the *Echoes Sentinel* of Stirling, New Jersey, who had defended the purpose of the hunt. It was signed by nine motion-picture actresses and featured a photograph of a negligee-clad woman in a provocative pose.

> You suggest that hunters have a "reverence for life." It is then something akin to the reverence the Marquis de Sade had for women. . . . Please spare our minds as you spare our bodies and don't try to ennoble your psychotic behavior by claiming that you are trimming the herd for the benefit of the herd (which you say consists of 400 deer). We've read your magazines where you admit to each other that it's fun . . . fun . . . fun . . . to . . . kill . . . kill . . . kill.
>
> The only herd that needs trimming is the herd of hunters. So please garb yourselves, you brave 150, in fawn color on December 19, and double your thrill . . . thrill . . . thrill.
>
> Sincerely yours, for the girls.

The Humane Society of the United States attacked the proposed hunt on humanitarian grounds, contending that the weapons specified were inefficient for making clean kills. Actually, the use of buckshot for deer hunting is required by a number of state wildlife codes, and, as its name denotes, it was developed originally as a specific means of killing deer. The standard 12-gauge load of No. 00 buckshot consists of nine .30-caliber slugs that, in the close-range shooting that the brushy cover of the Great Swamp required, is as deadly as any other load. A .45- or .50-caliber minie ball fired from a muzzleloading rifle has far more knockdown power than the famous Kentucky or Pennsylvania rifle used by such famed deerslayers as Daniel Boone. The hunter who selects a bow as his weapon automatically decreases his odds for taking a deer by about ninety percent. The Humane Society contended that, if the deer needed culling, it should be done by trained marksmen, specifically by National Park rangers. Why park rangers were specified is a mystery since the National Park Service was not involved in the management of the Great Swamp National Wildlife Refuge and skilled marksmanship is not one of the major requirements for employment as a park ranger.

On December 15, 1972, HS attorneys appealed to District Court Judge John Sirica in Washington, D. C., to stop the scheduled hunt. Sirica issued a temporary injunction which was upheld, two days later, on the eve of the proposed hunt, by a three-man panel consisting of Chief Judge David L. Bazelon, Senior Circuit Judge Charles Fahy, and Judge Carl McGowan. In siding with the antihunting groups, they ignored expert testimony from state and federal biologists who testified on the critical need for herd reduction.

Joined by Friends of Animals and DEER, HSUS continued the litigation until, in February, 1973, Judge Charles R. Richey of the U. S. District Court in Washington, D. C., ruled that hunting was one of the reasons the National Wildlife Refuge System had been established and that hunting is not inconsistent with the principles of sound wildlife management. His decision was upheld without written opinion by the U. S. Court of Appeals.

In the meantime the antihunting groups tried a new approach. They attacked the hunt in the fall of 1973 on ecological grounds, citing the National Environmental Policy Act of 1969. This law requires all federal agencies to file environmental-impact statements on any project having major impacts on the quality of the environment. Attorneys for HSUS justified their claims on the grounds that the hunters would trample vegetation and that expended buckshot would cause lead poisoning in waterfowl and deer. Again the stalling action worked, and no hunt was held while the U. S. Fish and Wildlife Service dutifully prepared its environmental-impact statement.

Biologists, in the meanwhile, were watching the deer herd with mounting concern. Pronounced browse lines were beginning to appear in the woodlands where the animals had eaten all food to a height of five feet, and signs of distress were beginning to appear in the animals themselves. Forty deer were definitely known to be victims of starvation or related malnutrition. A young buck found by refuge biologists on March 23, 1973, died before their eyes as it attempted to flee. It weighed forty-one pounds, less than half its normal weight, and it was heavily infested with worms, bots, and other external and internal parasites. State wildlife officers found another deer blinded by a massive calcified fibroma on its forehead, and had to destroy the suffering animal. Another with thirteen pounds of tumors between its legs was pulled down and killed by dogs. Between 1970 and 1974, the estimated deer population, in spite of these losses, soared from around four hundred to more than 650.

Somewhat ironically, the HSUS has a long and distinguished record for prosecuting owners of pets and livestock who keep their animals in overcrowded quarters leading to conditions no more pathetic than those its own actions were forcing on the deer in the Great Swamp.

On November 26, 1974, the antihunting forces, who were beginning to lose public favor as concrete evidence of overpopulation in the refuge became more widely recognized, obtained another restraining order blocking a hunt scheduled for December 10, from U. S. District Judge Frederick Lacey. They contended in their petition that the hunt was an unnecessarily cruel way of reducing the herd and that it would "cause irreparable loss of animal life." On December 6, however, Judge Lacey vacated his order, concluding that the hunt would best serve the public interest and that objections to it were unwarranted.

The opponents of the hunt promptly appealed to another judge, who issued another temporary restraining order. A three-judge tribunal, however, on the morning of the hunt itself, dismissed the order and upheld the decision of Judge Lacey. The hunt got underway at 11 a.m. when, at a signal from Refuge Manager George Gage, 137 hunters deployed over the refuge. Their progress was followed by the boos and catcalls of fifty-four pickets displaying banners and signs opposing the hunt and personally defaming the participants. After a brief and noisy display before the television cameras, they reboarded their chartered bus and returned to New York City.

One of the ironies of the Great Swamp case was that many of the placards and banners carried by the pickets singled out the National Rifle Association for special attack, although the NRA was only one of many groups recognizing the necessity for management of the deer herd. The president of the NRA at the time was Dr. C. R. Gutermuth who, as secretary of the North American Wildlife Foundation, had been largely responsible for the creation of the Great Swamp National Wildlife Refuge.

The Great Swamp situation typifies one of the major problems confronting efforts to maintain balanced wildlife populations in a world increasingly dominated by the works of man. A small but stridently vocal group has taken upon itself the task of undermining all constructive wildlife programs except for a few that meet its own ends. Whether deliberately or through ignorance, they distort the intent and objectives of wildlife management and discredit the accomplishments of the conservation movement. Their principal tools are fiction embroidered with half-truths and often with outright fabrication.

In 1974, Congress was debating the proposed Sikes Bill, a highly constructive piece of wildlife legislation that the conservation community had been trying to obtain for years. It authorized Congress to appropriate funds for wildlife management on the national forests and on the public lands administered by the Bureau of Land Management, on military reservations, and on lands administered by the Atomic Energy Commission. It called for cooperation between the state fish and wildlife agencies and federal land-management officials to expand wildlife-management programs on all federal lands, and authorized the collection of recreational-use fees from hunters, fishermen, and trappers using the lands. Although Congress has appropriated funds each year for fish and wildlife development by the U. S. Forest Service, Bureau of Land Management, and Armed Forces, the entire federal contribution has been little more than pennies per square mile. The Sikes Bill authorized general fund appropriations totaling $23.5 million to increase the federal share.

Just as the Sikes Bill was scheduled for vote, advertisements appeared in some of the major metropolitan newspapers. They stated that the bill, if passed, would open all of the public lands of the United States to hunting and the slaughter of wildlife. The advertisement was signed by the Committee for Humane Legislation, the lobbying arm of Friends of Animals, Inc. The fact is that the national forests and the public domain, with the exception of certain areas closed because of safety considerations, have always been open to regulated hunting under state laws.

Meanwhile, Alice Herrington, the president of Friends of Animals, had issued a newsletter to members, attacking the Sikes Bill and accusing Congressman John D. Dingell, chairman of the House Subcommittee on Fisheries, Wildlife and the Environment, of duplicity because of his pushing for the enactment of the Sikes Bill, and charging him with trying to circumvent the intent of the Marine Mammal Protection Act. Her newsletter generated such a flood of mail from emotional but well-intentioned protectionists that on November 1, 1974, Dingell was forced to take the unusual action of issuing an open letter to his colleagues in the House of Representatives. It stated in part:

> We have had a number of occasions to consider representations by Miss Herrington or organizations which she represents: The Committee for Humane Legislation, the Friends of Animals. She invariably acts out of an abundance of emotion and a paucity of facts, and the

few facts that she has seldom support the conclusions which she attempts to draw. The results of these confrontations is that her organization—far from being, as claimed, "the only professional lobby for animal protection" [in Washington], is scarcely heeded when conservation legislation is under consideration in the Congress and is little respected by responsible conservation organizations. As an example, she has claimed credit for the recent Endangered Species Act which was written by my Subcommittee without any advice or participation whatsoever from Miss Herrington or her organization. Nor was any comment or assistance ever offered by her.

Miss Herrington, in the same letter, mounted a major attack on H. R. 11537 [Sikes Bill] and on me personally as the Subcommittee Chairman who handled this bill which was supported by every national conservation organization. . . .

I cannot understand why people continue to support an organization with the well-deserved reputation for falsehoods and misstatements as this one. . . .

In spite of opposition generated by Friends of Animals, President Gerald Ford signed the Sikes Bill into law in October, 1974.

During the Great Swamp deer controversy, well-intentioned humanitarians suggested a number of alternatives to the use of public hunting as means of removing surplus deer. One of the most commonly advanced was the use of professional hunters—qualified marksmen—to do the killing on a selective basis aimed at taking only diseased and debilitated animals. On limited areas, such as the Great Swamp, which is an island of deer habitat surrounded by residential and industrial development, this has some feasibility as a method of herd control. The most effective method for reducing a localized deer population would be to kill pregnant does and newborn spotted fawns during the fawning season. But it is doubtful that this would be any more acceptable to humanitarians than the autumn hunting season so bitterly opposed. Also, most of the venison and hides that hunters converted to domestic use in the fall season would be wasted, and revenues accruing to the New Jersey Fish and Game Department through the sale of permits and licenses would be lost. Since any deer population has the capacity to double within two breeding seasons, pressures on the deer herd would have to be maintained by paid hunters on a regular basis. The U. S. Fish and Wildlife Service, which administers the refuge, has no funds for such a sustained program, and the New Jersey wildlife agency has no obligation or authority to use state funds and manpower to correct such problems on federal lands.

The term "trained marksmen" implies the use of rifles, which is unacceptable from a safety standpoint in thickly settled areas such as northern New Jersey. In heavy cover, such as that found on much of the deer range in Great Swamp, a charge of buckshot rarely carries much farther than the animal at which it is fired. But pinpoint accuracy is not required to kill a deer with a shotgun. Most of the skill involved is in approaching close enough for an effective shot.

Selective culling of the sick and infirm to reduce the incidence of disease, even by expert marksmen, is virtually impossible since infestations of parasites and symptoms of disease do not become obvious until the deer are in or approaching terminal stages of their ailment. Early stages of infections or infestations can be detected even by pathologists and veterinarians only after an animal has been killed or captured. Hunters of white-tailed deer, whether beginners or experts, rarely obtain much more than fleeting glimpses of their quarry as the animals dash through cover. The incidence of parasites or disease is a problem that can be minimized only by holding the entire population below the carrying capacity of the range.

The use of professional hunters to control deer and elk populations throughout the United States would impose a staggering financial burden on every state, since it would involve hiring an army of men whose salaries and expenses for transportation and equipment could not be less than $15,000 per man per year. This would convert deer and elk from financial assets to financial liabilities. It would still result in the deaths of as many deer or elk as sport hunters take annually under our present system, through which sport hunters pay substantial sums to the states for the privilege of removing surplus animals.

Others have suggested that predators, such as wolves, panthers, and coyotes, be reintroduced to cope with the overpopulation problem. While, from a biological viewpoint, this would be desirable, the fact is that most of our big-game ranges are fragmented and surrounded by beef and dairy farms, poultry-raising enterprises, and similar livestock ventures, a fact that precludes the introduction of wide-ranging predators anywhere except in large wilderness areas. Two square miles of good woodland cover may support forty or fifty healthy deer, but it takes a minimum of six square miles of similar cover to support a single wolf.

Others have suggested the use of chemical sterilants that inhibit reproduction. These substances have proved of some limited use in controlling coyotes, which will gulp down chunks of impregnated meat, but the random, rambling feeding habits of deer and other plant eaters preclude the application of drugs as a means of controlling these species.

Friends of Animals calls for the outlawing of all sport hunting and the total scuttling of our system of wildlife management. In her 1972 report to Friends of Animals, Ms. Herrington wrote:

> If the wildlife of America in all its diversity is to be saved, the people must reclaim their heredity and stewardship by acting to suppress the hunting triumvirate. This trilogy is comprised of the hunters, the "wildlife managers" and the munitions industry. Enrolled in this game of death are 20 million hunters, but their murderous deeds are only a small part of the planned ecological havoc perpetrated by about 6,000 self-styled "wildlife managers." This small group of men, with some slight knowledge of plant-and-animal, predator-prey relationships, functions today—*not* to save a world billions of years in the making—but to prostitute their knowledge in the service of the lucrative gun and bullet business. . . .
> A first step in freeing Mother Nature from the stranglehold of "management" is to remove the "managers," (the State Game Commissions and the Interior's Wildlife Service where the "managers" work) from the payroll of the munitions makers. A repeal of the Pittman-Robertson Act would do just that, would end the major revenue source which supports the false management concept.

Cleveland Amory of the Fund for Animals has made similar but less sweeping indictments of the wildlife-management profession, and also has called for the elimination of management programs. These allegations and the almost inevitable effects of the implementation of the recommendations deserve some analysis. The repeated charge that state management programs benefit only hunters and game species assumes that deer, waterfowl, ruffed grouse, and other game animals have value to no one except hunters. Any nonhunting birdwatcher, nature photographer, or wildlife enthusiast would sharply disagree. A hiker rounding a bend in the trail and confronting a bull moose or a canoeist flushing a flock of wood ducks has enjoyed a memorable esthetic experience. Deer watching has become a popular pastime in many places.

Any distinction between game and nongame species, moreover, is entirely arbitrary and artificial. Game animals are "game" in the sense that each species may be taken during a restricted open-hunting season, which, depending on the species and state laws, may be as short as one day or as long as six months. During the remainder of the year, each is essentially a nongame species. Limited moose hunting is now permitted in Minnesota, but in Maine, which has the largest moose population south of Canada, the moose has been accorded full protection for many years and is, for practical purposes, a nongame animal. In the Northeast, the ruffed grouse is one of the most popular game birds. In Missouri it is classified by state law as an endangered species.

Protectionists often react sharply when suggestions are made to reclassify predators, such as the cougar or wolf, as game animals on the assumption that hunters will then track down and kill the last of the animals. What they overlook is that the purpose of the action is to bring animals, now in legal limbo and subject to year-round persecution, under the protection of the game laws. When accorded such protection, they can no longer be trapped or poisoned and, if conditions warrant, they can be given full legal protection the year around.

The charge that state wildlife agencies have placed more program emphasis on species of interest to hunters than on nonhunted species carries more than a thread of validity. Until recent years, nearly all of the research and management effort has been directed at game species, although all states, for many years, have had laws that fully protect many nonhunted species. This, in part, is a carryover from the origins of wildlife conservation when sportsmen were trying to obtain protection for game species that were being harried toward extinction by market hunters and other commercial interests. The game animals were those most in need of stronger protection. In large part, it derives from the fact that sport hunters and fishermen have been the financial mainstays of state wildlife programs, and major contributors to funds at the federal level. Out of a combined budget of $315 million for fifty-one state fish and wildlife agencies in 1972, only four percent was derived from general fund appropriations paid by general taxpayers. Nearly all of the remainder was contributed directly or indirectly by sport hunters and anglers. In recent years most of the states have adopted and all are in the process of adopting programs for the benefit of nongame fish and wildlife in compliance with the Endangered Species Act of 1973. To date, most of this nongame conservation activity is still financed predominantly from funds derived from sportsmen. State legislatures have demonstrated a particularly tight-fisted attitude toward wildlife conservation. As of 1973, thirty-three state wildlife agencies received no financial assistance at all from general taxpayers. Of the eighteen remaining agencies, most received funds only for public services—searches for lost persons by conservation officers, enforcement of snowmobile laws, and similar tasks—unrelated to fish and wildlife conservation.

Even without the recent expansion of wildlife management into nongame fields, nongame wildlife and the nonhunting public benefit substantially from sportsmen-financed projects and programs. Conservation officers patrolling the fields and forests are as alert to detect vandals shooting songbirds or protected hawks as they are to apprehend deer poachers. From 1939 through June 30, 1972, the state fish and wildlife agencies acquired, developed, or managed 38.5 million acres of land and water for wildlife. Funds for this program were derived exclusively from the Pittman-Robertson Federal Aid in Wildlife Restoration Act and revenues from hunting-license fees, which Ms. Herrington would have repealed. Without these acquisitions by the state agencies, many of these areas, along with their wildlife and other natural values, would certainly have been lost to commercial development. Nearly all state wildlife management areas receive far more recreational use by the nonhunting public than they do by hunters whose monies purchased them. Many are popular picnic spots, and nearly all serious bird watchers know that state wildlife areas are among the most productive for expanding their life lists of birds.

Among the state wildlife areas acquired or developed since 1939 are 1,622 waterfowl areas that cost $104.7 million. They were acquired primarily to benefit sixteen species of ducks of interest to hunters. But more than ten times as many nongame birds—162 species—and many nongame mammals, reptiles, and amphibians are associated with and dependent upon the wetland ecosystems that these areas protect. From the standpoint of actual wildlife use, the state waterfowl-management areas could as appropriately be designated heron-management or shorebird-management areas. If biologists were developing an area for meadowlarks the end product would closely resemble one developed for mourning doves or quail.

Habitat improvement can be made for no species without improving the habitat of a whole range of ecologically related animals. Hedges and food plantings created for pheasants and quail are used as nesting cover and feeding areas by dozens of songbirds. Many of the nesting boxes that state wildlife agencies and sportsmen's clubs have erected by the thousands are also used by flying squirrels, many species of owls, and other cavity-nesting species.

Many protectionists who want more wolves oppose development of deer habitat—which usually involves patch cutting, burning, or girdling mature timber to favor low-growing shrubs and tree saplings. Neither wolves nor their prey can live in large unbroken blocks of mature forests. Intensive deer-wolf habitat management also substantially increases the populations of rabbits, snowshoe hares, grouse, and rodents fed upon by foxes and coyotes, and the supplies of fruits and berries with which they vary their diets. Contrary to Ms. Herrington's assessment, the purpose of wildlife management is not to destroy natural diversity; it is to restore and maintain diversity in wildlife habitats and species in a nation where economic incentives are largely geared to the creation of monocultures in plant cover. Without diversity in habitats, few species of wildlife can survive.

The repeal of the Pittman-Robertson Act or the abolition of sport hunting would set back the clock on wildlife conservation by nearly a century when there was an abundance of game laws but a paucity of enforcement and positive conservation action. The elimination of hunting-license revenues to the states would effectively end nearly all wildlife law enforcement and conservation effort at the state level. Reliance on the federal government to step into the breech would be futile, as Congress and most administrations have been almost as niggardly as the state legislatures in appropriating funds for wildlife protection. Congress is usually generous in its authorizations when writing bills, but its actual appropriations usually fall far short of needs. In 1962, Congress authorized an advance of $105 million from future duck-stamp sales to be used to accelerate the acquisition of wetlands by the U. S. Fish and Wildlife Service as waterfowl-production areas. On the eve of its expiration, this amendment has been funded far short of its authorization, even though the return of the advance is assured.

In fiscal year 1975, the U. S. Fish and Wildlife Service received general fund appropriations of $103.7 million for all programs, other than earmarked federal-aid funds and duck-stamp sale receipts. In 1972, while state fish and wildlife agencies had combined budgets of $315 million, the Fish and Wildlife Service budget was $75.6 million. State wildlife agencies spent $72 million—nearly as much as the entire federal budget—for the salaries and expenses of more than 5,800 law-enforcement officers. The federal allocation for the salaries and expenses for 158 fish and wildlife law-enforcement agents was less than $5.5 million. With many new responsibilities toward endangered species and marine mammals under recently enacted laws, the little band of federal officers is required to spend nearly as much time in ports of entry and airports checking for illegal shipments of Mexican turtle shells, cheetah pelts, whale teeth, and other foreign contraband as it does in the field enforcing laws for the benefit of domestic wildlife.

Repeal of the Pittman-Robertson Federal Aid in Wildlife Restoration Act would eliminate a program that since 1937 has made more than $600 million available to the states for wildlife-restoration programs and which, with inflation, brings in substantially larger sums in each successive year. Abolishing sport hunting also would eliminate those resources of funds as it would those from the Duck Stamp Act, which now brings in more than $10 million annually for purchasing refuge lands and protecting wetlands from drainage.

The elimination of regulated sport hunting would virtually end all state involvement in wildlife-conservation effort. It might make the antihunters and some protectionists happy. But it would thoroughly delight a great many poachers and meat hunters who would then be free to pursue their avocation with little fear of arrest or prosecution. The effect on the future of wildlife outside the national parks and refuges would be devastating.

Chapter 26

Wildlife for Tomorrow

The achievements of American wildlife-conservation efforts, despite the cries of alarmists and detractors of wildlife management, greatly exceed their failures. Most of the species and subspecies now listed as endangered by the Department of the Interior were rare, endangered, or threatened between fifty and seventy-five years ago. Many animals that are now considered relatively common—beavers, wild turkeys, egrets and a number of other wading birds, a dozen or more species of shorebirds, the wood duck, whistling swan, pronghorn, and Rocky Mountain elk would all have been candidates for the endangered-species list, had one existed earlier in this century. In 1910, many authorities considered the sea otter extinct and the trumpeter swan on the verge of extinction. The coyote, peccary, glossy ibis, armadillo, and opossum, if not more abundant than they were in 1920, are certainly far more widely distributed.

A few species, like the sea otter, have almost literally returned from the dead. The eastern panther was regarded as extinct by all major authorities for a half century after 1891. In 1948, however, Bruce S. Wright, director of the Northeastern Wildlife Station of the Wildlife Management Institute at the University of New Brunswick, began gathering evidence of a population in the forests west of the St. John Valley. Since that time, there have been indications of its spread into northern Maine, and observers too reliable to discredit have reported sightings of eastern panthers at widely spread intervals in the Northeast and along the Appalachians. The wide-ranging, solitary, and generally nocturnal hunting habits of the panther, coupled with its extreme wariness, make its undetected presence in a particular geographic area quite plausible. Although Wright followed hundreds of miles of panther trails and examined dozens of kills for more than twenty years, he did not once catch up with one of the animals. Nor was he able to obtain a fresh specimen, although the range of the animals was cut by roads and highways and heavily used by deer hunters. The only concrete evidences of the panther's existence that Wright was able to accumulate were the hundreds of photographs and sharply defined plaster casts of its tracks—clearly made by cat pugs more than four inches in diameter with the characteristic drag marks of long sinuous tails. The reversion of most of New England and the Appalachians from agricultural and grazing use to forest, and the restoration of deer, beavers, turkeys, snowshoe hares, and porcupines to the region make the continued spread of the eastern panther more than a reasonable possibility.

Wildlife conservation has faced and overcome great challenges in the past. It will face even more formidable ones in the immediate future. Although the rate of human population growth in the United States has slowed in comparison to that of the early 1950s it still pushes steadily toward the 300-million mark. Each new American, with his demands for food, clothing, housing, energy, and living space, will compete with wildlife for the necessities of existence. In an effort to make the United States self-sufficient in energy production, vast areas of the Great Plains, to which the pronghorn antelope, sage grouse, and prairie chicken have been restored, are to be stripmined for coal, and huge steam plants are already sending plumes of black sulfurous smoke across the prairies of Colorado, Utah, Montana, and Wyoming. The effect on water supplies in an already water-deficient area could be disastrous. Although legislation to require land reclamation in the wake of stripmining has been introduced in Congress, and passed by a number of state legislatures, federal regulation has not yet been implemented in the national preoccupation with the energy crisis. Although reclamation can restore some semblance of the original land contours, it rarely can restore the plant life that the area originally supported. This plant cover, in turn, governs the animal populations the land can support.

Oil spills, with their resultant deadly effects on sea birds, marine mammals, and lesser marine organisms, pose a constant and growing threat to coastal and marine life. The capacity of oil tankers has increased nearly tenfold since the wreck of the *Torrey Canyon* devastated the coasts of southern England. Massive leaks from supertankers have already occurred in South American waters, and the thought of a collision between two of these behemoths is a constant nightmare for marine biologists. The offshore exploration for oil on the East Coast poses further threats of pending catastrophe.

The capacity of American farms to sustain varied wildlife populations has been greatly diminished in recent years, especially in the Middle West and parts of the South. Instead of a variety of products, most farms now produce only wheat, soybeans, cotton, or corn on fields unrelieved by permanent cover for mile on mile. Most of the small wetlands that made the prairies of the Middle West the most productive waterfowl and waterbird producing area on the continent have been drained or filled to accommodate the massive farm machinery now in use. Thousands of miles of once-productive streams have been converted to sterile ditches whose waters and shores support little habitat for any form of life. If every proposed drainage, flood-control, water-diversion, and channelization project already on blueprints in the offices of the Soil Conservation Service, Bureau of Reclamation, and Corps of Engineers were implemented, there would be few free-running streams left in the United States.

Forestry, like agriculture, is becoming increasingly oriented toward the production of single species, principally pines and other rapidly growing softwoods with value to a relatively small range of wildlife species. As in agriculture, herbicides are used increasingly to suppress competing hardwoods and shrubs to favor development of cash-crop species. Clearcuts have become progressively larger, both on private and national-forest lands, in response to demands for domestic forest products and to the use of timber exports beginning during the Nixon Administration, to help restore the nation's balance of trade. Under this pressure, the U. S. Forest Service—operating under the Multiple Use-Sustained Yield Act of 1960 through which wildlife and recreation supposedly have equal standing with other uses of the national forests—has been forced to emphasize timber production over all other land values and uses.

The rapid proliferation and intrusion of second-home and recreational development, with attendant road construction into former wild areas, have eliminated much vital wildlife habitat. The town of Vail, Colorado, now a thriving ski resort favored by President Gerald Ford, occupies the site of the former wintering grounds of what was, a few years ago, one of the largest mule deer herds in Colorado. The stillness of northern cedar swamps and hillside thickets that formerly provided undisturbed winter refuges for deer, moose, grouse, and snowshoe hares now is constantly shattered by the whining roar of snowmobiles.

America's efforts to maintain a diverse wild population in the future will be complicated further by pressures to feed and clothe much of the world's population, many of whose national leaders show little interest in checking the population growth that is the root of their problems. Unless there is a sharp reversal of current trends or a major catastrophe, there will be six billion people on earth by the year 2000.

These economic and social forces are the major problems facing wildlife conservation in the last quarter of the twentieth century. In their solution or lack of solution lies the future of wildlife in the United States and in the world.

On the credit side, the 1970s may well go into history as the decade when America turned the corner on many of the most pressing environmental problems. While new sources of pollution cancel out much of the progress made by pollution-abatement efforts, the trend is not all downhill. The federal government, through the Environmental Protection Agency and the National Environmental Policy Act, now has machinery for enforcing strict adherence to air- and water-quality standards. Some of the most flagrant polluters have been closed down or required to install anti-pollution devices. Tougher state, county, and local laws have eliminated many sources of pollution by industry, municipalities, businesses, and individual landowners. The elimination or sharp curtailment of water pollution would restore to usefulness thousands of miles of streams and hundreds of thousands of acres of ponds, lakes, and estuaries that now support limited animal life.

An expansion of the recent and welcome movement of the Army Corps of Engineers toward substituting nonstructural alternatives for dams, levees, and channelization in flood-control efforts may save thousands of miles of free-running streams with their important fish and wildlife habitats. Changing public attitudes toward wetlands and stronger federal laws, like the Coastal Zone Management Act and comparable state laws, will save many acres of coastal marshes and other aquatic habitats that otherwise were slated for destruction.

The Two Objective—Multiple-Account policy of the Water Resources Council, adopted in 1973, requires all federal construction agencies to give as much consideration to environmental values—including fish, wildlife, and recreation—as they give to projected economic benefits. Alternative plans emphasizing both tangible and intangible benefits are now required before a water development project can be approved. This, too, gives much promise for slowing aquatic habitat destruction in the future.

The Environmental Protection Act requires all federal agencies to make detailed studies and public disclosure of the expected impacts of all of their projects on the environment, including fish and wildlife. These environmental-impact statements are subject to public as well as official review and comment. This, for the first time, gives environmentalists, including private citizens, an opportunity to influence projects and policies of federal agencies. Under this Act, the general use of DDT and some of the more persistent and poisonous insecticides has been prohibited or drastically curtailed. The gradual elimination of these substances from the environment may well make possible the restorations of bald eagles and brown pelicans in future years and may yet come in time to save the eastern peregrine falcon. Pest-control officials are beginning to explore more fully the integrated use of biological and environmental insect and weed controls.

Under the Endangered Species Act, all federal agencies controlling land or affecting the environment are required to make every effort to protect and maintain the habitats of any endangered species on lands or in projects under their jurisdiction. This program has already created positive results. The U. S. Forest Service, which formerly removed all diseased trees in forest-stand improvement operations, now has a standing policy of saving trees infected with redheart, a fungus disease that infects hardwoods. The red-cockaded woodpecker, which ranges throughout the Southeast, nests only in trees affected with this disease.

Both the Forest Service and the Bureau of Land Management, which together administer almost a third of the land area of the United States, have developed highly constructive conservation programs for eagles and other large raptors. The BLM has established extensive sanctuaries for birds of prey, and the Forest Service now refrains from cutting trees for several hundred yards around every active eagle nest. The Forest Service, in its logging programs, also has adopted a policy of saving dead snag trees—where this can be done without endangering human safety. Snag trees are preferred hunting perches and nesting sites for eagles and other large predatory birds and are feeding spots for woodpeckers, nuthatches, chickadees, and other insectivorous birds. Abandoned nesting holes hacked into dead standing trees by pileated woodpeckers are nesting cavities for bluebirds, chickadees, flying squirrels, and a host of other birds and mammals.

The U. S. Fish and Wildlife Service, as of fiscal year 1975, administers 373 national wildlife refuges comprising 33,903,802 acres. This will be greatly expanded, soon after this is written, as the Department of the Interior classifies lands withdrawn under the Alaska Native Claims Settlement Act for various public uses, including national wildlife refuges. Supplementing the National Wildlife Refuge System are 38.5 million acres of state wildlife management areas and refuges and 45 sanctuaries maintained by the National Audubon Society, which protect important segments of managed wildlife habitat from destruction by development.

Science in recent years has added important equipment to the wildlife manager's tool kit. Helicopters and fixed-wing aircraft are now used routinely by nearly all state and federal wildlife agencies. Their uses are legion, from law enforcement to herding antelope and counting deer and waterfowl. Coupled with aerial photography, they permit the censusing by numbers and by sex and age of herds and flocks with an exactitude hitherto impossible. Waterfowl censuses, made cooperatively by the state wildlife agencies, U. S. Fish and Wildlife Service, and Canadian Wildlife Service, undergo constant refinement. On these censuses, biologists fly at low levels on routes over thousands of miles of waterfowl habitat, counting ducks and geese and their broods to obtain an index of the breeding success and the water conditions on the nesting grounds. Other census crews work simultaneously from automobiles, canoes, and boats. Information gathered in the spring and summer censuses is analyzed at the Migratory Bird Research Laboratory in Laurel, Maryland, and becomes the basis for decisions on the waterfowl-hunting regulations that are released by the U. S. Fish and Wildlife Service in late summer. These are "framework" regulations specifying the number of days, within outside dates, that each state may select for its open season and the number of ducks and geese, by species, that a hunter may take in a day or hold in possession, and the methods legal for taking. If conditions warrant, the season on some species may be closed entirely, as it has been on canvasbacks and redhead ducks in recent years. These regulations are promulgated by the Fish and Wildlife Service in consultation with a nongovernmental advisory board consisting of representatives of all leading national conservation organizations, the governments of Canada and Mexico in accordance with the Migratory Bird Treaties, and with the state wildlife administrations.

Although census techniques for other migratory game birds differ by species, similar methods are used in establishing hunting regulations for rails, gallinules, snipe, woodcock, mourning and white-winged doves, and band-tailed pigeons.

The Migratory Bird Research Laboratory also is the repository for banding records for all species of migratory birds in North America. Through the use of computers, research workers know the species, sex, and general age of a bird that has carried a recovered band, the place it was banded, and where it was retrapped, killed, or found dead. Through the analysis of hundreds of thousands of band returns, federal biologists have accumulated an amazing amount of data on mortality rates and the causes of mortality, distribution and movements, longevity, and sex ratios by age classes for nearly all bird species. With migratory game birds, the banding returns also provide an index on relative hunting pressure, which is an important consideration in establishing hunting regulations.

The development of transistorized tracking devices has greatly expanded the knowledge of animal movements and habits. These instruments have been reduced progressively in size until they can now be attached without discomfort or inconvenience even to relatively small birds and mammals. They emit a distinctive radio signal that is picked up by receivers in the hands of distant operators who, by the process of triangulation, can pinpoint the exact location of the animal at any time. They are especially useful in disclosing the habits and movements of nocturnal species and those that frequent dense cover. If a transistorized animal is killed, its body can be recovered almost immediately, even though it may, in its last hours, have crawled into a cave or hole, where its detection would otherwise have been impossible.

Through other miracles of modern science, direct observation of nocturnal animals is now possible even on the darkest nights. Biologists today are using infrared "snooperscopes," which were developed for military use, to determine the habits of a number of species under conditions where observation was formerly impossible.

Factual information on the population status, life history, mortality, breeding habits, food habits, and similar factors is essential to the development of a sound management program for each species. Management may take many forms. It may involve habitat improvement. It can involve population regulation through full protection or regulated taking designed to hold certain populations in balance with their food supplies to prevent conflicts with agriculture and animal husbandry. Under certain circumstances, as with the Kirtland's warbler and the cowbird, competing species may have to be subjected to drastic reduction to assure the survival of an endangered species.

Annual hunting regulations in most states are established by a nonsalaried commission, consisting of from three to ten or more members selected in turn for their interest in wildlife and related natural resources. The commissioners select and employ a qualified salaried director who is responsible for the administration of the department and the implementation of policy established by the commission. Under the director, there are usually several assistant directors or division chiefs, each responsible for the administration of one of the functions of the agency—law enforcement, research, fisheries and wildlife management, business administration, and education and information.

At the federal level, under present organization, the agency primarily responsible for fish and wildlife resources is the U. S. Fish and Wildlife Service in the Department of the Interior. Liaison between the Secretary of the Interior and the director of the Service is through an Assistant Secretary of the Interior for Fish and Wildlife and Parks. Under the Director, there are three associate directors responsible for a group of administrative divisions and offices that carry out the various functions of the Service. The Fish and Wildlife Service maintains seven regional offices, each with its own staff and regional director.

The principal functions of the Service are to administer the National Wildlife Refuge System, promulgate regulations for taking migratory birds, serve as the lead agency in international conventions on wildlife conservation, conduct research, and enforce federal laws applying to wildlife. Among the more important of these are the Lacey Act of 1900, the Migratory Bird Treaty Act, the Endangered Species Act, and the Marine Mammal Protection Act. The Service also disburses to the states the monies collected under the Pittman-Robertson and Dingell-Johnson Federal Aid in Fish and Wildlife Restoration Acts.

The U. S. Fish and Wildlife Service maintains a number of fish hatcheries and administers several laws applying to fishing, but primary responsibility for fish resources is vested in the National Marine Fisheries Service in the National Oceanic and Atmospheric Administration of the Department of Commerce. NMFS shares with the Fish and Wildlife Service responsibility for enforcing the Marine Mammal Protection Act.

All federal land-management agencies—the U. S. Forest Service, Bureau of Land Management, Tennessee Valley Authority, the Armed Services and the Department of Defense—employ biologists to manage wildlife on their holdings, either directly or in cooperation with state fish and wildlife agencies. The Soil Conservation Service of the U. S. Department of Agriculture maintains a substantial staff of fish and wildlife biologists who advise and assist private landowners in planning and developing wildlife habitat on their lands.

These federal programs are funded primarily from general fund appropriations as part of the annual budget of the agency involved. By contrast, state fish and wildlife agencies are funded primarily from hunting- and fishing-license fees and from earmarked federal manufacturers' taxes on sporting arms and ammunition, certain items of fishing and archery tackle, and handguns, which are passed on to sportsmen-purchasers under the Pittman-Robertson Federal Aid in Wildlife Restoration and Dingell-Johnson Federal Aid to Fisheries Acts. Under this system, the principal beneficiaries of fish and game resources are taxed directly to support the programs that maintain the fish and wildlife on which their recreation depends.

From an administrative standpoint, this system has both advantages and disadvantages. The wildlife administrator is freed from the annual legislative battle for funds in which he must defend his budget requests before economy-minded appropriations committees, legislatures, and governors. He has a very good idea of how much money his agency will have in the coming year on the basis of current license revenues. Moreover, he is assured a reasonably substantial income for his agency through fat years and lean. Hunting- and fishing-license sales usually rise rather than fall during periods of unemployment, strikes, and layoffs. If the wildlife agencies depended solely upon legislative appropriations, their budgets would be among the first to be trimmed in times of economic stress. The method also has some flexibility, as license fees can be adjusted upward to meet rising costs, although many state legislatures hold veto powers over such license-fee hikes.

On the negative side, there is a limit to the height to which prices of hunting and fishing licenses can be raised without negative reaction. When fees rise sharply, many poorer and more casual sportsmen who have routinely bought licenses hang up their rods and guns. When nonresident license fees are raised sharply, out-of-state hunters and anglers stay in their home states or spend their vacations in other jurisdictions. With inflation, many states have reached this point of diminishing returns and are hard-pressed to maintain existing programs and unable to expand their programs into new fields of endeavor.

Justification for supporting fish and wildlife programs almost exclusively through taxes levied on a small segment of the American public has long faded and is diminishing rapidly. Forty or fifty years ago, interest in wildlife by the general public outside the hunting sector was confined to a few scientists and dedicated bird watchers and nature enthusiasts banded together in the Audubon Societies. Today there are millions of Americans actively engaged in bird watching and nature study. The National Audubon Society has nearly 400,000 active members, and perhaps as many more men and women are members of the various state Audubon Societies and state and local bird clubs not affiliated directly with the national association. The 1970 National Survey of Hunting and Fishing, conducted through the U. S. Fish and Wildlife Service, indicated that there were 28,231,000 serious bird watchers, amateur nature photographers, and nature hikers, as opposed to 14,332,000 hunters.

With increased urbanization, improved transportation, and more leisure time, many millions of Americans are seeking escape from the noise and bustle of city life by renewing their acquaintanceship with nature. Backpacking and hiking have grown so phenomenally that public-land administrative agencies have been forced to limit the numbers of hikers using trails and campgrounds in the national parks and wilderness systems. Some national wildlife refuges are so heavily used by picnickers, canoeists, and other nonhunting recreationists that primary purposes of the areas have been jeopardized. To all of these outdoor pastimes, the presence of wildlife is essential or adds materially to the outdoor experience.

A number of surveys have shown that the majority of these millions of nonhunters would be more than willing to be taxed to aid state and federal wildlife restoration and maintenance programs if an appropriate vehicle for such contributions existed. Congress and the state legislatures, with few exceptions, have demonstrated little recognition of this public concern.

The budget of the U. S. Fish and Wildlife Service for fiscal year 1976 totals $234 million. On face value, this appears to be a major public investment of taxpayers' funds in fish and wildlife conservation. But on analysis, the general taxpayer contributes only a fraction of the total, which, in spite of inflation, is a half-million dollars below that available in fiscal year 1975.

Of the total appropriation of $234 million, $22 million is money transferred from other agencies for partially mitigating fish and wildlife losses from water projects and reimbursing the Fish and Wildlife Service for services performed. It includes a modest allocation from the Land and Water Conservation Fund for land purchases for the benefit of endangered species. The Land and Water Conservation Fund revenues derive mainly from offshore oil leases and powerboat fuel-tax receipts. None of the $22 million comes from general tax revenues.

With these transfers subtracted, the funds allocated to the Service by Congress come to $212 million. But $92.5 million of that is derived from the manufacturers' excise taxes paid by sportsmen on sporting arms and ammunition ($57.7 million), fishing tackle ($18.6 million) and Duck Stamp revenues ($12 million) that are also paid by sport hunters. The sale of timber and other commodities from the national wildlife refuges brings in $4.2 million. Most of the refuge-resources sales receipts, however, go to the counties in which the refuges are located in lieu of taxes.

Subtracting the monies derived from sportsmen and that allotted the counties, brings the general funds appropriated to the Service to only $119.5 million.

But only part of this is available for basic fish and wildlife management. Of the total, $3.5 million is earmarked for state anadromous fish projects, $4 million for administration, and $6.5 million for interpretation and recreation.

Of the remaining $105.5 million, endangered species are allotted $7.5 million, an increase of $1.8 over fiscal year 1975, but only $1 million of this is for actual on-the-ground management. Planning and coordination receive $3.2 million, research $1.1 million, law enforcement $2.1 million, and increased space costs and pay raises in the Endangered Species Office $68,000. No funds are appropriated for grants-in-aid to state wildlife agencies for endangered species conservation work as called for by the Endangered Species Act of 1973.

Take away the funds requested for endangered species and $98 million remains with which to finance federal responsibilities for general fish and wildlife conservation. Approximately $25 million of this is for fisheries management, leaving $73 million for wildlife. But $17.1 million of this is scheduled for planning and biological services. This is used to try to minimize losses to fish and wildlife resources resulting from federal energy and water development, not to develop habitat and increase fish and wildlife populations.

The impressive $234-million budget for the U. S. Fish and Wildlife Service, under close scrutiny, withers rapidly in terms of general funds appropriated for overall wildlife enhancement to around $55.9 million.

Additionally, although budgets for the U. S. Fish and Wildlife Service have increased annually on paper, the increases have scarcely kept pace with inflation. Appropriations for resource-management projects have been essentially static since 1970. For Fish and Wildlife Service programs that received $54.2 million in 1970, the Administration requested only $64.4 in 1976, but in terms of 1970 purchasing power, the request is only for $56 million, a $1.8 million increase in six years. The remainder of the $112 million for resource-management projects for fiscal year 1976 is for new activities, such as supplementing the Endangered Species Act of 1973 and the Marine Mammal Protection Act of 1972, and for nonprogram expenses such as salary increases and higher space costs.

Congress in recent years has thrust upon the Fish and Wildlife Service new responsibilities that were formerly borne exclusively by the states without appropriating commensurate funds adequate for effective programs to meet the new commitments. Under an amendment to the 1936 Convention between the United States and the Mexican States for the Protection of Migratory Birds and Game Animals adopted in 1972, the Service received primary jurisdiction over thirty-two families of birds over the thirty-one covered by the original Convention. Among these was the family Corvidae, which includes the common crow, an agricultural pest in much of the United States. It was included because in Mexico the family includes a number of threatened species of jays and birds of paradise. The Marine Mammal Protection Act of 1972 preempted state jurisdiction over all marine mammals, even in state territorial waters, and the Endangered Species Act of 1973 gave the federal service sovereignty over 109 species of fish, birds, mammals, reptiles, and amphibians, the majority of which are nonmigratory. None of these programs has been funded anywhere near authorized appropriations.

In the meantime, because of budgetary and manpower shortages, the Fish and Wildlife Service has been struggling to keep some of its older programs afloat. Substantial numbers of its small law-enforcement staff, who formerly devoted most of their time to enforcing provisions of the Migratory Bird Treaty and Lacey Acts, now spend much of their time and energy in efforts geared to the protection of foreign endangered animals.

Although the National Wildlife Refuge System is continuing to expand, the rate of expansion is far below established goals, and wetland acquisition, long a high-priority objective in wildlife-conservation programs, is not keeping pace with destruction through drainage. In passing the Wetlands Loan Act of 1961, Congress established a goal of bringing under federal control at least seventy-five percent or 1,750,000 acres of the most important waterfowl wetlands in the prairie-pothole region of the nation. In addition to the expansion to major refuges, this law authorized the acquisition by purchase or long-term lease of privately owned marshes and potholes as breeding grounds for waterfowl and other aquatic birds. The Accelerated Wetlands Acquisition Program that was funded under the Wetlands Loan Act expires in fiscal year 1976. Of 750,000 acres of wetlands scheduled for acquisition for expanding the refuge system in 1961, only 405,000 acres were actually acquired at the end of fiscal year 1974. Waterfowl-production areas actually acquired at the end of fiscal year 1974 totaled 1,749,000 acres as opposed to the original 1961 goal of 2.5 million acres. When the Accelerated Wetlands Acquisition Program expires in fiscal year 1976, it will be more than 600,000 acres short of its 2.5 million-acre goal. Inflation in land prices has been a major stumbling block in the path of this constructive program which benefits many more species than ducks, but the problem has not been helped by the fact that Congress has not appropriated $19.1 million of the $105 million it authorized when the 1961 Act was passed. Unless Congress cancels the debt or extends the terms of the Wetlands Loan Act, repayment from future duck-stamp revenues must begin in fiscal year 1977. This, with expected additional inflation, will virtually cancel out any advantages that accrued to the budget of the U. S. Fish and Wildlife Service by raising the price of the duck stamp from $3 to $5 in 1974.

Meanwhile, many of the older refuges are almost literally falling apart. Although their existence protects substantial areas from drainage and commercial development, many have no resident managers and are virtually without protection or maintenance. On many, water-control structures and other past improvements are in a deplorable state of disrepair. Construction funds for the entire refuge system in fiscal year 1975 were $1,049,000 of which $325,000 was earmarked for pollution abatement. The backlog of refuge-facility rehabilitation needs is $60 million, and the gap between needs and accomplishment grows larger every year.

The American system of wildlife management and conservation has the best record of achievement of any in the world. It was built, brick on brick, by concerned Americans working together toward mutual goals, by concerned sportsmen struggling shoulder to shoulder with nonhunting bird and nature enthusiasts to establish national parks, refuges, and forests, and to develop sound laws for the protection of fish and wildlife and the habitats on which they depend. It was built by state and federal conservation agencies working together in mutual respect and mutual trust.

Unfortunately, at a time when economic pressures on wildlife and habitat and other natural areas are greater than at any time since the days of the market hunters and the land barons, these traditional working relationships show signs of divisiveness, largely over superficial issues. The national conservation movement is beginning to show rifts that, unless healed, could fragment the conservation forces from a united army into small, disorganized guerrilla bands harrying the outposts of the common enemy but doing little to check its advance.

In spite of its record of accomplishment, the American system of wildlife conservation, like any other manmade institution, is not perfect. It could be vastly strengthened and expanded. Large segments of the American public are demanding that this be done. Many nonhunters, although they benefit from sportsmen-financed state and federal programs in which they have little financial investment, resent what they consider the dictatorial powers of hunting and fishing interests over the regulation of America's fish and wildlife populations. Some wildlife administrators and sportsmen's groups have actively resisted opening the doors of administrative decision to nonhunters who are concerned for the future of wildlife.

While there probably can never be a common meeting ground between the extremists on either side of the spectrum, there is much common ground for a meeting of minds between the vastly broader segment of wildlife interest between. To achieve a meeting will require more communication and mutual understanding between hunters and nonhunters than has been apparent in the immediate past. Many nonhunters must come to realize that all hunters are not bloody-handed butchers lusting for the blood of Bambi but that the majority, by far, are decent, law-abiding citizens as concerned for the well-being of all wildlife as most of the nonhunters. Before making emotional snap judgments on management decisions, they should investigate the facts on which the professional biologists base decisions.

Most nonhunters need to learn more about the principles of wildlife management and the biological basis for its existence. They must recognize that the elimination of regulated hunting, although it would remove the human factor, would not prevent animal suffering, nor would it, in the long run, save the life of a single animal. It would merely substitute one form of death that may or may not be as quick as a hunter's bullet or shot charge for another. The nonhunter must learn to recognize that sport hunting, regulated to remove only a portion of the annual surplus and assure survival of the breeding population, is a legitimate and often necessary use of wildlife. He must recognize that his own actions as a nature observer or photographer in the wrong place and at the wrong time—as on the lambing grounds of wild sheep in spring—may be more damaging to the animal population than a limited regulated hunt in autumn.

On the other hand, sportsmen must admit more freely that not all of the members of their fraternity smell of roses. If sport hunting is to remain socially acceptable, they must do everything in their power to eliminate from their ranks the vandal, game hog, and slob hunter. They must insist on tough state laws that carry the penalty of automatic license revocation as well as fines for any deliberate violation of the game codes, which, in all states should be extended to include vandalism, illegal trespass, littering, and violation of hunting safety rules. They must insist upon mandatory comprehensive hunter-education programs that extend beyond learning how to cross a fence without shooting oneself into the ethics and etiquette of sportsmanship, wildlife habits, species identification, and game laws. They must initiate a meaningful dialog with reasonable segments of the nonhunting public with a goal toward resuming cooperation toward mutual goals. In their actions and behavior, they must respect the sensibilities of the nonhunter and recognize that wildlife has public values and uses beyond those for hunting. With this in mind, they should be in the forefront in supporting the creation of appropriate parks, sanctuaries, and similar natural areas where nonhunters can observe wildlife without disturbance by the gun.

With renewed respect and understanding, both sides should combine forces to build a truly balanced wildlife-restoration program in the United States. As a first step, every effort must be made to bring funding for existing federal wildlife programs up to full authorized levels. This would permit realization of the close federal-state cooperation foreseen by the authors of the Endangered Species and Marine Mammal Protection Acts and begin to restore the usefulness of the national wildlife refuges to something approaching their full potential for all forms of wildlife.

Secondly, sources of supplementary funding must be found to broaden existing state wildlife conservation and management programs to embrace nongame species in a more meaningful manner. Such a move would eliminate most of the criticism now directed at fish and wildlife agencies and confirm their frequently repeated—and in most cases, genuine—concern for all species of fish and wildlife.

Ideally, state nongame wildlife conservation and management programs should be financed through general-fund appropriations based on a percentage of receipts from traditional sources of financial support. Nonhunting conservationists frequently make the point that fish and wildlife belong to all of the people, but nearly all of the revenues for wildlife restoration and maintenance are derived from the small segment of the public that hunts and fishes. But the fallacy of depending heavily upon general-fund appropriations by Congress or the state legislatures for support of fish and wildlife programs is easily demonstrated.

In its 1975 report to the Council on Environmental Quality and the Department of the Interior on funding and potential funds for nongame programs, the Wildlife Management Institute recommended the use of an earmarked excise tax on camping or other outdoor recreational equipment that would bring in the minimum of $40 million determined to be needed to expand state fish and wildlife programs fully into the nongame field. This would be distributed to the states on a formula patterned loosely after that used in the time-tested Federal Aid in Fish and Wildlife Restoration Acts. These revenues would supplement funds now derived from hunting- and fishing-license receipts and existing federal-aid programs.

Additionally, each state fish and wildlife agency should provide some voice for nonhunting interests in its decision-making process. This could take the form of a citizens' nongame advisory committee comprised of nonhunting but broadminded and well-informed citizens, the use of the public hearing on major decisions, or, preferably, by specific representation on each state fish and wildlife commission of one or more spokesmen for the nonhunting public.

With these reforms, most of the grounds for criticism of the American system of wildlife management and conservation would be eliminated, and the future of an abundant and highly diversified wildlife population assured for the American of tomorrow.

Appendix

Common and scientific names of birds and mammals mentioned or referred to in text.

BIRDS

American Coot   *Fulica americana* (Gmelin)

American Woodcock   *Philohela minor* (Gmelin)

Attwater's Prairie Chicken   *Tympanuchus cupido attwateri* (Bendire)

Auk, Great   *Pinguinus impennis* (Linnaeus)

Bald Eagle   *Haliaeetus leucocephalus* (Linnaeus)

Bald Eagle, Southern   *Haliaeetus leucocephalus leucocephalus* (Linnaeus)

Band-tailed Pigeon   *Columba fasciata* (Say)

Barn Owl   *Tyto alba* (Scopoli)

Barred Owl   *Strix varia* (Barton)

Belted Kingfisher   *Megaceryle alcyon* (Linnaeus)

Black-bellied Plover   *Squatarola squatarola* (Linnaeus)

Black Rail   *Laterallus jamaicensis* (Gmelin)

Black Skimmer   *Rhynchops nigra* (Linnaeus)

Black Vulture   *Coragyps atratus* (Bechstein)

Bluebird, Eastern   *Sialia sialis* (Linnaeus)

Blue Grouse   *Dendragapus obscurus* (Say)

Blue Jay   *Cyanocitta cristata* (Linnaeus)

Bobwhite Quail   *Colinis virginianus* (Linnaeus)

Bobwhite, Masked   *Colinis virginianus ridgwayi* (Brewster)

Brant, Atlantic *Branta bernicla hrota* (Muller)

Brant, Black *Branta nigricans* (Lawrence)

Broad-winged Hawk *Buteo platypterus* (Vieillot)

Brown-headed Cowbird *Molothrus ater* (Boddaert)

Bufflehead *Bucephala albeola* (Linnaeus)

Burrowing Owl *Speotyto cunicularia* (Molina)

California Condor *Gymnogyps californianus* (Shaw)

California Quail *Lophortyx californica* (Shaw)

Canvasback *Aythya valisineria* (Wilson)

Carolina Parakeet *Conuropsis carolinensis* (Linnaeus)

Chukar Partridge *Alectoris graeca chukar* (Meisner)

Clapper Rail *Rallus longirostris* (Boddaert)

Common Crow *Corvus brachyrhynchos* (Brehm)

Common Gallinule *Gallinula chloropus* (Linnaeus)

Common Murre *Uria aalge* (Pontoppidan)

Common Raven *Corvus corax* (Linnaeus)

Common Snipe *Capella gallinago* (Linnaeus)

Condor, California *Gymnogyps californianus* (Shaw)

Cooper's Hawk *Accipiter cooperii* (Bonaparte)

Coot, American *Fulica americana* (Gmelin)

Cowbird, Brown-headed *Molothrus ater* (Boddaert)

Crane, Sandhill *Grus canadensis* (Linnaeus)

Crane, Whooping *Grus americana* (Linnaeus)

Crow, Common *Corvus brachyrhynchos* (Brehm)

Curlew, Eskimo *Numenius borealis* (Forster)

Dove, Mourning *Zenaidura macroura carolinensis* (Linnaeus)

Dove, Rock *Columba livia* (Gmelin)

Dove, White-winged *Zenaida asiatica* (Linnaeus)

Downy Woodpecker *Dendrocopos pubescens* (Linnaeus)

Duck, Black *Anas rubripes* (Brewster)

Duck, Labrador *Camptorhynchus labradorius* (Gmelin)

Duck, Ruddy *Oxyura jamaicensis rubida* (Gmelin)

Duck, Wood *Aix sponsa* (Linnaeus)

Eagle, Bald *Haliaeetus leucocephalus* (Linnaeus)

Eagle, Golden *Aquila chrysaëtos* (Linnaeus)

Eagle, Southern Bald   *Haliaeetus leucocephalus leucocephalus* (Linnaeus)

Eastern Bluebird   *Sialia sialis* (Linnaeus)

Eastern Meadowlark   *Sturnella magna* (Linnaeus)

Eastern Wild Turkey   *Meleagris gallopavo silvestris* (Vieillot)

Egret, Cattle   *Bubulcus ibis* (Linnaeus)

Egret, Common   *Casmerodius alba* (Linnaeus)

Egret, Snowy   *Leucophoyx thula* (Molina)

Eider, Common   *Somateria mollissima* (Linnaeus)

English Sparrow   *see* House Sparrow

Eskimo Curlew   *Numenius borealis* (Forster)

Ferruginous Hawk   *Buteo regalis* (Gray)

Flicker, Red-shafted   *Colaptes caper collaris* (Gmelin)

Flicker, Yellow-shafted   *Colaptes auratus* (Linnaeus)

Florida Wild Turkey   *Meleagris gallapavo osceola* (Scott)

Gallinule, Common   *Gallinula chloropus* (Linnaeus)

Gallinule, Purple   *Porphyrula martinica* (Linnaeus)

Gambel's Quail   *Lophortyx gambelii* (Gambel)

Golden Eagle   *Aquila chrysaëtos* (Linnaeus)

Goldeneye, Common   *Bucephala clangula* (Linnaeus)

Goose, Aleutian Canada   *Branta canadensis leucopareia* (Brandt)

Goose, Canada   *Branta canadensis* (Linnaeus)

Goose, Snow   *Chen hyperborea* (Pallas)

Goose, White-fronted   *Anser albifrons* (Scopoli)

Goshawk   *Accipiter gentilis* (Linnaeus)

Gray Partridge   *Perdix perdix* (Linnaeus)

Great Auk   *Pinguinus impennis* (Linnaeus)

Greater Prairie Chicken   *Tympanuchus cupido pinnatus* (Brewster)

Greater Yellowlegs   *Tringa melanoleuca* (Gmelin)

Grouse, Blue   *Dendragapus obscurus* (Say)

Grouse, Ruffed   *Bonasa umbellus* (Linnaeus)

Grouse, Sage   *Centrocercus urophasianus* (Bonaparte)

Grouse, Sharp-tailed   *Pedioecetes phasianellus* (Linnaeus)

Grouse, Spruce   *Canachites canadensis* (Linnaeus)

Gull, Herring   *Larus argentatus* (Pontoppidan)

Hairy Woodpecker   *Dendrocopus villosus* (Linnaeus)

Harris Hawk   *Parabuteo unicinctus harrisi* (Temminck)

Hawk, Broad-winged   *Buteo platypterus* (Vieillot)

Hawk, Cooper's   *Accipiter cooperii* (Bonaparte)

Hawk, Ferruginous   *Buteo regalis* (Gray)

Hawk, Harris   *Parabuteo unicinctus harrisi* (Temminck)

Hawk, Marsh   *Circus cyaneus hudsonius* (Linnaeus)

Hawk, Red-shouldered   *Buteo lineatus* (Gmelin)

Hawk, Red-tailed   *Buteo jamaicensis* (Gmelin)

Hawk, Rough-legged   *Buteo lagopus* (Pontoppidan)

Hawk, Sharp-shinned   *Accipiter striatus velox* (Vieillot)

Hawk, Sparrow   *Falco sparverius* (Linnaeus)

Heath Hen   *Tympanuchus cupido cupido* (Linnaeus)

Heron, Great Blue   *Ardea herodias* (Linnaeus)

Heron, Great White   *Ardea occidentalis* (Audubon)

Herring Gull   *Larus argentatus* (Pontoppidan)

Hooded Merganser   *Lophodytes cucullatus* (Linnaeus)

Horned Owl   *Bubo virginianus* (Gmelin)

House Sparrow   *Passer domesticus* (Linnaeus)

Hungarian Partridge   *See* Gray Partridge

Ibis, Glossy   *Plegadis falcinellus* (Linnaeus)

Ivory-billed Woodpecker   *Campephilus principalis* (Linnaeus)

Jay, Blue   *Cyanocitta cristata* (Linnaeus)

King Rail   *Rallus elegans* (Audubon)

Kingfisher, Belted   *Megaceryle alcyon* (Linnaeus)

Kirtland's Warbler   *Dendroica kirtlandii* (Baird)

Labrador Duck   *Camptorhynchus labradorius* (Gmelin)

Least Tern   *Sterna albifrons antillarum* (Pallas)

Lesser Prairie Chicken   *Tympanuchus pallidicinctus* (Ridgway)

Mallard   *Anas platyrhynchos* (Linnaeus)

Marsh Hawk   *Circus cyaneus hudsonius* (Linnaeus)

Masked Bobwhite   *Colinis virginianus ridgwayi* (Brewster)

Meadowlark, Eastern   *Sturnella magna* (Linnaeus)

Meadowlark, Western   *Sturnella neglecta* (Audubon)

Merganser, Common   *Mergus merganser* (Linnaeus)

Merganser, Hooded *Lophodytes cucullatus* (Linnaeus)

Merganser, Red-breasted *Mergus serrator* (Linnaeus)

Merriam's Wild Turkey *Meleagris gallapavo merriami* (Nelson)

Mountain Quail *Oreortyx picta palmeri* (Douglas)

Mourning Dove *Zenaidura macroura carolinensis* (Linnaeus)

Murre, Common *Uria aalge* (Pontoppidan)

Osprey *Pandion haliaetus* (Linnaeus)

Owl, Barn *Tyto alba* (Scopoli)

Owl, Barred *Strix varia* (Barton)

Owl, Burrowing *Speotyto cunicularia* (Molina)

Owl, Horned *Bubo virginianus* (Gmelin)

Owl, Screech *Otus asio* (Linnaeus)

Owl, Snowy *Nyctea nyctea* (Linnaeus)

Parakeet, Carolina *Conuropsis carolinensis* (Linnaeus)

Passenger Pigeon *Ectopistes migratorius* (Linnaeus)

Partridge, Chukar *Alectoris graeca chukar* (Meisner)

Partridge, Gray *Perdix perdix* (Linnaeus)

Partridge, Hungarian *See* Gray Partridge

Pelican, Brown *Pelecanus occidentalis* (Linnaeus)

Pheasant, Ring-necked *Phasianus colchicus torquatus* (Linnaeus)

Pigeon, Band-tailed *Columba fasciata* (Say)

Pigeon, Passenger *Ectopistes migratorius* (Linnaeus)

Pileated Woodpecker *Dryocopus pileatus* (Linnaeus)

Pintail *Anas acuta* (Linnaeus)

Plover, Black-bellied *Squatarola squatarola* (Linnaeus)

Plover, Upland *Bartramia longicauda* (Bechstein)

Prairie Chicken, Attwater's *Tympanuchus cupido attwateri* (Bendire)

Prairie Chicken, Greater *Tympanuchus cupido pinnatus* (Brewster)

Prairie Chicken, Lesser *Tympanuchus pallidicinctus* (Ridgway)

Ptarmigan, Rock *Lagopus mutus* (Montin)

Ptarmigan, White-tailed *Lagopus leucurus* (Richardson)

Ptarmigan, Willow *Lagopus lagopus* (Linnaeus)

Purple Gallinule *Porphyrula martinica* (Linnaeus)

Quail, Bobwhite *Colinis virginianus* (Linnaeus)

Quail, California *Lophortyx californica* (Shaw)

Quail, Gambel's   *Lophortyx gambelii* (Gambel)
Quail, Masked Bobwhite   *Colinus virginianus ridgwayi* (Brewster)
Quail, Mountain   *Oreotyx picta palmeri* (Douglas)
Quail, Scaled   *Callipepla squamata* (Vigors)
Rail, Black   *Laterallus jamaicensis* (Gmelin)
Rail, Clapper   *Rallus longirostris* (Boddaert)
Rail, King   *Rallus elegans* (Audubon)
Rail, Virginia   *Rallus limicola* (Vieillot)
Rail, Yellow   *Coturnicops noveboracensis* (Gmelin)
Raven, Common   *Corvus corax* (Linnaeus)
Red-breasted Merganser   *Mergus serrator* (Linnaeus)
Red-cockaded Woodpecker   *Dendrocopus borealis* (Vieillot)
Red-shafted Flicker   *Colaptes caper collaris* (Gmelin)
Red-shouldered Hawk   *Buteo lineatus* (Gmelin)
Red-tailed Hawk   *Buteo jamaicensis* (Gmelin)
Ring-necked Pheasant   *Phasianus colchicus torquatus* (Linnaeus)
Rio Grande Wild Turkey   *Meleagris gallapavo intermedia* (Sennett)
Robin   *Turdus migratorius* (Linnaeus)
Rock Dove   *Columba livia* (Gmelin)
Rock Ptarmigan   *Lagopus mutus* (Montin)
Roseate Tern   *Sterna dougalli* (Montagu)
Rough-legged Hawk   *Buteo lagopus* (Pontoppidan)
Ruddy Duck   *Oxyura jamaicensis rubida* (Gmelin)
Ruffed Grouse   *Bonasa umbellus* (Linnaeus)
Sage Grouse   *Centrocercus urophasianus* (Bonaparte)
Sandhill Crane   *Grus canadensis* (Linnaeus)
Scaled Quail   *Callipepla squamata* (Vigors)
Scaup, Greater   *Aythya marila* (Linnaeus)
Scaup, Lesser   *Aythya affinis* (Eyton)
Screech Owl   *Otus asio* (Linnaeus)
Sharp-shinned Hawk   *Accipiter striatus velox* (Vieillot)
Sharp-tailed Grouse   *Pedioecetes phasianellus* (Linnaeus)
Shoveler   *Spatula clypeata* (Linnaeus)
Skimmer, Black   *Rhynchops nigra* (Linnaeus)

Snipe, Common   *Capella gallinago* (Linnaeus)

Snowy Owl   *Nyctea nyctea* (Linnaeus)

Sora   *Porzana carolina* (Linnaeus)

Sparrow, English   *See* House Sparrow

Sparrow Hawk   *Falco sparverius* (Linnaeus)

Sparrow, House   *Passer domesticus* (Linnaeus)

Spoonbill, Roseate   *Ajaia ajaia* (Linnaeus)

Spruce Grouse   *Canachites canadensis* (Linnaeus)

Starling   *Sturnus vulgaris* (Linnaeus)

Swan, Trumpeter   *Olor buccinator* (Richardson)

Swan, Whistling   *Olor columbianus* (Ord)

Teal, Blue-winged   *Anas discors* (Linnaeus)

Teal, Green-winged   *Anas carolinensis* (Gmelin)

Tern, Least   *Sterna albifrons antillarum* (Pallas)

Tern, Roseate   *Sterna dougalli* (Montagu)

Turkey, Eastern Wild   *Meleagris gallopavo silvestris* (Vieillot)

Turkey, Florida Wild   *Meleagris gallopavo osceola* (Scott)

Turkey, Merriam's Wild   *Meleagris gallopavo merriami* (Nelson)

Turkey, Rio Grande Wild   *Meleagris gallopavo intermedia* (Sennett)

Turkey Vulture   *Cathartes aura* (Linnaeus)

Upland Plover   *Bartramia longicauda* (Bechstein)

Virginia Rail   *Rallus limicola* (Vieillot)

Vulture, Black   *Coragyps atratus* (Bechstein)

Vulture, Turkey   *Cathartes aura* (Linnaeus)

Warbler, Kirtland's   *Dendroica kirtlandii* (Baird)

Western Meadowlark   *Sturnella neglecta* (Audubon)

White-tailed Ptarmigan   *Lagopus leucurus* (Richardson)

White-winged Dove   *Zenaida asiatica* (Linnaeus)

Whooping Crane   *Grus americana* (Linnaeus)

Widgeon, American   *Mareca americana* (Gmelin)

Willow Ptarmigan   *Lagopus lagopus* (Linnaeus)

Woodcock, American   *Philohela minor* (Gmelin)

Wood Duck   *Aix sponsa* (Linnaeus)

Woodpecker, Hairy   *Dendrocopos villosus* (Linnaeus)

Woodpecker, Ivory-billed   *Campephilus principalis* (Linnaeus)
Woodpecker, Pileated   *Dryocopus pileatus* (Linnaeus)
Woodpecker, Red-cockaded   *Dendrocopus borealis* (Vieillot)
Yellowlegs, Greater   *Tringa melanoleuca* (Gmelin)
Yellow Rail   *Coturnicops noveboracensis* (Gmelin)
Yellow-shafted Flicker   *Colaptes auratus* (Linnaeus)

MAMMALS

American Elk   *See* Wapiti
Antelope, Pronghorn   *See* Pronghorn
Arctic Hare   *Lepus arcticus*
Atlantic Killer Whale   *Grampus orca* (Linnaeus)
Atlantic Right Whale   *Eubalaena glacialis* (Borowski)
Badger   *Taxidea taxus*
Badlands Bighorn Sheep   *Ovis canadensis auduboni* (Merriam)
Barren Ground Caribou   *Rangifer tarandus arcticus* (Richardson)
Beaked Whales   *Berardius* (spp.) (Duvernoy)
Bear, Black   *Ursus americanus*
Bear, Grizzly   *Ursus horribilis*
Bear, Polar   *Thalarctos maritimus*
Beaver   *Castor canadensis*
Bighorn Sheep, Badlands   *Ovis canadensis auduboni* (Merriam)
Bighorn Sheep, California   *Ovis canadensis californiana* (Douglas)
Bighorn Sheep, Desert   *Ovis canadensis mexicana* (Merriam) & O. c.
   nelsoni (Merriam)
Bighorn Sheep, Rocky Mountain   *Ovis canadensis canadensis* (Shaw)
Bison, Plains   *Bison bison* (Linnaeus)
Bison, Wood   *Bison bison athabascae* (Rhoads)
Black Bear   *Ursus americanus*
Black-footed Ferret   *Mustela nigripes* (Audubon & Bachman)
Black-footed Lemming   *Lemmus nigripes* (True)

Black Rat   *Rattus rattus*

Black-tailed Deer   *Dama hemionus*

Black-tailed Deer, Columbian   *Dama hemionus columbiana* (Richardson)

Black-tailed Jackrabbit   *Lepus californicus*

Black-tailed Prairie Dog   *Cynomys ludovicianus*

Blue Whale   *Sibbaldus musculus* (Linnaeus)

Bobcat   *Lynx rufus*

Bog Lemming   *Synaptomys* (spp.) (Baird)

Bottle-nosed Dolphin   *Tursiops* (spp.) (Gervais)

Bottle-nosed Whale   *Hyperoodon ampullatus* (Forster)

Bowhead Whale   *Balaena mysticetus* (Linnaeus)

Buffalo   *See* Bison

California Bighorn Sheep   *Ovis canadensis californiana* (Douglas)

Caribou, Barren Ground   *Rangifer tarandus arcticus* (Richardson)

Caribou, Woodland   *Rangifer tarandus caribou* (Gmelin)

Chipmunk, Eastern   *Tamias striatus*

Chipmunk, Least   *Eutamias minimus*

Collared Lemming   *Dicrostonyx hudsonius*

Collared Peccary   *Tayassu tajacu angulatus*

Columbian Black-tailed Deer   *Dama hemionus columbiana* (Richardson)

Cottontail, Desert   *Sylvilagus audubonii*

Cottontail, Eastern   *Sylvilagus floridanus*

Cottontail, New England   *Sylvilagus transitionalis* (Bangs)

Cougar   *See* Lion, Mountain; Panther, Eastern

Coyote   *Canis latrans*

Dall's Sheep   *Ovis dalli*

Deer, Black-tailed   *Dama hemionus*

Deer, Columbian Black-tailed   *Dama hemionus columbiana* (Richardson)

Deer, Key   *Dama virginiana clavia* (Barbour & G. M. Allen)

Deer, Northern White-tailed   *Dama virginiana borealis* (Miller)

Deer, Rocky Mountain Mule *Dama hemionus hemionus* (Refinesque)

Deer, White-tailed *Dama virginiana*

Delmarva Fox Squirrel *Sciurus niger cinerius* (Linnaeus)

Desert Bighorn Sheep *Ovis canadensis mexicana* and *O. c. nelsoni* (Merriam)

Desert Cottontail *Sylvilagus audubonii*

Dolphin *Delphinus* (spp.) (Linnaeus)

Dolphin, Bottle-nosed *Tursiops* (spp.) (Gervais)

Eastern Chipmunk *Tamias striatus*

Eastern Cottontail *Sylvilagus floridanus*

Eastern Elk *Cervus canadensis canadensis* (Erxleben)

Eastern Panther *Felis concolor cougar* (Kerr)

Eastern Spotted Skunk *Spilogale putorius*

Eastern Timber Wolf *Canis lupus lycaon* (Schreber)

Elk, American *See* Wapiti

Elk, Eastern *Cervus canadensis canadensis* (Erxleben)

Elk, Merriam's *Cervus merriami* (Nelson)

Ferret, Black-footed *Mustela nigripes* (Audubon & Bachman)

Fin-backed Whale *Balaenoptera physalus* (Linnaeus)

Fisher *Martes pennanti*

Florida Panther *Felis concolor coryi* (Bangs)

Flying Squirrel, Northern *Glaucomys sabrinus*

Flying Squirrel, Southern *Glaucomys volans*

Fox, Gray *Urocyon cinereoargenteus*

Fox, Kit *Vulpes macrotis*

Fox, Red *Vulpes fulva*

Fox Squirrel *Sciurus niger*

Fox Squirrel, Delmarva *Sciurus niger cinerius* (Linnaeus)

Fox, Swift *Vulpes velox*

Franklin's Ground Squirrel *Spermophilus franklinii* (Sabine)

Fur Seal, Northern *Callorhinus ursinus*

Goat, Mountain *Oreamnos montanus*

Golden-mantled Ground Squirrel *Spermophilus lateralis*

Gray Fox *Urocyon cinereoargenteus*

Gray Squirrel   *Sciurus carolinensis*

Gray Whale   *Eschrichtius gibbosus* (Erxleben)

Gray Wolf   *Canis lupus*

Grizzly Bear   *Ursus horribilis*

Ground Squirrel, Franklin's   *Spermophilus franklinii* (Sabine)

Ground Squirrel, Golden-mantled   *Spermophilus lateralis*

Hare, Arctic   *Lepus arcticus*

Harp Seal   *Phoca groenlandica* (Erxleben)

Hoary Marmot   *Marmota pruinosa*

House Mouse   *Mus musculus*

Humpback Whale   *Megaptera novaengliae* (Borowski)

Indian Mongoose   *Herpestes javanicus*

Jackrabbit, Black-tailed   *Lepus californicus*

Jackrabbit, White-tailed   *Lepus townsendi*

Jaguar   *Felis onca*

Javelina   *See* Peccary, Collared

Kangaroo Rat, Ord's   *Dipodomys ordii*

Key Deer   *Dama virginiana clavia* (Barbour & G. M. Allen)

Killer Whale, Atlantic   *Grampus orca* (Linnaeus)

Killer Whale, Pacific   *Grampus rectipinna* (Cope)

Kit Fox   *Vulpes macrotis*

Least Chipmunk   *Eutamias minimus*

Lemming, Black-footed   *Lemmus nigripes* (True)

Lemming, Bog   *Synaptomys* (spp.)

Lemming, Collared   *Dicrostonyx hudsonius*

Lion, Mountain   *Felis concolor*

Lynx, Canada   *Lynx canadensis*

Man   *Homo sapiens*

Marmot, Hoary   *Marmota pruinosa*

Marmot, Yellow-bellied   *Marmota flaviventris*

Marten   *Martes americana*

Merriam's Elk   *Cervus merriami* (Nelson)

Mink   *Mustela vison*

Mink, Sea   *Mustela macradon* (Prentiss)

Mongoose, Indian   *Herpestes javanicus*

Moose   *Alces americana*
Moose, Shiras'   *Alces alces shirasi* (Nelson)
Mountain Caribou   *Rangifer tarandus montanus* (Thompson-Seton)
Mountain Goat   *Oreamnos montanus*
Mountain Lion   *Felis concolor*
Mountain Sheep   *Ovis canadensis*
Mouse, House   *Mus musculus*
Mouse, White-footed   *Peromyscus* (spp.) (Gloger)
Mule Deer, Rocky Mountain   *Dama hemionus hemionus* (Rafinesque)
Musk-ox   *Ovibos moschatus*
Muskrat   *Ondatra zibethica*
Norway Rat   *Rattus norvegicus*
Opossum   *Didelphis marsupialis*
Otter, River   *Lutra canadensis*
Otter, Sea   *Enhydra lutris*
Panther, Eastern   *Felis concolor cougar* (Kerr)
Panther, Florida   *Felis concolor coryi* (Bangs)
Peccary, Collared   *Tayassu angulatus*
Polar Bear   *Thalarctos maritimus*
Porcupine   *Erethizon dorsatum*
Porpoises   *Stenella* (spp.) (Gray)
Prairie Dog, Black-tailed   *Cynomys ludovicianus*
Prairie Dog, White-tailed   *Cynomys leucurus* (Merriam)
Pronghorn   *Antilocapra americana*
Rabbit, Black-tailed Jack   *Lepus californius*
Rabbit, Cottontail   *See* Cottontail
Rabbit, Black-tailed Jack   *Lepus californicus*
Sea Mink   *Mustela macradon* (Prentiss)
Sea Otter   *Enhydra lutris*
Seal, Harp   *Phoca groenlandica* (Erxleben)
Seal, Northern Fur   *Callorhinus ursinus*
Sei Whale   *Balaenopterus borealis* (Lesson)
Sheep, Audubon Bighorn   *Ovis canadensis auduboni* (Merriam)
Sheep, California Bighorn   *Ovis canadensis californiana* (Douglas)
Sheep, Dall's   *Ovis dalli*

Sheep, Desert Bighorn   *Ovis canadensis mexicana* and *O. c. nelsoni*
(Merriam)

Sheep, Mountain   *Ovis canadensis*

Sheep, Rocky Mountain Bighorn   *Ovis canadensis canadensis* (Shaw)

Sheep, Stone   *Ovis canadensis stonei* (J. A. Allen)

Skunk, Eastern Spotted   *Spilogale putorius*

Skunk, Striped   *Mephitis mephitis*

Skunk, Western Spotted   *Spilogale gracilis*

Sperm Whale   *Physeter catodon* (Linnaeus)

Squirrel, Delmarva Fox   *Sciurus niger cinerius* (Linnaeus)

Squirrel, Franklin's Ground   *Spermophilus franklinii* (Sabine)

Squirrel, Golden-mantled Ground   *Spermophilus lateralis*

Squirrel, Gray   *Sciurus carolinensis*

Squirrel, Northern Flying   *Glaucomys sabrinus*

Squirrel, Red   *Tamiasciurus hudsonicus*

Squirrel, Southern Flying   *Glaucomys volans*

Swift Fox   *Vulpes velox*

Walrus   *Odobenus rosmarus*

Wapiti   *Cervus canadensis*

Whale, Atlantic Killer   *Grampus orca* (Linnaeus)

Whale, Atlantic Right   *Eubalaena glacialis* (Borowski)

Whale, Blue   *Sibbaldus musculus* (Linnaeus)

Whale, Bowhead   *Balaena mysticetus* (Linnaeus)

Whale, Fin-backed   *Balaenoptera physalus* (Linnaeus)

Whale, Gray   *Eschrichtius gibbosus* (Erxleben)

Whale, Humpbacked   *Megaptera novaengliae* (Borowski)

Whale, Pacific Killer   *Grampus rectipinna* (Cope)

Whale, Pacific Right   *Eubalaena sieboldii* (Gray)

Whale, Sei   *Balaenopterus borealis* (Lesson)

Whale, Sperm   *Physeter catodon* (Linnaeus)

Wolf, Eastern Timber   *Canis lupus lycaon* (Schreber)

Wolf, Red   *Canis niger*

Wolverine   *Gulo luscus*

Woodchuck   *Marmota monax*

References

CHAPTER 1

pp. 4–5. Hays, W. J. 1871. Notes on the range of some of the animals in America at the time of the arrival of the white men. American Notes, 5:387–392.   *pp. 4–13.* Seton, Ernest Thompson. 1926. Lives of game animals. Doubleday, Doran, and Co. Garden City, New York.   *pp. 5–8.* Josephy, Alvin M. Jr. (ed.) 1961. The American heritage book of Indians. American Heritage Publishing Co., Inc. New York.   *p. 8.* Hodge, F. W. and T. H. Lewis. 1906. Spanish explorers in the southern United States, 1528–1543. Scribner's, New York.   *pp. 9–10.* Ford, Alice. 1964. John James Audubon. University of Oklahoma Press, Norman.   *p. 10.* Parkman, Francis. 1872. The Oregon Trail: sketches of prairie and Rocky Mountain life. Boston.   *p. 10.* Murphy, Virginia Reed. 1891. Across the plains with the Donner party: a personal narrative of the overland trip to California. Century Magazine, XLII (53) pp. 409–429.   *pp. 13–14.* Anderson, George S. 1893. A buffalo story, *in* American Big Game Hunting. Forest and Stream Publishing Co., New York.   *pp. 14–17.* Seton, Ernest Thompson. 1926. op. cit.   *pp. 17–18.* Holman, John P. 1938. George Bird Grinnell. Journal of Mammalogy, 19 (3).   *pp. 17–18.* Reiger, John F. (ed.) 1972. The passing of the great west: selected papers of George Bird Grinnell. Winchester Press, New York.   *pp. 18–19.* Grinnell, George Bird. 1893. In buffalo days, *in* American Big Game Hunting. Forest and Stream Publishing Co., New York.

CHAPTER 2

pp. 20–26. Seton, Ernest Thompson. 1926. op. cit.   *pp. 20–26.* Hays, W. J. 1871. op. cit.   *pp. 20–26.* Grossman, Mary Louise and Shelly, and John N. Hamlet. 1969. Our vanishing wilderness. Grossett and Dunlap, Madison Square Press, New York.   *pp. 23–24.* Hyde, George E. 1962. Indians of the woodlands from prehistoric times to 1725. University of Oklahoma Press, Norman.   *p. 26.* Burrage, Henry S. (ed.) 1932. Early English and French voyages: original narratives of early American history. Charles Scribner's Sons, New York. (Copies are translated from the original manuscripts.)

CHAPTER 3

p. 27. Burrage, Henry S. (ed.) 1932. op. cit.   *p. 28.* Matthiessen, Peter. 1959. Wildlife in America. The Viking Press, New York.   *pp. 28–29.* Cumming, W. P., R. E. Skelton, and D. P. Quinn. 1971. The discovery of North America. American Heritage Press, New York.   *pp. 28–29.* Hodge, F. W., and T. H. Lewis. 1906. op. cit.   *pp. 28–29.* Hammond, George P.

and Agapito Rey. 1953. Don Juan de Oñate, colonizer of New Mexico. 1595–1628. University of New Mexico Press Vol. V. Coronado Historical Series, Albuquerque. *p. 30.* Smith, John. 1907. The generall historie of Virginia, New England, and the Summer Isles, together with the true travels, adventures, and observations, and a sea grammer (copy from the original manuscript). James MacLehose and Sons, Glasgow, Scotland. *pp. 30–31.* Bradford, William. 1898. Bradford's history of "Plimouth Plantation" (copy from the original manuscript). Commonwealth of Massachusetts, Boston. *p. 32.* Wood, William. 1635. New England's prospect. London, England. *p. 32.* Josselyn, John. 1865. New England's rarities (copy from the original manuscript). William Veazie, Boston, Massachusetts. *pp. 32–35.* VanDersal, William R. 1943. The American land. Oxford University Press, New York. *pp. 35–36.* Young, Stanley P., and Edward A. Goldman. 1944. The wolves of North America. Wildlife Management Institute. Washington, D.C. *pp. 36–37.* Lewis, Alonzo, and James R. Newhall, 1890. History of Lynn, Essex County, Massachusetts, including Lynfield, Saugus, Swampscott, and Nahant: 1629–1864. Geo. C. Herbert, Lynn, Massachusetts. *p. 37.* Burrage, Henry S. (ed.) 1932. op. cit. *pp. 38–39.* Forbush, Edward Howe. 1925. Birds of Massachusetts and other New England states. Massachusetts Board of Agriculture, Boston. *p. 38.* Josselyn, John. 1865. op. cit. *p. 38.* Wood, William. 1635. op. cit. *p. 38.* Lewis, Alonzo, and James R. Newhall. 1890. op. cit. *p. 39.* Josselyn, John. 1865. op. cit. *pp. 39–40.* Allen, Glover M. 1930. History of the Virginia deer in New England *in* Proceedings of the New England Game Conference (1929) 19–41. *p. 40.* Judd, Sylvester. 1905. History of Hadley, including the early history of Hatfield, South Hadley, Amherst, and Granby, Massachusetts. H. R. Huntington and Co., Springfield, Massachusetts.

CHAPTER 4

pp. 41–54. Lavender, David. 1965. The American heritage history of the great west. Editor in charge, Alvin M. Josephy, American Heritage Publishing Co., New York. *p. 41.* Burrage, Henry S. (ed.) 1932. op. cit. *pp. 43–45.* Lewis, Meriwether, and William Clark. 1904. Original Journals of the Lewis and Clark Expedition, 1804–1806. Reuben Gold Thwaites, New York. *p. 44.* Allen, Glover M. 1942. Extinct and vanishing mammals of the western hemisphere with the marine mammals of all the oceans. American Committee for International Wild Life Protection, special publication number 11. New York. *pp. 45–54.* Coues, Elliott (ed.) 1897. New light on the early history of the greater Northwest. Manuscript journals of Alexander Henry and David Thompson. New York. *pp. 44–47.* Armour, David A. 1966. Massacre at Mackinac—1763. Mackinac Island State Park Commission. Mackinac Island. *pp. 45–54.* Henry, Alexander. 1901. Travels and adventures in Canada and the Indian Territories—Alexander Henry, Fur Trader, 1760–1776. Boston. *pp. 50–51.* Irving, Washington. 1855. Astoria; or anecdotes of an enterprise beyond the Rocky Mountains. New York. *pp. 51–54.* Osborne, Russell. 1965. Journal of a trapper (1834–1843). Aubrey L. Haines, editor. University of Nebraska Press.

CHAPTER 5

pp. 55–58. Morton, Thomas. 1637. New English Canaan or New Canaan. Amsterdam.   *pp. 55–58.* Beals, Carlton. 1955. The rebels of Merry Mount. American Heritage VI (4) 56, 59, 101 (June).   *p. 56.* Bradford, William. 1898. op. cit.   *p. 57.* ibid.   *pp. 58–59.* Greener, W. W. 1885. The gun: its development with notes on shooting. Cassell and Co. London, England. *pp. 58–60.* Herbert, Henry William. 1848. Frank Forester's field sports of the United States and British Provinces of North America. Stringer and Townsend, New York.   *p. 61.* Phillips, John C. 1929. Shooting stands of eastern Massachusetts. Riverside Press, Cambridge, Massachusetts. *p. 62.* Herbert, Henry William. 1848. op. cit.   *pp. 63–65.* Forbush, Edward Howe. 1925. op. cit.   *p. 64.* Herbert, Henry William. 1848. op. cit. *pp. 64–65.* Mershon, William B. 1932. Recollections of my fifty years of hunting and fishing. The Stratford Company, Boston.

CHAPTER 6

pp. 69–70. Morris, Richard B. 1973. The southern plantations, *in* The Life History of the United States, part 3. 68–74. Time, Inc., New York. *p. 69.* Seton, Ernest Thompson. 1926. op. cit.   *pp. 70–71.* Rosen, George. 1958. A history of public health. MD Publications Inc., New York. *pp. 71–72.* Allen, Glover M. 1930. op. cit.   *p. 72.* Herbert, Henry William. 1848. op. cit.   *p. 73.* VanDuser, William A. 1848. Letter to the editor, Spirit of the Times, June 1. (unpub.)   *p. 73.* Valentine, D. J. 1850. An act to digest all laws respecting the preservation of game in our city and the County of New York. Minutes of New York Sportsmen's Club. (unpub.)   *p. 73.* Clepper, Henry (ed.) 1971. Leaders in American conservation. The Ronald Press, New York.   *p. 74.* Herbert, Henry William. 1847. Letter to William A. VanDuser, Secretary of the New York Sportsmen's Club, January 10. (unpub.)   *p. 74.* VanDuser, William A. 1846. Secretary's report, New York Sportsmen's Club, December 8. (unpub.) *p. 74.* VanDuser, William A. 1949. Letter to William A. Gardiner, December 20. (unpub.)   *p. 75.* Herbert, Henry William. 1848. op. cit.

CHAPTER 7

p. 77. National Park Service. 1958. Yellowstone National Park, leaflet NP Yel 7007.   *pp. 78–79.* Anderson, George S. 1895. Protection of Yellowstone Park, *in* Hunting in Many Lands, Forest and Stream Publishing Co. New York.   *pp. 79–81.* Morison, Elting E. (ed.) 1951. The letters of Theodore Roosevelt, 1869–1898. Harvard University Press, Cambridge, Massachusetts.   *p. 81.* Roosevelt, Theodore. 1895. Hunting in the cattle country, *in* Hunting in Many Lands, Forest and Stream Publishing Co. New York.   *pp. 82–83.* Anderson, George S. 1895. op. cit.   *pp. 83–85.* Anonymous. 1895. Adverse to park segregation. Forest and Stream XLIV (12): 221.   *p. 84.* Anonymous. 1893. The menace to Yellowstone Park. (Editorial from) Springfield Republican *in* Forest and Stream, XL (1):9. *pp. 85–89.* Anderson, George S. 1895. op. cit.   *p. 85.* Anonymous. 1893.

(a). Railroad routes to Cooke. Forest and Stream, XLI (35):537.   *p. 85.* Anonymous. 1893. (b) Will Speaker Crisp be deceived? Forest and Stream XL (8):155.   *pp. 87–89.* Anonymous. 1894. Howell in the toils. Forest and Stream, XLIII (7):133.   *pp. 88–89.* Anonymous. 1894 (a). Save the park buffalo! Forest and Stream, XLII (15):309.   *pp. 89–90.* Congress of the United States. 1894. National Park Protective Act, May 7.   *pp. 89–90.* Russell, Carl P. A history of the National Park Service. National Parks, 33 (140):6–11.   *pp. 89–90.* Everhardt, William C. 1972. The National Park Service. Praeger Library of the U. S. Government Departments and Agencies. Praeger Publishers, New York.   *pp. 88–89.* Yard, Robert Sterling. 1919. The book of the national parks. Charles Scribner's Sons, New York.

CHAPTER 8

pp. 91–105. Frank, Bernard. 1955. Our national forests. University of Oklahoma Press, Norman.   *pp. 92–106.* Public Land Law Review Commission. 1970. One third of the nation's land: a report to the President and to the Congress by the Public Land Law Review Commission. U. S. Government Printing Office, Washington, D.C.   *pp. 92–105.* Ise, John. 1920. The United States Forest Policy. Yale University Press, New Haven, Connecticut.   *pp. 93–95.* Schurz, Carl. 1907. Reminiscenses. McClure Co., New York.   *pp. 93–95.* Schurz, Carl. 1907. Collected writings. McClure Co., New York.   *pp. 93–95.* Schurz, Carl. 1877. Report of the Secretary of the Interior. U. S. Government Printing Office, Washington, D.C. *p. 94.* Holbrook, Stewart H. 1958. Daylight in the swamp. American Heritage IX (6):11–19, Oct.   *p. 94.* Holbrook, Stewart H. 1956. Fire makes wind; wind makes fire. American Heritage VII (5):52–57.   *pp. 95–105.* Pinchot, Gifford. 1947. Breaking new ground. Harcourt, Brace and Co., New York.   *p. 96.* Boone and Crockett Club. 1891. Minutes of meeting, April 8. (unpub.)   *p. 97.* Roosevelt, Theodore, and George Bird Grinnell (eds.). 1893. American big-game hunting. Forest and Stream Publishing Company, New York.   *pp. 98–105.* Greeley, William B. 1953. Forest Policy. McGraw-Hill Book Company, New York.   *p. 98.* Anonymous. 1894 (b.). Troops for the forests! Forest and Stream XLII (9):177.   *p. 101.* Franc, Otto. 1897. Letter to Archibald Rogers, April 9. (unpub.)   *p. 103.* Pinchot, Gifford. 1898. Report to the Boone and Crockett Club, January 8. (unpub.)

CHAPTER 9

pp. 108–109. Einarsen, Arthur S. 1945. The pheasant in the Pacific Northwest, *in* The Ring-necked Pheasant and its Management in North America, Wildlife Management Institute, Washington, D.C.   *p. 109.* United States Cartridge Company. 1898. Where to hunt American game. Lowell, Mass. *p. 110.* Greener, W. W. 1885. op. cit.   *pp. 110–111.* Whitehead, Charles E. 1895. Game laws, *in* Hunting in Many Lands. Forest and Stream Publishing Co.   *p. 111.* Roosevelt, Theodore. 1894. Letter to George Bird Grinnell, January 13. (unpub.)   *pp. 113–114.* Clepper, Henry (ed.). 1971. op. cit.

CHAPTER 10

pp. 117–128. Hagedorn, Hermann. 1941. Theodore Roosevelt, *in* The National Encyclopedia. P. F. Collier and Son, Corp. New York. *pp. 117–128.* Palmer, E. Laurence. 1958. Theodore Roosevelt and conservation—1858–1958. Theodore Roosevelt Centennial Commission. New York. *pp. 117–128.* Greeley, William B. 1943. op. cit. *pp. 117–128.* Baker, Gladys L., Wayne D. Rasmussen, Vivian Wiser, and Jane M. Potter, 1963. Century of service: the first 100 years of the United States Department of Agriculture. U. S. Government Printing Office, Washington, D.C. *pp. 117–128.* Ise, John. 1920. op. cit. *pp. 117–128.* Pinchot, Gifford. 1947. op. cit. *pp. 120–122.* Wolman, Abel. 1963. Water resources. National Academy of Sciences. National Research Council, Washington, D.C. *p. 122.* Congress of the United States. 1900. Act of May 25, 1900. 31 Stat. 187. *pp. 122–123.* DuMont, Philip A. 1966. Refuges and sanctuaries, *in* Birds in Our Lives. Bureau of Sport Fisheries and Wildlife, U. S. Department of the Interior. Washington, D.C. *pp. 123–124.* U. S. Department of Agriculture. 1974. The principal laws relating to Forest Service Activities. Agriculture handbook No. 453. U. S. Department of Agriculture, Washington, D.C. *p. 123.* Anonymous. 1893. The reservation of Afognak. Forest and Stream, XL (2):23.

CHAPTER 11

pp. 129–138. Pearson, T. Gilbert. 1937. Adventures in bird protection. Appleton-Century, New York. *p. 130.* Anonymous. 1894 (c). The absolute prohibition of traffic in game. Forest and Stream, XLII (6):111. *p. 131.* Congress of the United States. 1900. Act of May 25. *pp. 138–142.* Hornaday, William T. 1931. Thirty years war for wild life. Charles Scribner's Sons, New York. *pp. 138–142.* Hornaday, William T. 1924. American bison in 1924. *in* Hunting and Conservation. Yale University Press, New Haven, Connecticut. *pp. 138–142.* Garretson, Martin S. 1938. The American bison. New York Zoological Society, New York. *p. 141.* U. S. Fish and Wildlife Service. 1967. National Bison Range. U. S. Department of the Interior, Washington, D.C. *p. 142.* U. S. Fish and Wildlife Service. 1971. Big game inventory for 1970. Wildlife leaflet 497. U. S. Department of the Interior. Washington, D.C. *p. 142.* Roop, Larry. 1971. Trail of the bison. Wyoming Wildlife, XXXV (7) 18–23, July.

CHAPTER 12

pp. 143–146. Forbush, Edward Howe. 1925. op. cit. *pp. 146–148.* Grinnell, George Bird. 1901. American duck hunting. Forest and Stream Publishing Co., New York. *p. 146.* Greener, W. W. 1885. op. cit. *p. 147.* Sowls, Lyle K. 1955. Prairie ducks. Stackpole Company, Harrisburg, Pennsylvania. *p. 148.* Anonymous. 1894 (c). op. cit. *p. 150.* Lacey, John F. 1905. Letter to Judge D. C. Beaman, February 5 (unpub.). *pp. 150–152.* Pearson, T. Gilbert. 1937. op. cit. *pp. 152–155.* Hornaday, William T. 1931. op. cit. *p. 152.* Hawes, Harry Bartow. 1935. Fish and game—

now or never. Appleton-Century Co., New York.   *p. 153.* Boone and Crockett Club. 1915. Report of the game conservation committee (unpub). *pp. 153–155.* Grinnell, George Bird, and Charles Sheldon. 1924. Federal migratory bird legislation *in* Hunting and Conservation. Yale University Press, New Haven, Connecticut.   *p. 155.* Day, Albert M. 1949. North American waterfowl. The Stackpole Co., Harrisburg, Pennsylvania.

CHAPTER 13

pp. 157–160. Gordon, Seth. 1937. Game administration policies and methods. Transactions of the Second North American Wildlife Conference. American Wildlife Institute, Washington, D.C.   *pp. 161–162.* Einarsen, Arthur S. 1945. op. cit.   *p. 162.* Forbush, Edward Howe. 1907. Useful birds and their protection. Massachusetts Board of Agriculture, Boston. *pp. 163–164.* Latham, Roger W. 1960. Bounties are bunk. National Wildlife Federation, Washington, D.C.   *pp. 163–164.* Gordon, Seth. 1974. Bounty frauds clean-up. Pennsylvania Game News. 45 (6):13–16 (June).   *p. 165.* Nelson, E. W. 1917. Address. Proceedings of the International Association of Game, Fish and Conservation Commissioners. Saint Paul, Minn., Aug. 28.   *pp. 165–168.* Gordon, Seth. 1974. op. cit.   *p. 168.* Seton, Ernest Thompson. 1926. op. cit.   *p. 169.* Westcott, George W. (ed.) 1936. Massachusetts agricultural census figures by counties for 1925 and 1935; state totals from 1880 to 1935. Massachusetts State College, U. S. Department of Agricuture and County Extension Service in Agriculture and Home Economics, Boston.   *p. 171.* Foote, Leonard E. 1946. A history of wild game in Vermont. Vermont Fish and Game Service, Montpelier.   *p. 171.* Seton, Ernest Thompson. 1926. op. cit.

CHAPTER 14

p. 176. Kalbfus, Joseph. 1912. The law of Pennsylvania denying to aliens the right to hunt or shoot or even to be possessed of a shotgun or rifle in this commonwealth. Proceedings of the 6th Biennial Meeting of the National Association of Game Wardens and Commissioners, Boston, August 29–Sept. 2.   *p. 178.* Clepper, Henry (ed.). 1971. op. cit.   *pp. 178–189.* Hornaday, William T. 1931. op. cit.   *pp. 178–189.* Hornaday, William T. 1913. Our vanishing wild life, its extermination and preservation. New York Zoological Society, New York.   *pp. 178–189.* Hornaday, William T. 1920. Statement of the permanent wild life protective fund, June.   *p. 179.* Hornaday, William T. 1931. op. cit.   *pp. 180–181.* ibid.   *pp. 181–184.* Pearson, T. Gilbert. 1937. op. cit.   *pp. 183–184.* Hawes, Harry Bartow. 1935. op. cit.   *p. 184.* Anonymous. 1919. Sportsmen, attention! Bulletin, American Game Protective Association, VII (2):28.   *p. 185.* Holland, Ray P. 1922. The public shooting ground—game refuge bill. Bulletin, American Game Protective Association 11 (3):3–5.   *pp. 185–186.* Walcott, Frederic C. 1921. The necessity of free shooting grounds. Bulletin, American Game Protective Association, 10 (2):8–9.   *p. 186.* Anonymous. 1925. S. 2913-H.R. 745. Bulletin, American Game Protective Association. 14 (1):10.   *pp. 187–194.* Phillips, John C. 1932. The American Wild

Fowlers—a brief history of the association, 1927–1931. Privately printed. Boston, Massachusetts. *pp. 187–194.* Phillips, John C., and Frederick C. Lincoln. 1932. American waterfowl. Houghton Mifflin Co., Boston.

CHAPTER 15

pp. 195–201. Pearson, T. Gilbert. 1937. op. cit. *p. 199.* Shantz, H. L. 1943. Remarks. Transactions of the 8th North American Wildlife Conference. Washington, D.C. *pp. 201–204.* Gordon, Seth. 1974. a. op. cit. *pp. 204–210.* Shantz, H. L. 1943. op. cit. *pp. 204–210.* Graves, H. S. 1916. Game protection on the national forests. Bulletin, American Game Protective Association, 5 (2):18–19. *pp. 204–210.* Graves, H. S., and E. W. Nelson. 1919. Our national elk herds. Bulletin, American Game Protective Association 8 (1):1–9. *pp. 204–210.* Cahalane, Victor H. 1943. Elk management and herd regulation—Yellowstone National Park. Transactions 9th North American Wildlife Conference, Washington, D.C. *pp. 210–214.* Pearson, T. Gilbert. 1937. op. cit. *pp. 210–214.* Forbush, Edward Howe. 1925. op. cit. *pp. 210–214.* Massachusetts, Commonwealth of. 1860–1948. Acts and resolves of the General Court of Massachusetts. Commonwealth of Massachusetts, Boston. *pp. 210–214.* Massachusetts, Commonwealth of. 1920–1950. Annual reports of the director of fisheries and game. Boston. *pp. 214–216.* Flader, Susan L. 1973. Thinking like a mountain: a biographical study of Aldo Leopold. Forest History, 17 (1):14–28, April. *pp. 214–216.* Leopold, Aldo. 1933. Game management. Charles Scribner's Sons, New York. *pp. 214–216.* Clepper, Henry (ed.), 1971. op. cit.

CHAPTER 16

pp. 217–218. Bennett, Hugh Hammond. 1955. Elements of soil conservation. McGraw-Hill Book Co., New York. *pp. 218–222.* U. S. Senate. 1940. Special Committee on the Conservation of Wildlife Resources, pursuant to S. Res. 246. U. S. Government Printing Office, Washington, D.C. *p. 221.* Darling, Jay N. 1960. Letter to James B. Trefethen, April 24 (unpub.). *pp. 221–222.* Darling, Jay N. 1960 (a). Letter to James B. Trefethen (unpub.). *pp. 222–224.* Phillips, John C. 1929. op. cit. *pp. 225–226.* Darling, Jay N. 1960. Letter to Seth Gordon, April 16 (unpub.). *pp. 226–227.* Gutermuth, C. R. 1935. Letter to Jay N. Darling, July 25 (unpub.). *p. 227.* Darling, Jay N. 1935. Letter to C. R. Gutermuth, July 27 (unpub.). *p. 227.* Anonymous. 1935. Institute proposes federation. American Wildlife 24 (5):67, 74. *pp. 228–229.* U. S. Senate. 1940. op. cit. *p. 229.* American Wildlife Institute. 1936. Proceedings of the North American Wildlife Conference. Washington, D.C.

CHAPTER 17

p. 232. Taylor, Walter P. (ed.). 1956. The deer of North America. Stackpole Co., Harrisburg, Pennsylvania. *pp. 232–233.* U. S. Senate. 1940.

op. cit.   *p. 233*. Congress of the United States. 1934. Fish and Wildlife
Coordination Act of March 10.   *pp. 234–246*. Bennett, Hugh Hammond.
1955. op. cit.   *pp. 234–236*. Graham, Edward H. 1944. Natural principles
of land use. Oxford University Press, New York.   *pp. 234–236*. Gabrielson, Ira N. Wildlife conservation. The Macmillan Company, New York.
p. 236. Day, Albert M. 1949. op. cit.

CHAPTER 18

   p. 238. Leopold, Aldo. 1930. An American game policy. Proceedings of
the Seventeenth American Game Conference. American Game Protective
Association, Washington, D.C.   *p. 230*. DeLaBarre, Cecil F. 1946. Cooperative wildlife management in Virginia. Transactions of the Eleventh
North American Wildlife Conference. Wildlife Management Institute,
Washington, D.C.   *p. 240*. Maunder, Elwood. 1974. Clinton R. Guth-
muth—pioneer conservationist and the Natural Resources Council of America. Forest History Society, Santa Cruz, California.   *pp. 241–242*. Hocg-
b̃aum, H. Albert. 1944. The canvasback on a prairie marsh. American
Wildlife Institute, Washintgon, D.C.

CHAPTER 19

   p. 244. Gabrielson, Ira N. 1946. What is coming for wildlife? Transactions of the Fourteenth North American Wildlife Conference, 28–35. Wildlife Management Institute, Washington, D.C.   *p. 244*. Mitchell, Glenn E.
1949. The big-game resource. Transactions of the Fourteenth North American Wildlife Conference, 538–543. Wildlife Management Institute, Washington, D.C.   *pp. 244–255*. Rutherford, Robert M. 1946. Pittman-Robertson program accomplishment and prospects. Transactions of the Eleventh North American Wildlife Conference, 427–457. Wildlife Management
Institute, Washington, D.C.   *pp. 244–255*. Rutherford, Robert M. 1949.
Ten years of Pittman-Robertson wildlife restoration. Wildlife Management
Institute, Washington, D.C.   *pp. 244–255*. Rutherford, Robert M. 1954.
Five years of Pittman-Robertson wildlife restoration, 1949–1953. Wildlife
Management Institute, Washington, D.C.   *pp. 244–255*. U. S. Fish and
Wildlife Service. 1975. Thirty-five years of shared wildlife management.
U. S. Department of the Interior, Washington, D.C.   *p. 247*. Hunter,
Gilbert N., Theodor R. Swen, and George W. Jones. 1949. The trapping
and transplanting of Rocky Mountain bighorn sheep. Transactions of the
Eleventh North American Wildlife Conference, 364–373. Washington, D.C.
pp. 248–251. Beuchner, Helmut K. 1950. Range ecology of the pronghorn
on the Wichita Mountains Wildlife Refuge. Transactions of the Fifteenth
North American Wildlife Conference. Wildlife Management Institute,
Washington, D.C.   *pp. 248–251*. Lay, Daniel A. 1946. Controlled antelope hunts and problems of administering public hunting. Transactions of
the Eleventh North American Wildlife Conference, 247-279. Wildlife Management Institute, Washington, D.C.   *pp. 249–250*. Pearson, T. Gilbert.
1946. op. cit.   *p. 251*. Mussehl, Thomas W., and F. W. Howell (eds.).
1971. Game management in Montana. Montana Game and Fish Depart-

ment, Helena.   *pp. 251–255.* Mosby, Henry S. 1973. Restoration and introductions of the wild turkey, *in* Wild Turkey Management; Current Problems and Programs. Missouri Chapter of the Wildlife Society and University of Missouri Press, Columbia.   *p. 252.* Blakey, Harold L. 1941. Status and management of the wild turkey. American Wildlife, May–June, 139–142.

CHAPTER 20

pp. 257–266. Wildlife Management Institute. 1950–1960. Outdoor News Bulletin.   *pp. 262–266.* Maunder, Elwood. 1974. op. cit.   *pp. 263–264.* Udall, Stewart L. 1963. The quiet crisis. Holt, Rinehart, and Winston, New York.   *p. 266.* Outdoor Recreation Resources Review Commission. 1962. Outdoor recreation in America. U. S. Government Printing Office, Washington, D.C.

CHAPTER 21

p. 270. U. S. Forest Service. 1965. Timber trends in the United States. U. S. Government Printing Office, Washington, D.C.   *pp. 271–273.* Hickey, J. J. 1966. Birds and pesticides, *in* Birds in Our Lives. U. S. Department of the Interior, Washington, D.C.   *pp. 271–273.* Linduska, Joseph P. 1948. Insecticides vs. wildlife. Transactions of the Thirteenth North American Wildlife Conference. Wildlife Management Institute, Washington, D.C.   *p. 271.* Couch, Leo K. 1948. Effects of DDT on wildlife in a Mississippi River bottomland. Transactions of the Eleventh North American Wildlife Conference, Washington, D.C.   *pp. 273–274.* Brower, David (ed.). 1961. Wilderness, America's living heritage. Sierra Club, San Francisco, California.   *p. 275.* Outdoor Recreation Resources Review Commission. 1962. op. cit.   *p. 276.* President's Council on Recreation and Natural Beauty. 1968. From sea to shining sea: our natural environment. U. S. Government Printing Office, Washington, D.C.   *pp. 276–277.* National Park Service. 1974. National Park Service studies show fires may help national parks. NPS news release, December 12.   *pp. 272–277.* Loope, Lloyd L. and George E. Gruell. 1973. The ecological role of fire in the Jackson Hole area, northwestern Wyoming. Journal of Quarternary Research, 3 (3):425–443.

CHAPTER 22

p. 279. Hornaday, Wiliam T. 1931. op. cit.   *pp. 279–294.* Cain, Stanley A. 1972. Predator control—1971. Report to the Council on Environmental Quality and the Department of the Interior by the Advisory Committee on Predator Control. Institute for Environmental Quality, University of Michigan, Ann Arbor.   *p. 295.* Williamson, Lonnie L. (ed.) 1974. Hopes for new wolf population remain high. Outdoor News Bulletin 28 (22):1. Wildlife Management Institute, Washington, D.C.   *p. 292.* Regenstein, Lewis. 1972. Extinction of eastern timber wolf threatened by government project. Washington *Post*, November 28.   *pp. 292–293.* Rupp,

Craig. 1973. Letter to Lewis Regenstein, January 10.   *p. 293.* U. S. Fish and Wildlife Service. 1972. Assistant Secretary Reed calls for moratorium on taking of endangered eastern timber wolf. Multilithed, December 12. *p. 295.* n.d. North American Wolf Society. Brochure.

CHAPTER 23

pp. 296–315. U. S. Fish and Wildlife Service. 1973. Theatened wildlife of the United States. U. S. Department of the Interior, Washington, D.C. *pp. 296–315.* U. S. Fish and Wildlife Service. 1974. United States list of endangered fauna. U. S. Department of the Interior, Washington, D.C., May.   *p. 298.* Allen, Glover M. 1942. op. cit.   *pp. 302–324.* Maunder, Elwood. 1974. op. cit.   *p. 302.* Jackson, Bud. 1950. Memorandum to Richard Borden, April 24.   *p. 305.* Klimstra, W. D., D. J. Hardin and N. Silva. 1969. Key deer investigations. Annual Report 1968–69. Cooperative Wildlife Research Laboratory. Southern Illinois University. Carbondale, Illinois.   *p. 306.* McNulty, F. 1966. The whooping crane—the bird that defies extinction. E. P. Dutton and Co., New York.   *pp. 308–309.* Anonymous. 1972. Trouble for Michigan's bird of fire. Audubon 74:34–35. *pp. 309–310.* Clement, Roland C. 1969. The status of the California condor. National Geographic Society Research Reports, 1964 Projects, 163–169. *pp. 314–315.* Nowak, Ron. 1974. Red wolf: our most endangered mammal. National Parks and Conservation, August 9–12.

CHAPTER 24

pp. 316–323. Hill, David O. 1975. Vanishing giants. Audubon, January. *pp. 316–322.* Allen, Glover M. 1942. op. cit.   *pp. 320–339.* U. S. Congress. 1971. Marine mammals. Hearings before the Subcommittee on Fisheries and Wildlife Conservation of the Committee on Merchant Marine and Fisheries, House of Representatives, Ninety Second Congress—First Session. U. S. Government Printing Office, Washington, D.C.   *pp. 323–325.* Reiger, George. 1975. Dolphin sacred, porpoise profane. Audubon, January. *pp. 330–331.* Simpson, Elizabeth. 1967. Report of sealing in the Pribilof Islands. World Federation for the Protection of Animals. Zurich, Switzerland.   *pp. 332–335.* Kenyon, Karl W. 1972. The return of the sea otter, *in* Sea Otter in Eastern North Pacific Waters. Compiled by Alice Seed. Pacific Search, Seattle, Washington.   *pp. 333–335.* Palmer, Lucille. 1972. The sea otter hunters, 1741–1911. *in* Sea Otter in Eastern North Pacific Waters. Compiled by Alice Seed. Pacific Search, Seattle, Washington.

CHAPTER 25

pp. 341–342. Maunder, Elwood. 1974. op. cit.   *pp. 342–345.* McDowell, Bob. 1975. The Great Swamp deer hunt. New Jersey Outdoors 2 (1):26–27. *pp. 342–345.* Roscoe, Douglas, and George P. Howard. 1974–1975. The face of famine. The Conservationist, December–January.   *p. 343.* n.d. Report of Friends of Animals.   *p. 346.* Williamson, Lonnie L. (ed.). 1974. Sikes Act signed by President, Outdoor News Bulletin, 28 (22), November 1.

Wildlife Management Institute, Washington, D.C.   *pp. 346–347.* Dingell, John D. 1974. Letters to all members of the U. S. House of Representatives, November 1.   *p. 349.* Herrington, Alice. 1972. Letter to "Dear Friends." Friends of Animals, Inc., New York.   *p. 349.* Amory, Cleveland, 1975. Man kind? our incredible war on wildlife. Harper and Row, New York. *pp. 352–354.* U. S. Fish and Wildlife Service. 1975. Statistical summary for fish and wildlife restoration. Division of Federal Aid, Washington, D.C.

CHAPTER 26

p. 361. Wildlife Management Institute. 1973. National survey of state fish and wildlife funding, Washington, D.C.   *p. 362.* U. S. Bureau of Sport Fisheries and Wildlife. 1971. National survey of hunting and fishing. U. S. Government Printing Office, Washington, D.C.   *pp. 365–366.* Greenwalt, Lynn A. 1974. Letter to Senator Lee Metcalf on status of the National Wildlife Refuge System, November 15.   *p. 368.* Wildlife Management Institute. 1975. Current investments, projected needs, and potential new sources of income for nongame fish and wildlife programs in the United States, Washington, D.C.

Index